TO BE TRUTHFUL, I DON'T KNOW A LOT ABOUT
DIFFICULT SUBJECTS, BUT NOW THAT I'VE
BEEN GIVEN THE OPPORTUNITY TO WRITE
SOMETHING HERE, I STRUGGLED TO CREATE
A GREAT QUOTE OR SAYING THAT WOULD LIVE
ON THROUGH THE CENTURIES. I REALLY TRIED
HARD, AND IT'S NOT SUPPOSED TO BE A JOKE
OR ANYTHING. WHAT DO YOU THINK OF THIS:

"THERE ARE NO NUDISTS IN COLD AREAS."
- TSUGUMI OHBA

Tsugumi Ohba
Born in Tokyo.
Hobby: Collecting teacups.
Day and night, develops manga plots
while holding knees on a chair.

Takeshi Obata was born in 1969 in Niigata, Japan, and
is the artist of the wildly popular SHONEN JUMP title
Hikaru no Go, which won the 2003 Tezuka Shinsei
"New Hope" award and the Shogakukan Manga award.
Obata is also the artist of **Arabian Majin Bokentan
Lamp Lamp, Ayatsuri Sakon,** and **Cyborg Jichan G.**

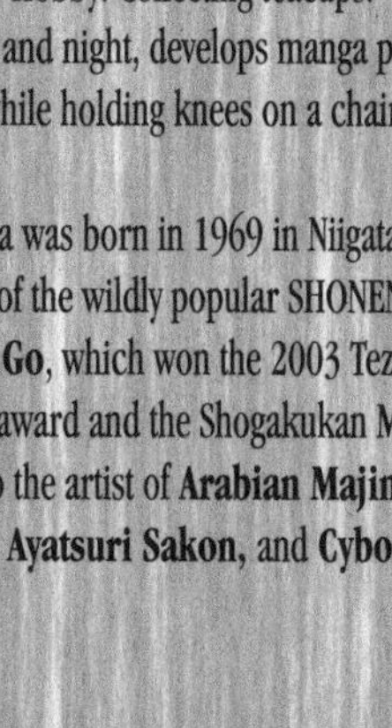

DEATH NOTE VOL 11
SHONEN JUMP ADVANCED Manga Edition

STORY BY TSUGUMI OHBA
ART BY TAKESHI OBATA

Translation & Adaptation/Tetsuichiro Miyaki
Touch-up Art & Lettering/Gia Cam Luc
Design/Sean Lee
Editor/Pancha Diaz

Printed in the U.S.A.

Published by VIZ Media, LLC
P.O. Box 77010
San Francisco, CA 94107

13
First printing, May 2007
Thirteenth printing, September 2014

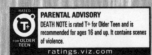

www.viz.com

THE WORLD'S MOST
CUTTING-EDGE MANGA

SHONEN
JUMP
ADVANCED
www.shonenjump.com

SHONEN JUMP ADVANCED MANGA

DEATH NOTE

デスノート

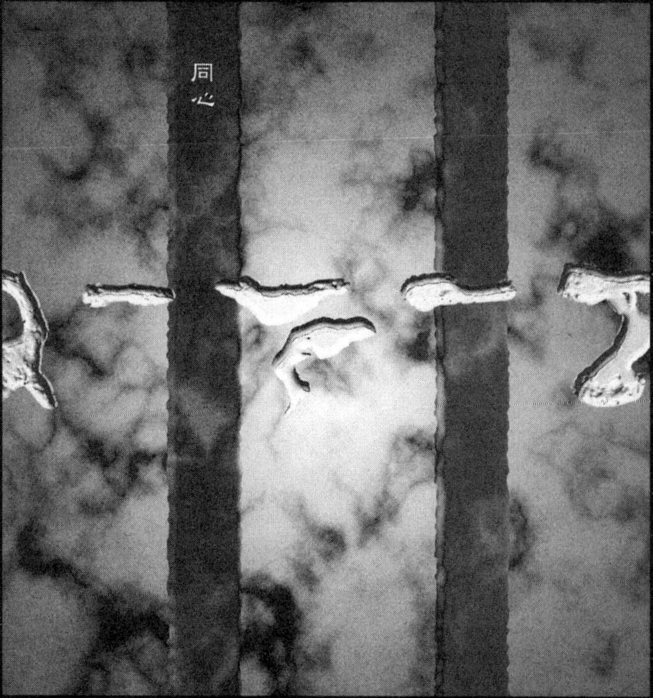
同心

Vol. 11

Kindred Spirit

Story by Tsugumi Ohba

Art by Takeshi Obata

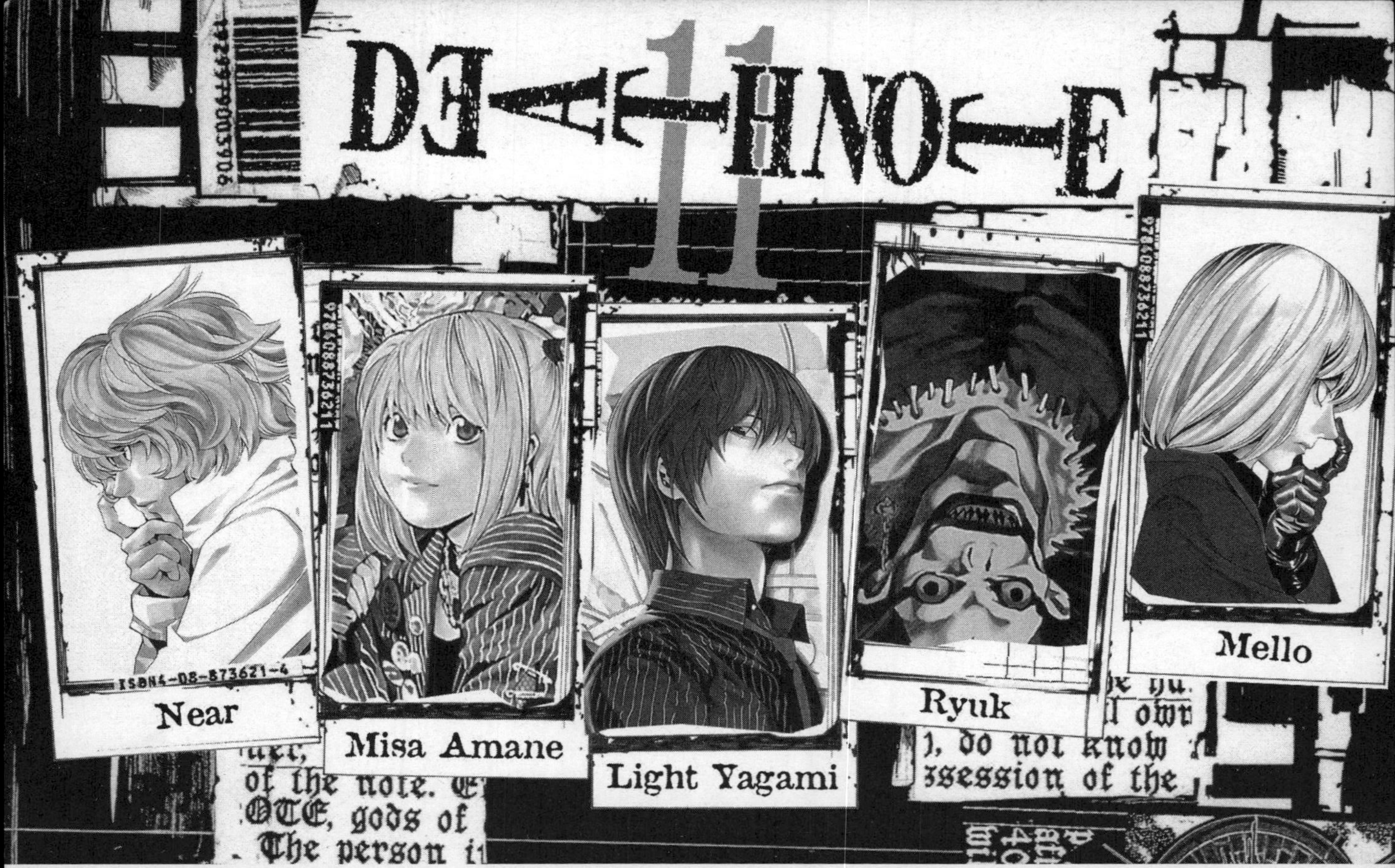

DEATH NOTE
11
ISBN4-08-873621-4
Near
Misa Amane
Light Yagami
Ryuk
Mello
of the note.
OTE, gods of
The person
, do not know
ssession of the

Lidner
Gevanni
Rester
Sayu Yagami
Sachiko Yagami
Soichiro Yagami
Kiyomi Takada
Teru Mikami
Matsuda
Ide
Aizawa
Mogi

"THE HUMAN WHOSE NAME IS WRITTEN IN THIS NOTE SHALL DIE"... LIGHT YAGAMI, A STRAIGHT-A HIGH SCHOOL HONORS STUDENT, PICKS UP THE "DEATH NOTE" DROPPED BY THE SHINIGAMI RYUK INTO THE HUMAN WORLD. INITIALLY HORRIFIED BY THE NOTEBOOK'S POWERS, LIGHT EVENTUALLY DECIDES TO USE THE DEATH NOTE TO PURGE THE WORLD OF VIOLENT CRIMINALS AND CREATE AN IDEAL SOCIETY. L, A SECRETIVE GENIUS WHO SPECIALIZES IN SOLVING UNSOLVED CASES, STRIVES TO TRACK DOWN KIRA, SETTING OFF AN ALMIGHTY BATTLE OF THE WITS BETWEEN LIGHT AND HIMSELF. BUT LIGHT FINALLY MANAGES TO GET RID OF L, LEAVING KIRA SEEMINGLY UNOPPOSED.

FOUR YEARS HAVE PASSED, AND LIGHT HAS TAKEN THE ROLE OF "THE SECOND L" WHILE CONTINUING TO SHAPE THE WORLD AS KIRA. BUT L'S TWO PROTÉGÉS HAVE BEGUN TO MAKE THEIR MOVE. AFTER DISCOVERING THE EXISTENCE OF THE DEATH NOTE, THEY BOTH CONCLUDE THAT ACQUIRING THE NOTEBOOK IS THE QUICKEST WAY TO GET KIRA, AND A SCRAMBLE FOR THE DEATH NOTE BEGINS.

MELLO'S INGENIOUS PLAN TO GET THE NOTEBOOK SUCCEEDS, AND HE LEARNS ABOUT THE FAKE "13 DAY RULE," BUT THE JAPANESE INVESTIGATION TEAM MANAGES TO REGAIN THE NOTEBOOK AND MELLO IS FORCED INTO HIDING. BUT RETRIEVING THE DEATH NOTE IS NOT WITHOUT COST, AND SOICHIRO YAGAMI IS FATALLY WOUNDED. AFTER A SERIES OF FURTHER INCIDENTS IN THE U.S., MELLO AND NEAR EXCHANGE INFORMATION. AFTER LEARNING OF THE FAKE "13 DAY RULE," NEAR BEGINS TO SUSPECT THAT THE NEW L IS KIRA, AND STARTS TO STIR THINGS UP IN THE JAPANESE TASK FORCE. NEAR'S MEDDLING WORKS, AND THE TASK FORCE MEMBERS, ESPECIALLY AIZAWA, BEGIN TO SUSPECT LIGHT. WITH NEW INFORMATION FROM AIZAWA, NEAR BECOMES CONFIDENT THAT THE NEW L IS LIGHT!

DEATH NOTE
Vol. 11

CONTENTS

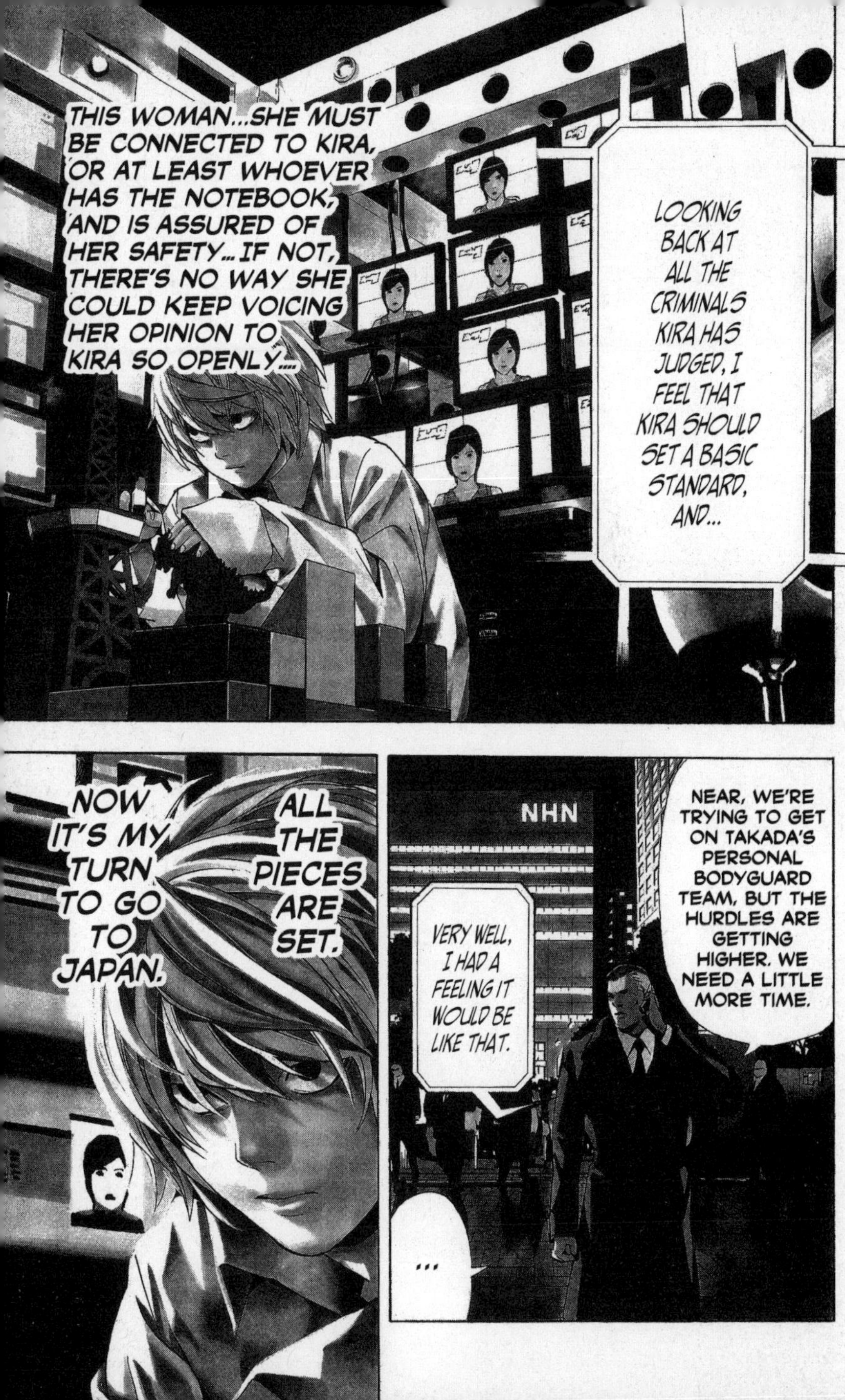
LOOKING BACK AT ALL THE CRIMINALS KIRA HAS JUDGED, I FEEL THAT KIRA SHOULD SET A BASIC STANDARD, AND...
THIS WOMAN...SHE MUST BE CONNECTED TO KIRA, OR AT LEAST WHOEVER HAS THE NOTEBOOK, AND IS ASSURED OF HER SAFETY...IF NOT, THERE'S NO WAY SHE COULD KEEP VOICING HER OPINION TO KIRA SO OPENLY...
NHN
NEAR, WE'RE TRYING TO GET ON TAKADA'S PERSONAL BODYGUARD TEAM, BUT THE HURDLES ARE GETTING HIGHER. WE NEED A LITTLE MORE TIME.
VERY WELL, I HAD A FEELING IT WOULD BE LIKE THAT.
...
ALL THE PIECES ARE SET.
NOW IT'S MY TURN TO GO TO JAPAN.

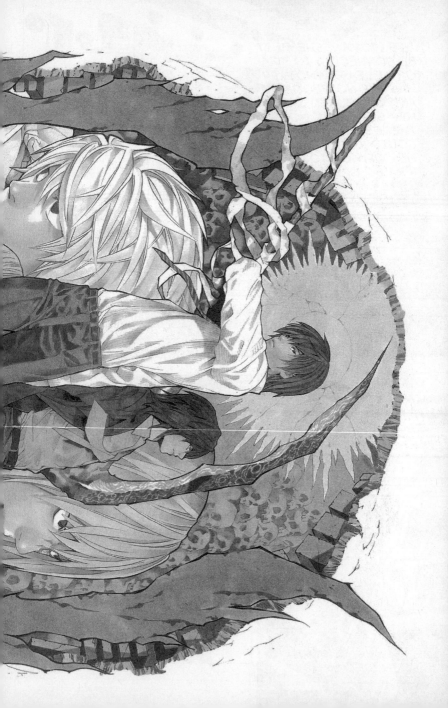

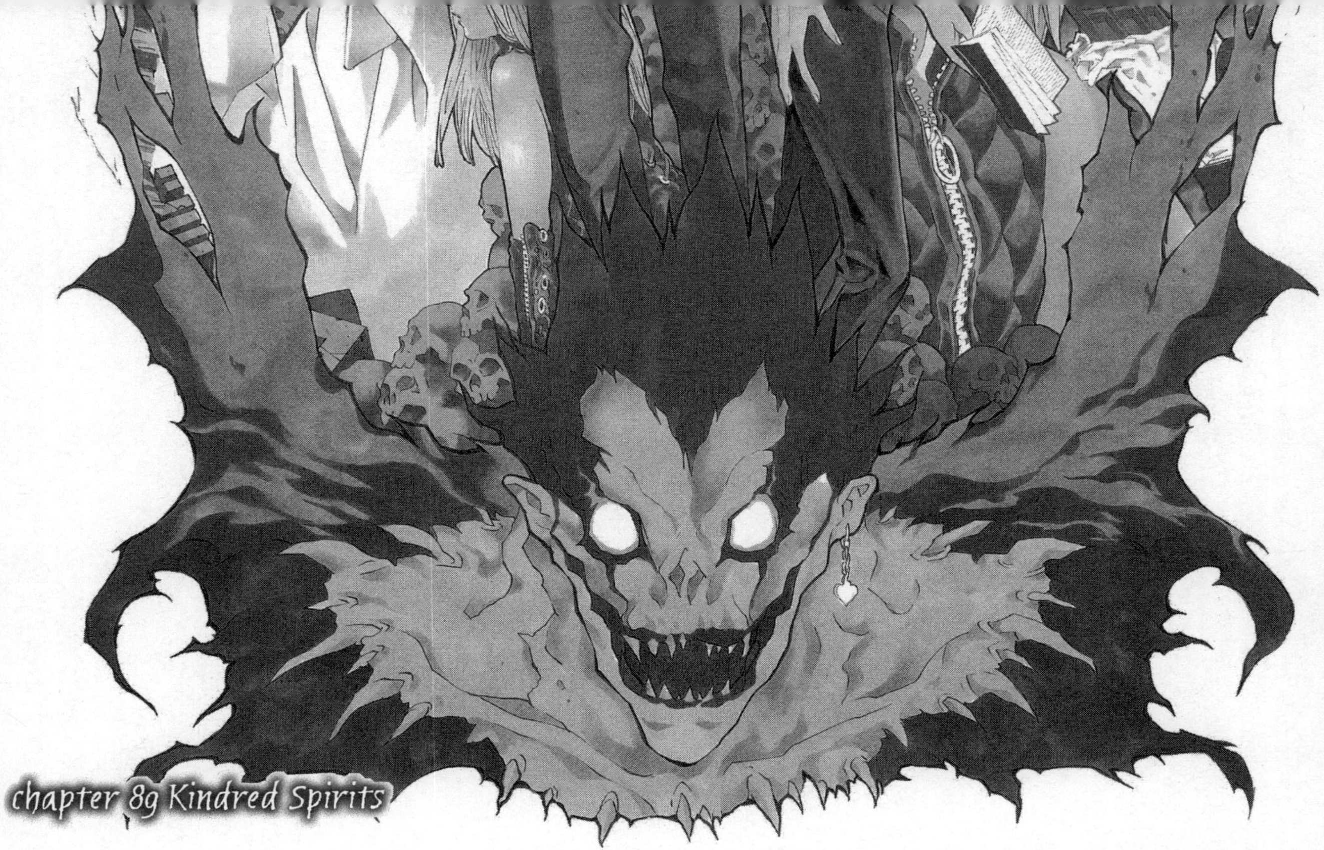
chapter 89 Kindred Spirits

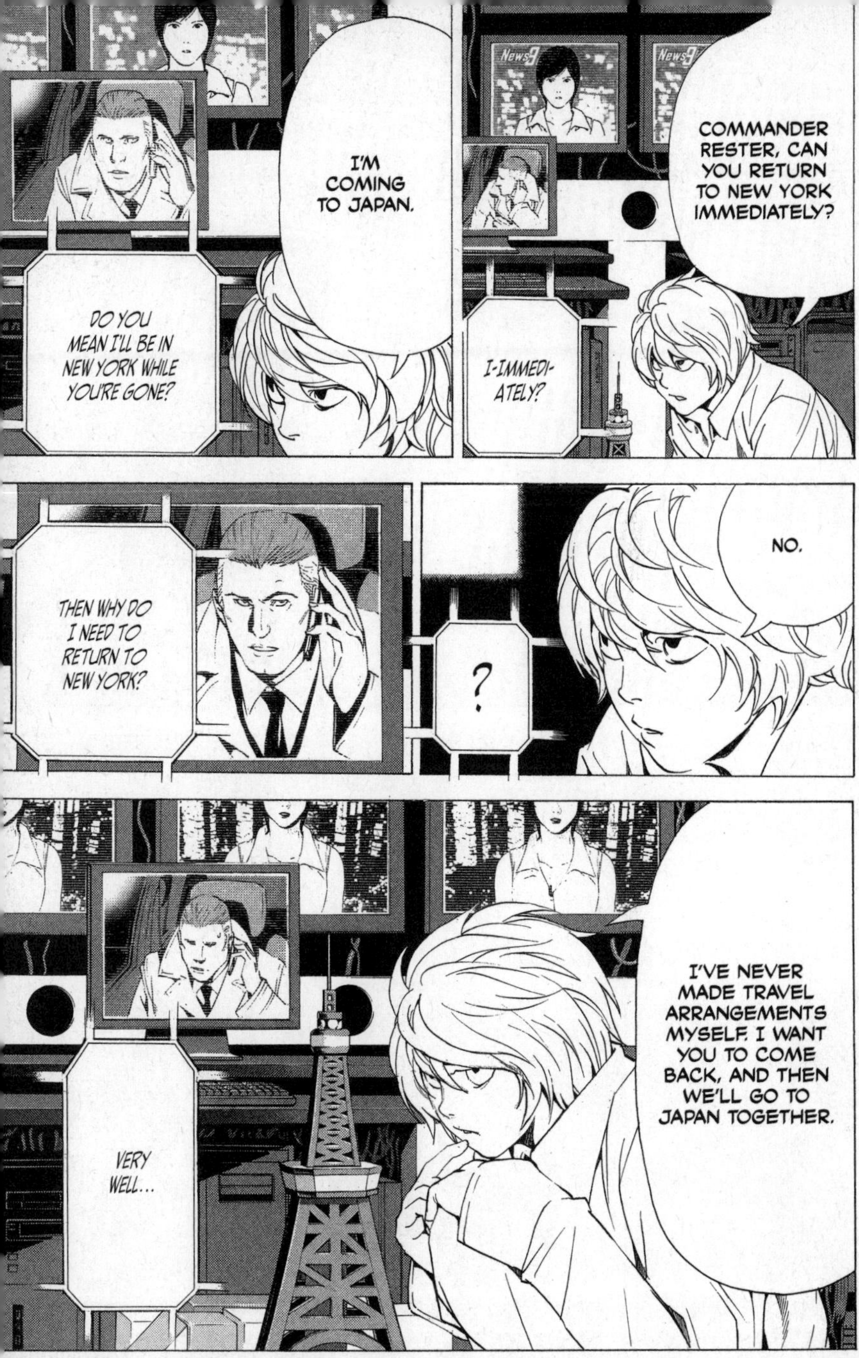
COMMANDER RESTER, CAN YOU RETURN TO NEW YORK IMMEDIATELY?
I-IMMEDI-ATELY?
I'M COMING TO JAPAN.
DO YOU MEAN I'LL BE IN NEW YORK WHILE YOU'RE GONE?
NO.
?
THEN WHY DO I NEED TO RETURN TO NEW YORK?
I'VE NEVER MADE TRAVEL ARRANGEMENTS MYSELF. I WANT YOU TO COME BACK, AND THEN WE'LL GO TO JAPAN TOGETHER.
VERY WELL...

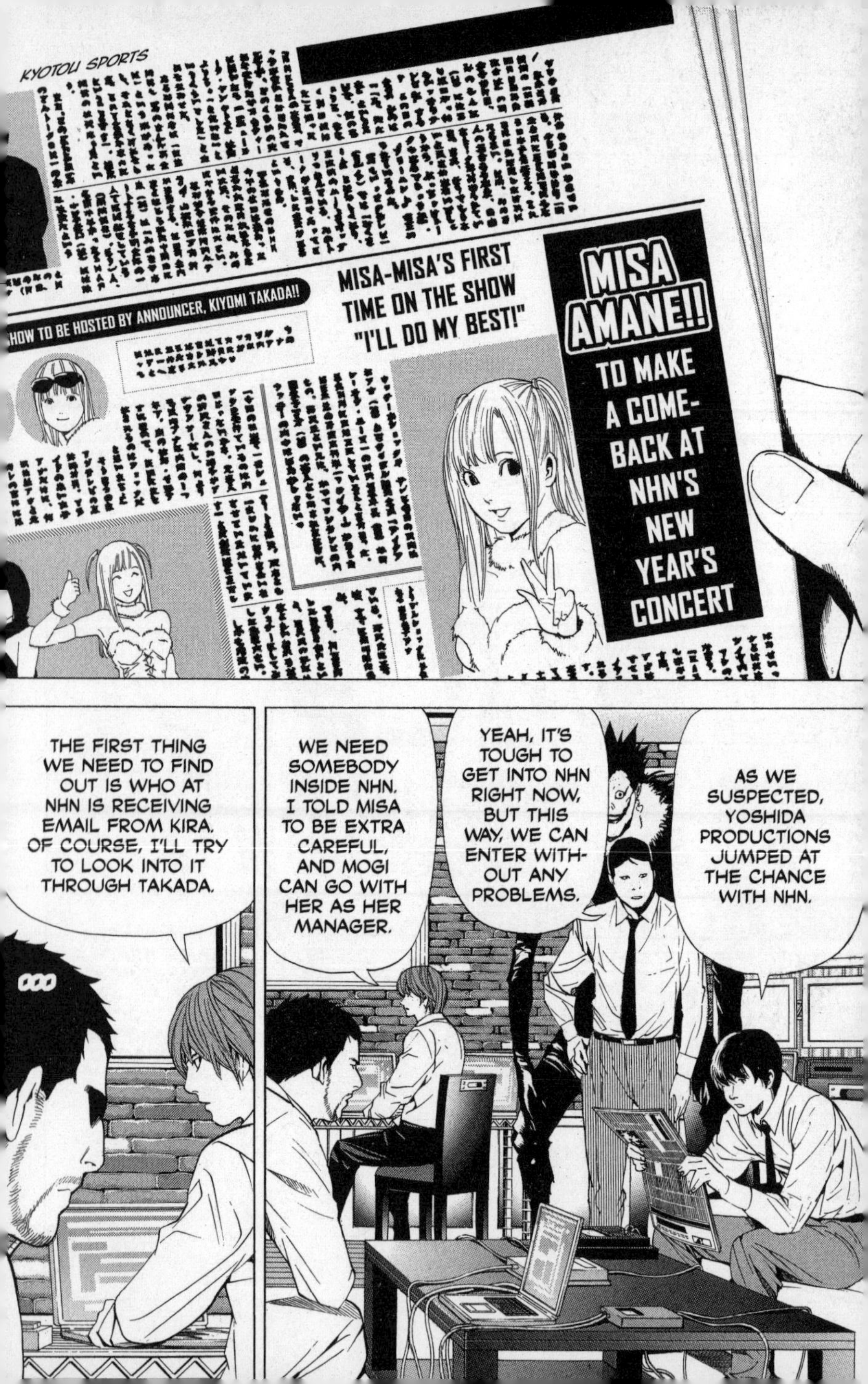
KYOTOU SPORTS
MISA AMANE!!
TO MAKE A COME-BACK AT NHN'S NEW YEAR'S CONCERT
MISA-MISA'S FIRST TIME ON THE SHOW "I'LL DO MY BEST!"
SHOW TO BE HOSTED BY ANNOUNCER, KIYOMI TAKADA!!
AS WE SUSPECTED, YOSHIDA PRODUCTIONS JUMPED AT THE CHANCE WITH NHN.
YEAH, IT'S TOUGH TO GET INTO NHN RIGHT NOW, BUT THIS WAY, WE CAN ENTER WITHOUT ANY PROBLEMS.
WE NEED SOMEBODY INSIDE NHN. I TOLD MISA TO BE EXTRA CAREFUL, AND MOGI CAN GO WITH HER AS HER MANAGER.
THE FIRST THING WE NEED TO FIND OUT IS WHO AT NHN IS RECEIVING EMAIL FROM KIRA. OF COURSE, I'LL TRY TO LOOK INTO IT THROUGH TAKADA.

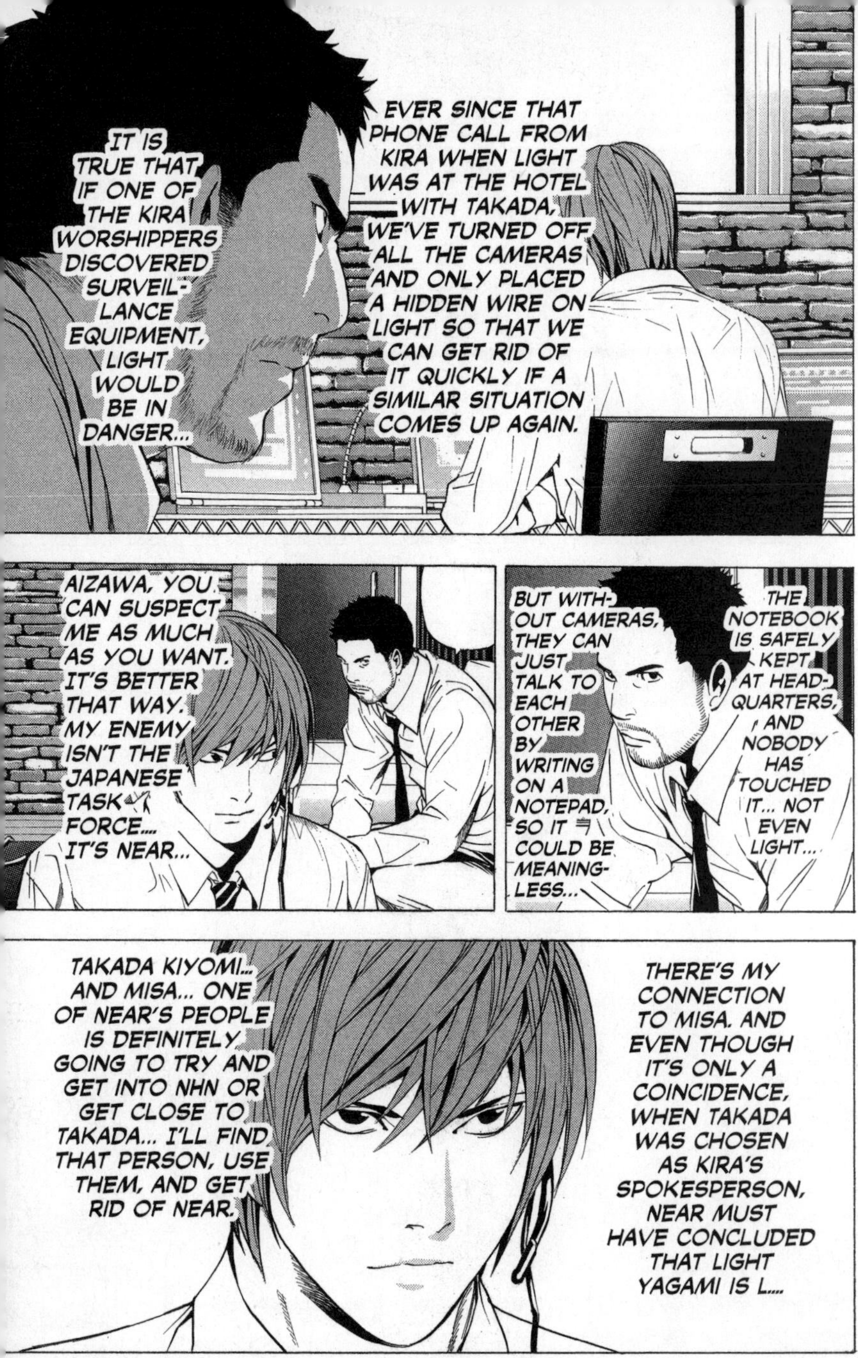
EVER SINCE THAT PHONE CALL FROM KIRA WHEN LIGHT WAS AT THE HOTEL WITH TAKADA, WE'VE TURNED OFF ALL THE CAMERAS AND ONLY PLACED A HIDDEN WIRE ON LIGHT SO THAT WE CAN GET RID OF IT QUICKLY IF A SIMILAR SITUATION COMES UP AGAIN.
IT IS TRUE THAT IF ONE OF THE KIRA WORSHIPPERS DISCOVERED SURVEIL-LANCE EQUIPMENT, LIGHT WOULD BE IN DANGER...
THE NOTEBOOK IS SAFELY KEPT AT HEAD-QUARTERS, AND NOBODY HAS TOUCHED IT... NOT EVEN LIGHT...
BUT WITH-OUT CAMERAS, THEY CAN JUST TALK TO EACH OTHER BY WRITING ON A NOTEPAD, SO IT COULD BE MEANING-LESS...
AIZAWA, YOU CAN SUSPECT ME AS MUCH AS YOU WANT. IT'S BETTER THAT WAY. MY ENEMY ISN'T THE JAPANESE TASK FORCE.... IT'S NEAR...
THERE'S MY CONNECTION TO MISA. AND EVEN THOUGH IT'S ONLY A COINCIDENCE, WHEN TAKADA WAS CHOSEN AS KIRA'S SPOKESPERSON, NEAR MUST HAVE CONCLUDED THAT LIGHT YAGAMI IS L....
TAKADA KIYOMI... AND MISA... ONE OF NEAR'S PEOPLE IS DEFINITELY GOING TO TRY AND GET INTO NHN OR GET CLOSE TO TAKADA... I'LL FIND THAT PERSON, USE THEM, AND GET RID OF NEAR.

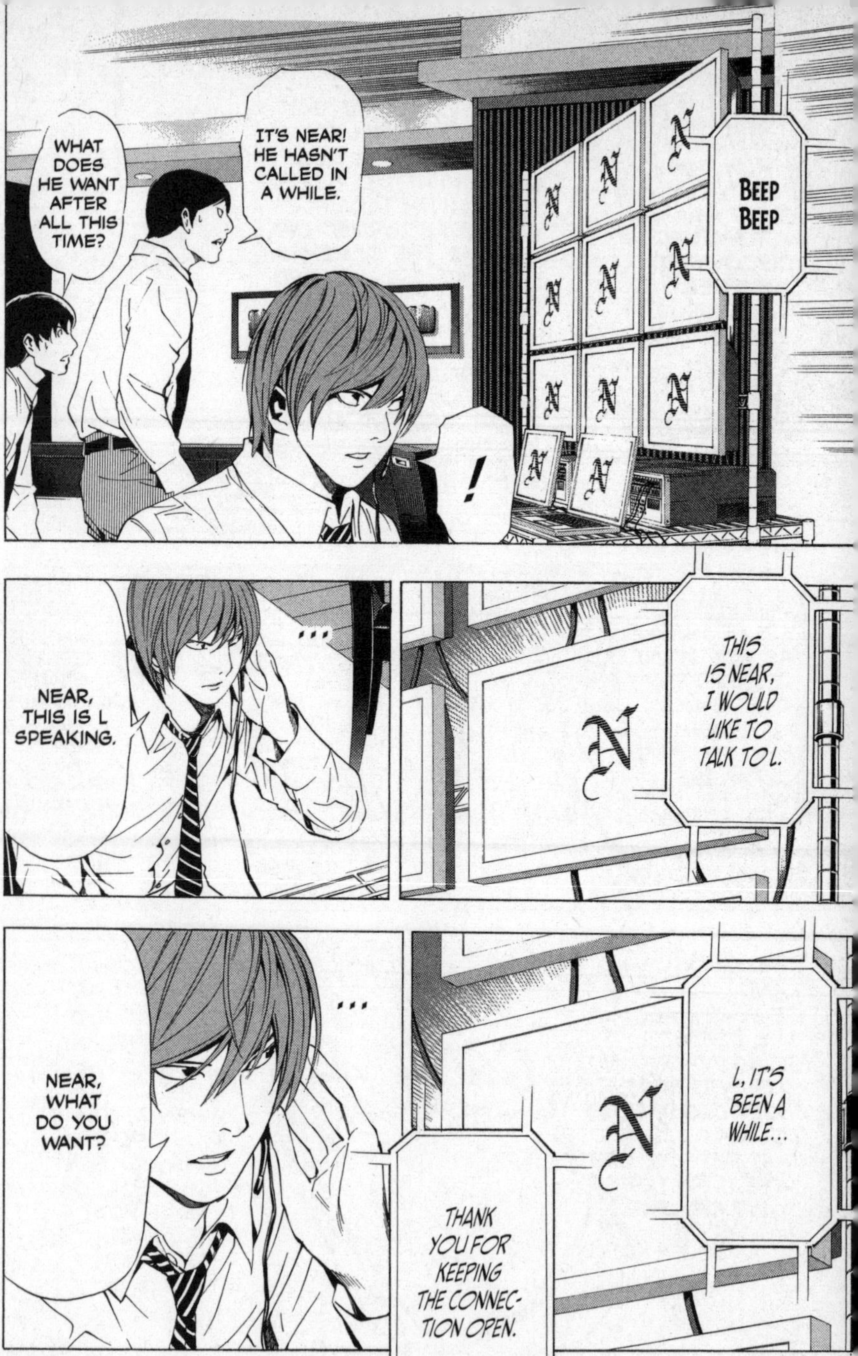
BEEP BEEP
IT'S NEAR! HE HASN'T CALLED IN A WHILE.
WHAT DOES HE WANT AFTER ALL THIS TIME?
!
THIS IS NEAR, I WOULD LIKE TO TALK TO L.
...
NEAR, THIS IS L SPEAKING.
L, IT'S BEEN A WHILE...
THANK YOU FOR KEEPING THE CONNEC-TION OPEN.
...
NEAR, WHAT DO YOU WANT?

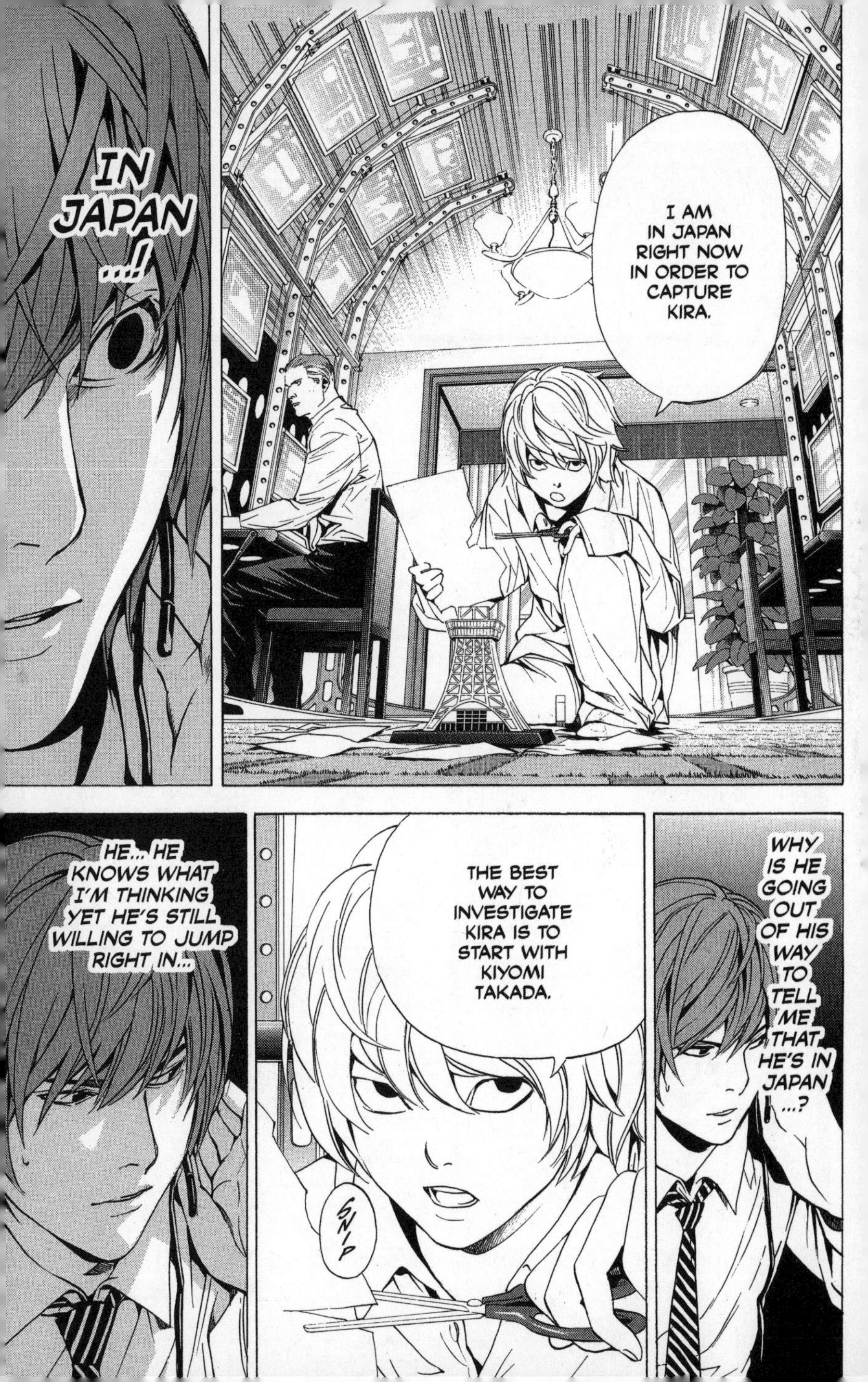
I AM IN JAPAN RIGHT NOW IN ORDER TO CAPTURE KIRA.
IN JAPAN ...!
WHY IS HE GOING OUT OF HIS WAY TO TELL ME THAT HE'S IN JAPAN ...?
THE BEST WAY TO INVESTIGATE KIRA IS TO START WITH KIYOMI TAKADA.
SNIP
HE... HE KNOWS WHAT I'M THINKING YET HE'S STILL WILLING TO JUMP RIGHT IN...

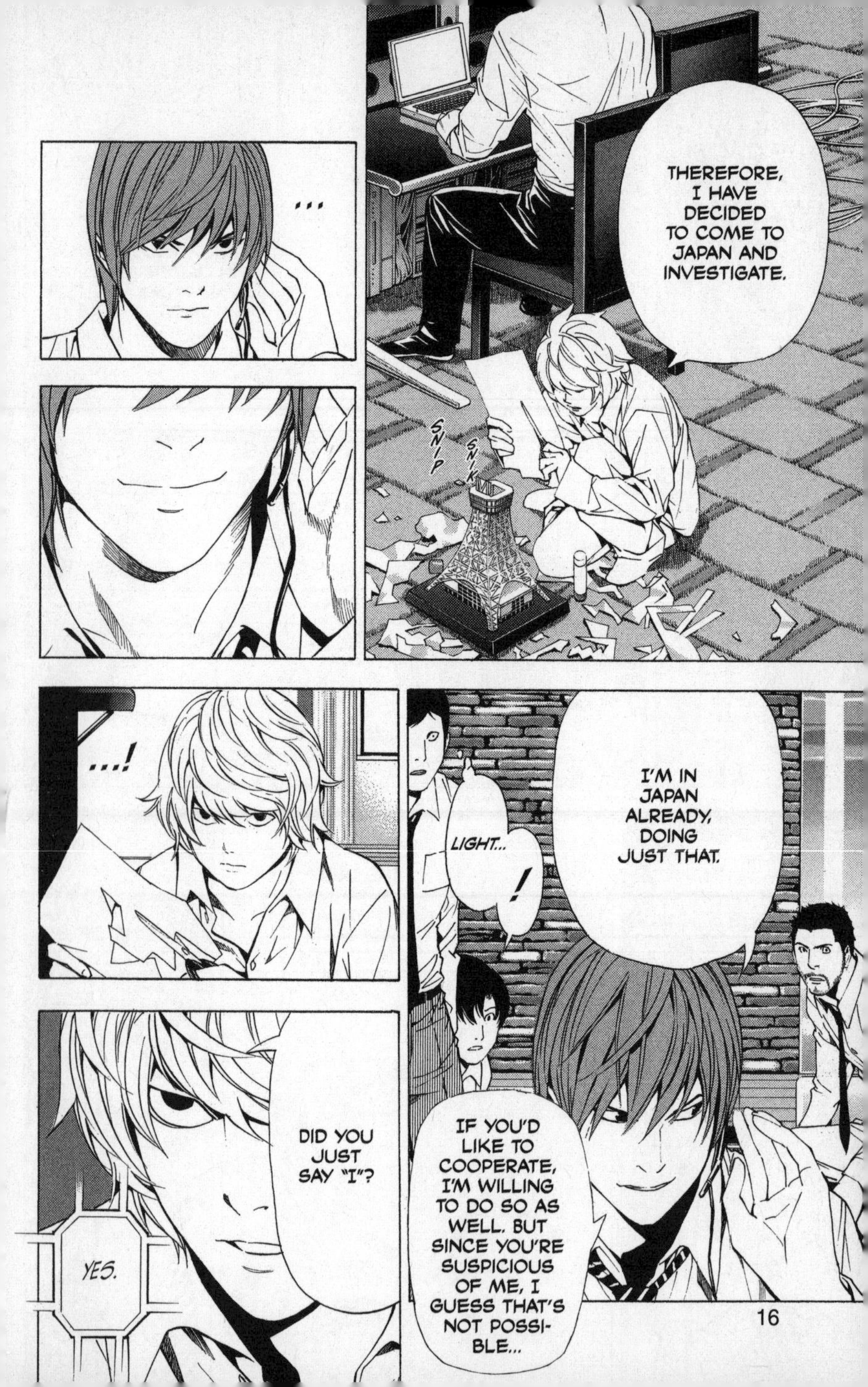
THEREFORE, I HAVE DECIDED TO COME TO JAPAN AND INVESTIGATE.
SNIP
SNIK
...
I'M IN JAPAN ALREADY, DOING JUST THAT.
LIGHT...
!
IF YOU'D LIKE TO COOPERATE, I'M WILLING TO DO SO AS WELL. BUT SINCE YOU'RE SUSPICIOUS OF ME, I GUESS THAT'S NOT POSSIBLE...
...!
DID YOU JUST SAY "I"?
YES.

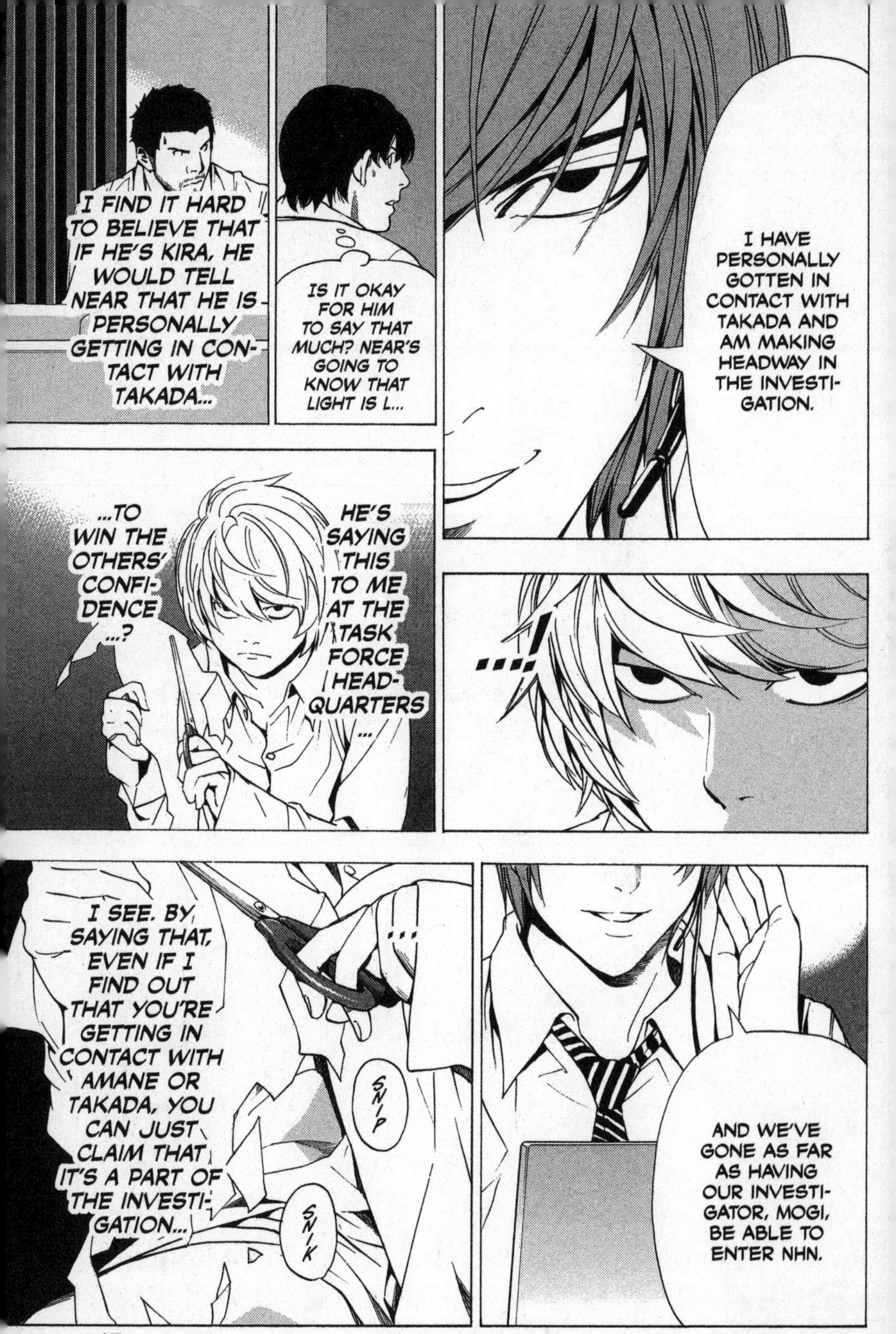

I HAVE PERSONALLY GOTTEN IN CONTACT WITH TAKADA AND AM MAKING HEADWAY IN THE INVESTIGATION.
IS IT OKAY FOR HIM TO SAY THAT MUCH? NEAR'S GOING TO KNOW THAT LIGHT IS L...
I FIND IT HARD TO BELIEVE THAT IF HE'S KIRA, HE WOULD TELL NEAR THAT HE IS PERSONALLY GETTING IN CONTACT WITH TAKADA...
...!
HE'S SAYING THIS TO ME AT THE TASK FORCE HEADQUARTERS...
...TO WIN THE OTHERS' CONFIDENCE...?
AND WE'VE GONE AS FAR AS HAVING OUR INVESTIGATOR, MOGI, BE ABLE TO ENTER NHN.
...
I SEE. BY SAYING THAT, EVEN IF I FIND OUT THAT YOU'RE GETTING IN CONTACT WITH AMANE OR TAKADA, YOU CAN JUST CLAIM THAT IT'S A PART OF THE INVESTIGATION...
SNIP
SNIK

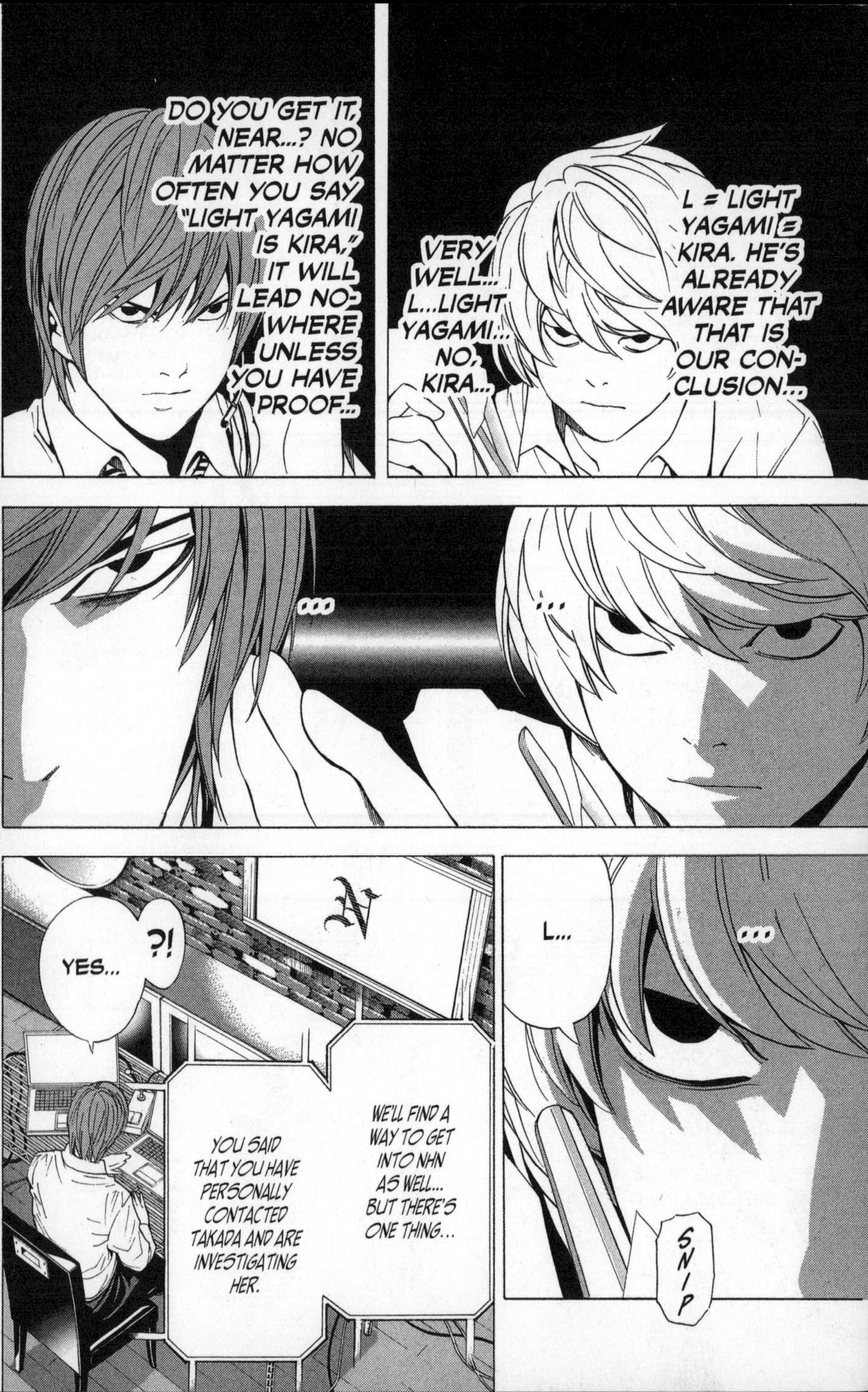
L = LIGHT YAGAMI = KIRA. HE'S ALREADY AWARE THAT THAT IS OUR CONCLUSION...
VERY WELL... L...LIGHT YAGAMI... NO, KIRA...
DO YOU GET IT, NEAR...? NO MATTER HOW OFTEN YOU SAY "LIGHT YAGAMI IS KIRA," IT WILL LEAD NOWHERE UNLESS YOU HAVE PROOF...
...
...
...
L...
SNIP
?!
YES...
WE'LL FIND A WAY TO GET INTO NHN AS WELL... BUT THERE'S ONE THING...
YOU SAID THAT YOU HAVE PERSONALLY CONTACTED TAKADA AND ARE INVESTIGATING HER.

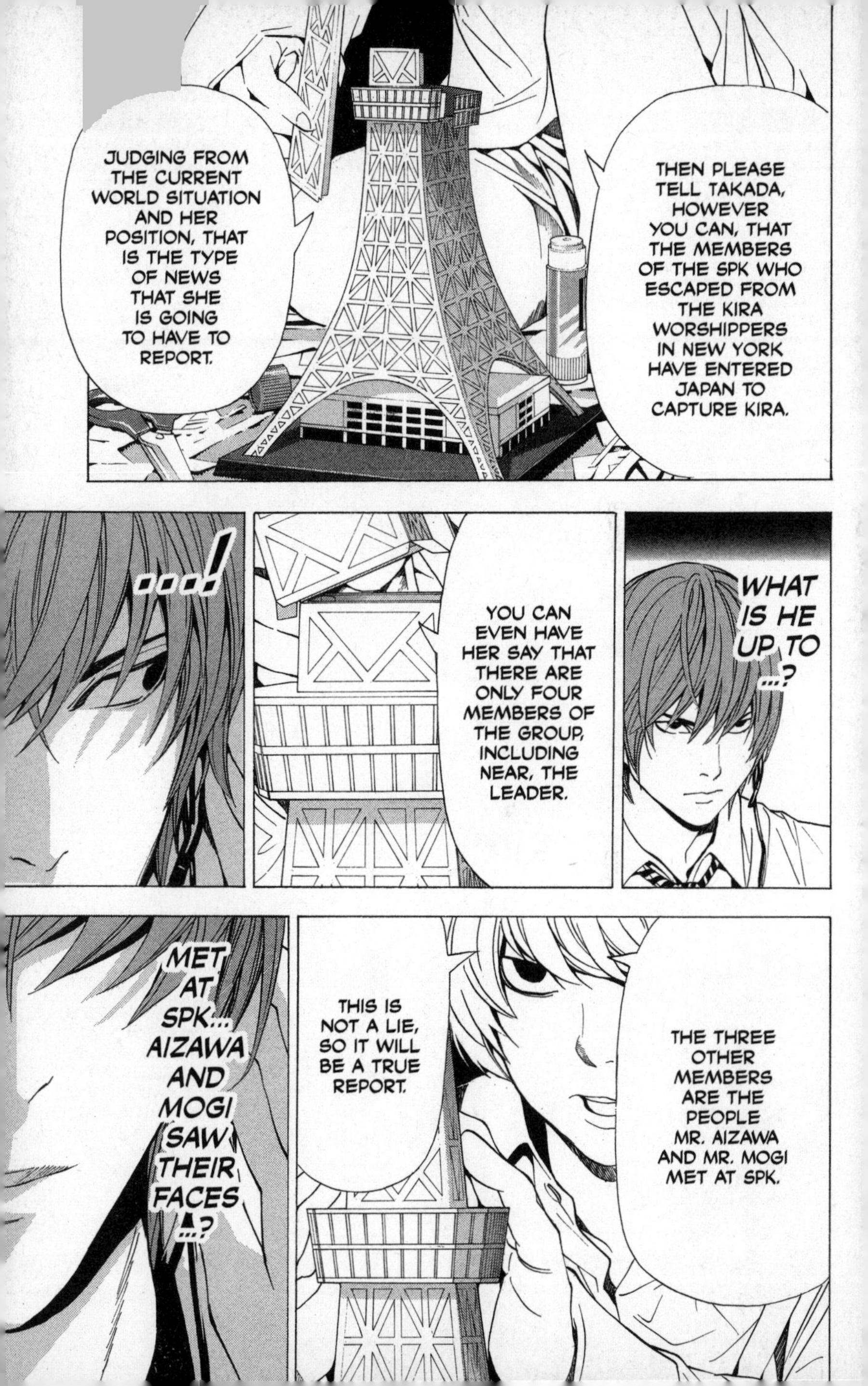
THEN PLEASE TELL TAKADA, HOWEVER YOU CAN, THAT THE MEMBERS OF THE SPK WHO ESCAPED FROM THE KIRA WORSHIPPERS IN NEW YORK HAVE ENTERED JAPAN TO CAPTURE KIRA.
JUDGING FROM THE CURRENT WORLD SITUATION AND HER POSITION, THAT IS THE TYPE OF NEWS THAT SHE IS GOING TO HAVE TO REPORT.
WHAT IS HE UP TO ...?
YOU CAN EVEN HAVE HER SAY THAT THERE ARE ONLY FOUR MEMBERS OF THE GROUP, INCLUDING NEAR, THE LEADER.
...!
THE THREE OTHER MEMBERS ARE THE PEOPLE MR. AIZAWA AND MR. MOGI MET AT SPK.
THIS IS NOT A LIE, SO IT WILL BE A TRUE REPORT.
MET AT SPK... AIZAWA AND MOGI SAW THEIR FACES ...?

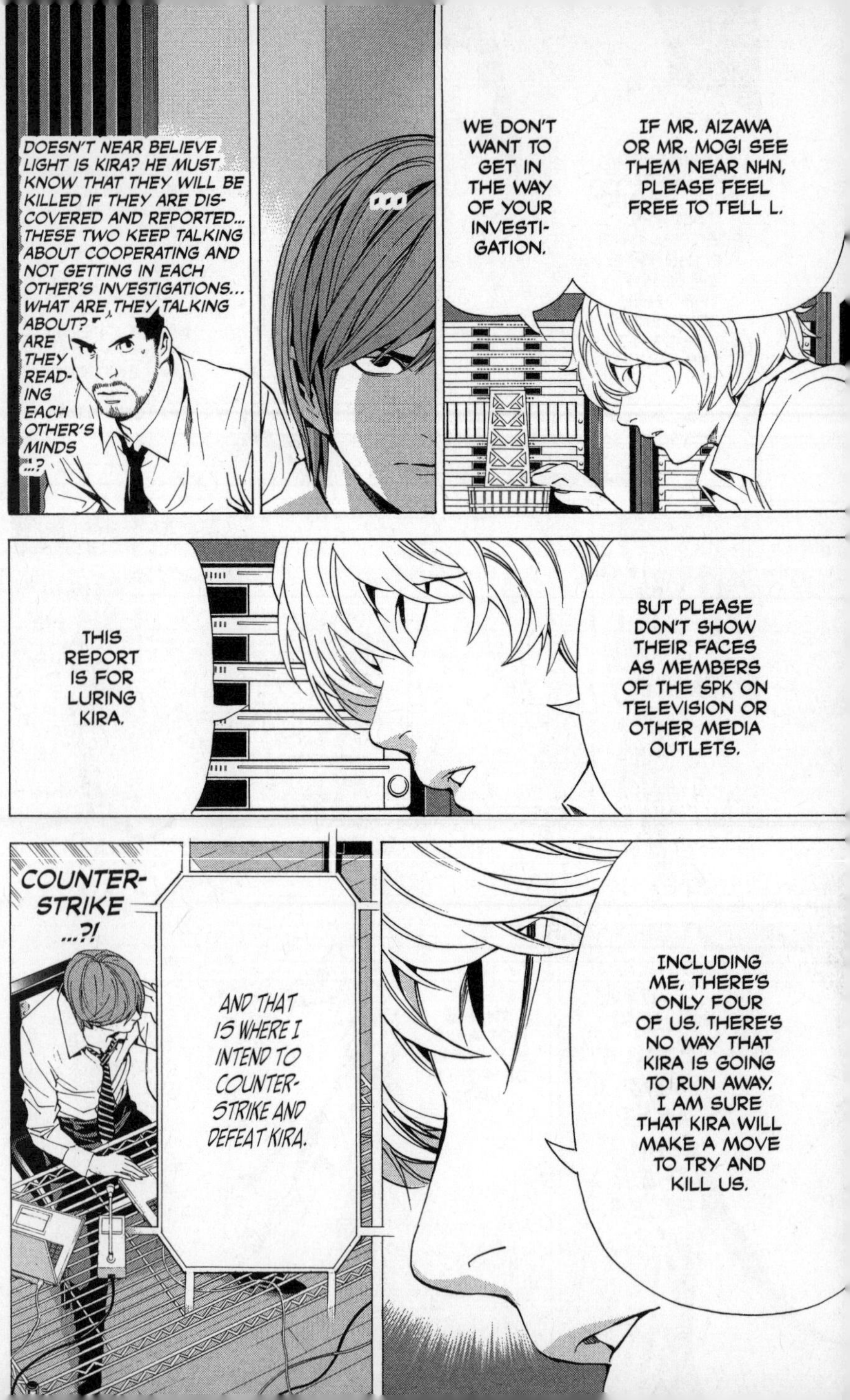
IF MR. AIZAWA OR MR. MOGI SEE THEM NEAR NHN, PLEASE FEEL FREE TO TELL L.
WE DON'T WANT TO GET IN THE WAY OF YOUR INVESTIGATION.
...
DOESN'T NEAR BELIEVE LIGHT IS KIRA? HE MUST KNOW THAT THEY WILL BE KILLED IF THEY ARE DISCOVERED AND REPORTED... THESE TWO KEEP TALKING ABOUT COOPERATING AND NOT GETTING IN EACH OTHER'S INVESTIGATIONS... WHAT ARE THEY TALKING ABOUT? ARE THEY READING EACH OTHER'S MINDS ...?
BUT PLEASE DON'T SHOW THEIR FACES AS MEMBERS OF THE SPK ON TELEVISION OR OTHER MEDIA OUTLETS.
THIS REPORT IS FOR LURING KIRA.
INCLUDING ME, THERE'S ONLY FOUR OF US. THERE'S NO WAY THAT KIRA IS GOING TO RUN AWAY. I AM SURE THAT KIRA WILL MAKE A MOVE TO TRY AND KILL US.
AND THAT IS WHERE I INTEND TO COUNTER-STRIKE AND DEFEAT KIRA.
COUNTER-STRIKE ...?!

READ THIS WAY

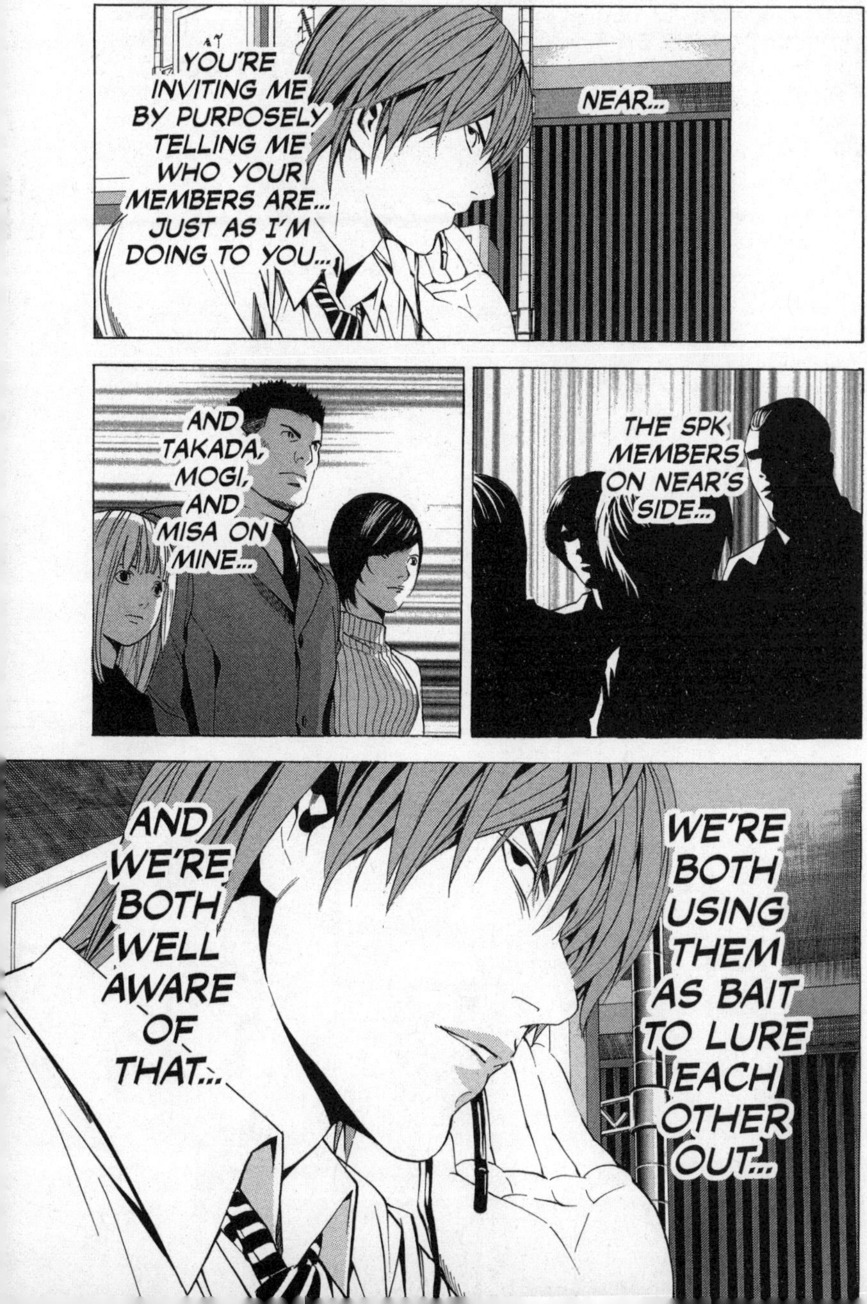
NEAR...
YOU'RE INVITING ME BY PURPOSELY TELLING ME WHO YOUR MEMBERS ARE... JUST AS I'M DOING TO YOU...
THE SPK MEMBERS ON NEAR'S SIDE...
AND TAKADA, MOGI, AND MISA ON MINE...
WE'RE BOTH USING THEM AS BAIT TO LURE EACH OTHER OUT...
AND WE'RE BOTH WELL AWARE OF THAT...

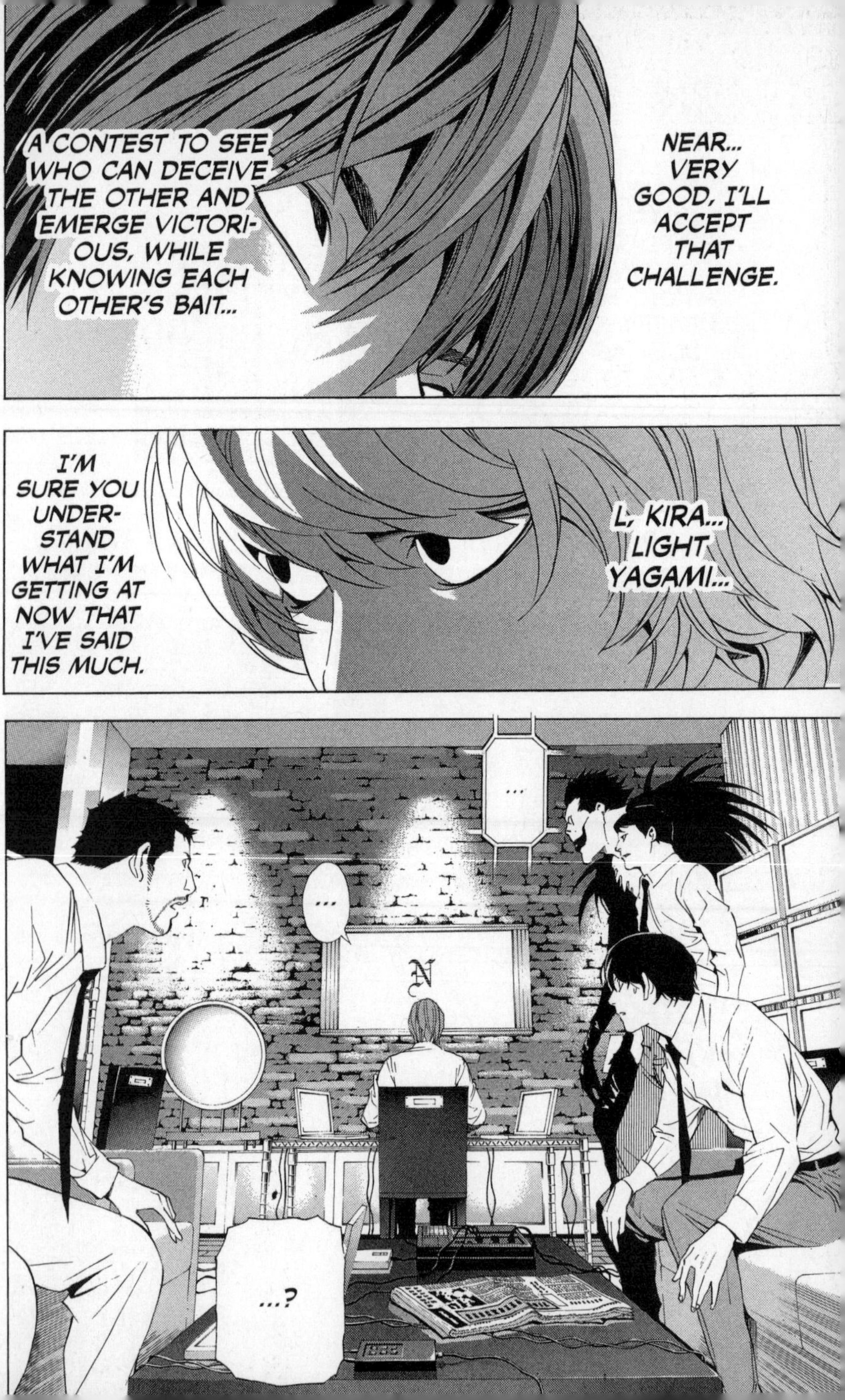
A CONTEST TO SEE WHO CAN DECEIVE THE OTHER AND EMERGE VICTORIOUS, WHILE KNOWING EACH OTHER'S BAIT...
NEAR... VERY GOOD, I'LL ACCEPT THAT CHALLENGE.
L, KIRA... LIGHT YAGAMI...
I'M SURE YOU UNDERSTAND WHAT I'M GETTING AT NOW THAT I'VE SAID THIS MUCH.
...
...
...?

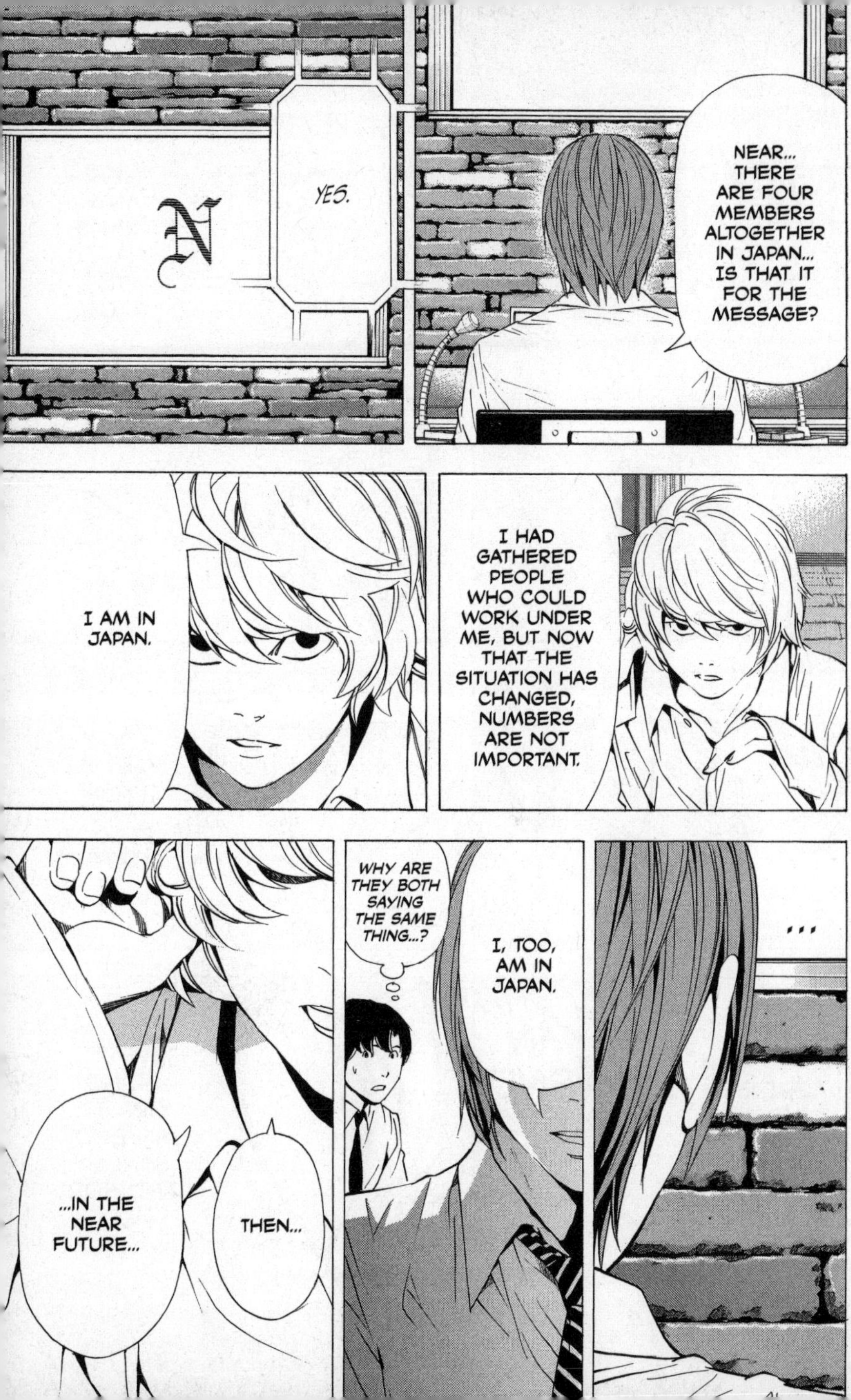
NEAR... THERE ARE FOUR MEMBERS ALTOGETHER IN JAPAN... IS THAT IT FOR THE MESSAGE?
YES.
N
I HAD GATHERED PEOPLE WHO COULD WORK UNDER ME, BUT NOW THAT THE SITUATION HAS CHANGED, NUMBERS ARE NOT IMPORTANT.
I AM IN JAPAN.
...
I, TOO, AM IN JAPAN.
WHY ARE THEY BOTH SAYING THE SAME THING...?
THEN...
...IN THE NEAR FUTURE...

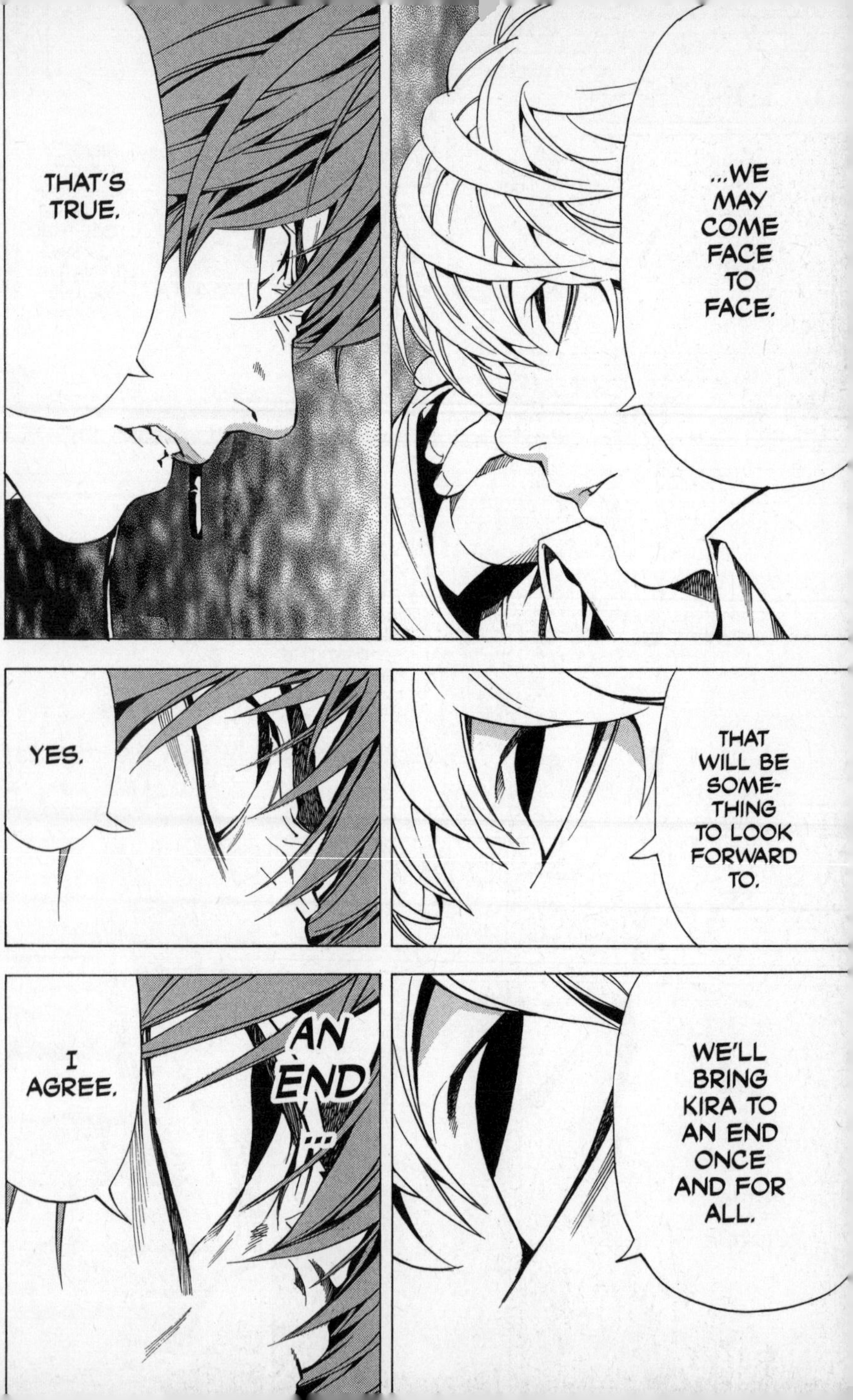
...WE MAY COME FACE TO FACE.
THAT'S TRUE.
THAT WILL BE SOME-THING TO LOOK FORWARD TO.
YES.
WE'LL BRING KIRA TO AN END ONCE AND FOR ALL.
AN END ...
I AGREE.

READ THIS WAY

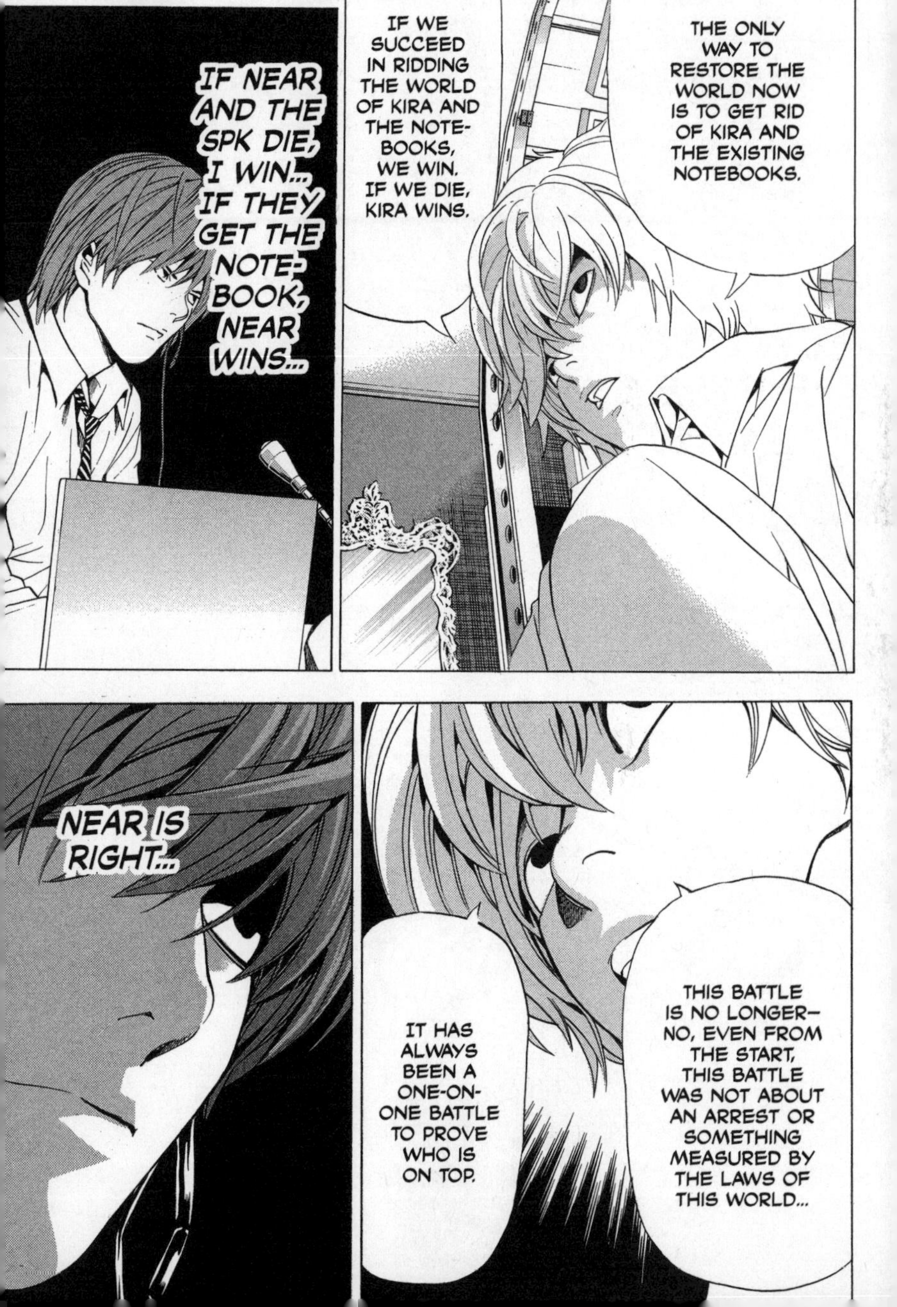
THE ONLY WAY TO RESTORE THE WORLD NOW IS TO GET RID OF KIRA AND THE EXISTING NOTEBOOKS.
IF WE SUCCEED IN RIDDING THE WORLD OF KIRA AND THE NOTE-BOOKS, WE WIN. IF WE DIE, KIRA WINS.
IF NEAR AND THE SPK DIE, I WIN... IF THEY GET THE NOTE-BOOK, NEAR WINS...
THIS BATTLE IS NO LONGER— NO, EVEN FROM THE START, THIS BATTLE WAS NOT ABOUT AN ARREST OR SOMETHING MEASURED BY THE LAWS OF THIS WORLD...
IT HAS ALWAYS BEEN A ONE-ON-ONE BATTLE TO PROVE WHO IS ON TOP.
NEAR IS RIGHT...

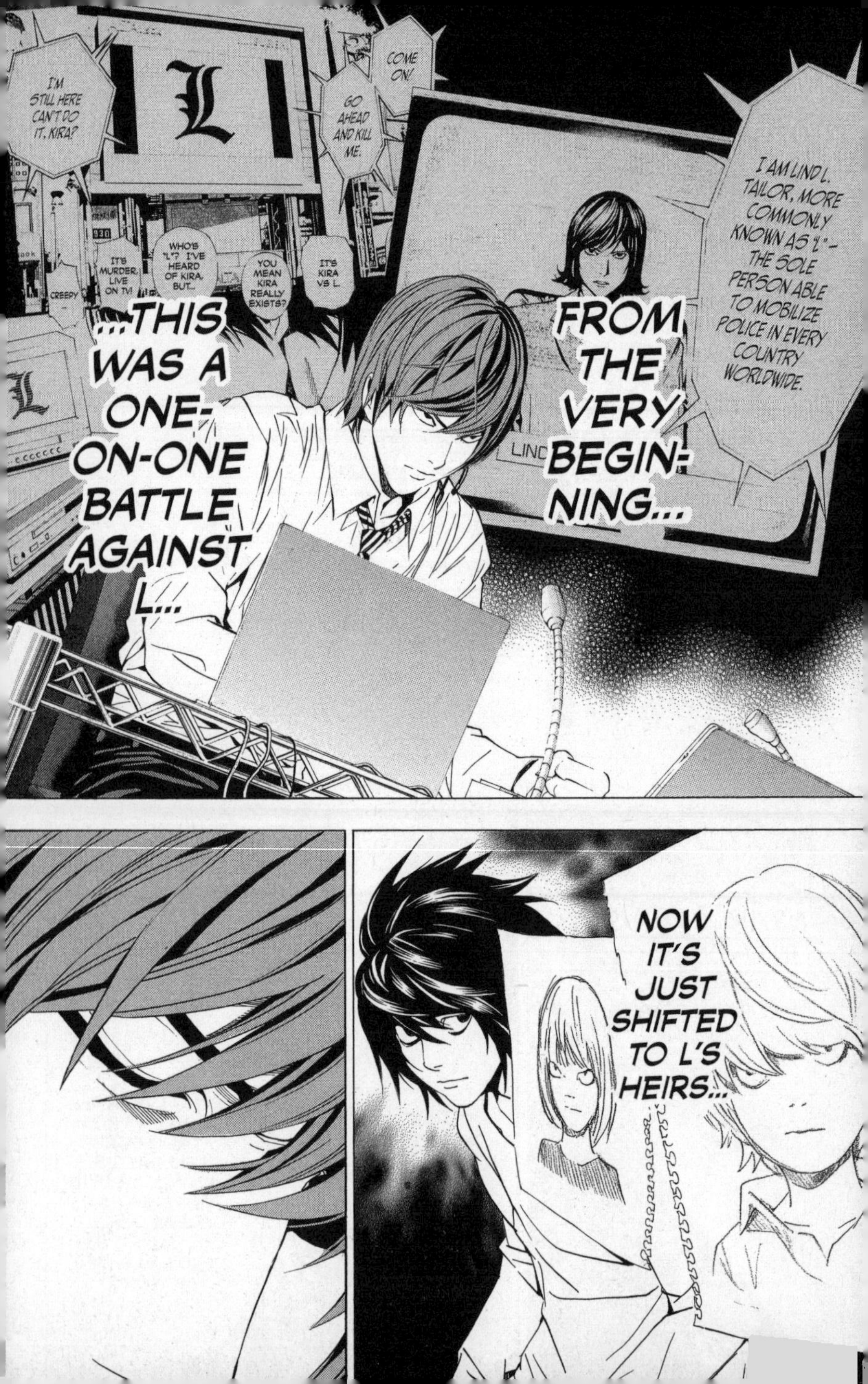
I AM LIND L. TAILOR, MORE COMMONLY KNOWN AS "L" – THE SOLE PERSON ABLE TO MOBILIZE POLICE IN EVERY COUNTRY WORLDWIDE.
LIND
FROM THE VERY BEGIN-NING...
...THIS WAS A ONE-ON-ONE BATTLE AGAINST L...
COME ON!
GO AHEAD AND KILL ME.
I'M STILL HERE CAN'T DO IT, KIRA?
IT'S KIRA VS L.
YOU MEAN KIRA REALLY EXISTS?
WHO'S "L"? I'VE HEARD OF KIRA, BUT...
IT'S MURDER, LIVE ON TV!
CREEPY
NOW IT'S JUST SHIFTED TO L'S HEIRS...

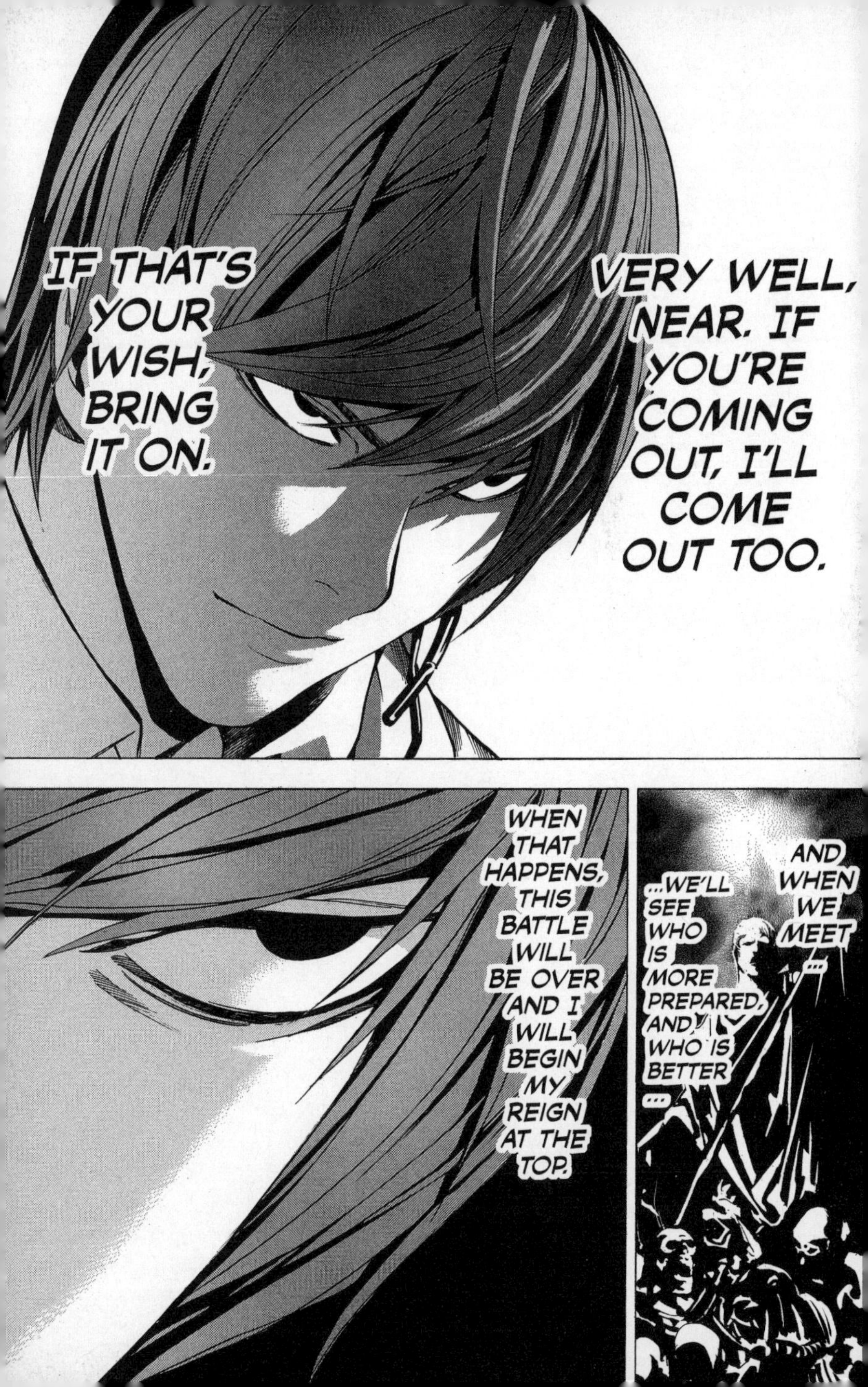
VERY WELL, NEAR. IF YOU'RE COMING OUT, I'LL COME OUT TOO.
IF THAT'S YOUR WISH, BRING IT ON.
AND WHEN WE MEET...
...WE'LL SEE WHO IS MORE PREPARED, AND WHO IS BETTER...
WHEN THAT HAPPENS, THIS BATTLE WILL BE OVER AND I WILL BEGIN MY REIGN AT THE TOP.

DEATH NOTE
How to use it
LX

- After a god of death has brought the DEATH NOTE to the human world and given its ownership to a human, the god of death may have the right to kill the human using his/her own DEATH NOTE for reasons such as disliking the owner.

死神が人間界にデスノートを持ち込み人間に所有権を与えたものの、
その人間が気に入らない等の理由から、
その人間を自分のノートで殺す事は一向に構わない。

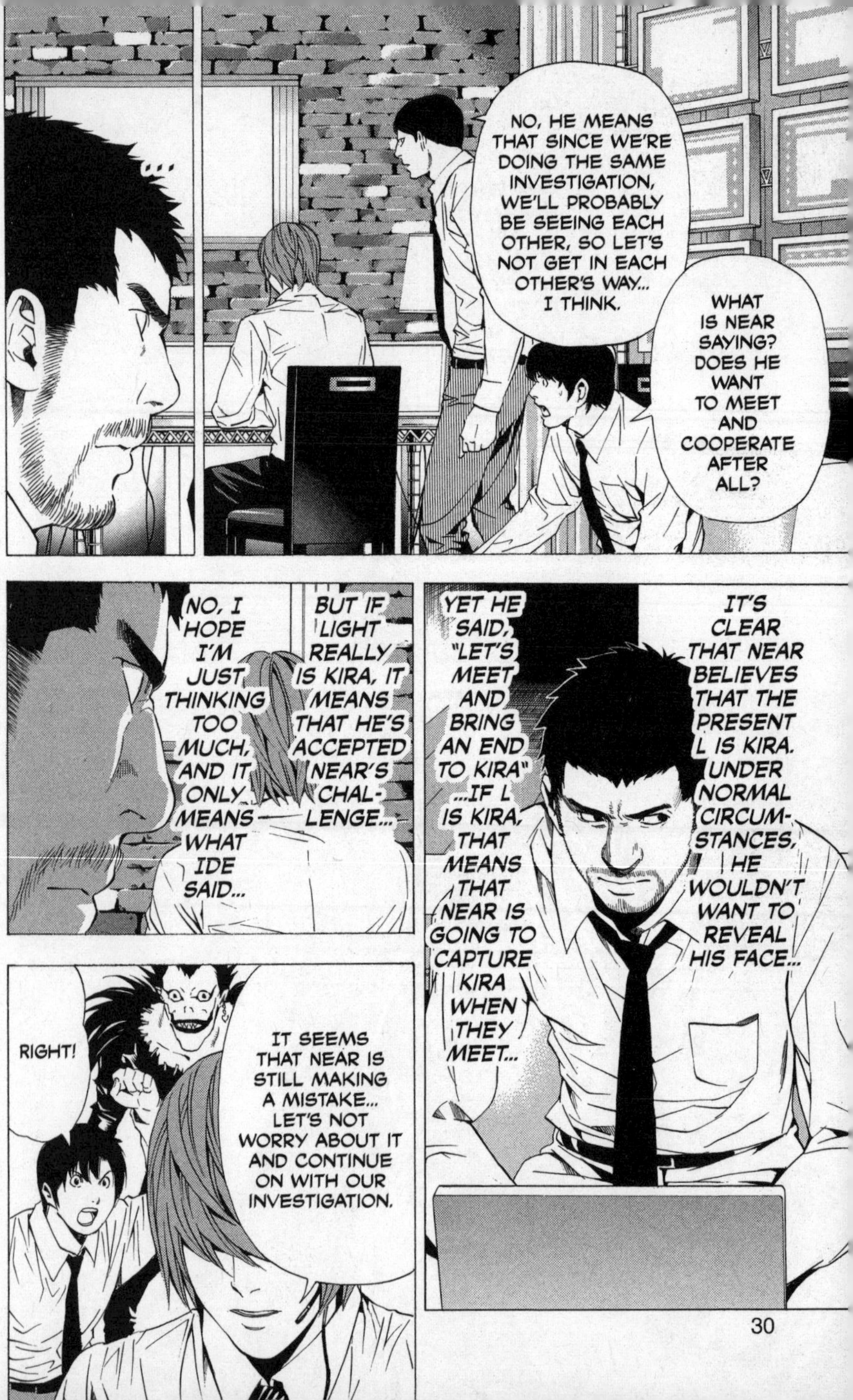
WHAT IS NEAR SAYING? DOES HE WANT TO MEET AND COOPERATE AFTER ALL?
NO, HE MEANS THAT SINCE WE'RE DOING THE SAME INVESTIGATION, WE'LL PROBABLY BE SEEING EACH OTHER, SO LET'S NOT GET IN EACH OTHER'S WAY... I THINK.
...
IT'S CLEAR THAT NEAR BELIEVES THAT THE PRESENT L IS KIRA. UNDER NORMAL CIRCUMSTANCES, HE WOULDN'T WANT TO REVEAL HIS FACE...
YET HE SAID, "LET'S MEET AND BRING AN END TO KIRA" ...IF L IS KIRA, THAT MEANS THAT NEAR IS GOING TO CAPTURE KIRA WHEN THEY MEET...
BUT IF LIGHT REALLY IS KIRA, IT MEANS THAT HE'S ACCEPTED NEAR'S CHALLENGE...
NO, I HOPE I'M JUST THINKING TOO MUCH, AND IT ONLY MEANS WHAT IDE SAID...
IT SEEMS THAT NEAR IS STILL MAKING A MISTAKE... LET'S NOT WORRY ABOUT IT AND CONTINUE ON WITH OUR INVESTIGATION.
RIGHT!

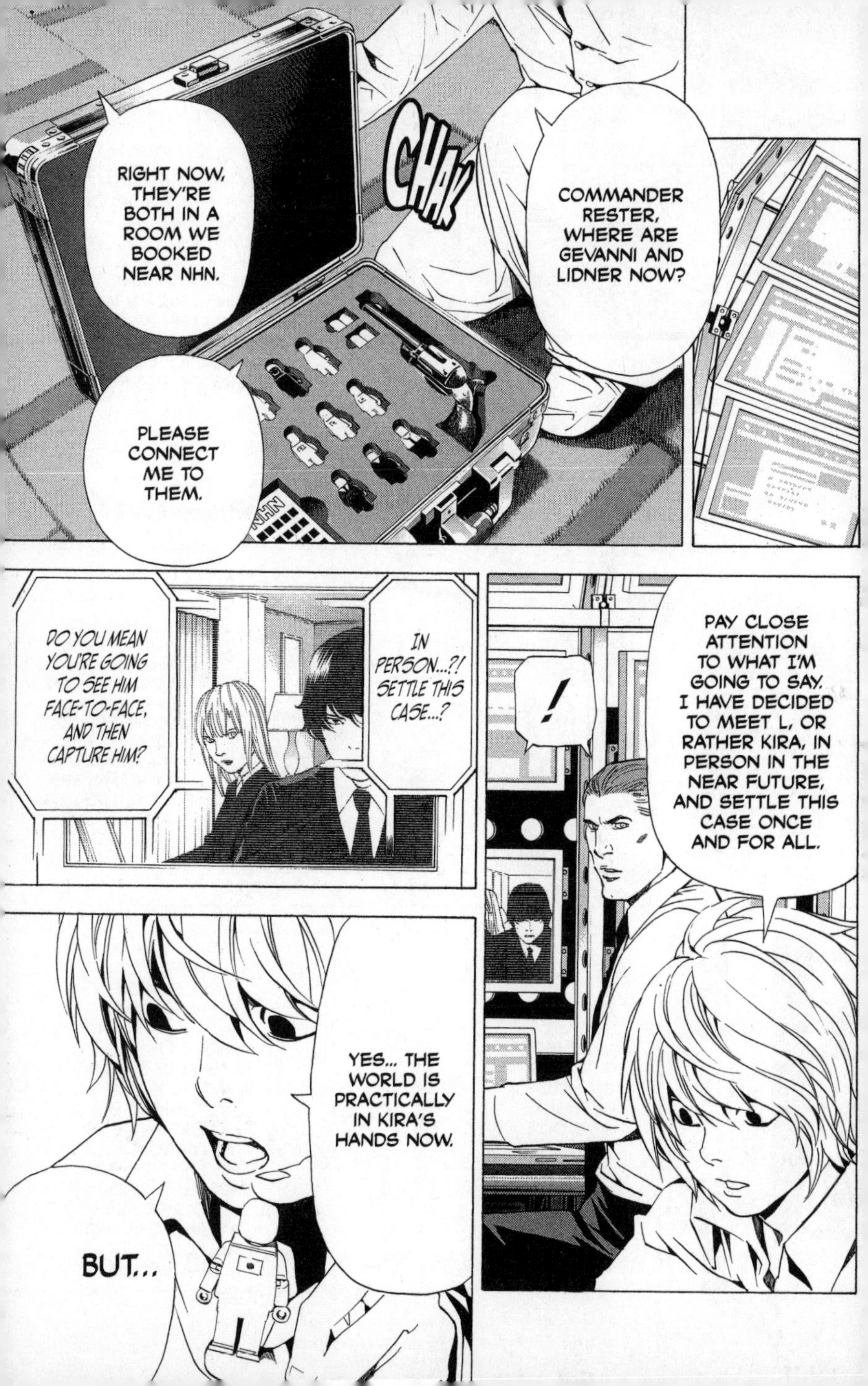
COMMANDER RESTER, WHERE ARE GEVANNI AND LIDNER NOW?
CHAK
RIGHT NOW, THEY'RE BOTH IN A ROOM WE BOOKED NEAR NHN.
PLEASE CONNECT ME TO THEM.
PAY CLOSE ATTENTION TO WHAT I'M GOING TO SAY. I HAVE DECIDED TO MEET L, OR RATHER KIRA, IN PERSON IN THE NEAR FUTURE, AND SETTLE THIS CASE ONCE AND FOR ALL.
!
IN PERSON...?! SETTLE THIS CASE...?
DO YOU MEAN YOU'RE GOING TO SEE HIM FACE-TO-FACE, AND THEN CAPTURE HIM?
YES... THE WORLD IS PRACTICALLY IN KIRA'S HANDS NOW.
BUT...

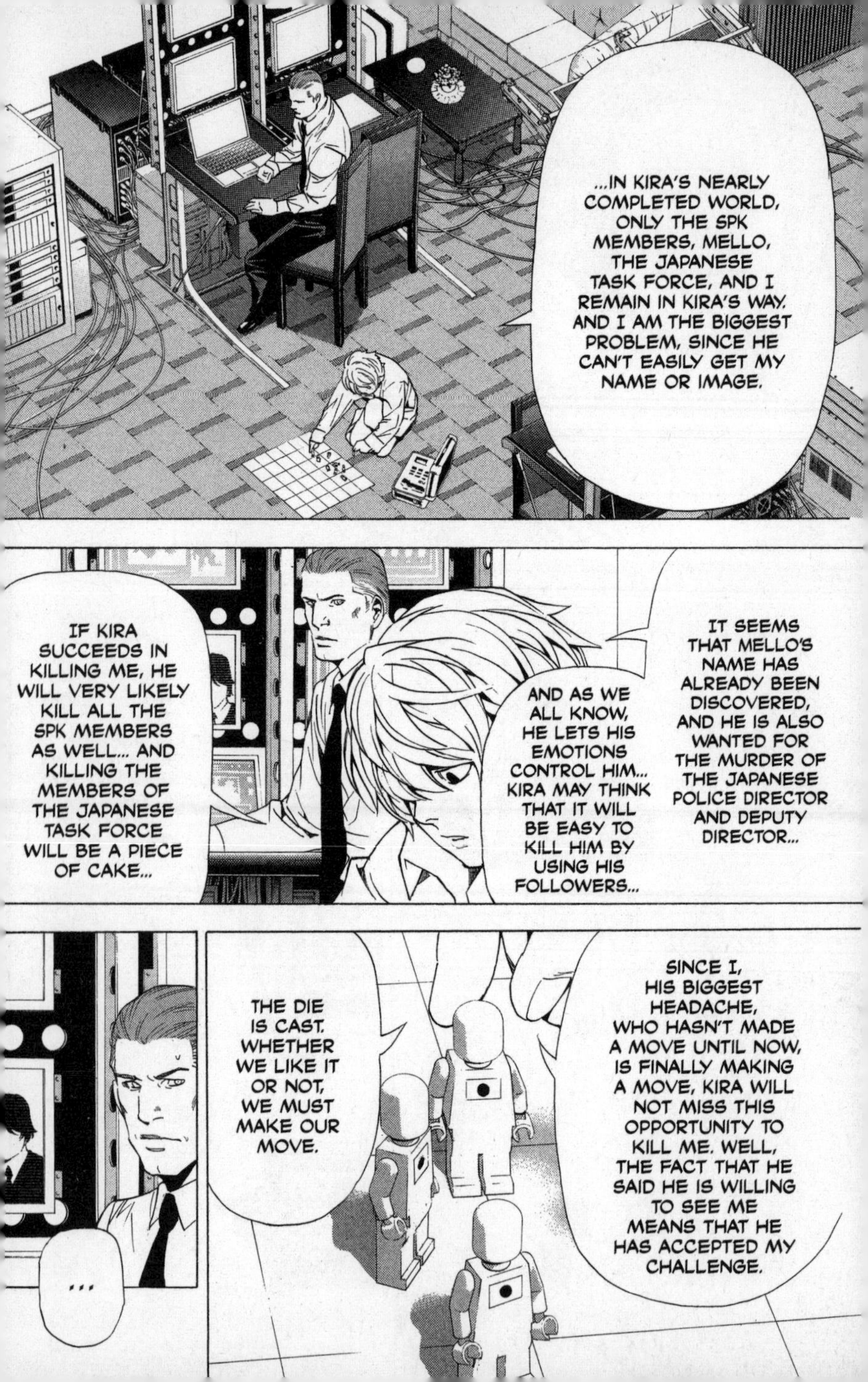
...IN KIRA'S NEARLY COMPLETED WORLD, ONLY THE SPK MEMBERS, MELLO, THE JAPANESE TASK FORCE, AND I REMAIN IN KIRA'S WAY. AND I AM THE BIGGEST PROBLEM, SINCE HE CAN'T EASILY GET MY NAME OR IMAGE.
IT SEEMS THAT MELLO'S NAME HAS ALREADY BEEN DISCOVERED, AND HE IS ALSO WANTED FOR THE MURDER OF THE JAPANESE POLICE DIRECTOR AND DEPUTY DIRECTOR...
AND AS WE ALL KNOW, HE LETS HIS EMOTIONS CONTROL HIM... KIRA MAY THINK THAT IT WILL BE EASY TO KILL HIM BY USING HIS FOLLOWERS...
IF KIRA SUCCEEDS IN KILLING ME, HE WILL VERY LIKELY KILL ALL THE SPK MEMBERS AS WELL... AND KILLING THE MEMBERS OF THE JAPANESE TASK FORCE WILL BE A PIECE OF CAKE...
SINCE I, HIS BIGGEST HEADACHE, WHO HASN'T MADE A MOVE UNTIL NOW, IS FINALLY MAKING A MOVE, KIRA WILL NOT MISS THIS OPPORTUNITY TO KILL ME. WELL, THE FACT THAT HE SAID HE IS WILLING TO SEE ME MEANS THAT HE HAS ACCEPTED MY CHALLENGE.
THE DIE IS CAST. WHETHER WE LIKE IT OR NOT, WE MUST MAKE OUR MOVE.
...

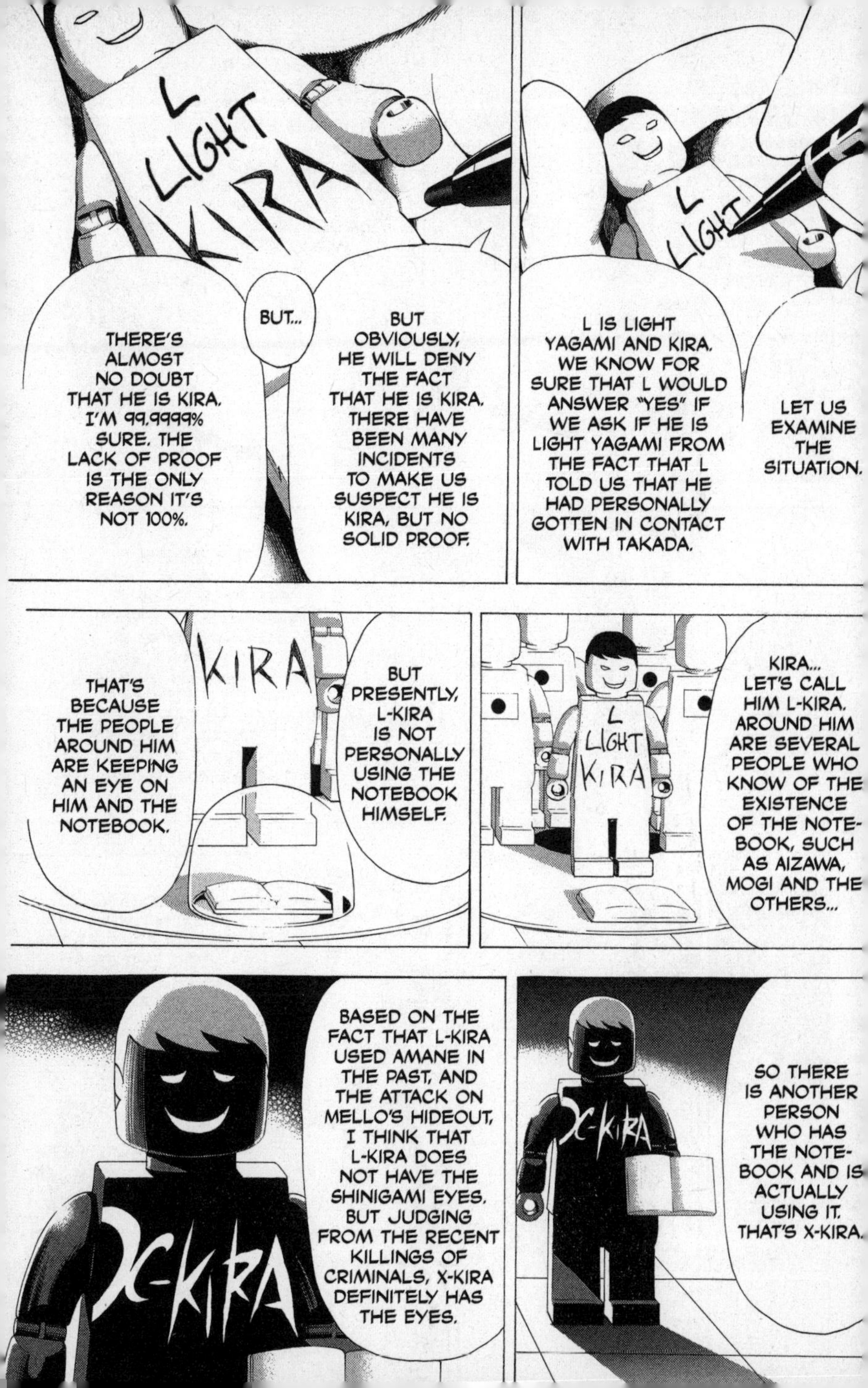

L
LIGHT
LET US EXAMINE THE SITUATION.
L IS LIGHT YAGAMI AND KIRA. WE KNOW FOR SURE THAT L WOULD ANSWER "YES" IF WE ASK IF HE IS LIGHT YAGAMI FROM THE FACT THAT L TOLD US THAT HE HAD PERSONALLY GOTTEN IN CONTACT WITH TAKADA.
L
LIGHT
KIRA
BUT OBVIOUSLY, HE WILL DENY THE FACT THAT HE IS KIRA. THERE HAVE BEEN MANY INCIDENTS TO MAKE US SUSPECT HE IS KIRA, BUT NO SOLID PROOF.
BUT...
THERE'S ALMOST NO DOUBT THAT HE IS KIRA. I'M 99.9999% SURE. THE LACK OF PROOF IS THE ONLY REASON IT'S NOT 100%.
KIRA... LET'S CALL HIM L-KIRA. AROUND HIM ARE SEVERAL PEOPLE WHO KNOW OF THE EXISTENCE OF THE NOTE-BOOK, SUCH AS AIZAWA, MOGI AND THE OTHERS...
L
LIGHT
KIRA
BUT PRESENTLY, L-KIRA IS NOT PERSONALLY USING THE NOTEBOOK HIMSELF.
KIRA
THAT'S BECAUSE THE PEOPLE AROUND HIM ARE KEEPING AN EYE ON HIM AND THE NOTEBOOK.
SO THERE IS ANOTHER PERSON WHO HAS THE NOTE-BOOK AND IS ACTUALLY USING IT. THAT'S X-KIRA.
X-KIRA
BASED ON THE FACT THAT L-KIRA USED AMANE IN THE PAST, AND THE ATTACK ON MELLO'S HIDEOUT, I THINK THAT L-KIRA DOES NOT HAVE THE SHINIGAMI EYES. BUT JUDGING FROM THE RECENT KILLINGS OF CRIMINALS, X-KIRA DEFINITELY HAS THE EYES.
X-KIRA

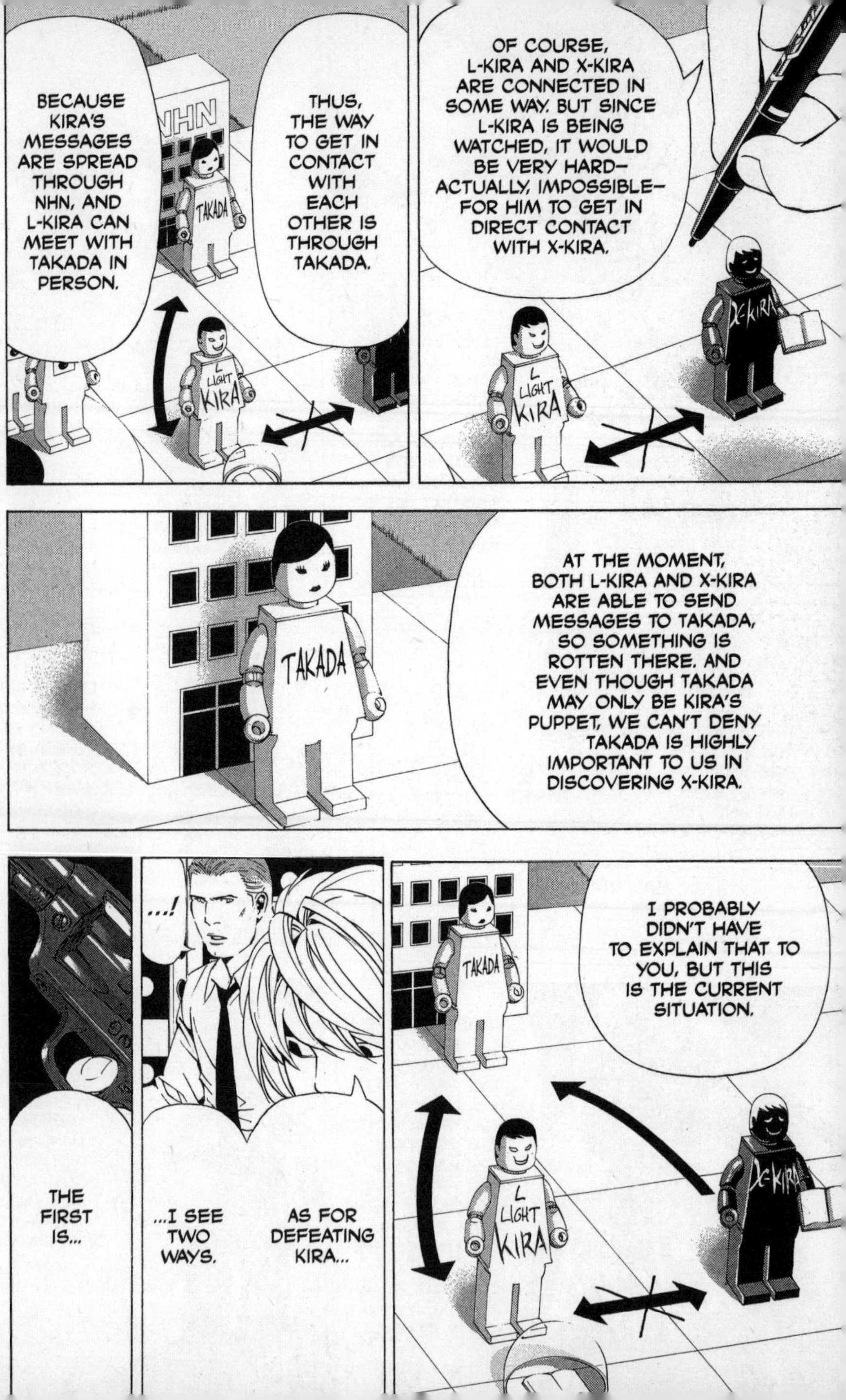
OF COURSE, L-KIRA AND X-KIRA ARE CONNECTED IN SOME WAY. BUT SINCE L-KIRA IS BEING WATCHED, IT WOULD BE VERY HARD—ACTUALLY, IMPOSSIBLE—FOR HIM TO GET IN DIRECT CONTACT WITH X-KIRA.
X-KIRA
L LIGHT KIRA
THUS, THE WAY TO GET IN CONTACT WITH EACH OTHER IS THROUGH TAKADA.
BECAUSE KIRA'S MESSAGES ARE SPREAD THROUGH NHN, AND L-KIRA CAN MEET WITH TAKADA IN PERSON.
NHN
TAKADA
L LIGHT KIRA
AT THE MOMENT, BOTH L-KIRA AND X-KIRA ARE ABLE TO SEND MESSAGES TO TAKADA, SO SOMETHING IS ROTTEN THERE. AND EVEN THOUGH TAKADA MAY ONLY BE KIRA'S PUPPET, WE CAN'T DENY TAKADA IS HIGHLY IMPORTANT TO US IN DISCOVERING X-KIRA.
TAKADA
I PROBABLY DIDN'T HAVE TO EXPLAIN THAT TO YOU, BUT THIS IS THE CURRENT SITUATION.
TAKADA
X-KIRA
L LIGHT KIRA
...!
AS FOR DEFEATING KIRA...
...I SEE TWO WAYS.
THE FIRST IS...

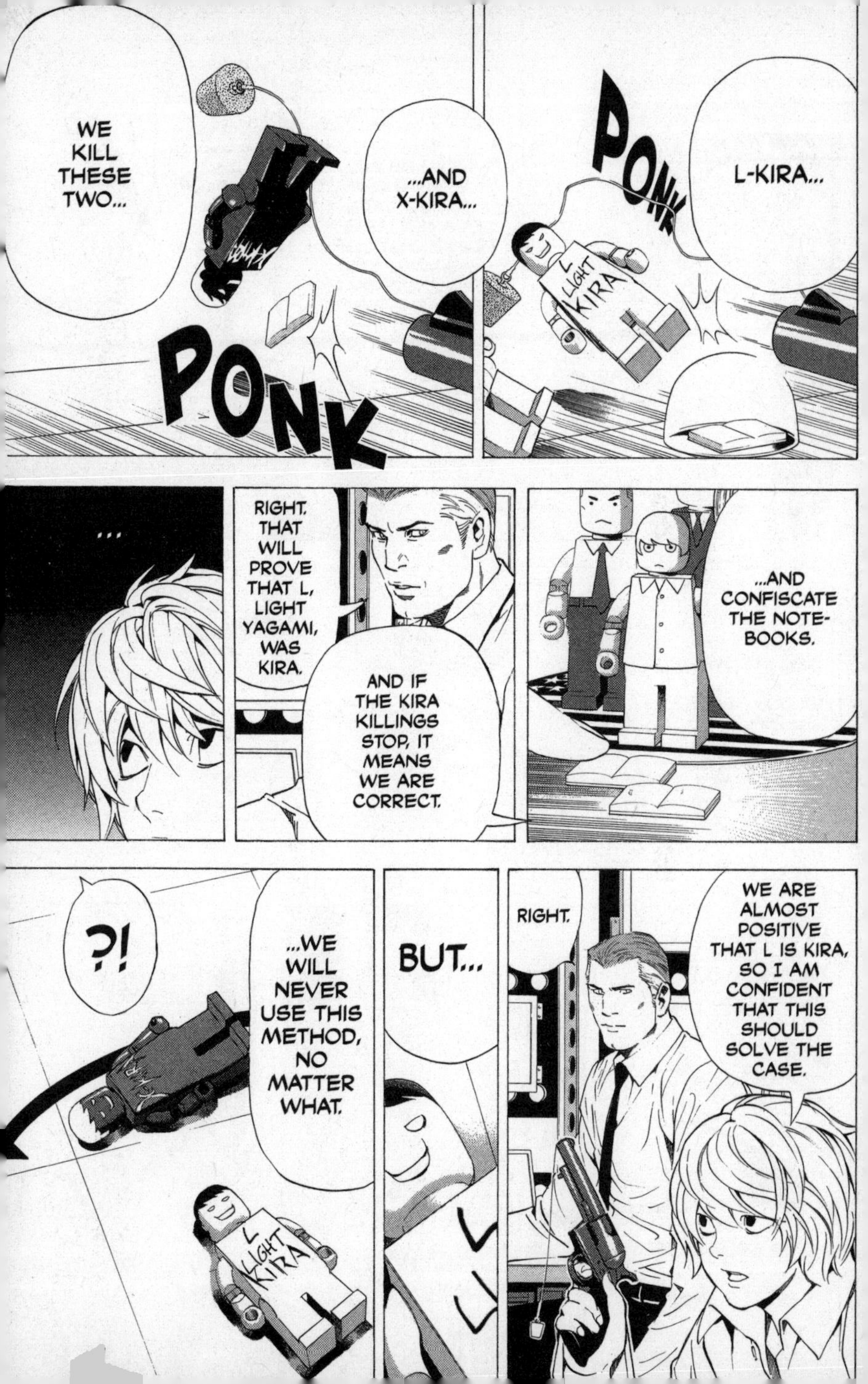
L-KIRA...
PONK
L LIGHT KIRA
...AND X-KIRA...
WE KILL THESE TWO...
PONK
...AND CONFISCATE THE NOTE-BOOKS.
RIGHT. THAT WILL PROVE THAT L, LIGHT YAGAMI, WAS KIRA.
AND IF THE KIRA KILLINGS STOP, IT MEANS WE ARE CORRECT.
...
WE ARE ALMOST POSITIVE THAT L IS KIRA, SO I AM CONFIDENT THAT THIS SHOULD SOLVE THE CASE.
RIGHT.
BUT...
...WE WILL NEVER USE THIS METHOD, NO MATTER WHAT.
?!
L LIGHT KIRA

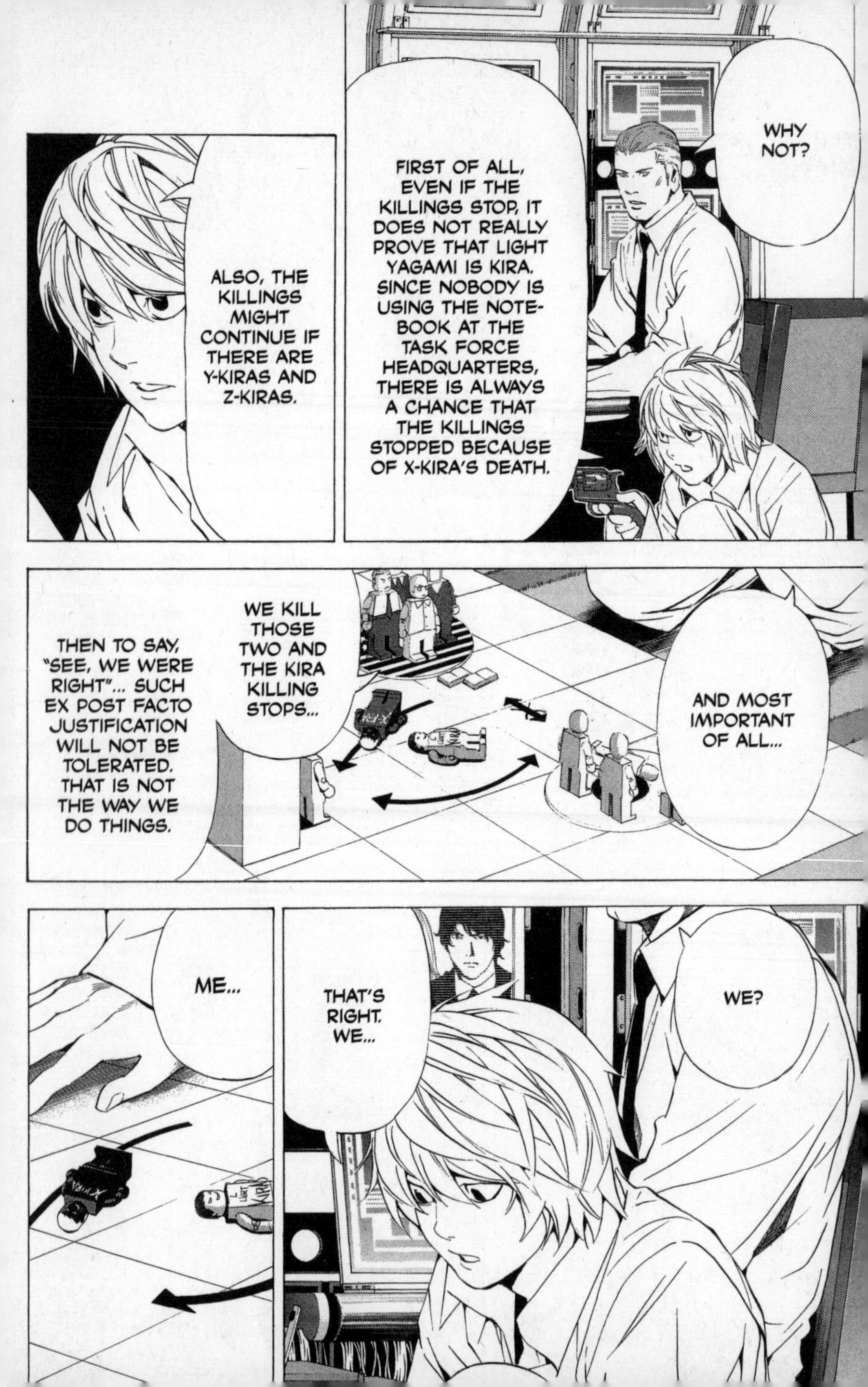
WHY NOT?
FIRST OF ALL, EVEN IF THE KILLINGS STOP, IT DOES NOT REALLY PROVE THAT LIGHT YAGAMI IS KIRA. SINCE NOBODY IS USING THE NOTE-BOOK AT THE TASK FORCE HEADQUARTERS, THERE IS ALWAYS A CHANCE THAT THE KILLINGS STOPPED BECAUSE OF X-KIRA'S DEATH.
ALSO, THE KILLINGS MIGHT CONTINUE IF THERE ARE Y-KIRAS AND Z-KIRAS.
AND MOST IMPORTANT OF ALL...
WE KILL THOSE TWO AND THE KIRA KILLING STOPS...
THEN TO SAY, "SEE, WE WERE RIGHT"... SUCH EX POST FACTO JUSTIFICATION WILL NOT BE TOLERATED. THAT IS NOT THE WAY WE DO THINGS.
WE?
THAT'S RIGHT. WE...
ME...

READ THIS WAY

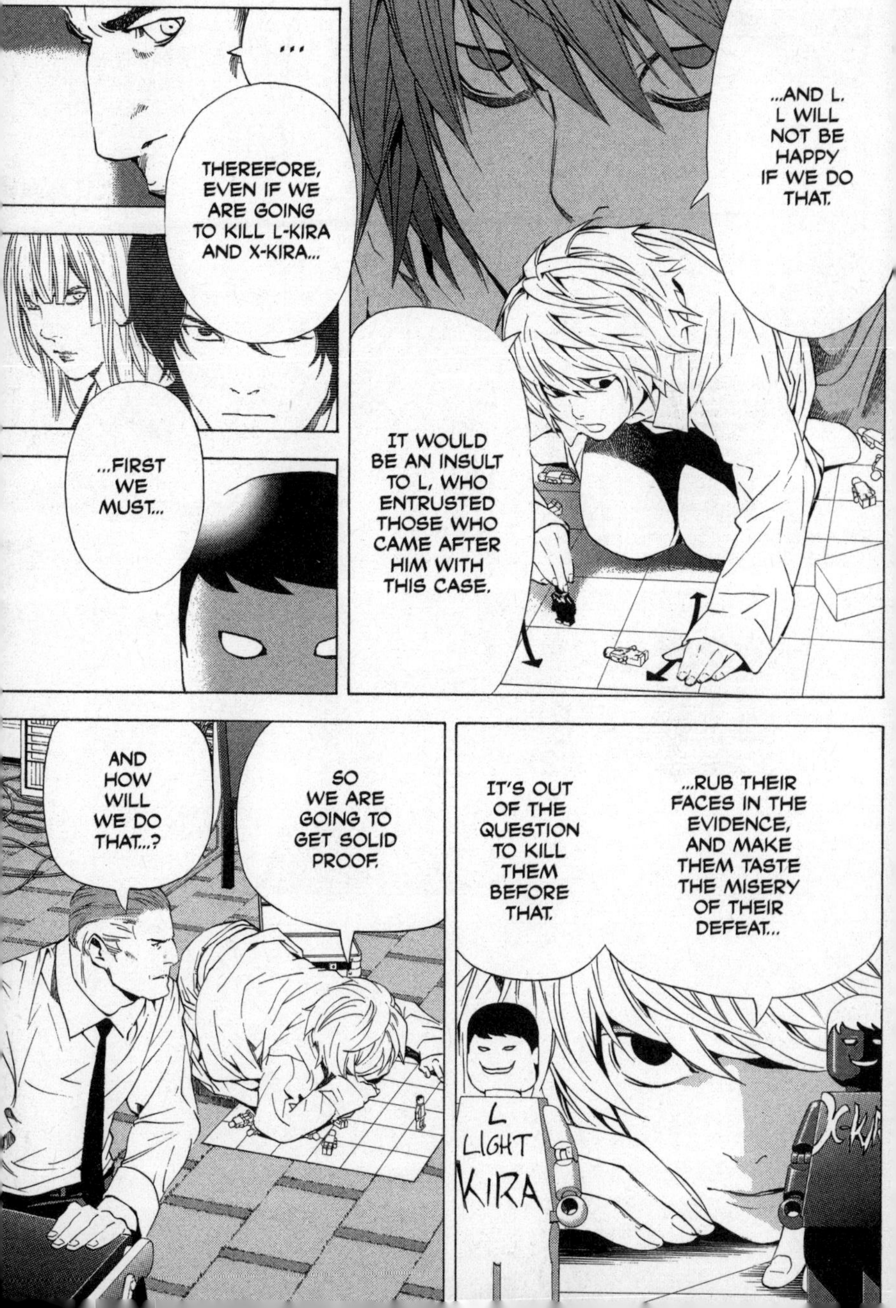
...AND L. L WILL NOT BE HAPPY IF WE DO THAT.
IT WOULD BE AN INSULT TO L, WHO ENTRUSTED THOSE WHO CAME AFTER HIM WITH THIS CASE.
...
THEREFORE, EVEN IF WE ARE GOING TO KILL L-KIRA AND X-KIRA...
...FIRST WE MUST...
...RUB THEIR FACES IN THE EVIDENCE, AND MAKE THEM TASTE THE MISERY OF THEIR DEFEAT...
IT'S OUT OF THE QUESTION TO KILL THEM BEFORE THAT.
L
LIGHT
KIRA
SO WE ARE GOING TO GET SOLID PROOF.
AND HOW WILL WE DO THAT...?

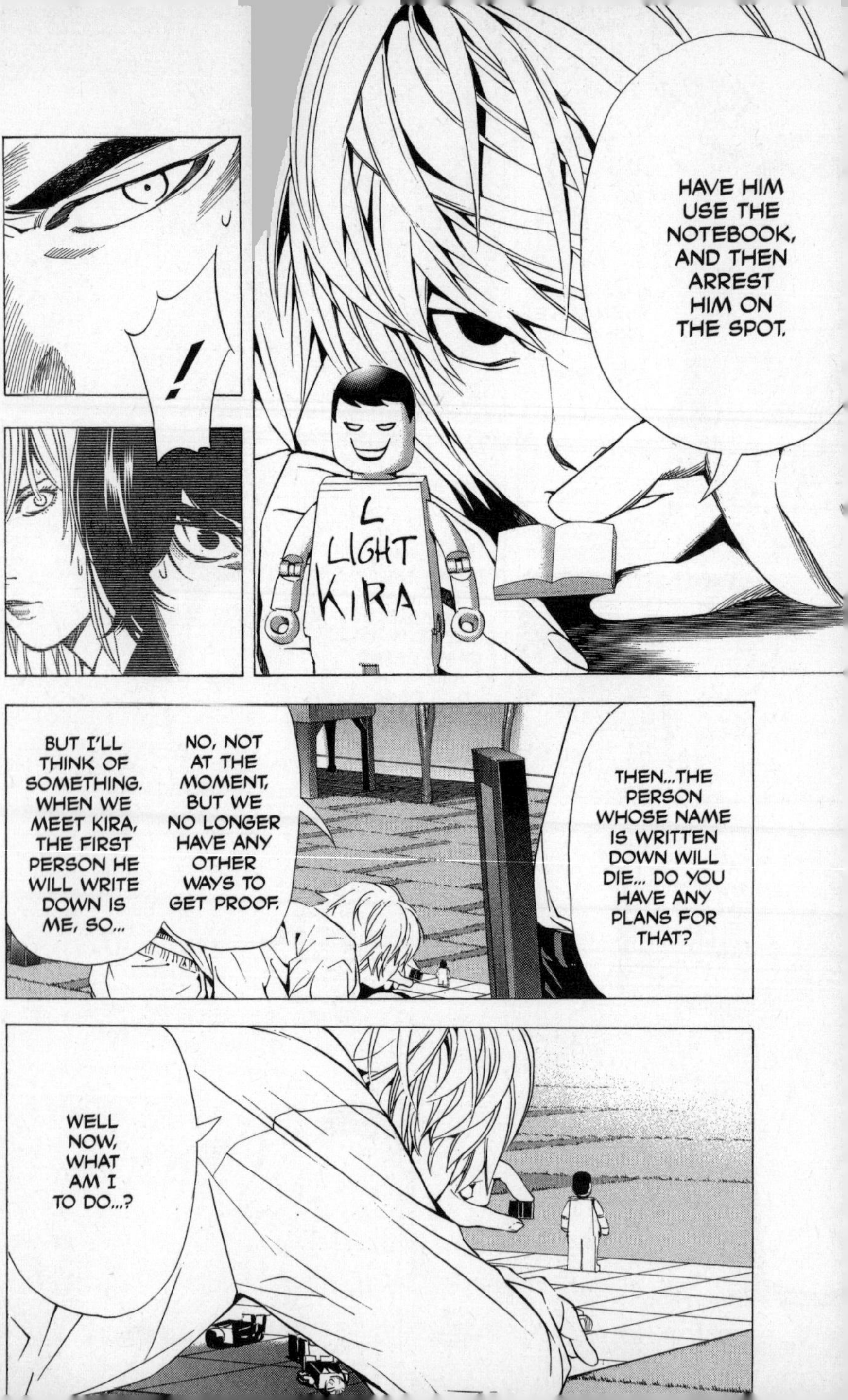
HAVE HIM USE THE NOTEBOOK, AND THEN ARREST HIM ON THE SPOT.
L
LIGHT
KIRA
!
THEN...THE PERSON WHOSE NAME IS WRITTEN DOWN WILL DIE... DO YOU HAVE ANY PLANS FOR THAT?
NO, NOT AT THE MOMENT, BUT WE NO LONGER HAVE ANY OTHER WAYS TO GET PROOF.
BUT I'LL THINK OF SOMETHING. WHEN WE MEET KIRA, THE FIRST PERSON HE WILL WRITE DOWN IS ME, SO...
WELL NOW, WHAT AM I TO DO...?

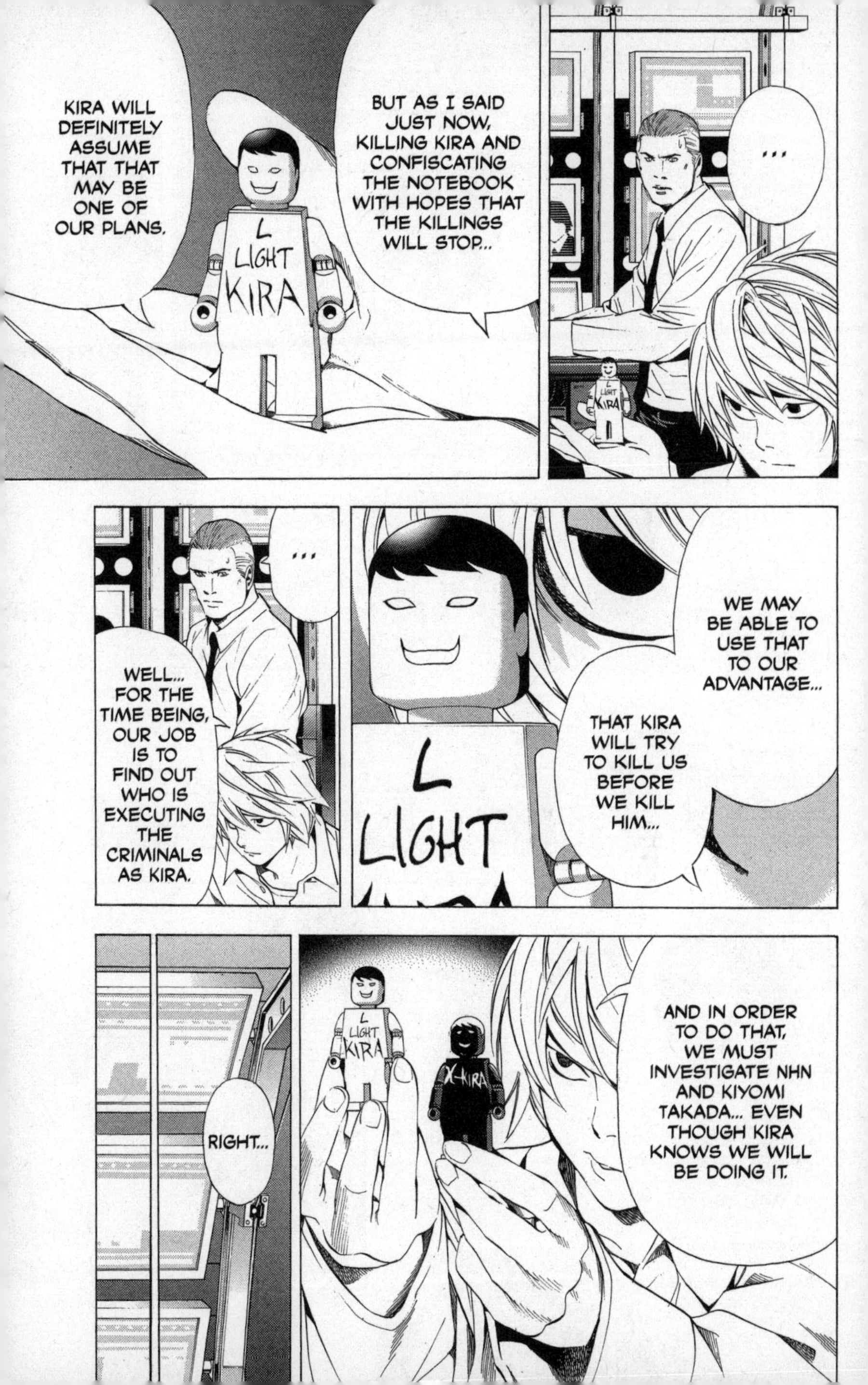
...
L
LIGHT
KIRA
BUT AS I SAID JUST NOW, KILLING KIRA AND CONFISCATING THE NOTEBOOK WITH HOPES THAT THE KILLINGS WILL STOP...
KIRA WILL DEFINITELY ASSUME THAT THAT MAY BE ONE OF OUR PLANS.
L
LIGHT
KIRA
WE MAY BE ABLE TO USE THAT TO OUR ADVANTAGE...
THAT KIRA WILL TRY TO KILL US BEFORE WE KILL HIM...
L
LIGHT
...
WELL... FOR THE TIME BEING, OUR JOB IS TO FIND OUT WHO IS EXECUTING THE CRIMINALS AS KIRA.
AND IN ORDER TO DO THAT, WE MUST INVESTIGATE NHN AND KIYOMI TAKADA... EVEN THOUGH KIRA KNOWS WE WILL BE DOING IT.
L
LIGHT
KIRA
X-KIRA
RIGHT...

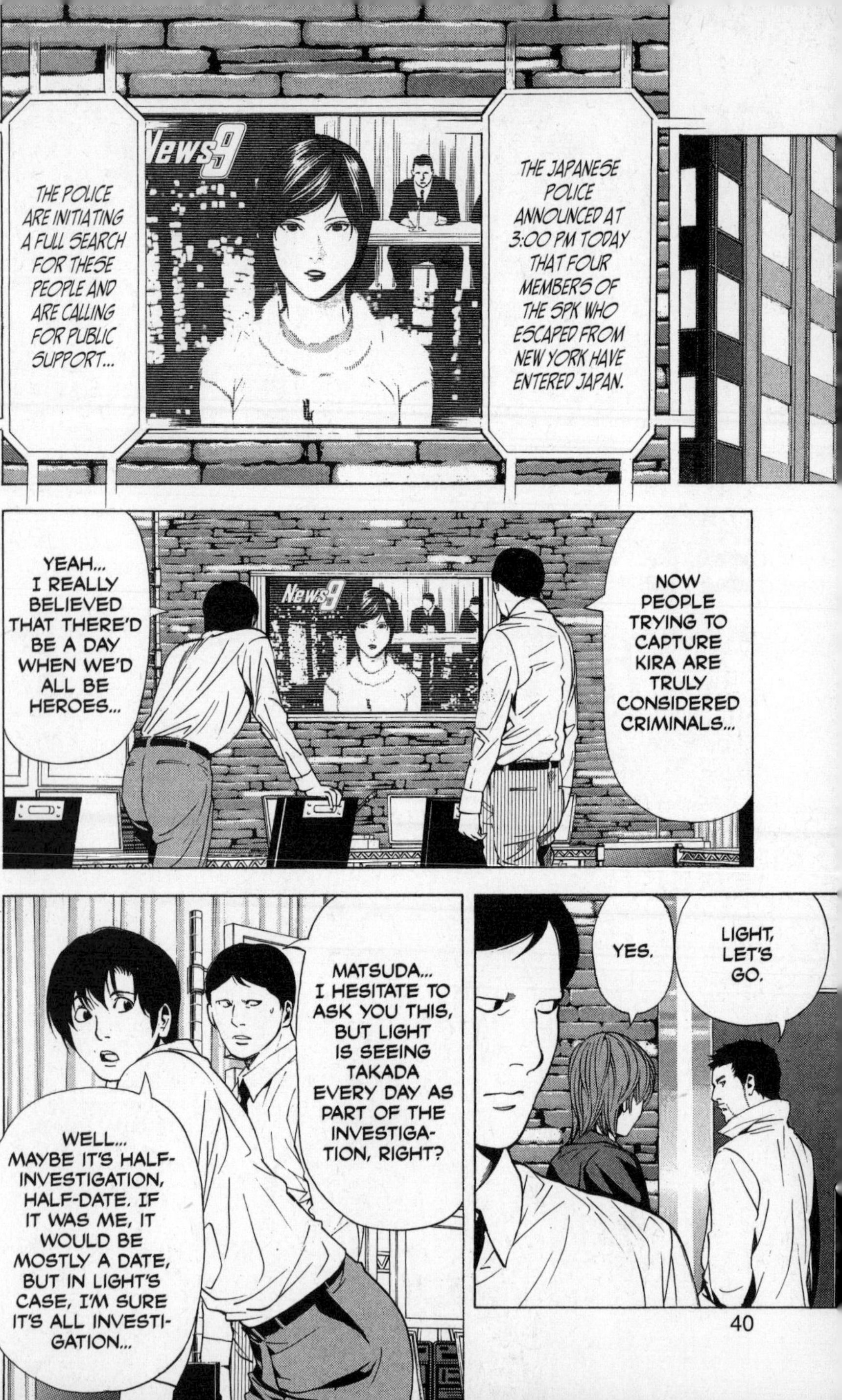
THE JAPANESE POLICE ANNOUNCED AT 3:00 PM TODAY THAT FOUR MEMBERS OF THE SPK WHO ESCAPED FROM NEW YORK HAVE ENTERED JAPAN.
News9
THE POLICE ARE INITIATING A FULL SEARCH FOR THESE PEOPLE AND ARE CALLING FOR PUBLIC SUPPORT...
NOW PEOPLE TRYING TO CAPTURE KIRA ARE TRULY CONSIDERED CRIMINALS...
News9
YEAH... I REALLY BELIEVED THAT THERE'D BE A DAY WHEN WE'D ALL BE HEROES...
LIGHT, LET'S GO.
YES.
MATSUDA... I HESITATE TO ASK YOU THIS, BUT LIGHT IS SEEING TAKADA EVERY DAY AS PART OF THE INVESTIGATION, RIGHT?
WELL... MAYBE IT'S HALF-INVESTIGATION, HALF-DATE. IF IT WAS ME, IT WOULD BE MOSTLY A DATE, BUT IN LIGHT'S CASE, I'M SURE IT'S ALL INVESTIGATION...

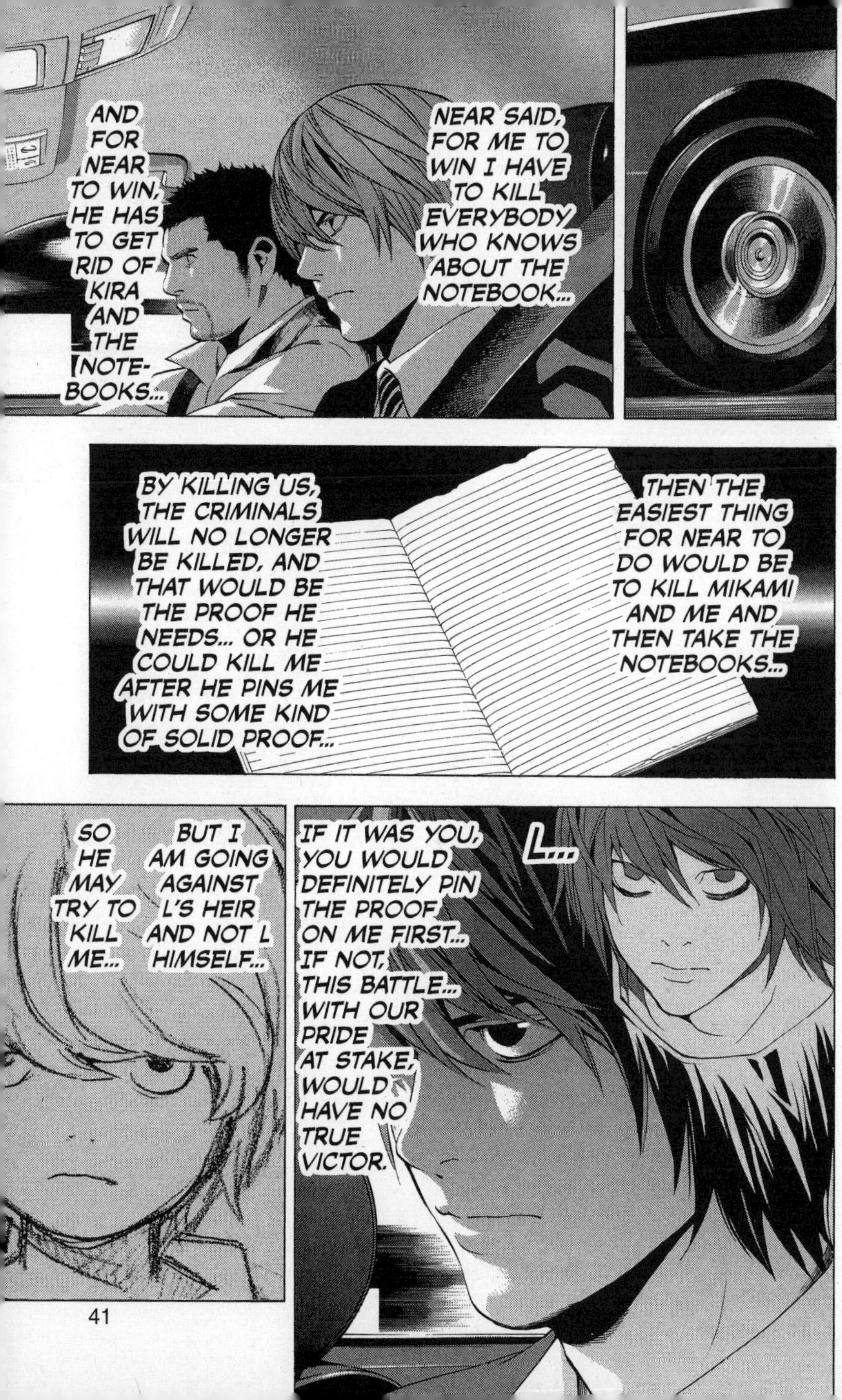
NEAR SAID, FOR ME TO WIN I HAVE TO KILL EVERYBODY WHO KNOWS ABOUT THE NOTEBOOK...
AND FOR NEAR TO WIN, HE HAS TO GET RID OF KIRA AND THE NOTE-BOOKS...
THEN THE EASIEST THING FOR NEAR TO DO WOULD BE TO KILL MIKAMI AND ME AND THEN TAKE THE NOTEBOOKS...
BY KILLING US, THE CRIMINALS WILL NO LONGER BE KILLED, AND THAT WOULD BE THE PROOF HE NEEDS... OR HE COULD KILL ME AFTER HE PINS ME WITH SOME KIND OF SOLID PROOF...
L...
IF IT WAS YOU, YOU WOULD DEFINITELY PIN THE PROOF ON ME FIRST... IF NOT, THIS BATTLE... WITH OUR PRIDE AT STAKE, WOULD HAVE NO TRUE VICTOR.
BUT I AM GOING AGAINST L'S HEIR AND NOT L HIMSELF...
SO HE MAY TRY TO KILL ME...

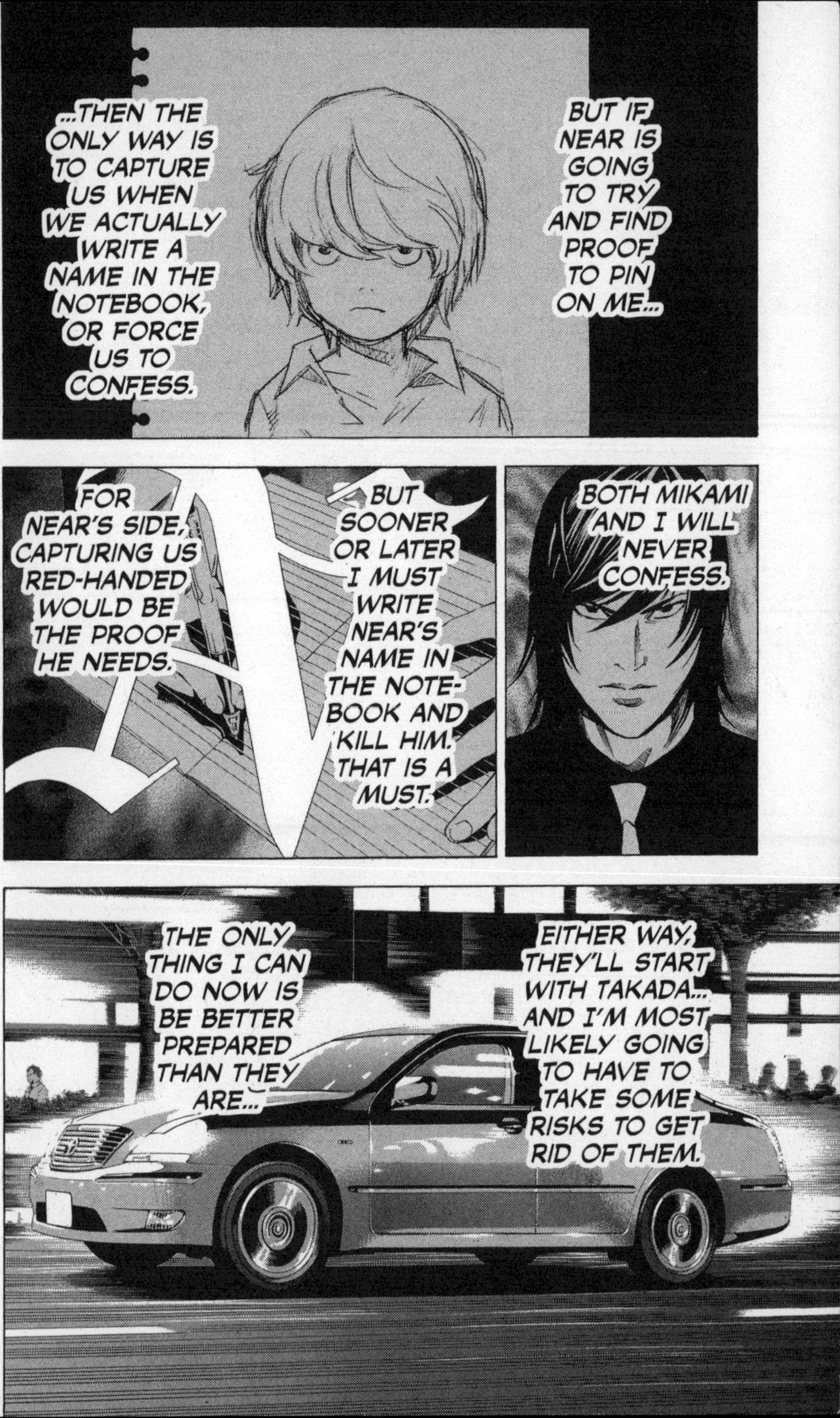
BUT IF NEAR IS GOING TO TRY AND FIND PROOF TO PIN ON ME...
...THEN THE ONLY WAY IS TO CAPTURE US WHEN WE ACTUALLY WRITE A NAME IN THE NOTEBOOK, OR FORCE US TO CONFESS.
BOTH MIKAMI AND I WILL NEVER CONFESS.
BUT SOONER OR LATER I MUST WRITE NEAR'S NAME IN THE NOTE-BOOK AND KILL HIM. THAT IS A MUST.
FOR NEAR'S SIDE, CAPTURING US RED-HANDED WOULD BE THE PROOF HE NEEDS.
EITHER WAY, THEY'LL START WITH TAKADA... AND I'M MOST LIKELY GOING TO HAVE TO TAKE SOME RISKS TO GET RID OF THEM.
THE ONLY THING I CAN DO NOW IS BE BETTER PREPARED THAN THEY ARE...

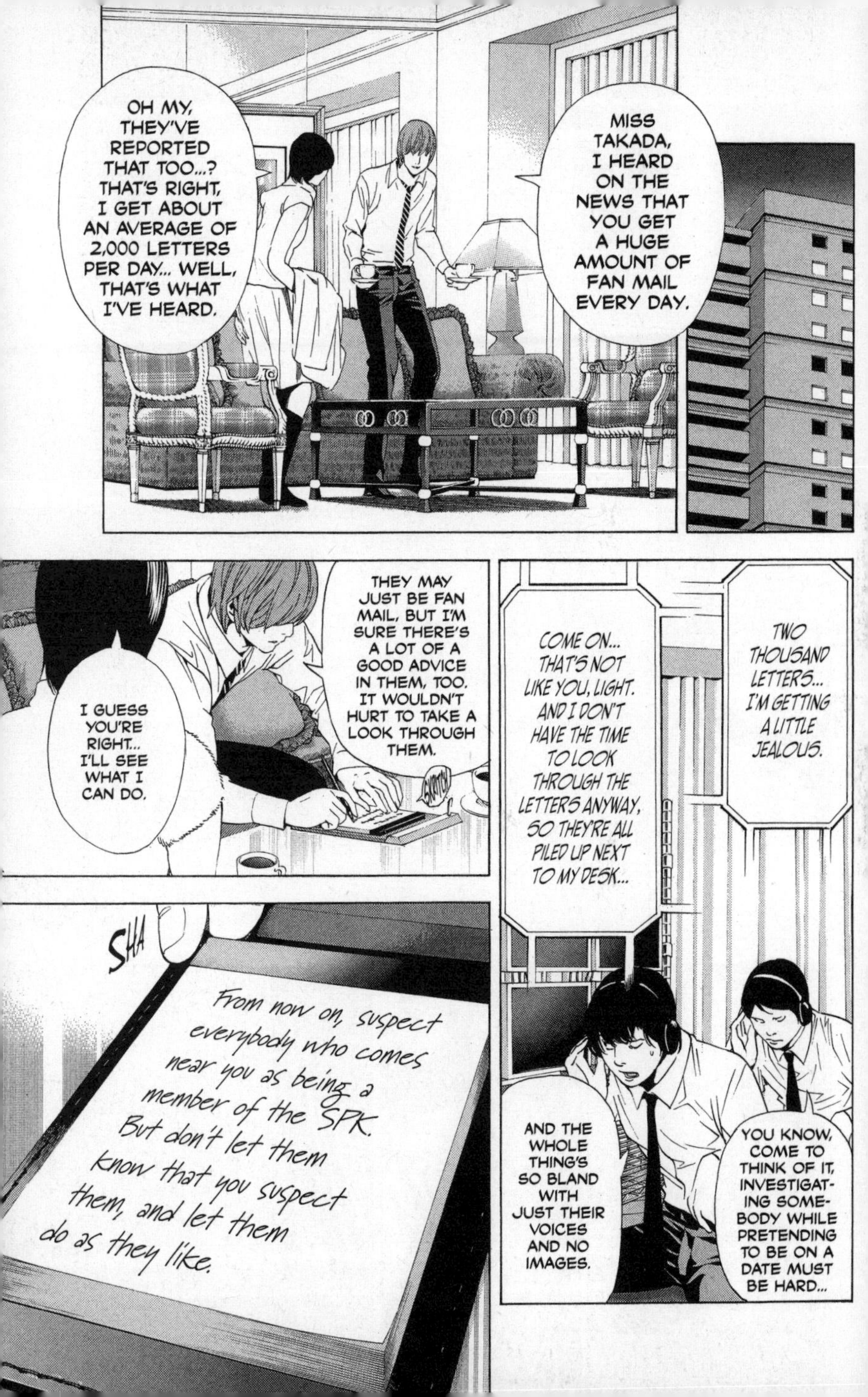
MISS TAKADA, I HEARD ON THE NEWS THAT YOU GET A HUGE AMOUNT OF FAN MAIL EVERY DAY.
OH MY, THEY'VE REPORTED THAT TOO...? THAT'S RIGHT, I GET ABOUT AN AVERAGE OF 2,000 LETTERS PER DAY... WELL, THAT'S WHAT I'VE HEARD.
TWO THOUSAND LETTERS... I'M GETTING A LITTLE JEALOUS.
COME ON... THAT'S NOT LIKE YOU, LIGHT. AND I DON'T HAVE THE TIME TO LOOK THROUGH THE LETTERS ANYWAY, SO THEY'RE ALL PILED UP NEXT TO MY DESK...
THEY MAY JUST BE FAN MAIL, BUT I'M SURE THERE'S A LOT OF A GOOD ADVICE IN THEM, TOO. IT WOULDN'T HURT TO TAKE A LOOK THROUGH THEM.
SKRITCH
I GUESS YOU'RE RIGHT... I'LL SEE WHAT I CAN DO.
YOU KNOW, COME TO THINK OF IT, INVESTIGATING SOMEBODY WHILE PRETENDING TO BE ON A DATE MUST BE HARD...
AND THE WHOLE THING'S SO BLAND WITH JUST THEIR VOICES AND NO IMAGES.
SHA
From now on, suspect everybody who comes near you as being a member of the SPK. But don't let them know that you suspect them, and let them do as they like.

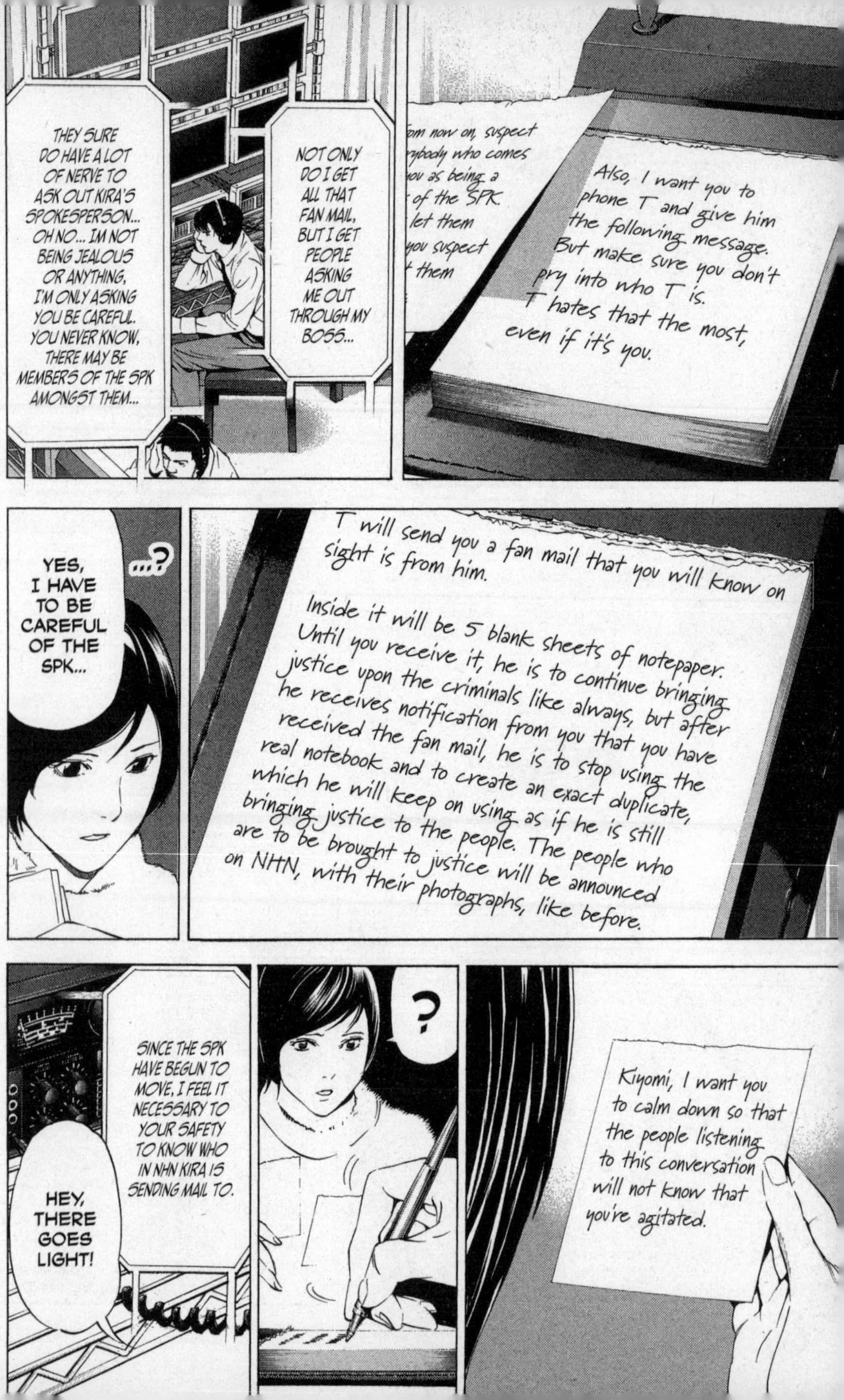
om now on, suspect
rybody who comes
ou as being a
of the SPK.
let them
you suspect
them
Also, I want you to phone T and give him the following message. But make sure you don't pry into who T is. T hates that the most, even if it's you.
NOT ONLY DO I GET ALL THAT FAN MAIL, BUT I GET PEOPLE ASKING ME OUT THROUGH MY BOSS...
THEY SURE DO HAVE A LOT OF NERVE TO ASK OUT KIRA'S SPOKESPERSON... OH NO... IM NOT BEING JEALOUS OR ANYTHING, I'M ONLY ASKING YOU BE CAREFUL. YOU NEVER KNOW, THERE MAY BE MEMBERS OF THE SPK AMONGST THEM...
T will send you a fan mail that you will know on sight is from him.
Inside it will be 5 blank sheets of notepaper. Until you receive it, he is to continue bringing justice upon the criminals like always, but after he receives notification from you that you have received the fan mail, he is to stop using the real notebook and to create an exact duplicate, which he will keep on using as if he is still bringing justice to the people. The people who are to be brought to justice will be announced on NHN, with their photographs, like before.
...?
YES, I HAVE TO BE CAREFUL OF THE SPK...
Kiyomi, I want you to calm down so that the people listening to this conversation will not know that you're agitated.
?
SINCE THE SPK HAVE BEGUN TO MOVE, I FEEL IT NECESSARY TO YOUR SAFETY TO KNOW WHO IN NHN KIRA IS SENDING MAIL TO.
HEY, THERE GOES LIGHT!

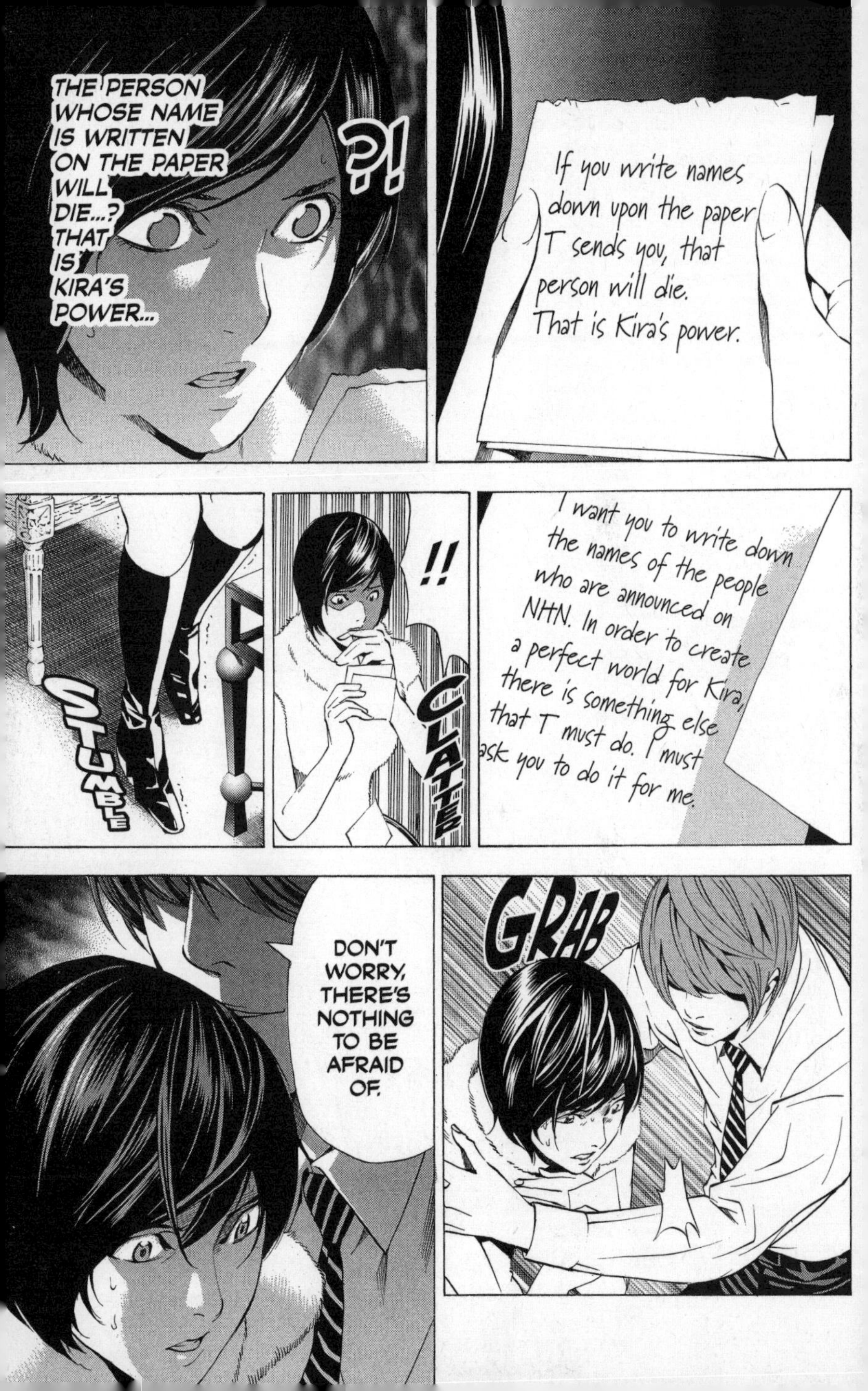
If you write names down upon the paper T sends you, that person will die. That is Kira's power.
THE PERSON WHOSE NAME IS WRITTEN ON THE PAPER WILL DIE...? THAT IS KIRA'S POWER...
?!
I want you to write down the names of the people who are announced on NHN. In order to create a perfect world for Kira, there is something else that T must do. I must ask you to do it for me.
!!
CLATTER
STUMBLE
GRAB
DON'T WORRY, THERE'S NOTHING TO BE AFRAID OF.

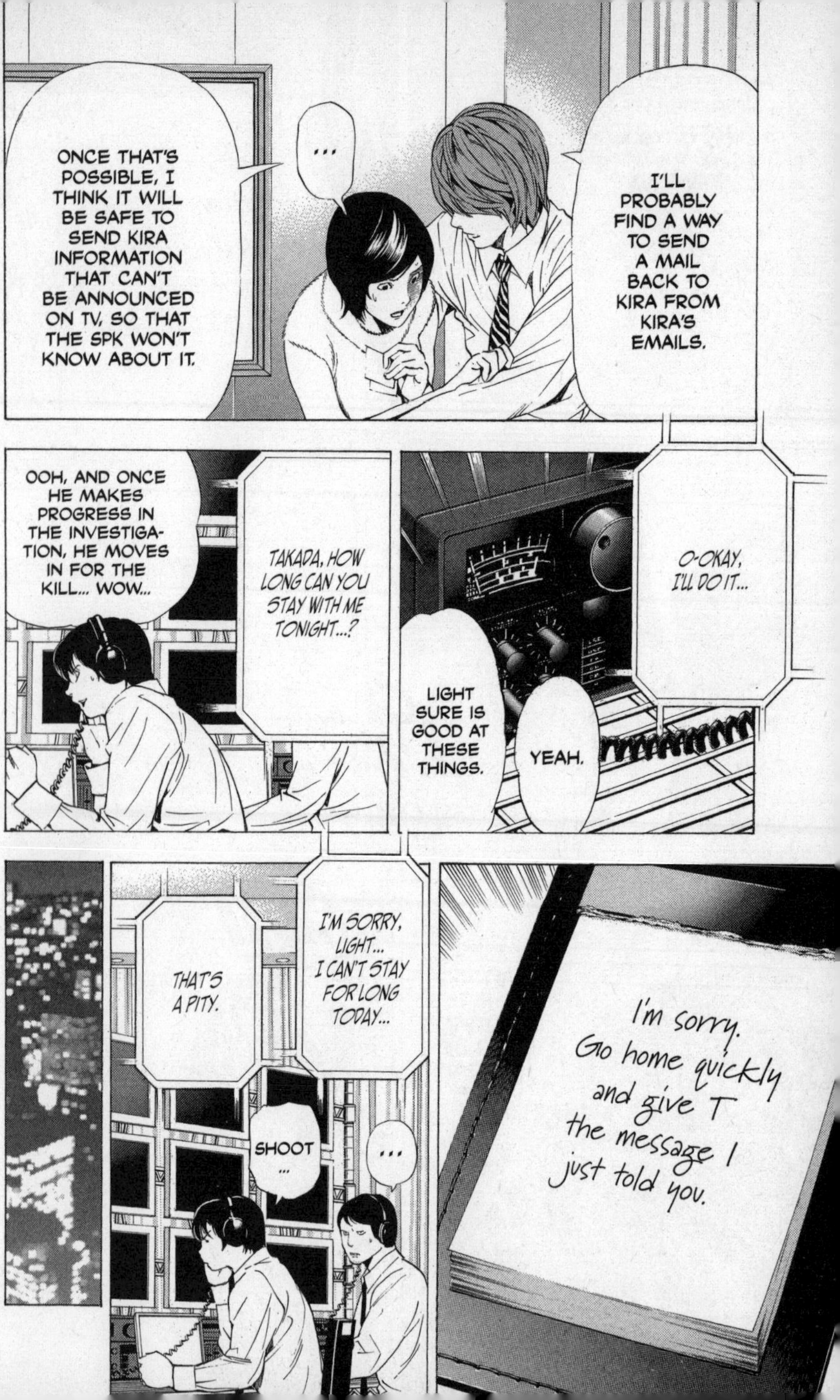
I'LL PROBABLY FIND A WAY TO SEND A MAIL BACK TO KIRA FROM KIRA'S EMAILS.
...
ONCE THAT'S POSSIBLE, I THINK IT WILL BE SAFE TO SEND KIRA INFORMATION THAT CAN'T BE ANNOUNCED ON TV, SO THAT THE SPK WON'T KNOW ABOUT IT.
O-OKAY, I'LL DO IT...
LIGHT SURE IS GOOD AT THESE THINGS.
YEAH.
TAKADA, HOW LONG CAN YOU STAY WITH ME TONIGHT...?
OOH, AND ONCE HE MAKES PROGRESS IN THE INVESTIGA-TION, HE MOVES IN FOR THE KILL... WOW...
I'm sorry. Go home quickly and give T the message I just told you.
I'M SORRY, LIGHT... I CAN'T STAY FOR LONG TODAY...
THAT'S A PITY.
...
SHOOT ...

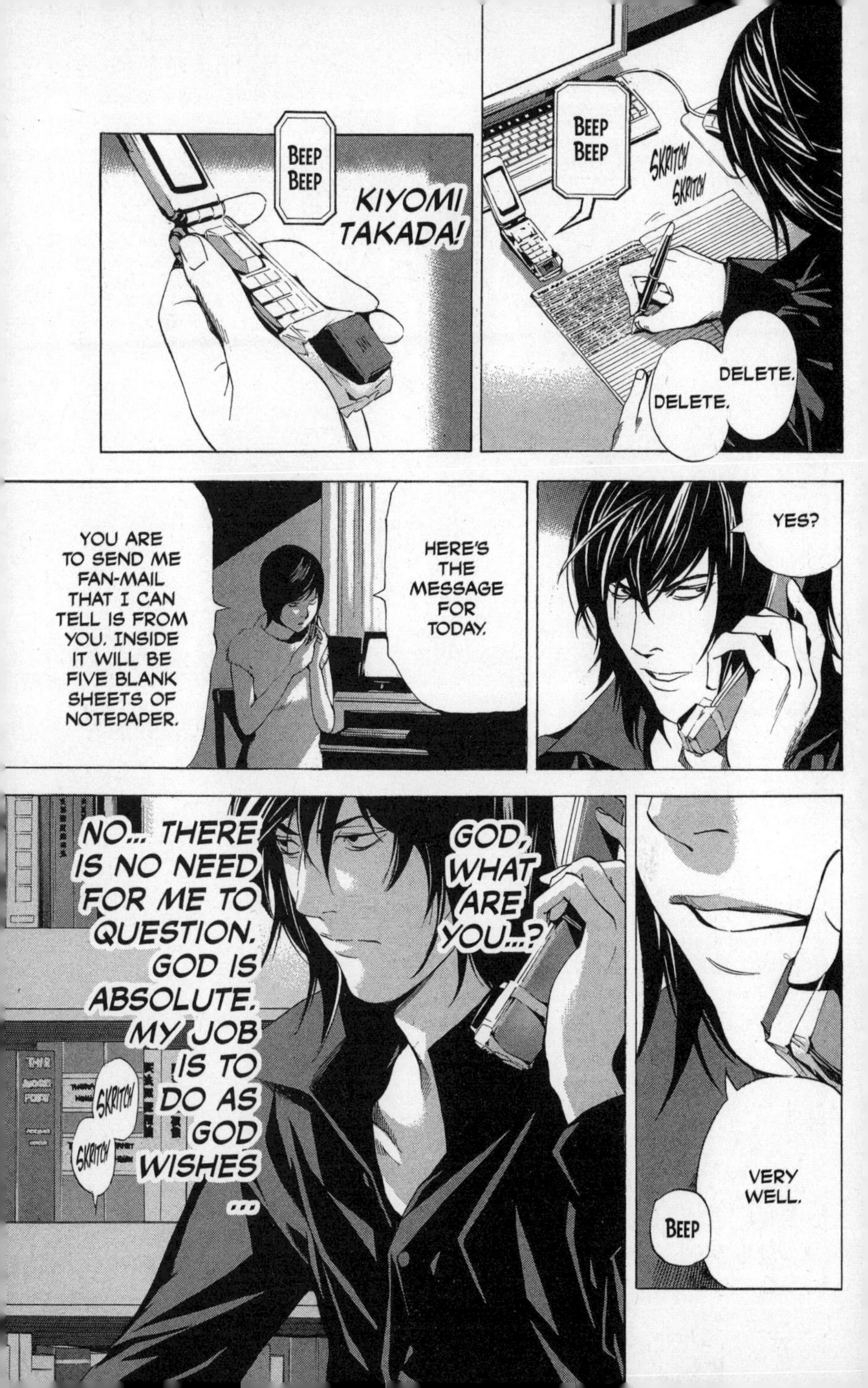
BEEP BEEP
SKRITCH SKRITCH
DELETE.
DELETE.
BEEP BEEP
KIYOMI TAKADA!
YES?
HERE'S THE MESSAGE FOR TODAY.
YOU ARE TO SEND ME FAN-MAIL THAT I CAN TELL IS FROM YOU. INSIDE IT WILL BE FIVE BLANK SHEETS OF NOTEPAPER.
VERY WELL.
BEEP
GOD, WHAT ARE YOU...?
NO... THERE IS NO NEED FOR ME TO QUESTION. GOD IS ABSOLUTE. MY JOB IS TO DO AS GOD WISHES ...
SKRITCH
SKRITCH

DEATH NOTE
How to use it
LXI

⊙ Even if a new victim's name, cause of death, or situation of death is written on top of the originally written name, cause of death or situation of death, there will be no effect on the original victim's death. The same thing will also apply to erasing what was written with a pencil, or whitening out what was written with a pen, in an attempt to rewrite it.

名前や死の状況が書き込まれた上に重ねて名前等を書き込んでも、
上に書かれた方は無効であり、
既に書き込まれてあった方の死・死因・死の状況には何の影響も及ばない。
鉛筆で書いた物を消したり、修正液等で消した上から書き直しても同様である。

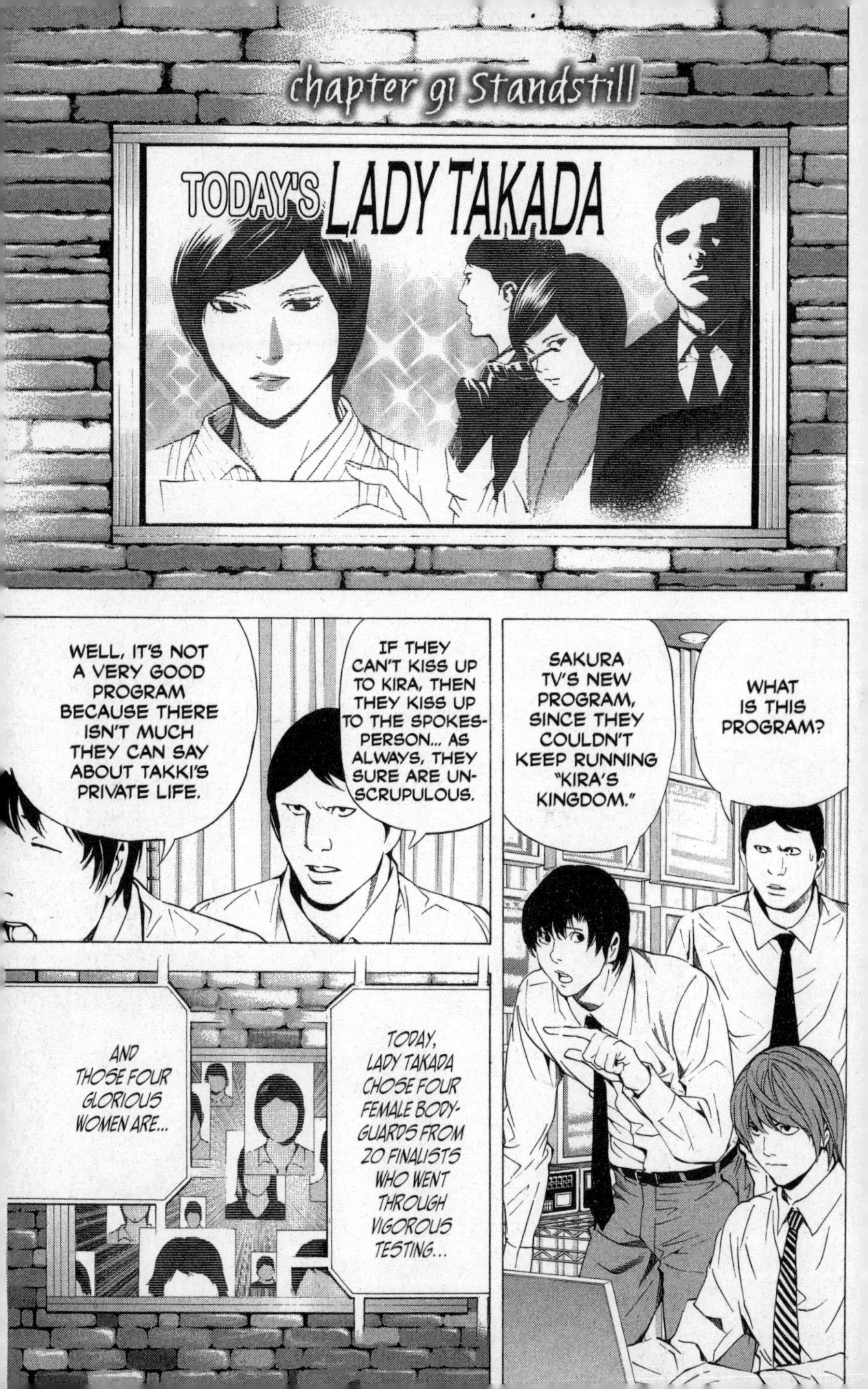
chapter 91 Standstill
TODAY'S LADY TAKADA
WHAT IS THIS PROGRAM?
SAKURA TV'S NEW PROGRAM, SINCE THEY COULDN'T KEEP RUNNING "KIRA'S KINGDOM."
IF THEY CAN'T KISS UP TO KIRA, THEN THEY KISS UP TO THE SPOKES-PERSON... AS ALWAYS, THEY SURE ARE UN-SCRUPULOUS.
WELL, IT'S NOT A VERY GOOD PROGRAM BECAUSE THERE ISN'T MUCH THEY CAN SAY ABOUT TAKKI'S PRIVATE LIFE.
TODAY, LADY TAKADA CHOSE FOUR FEMALE BODY-GUARDS FROM 20 FINALISTS WHO WENT THROUGH VIGOROUS TESTING...
AND THOSE FOUR GLORIOUS WOMEN ARE...

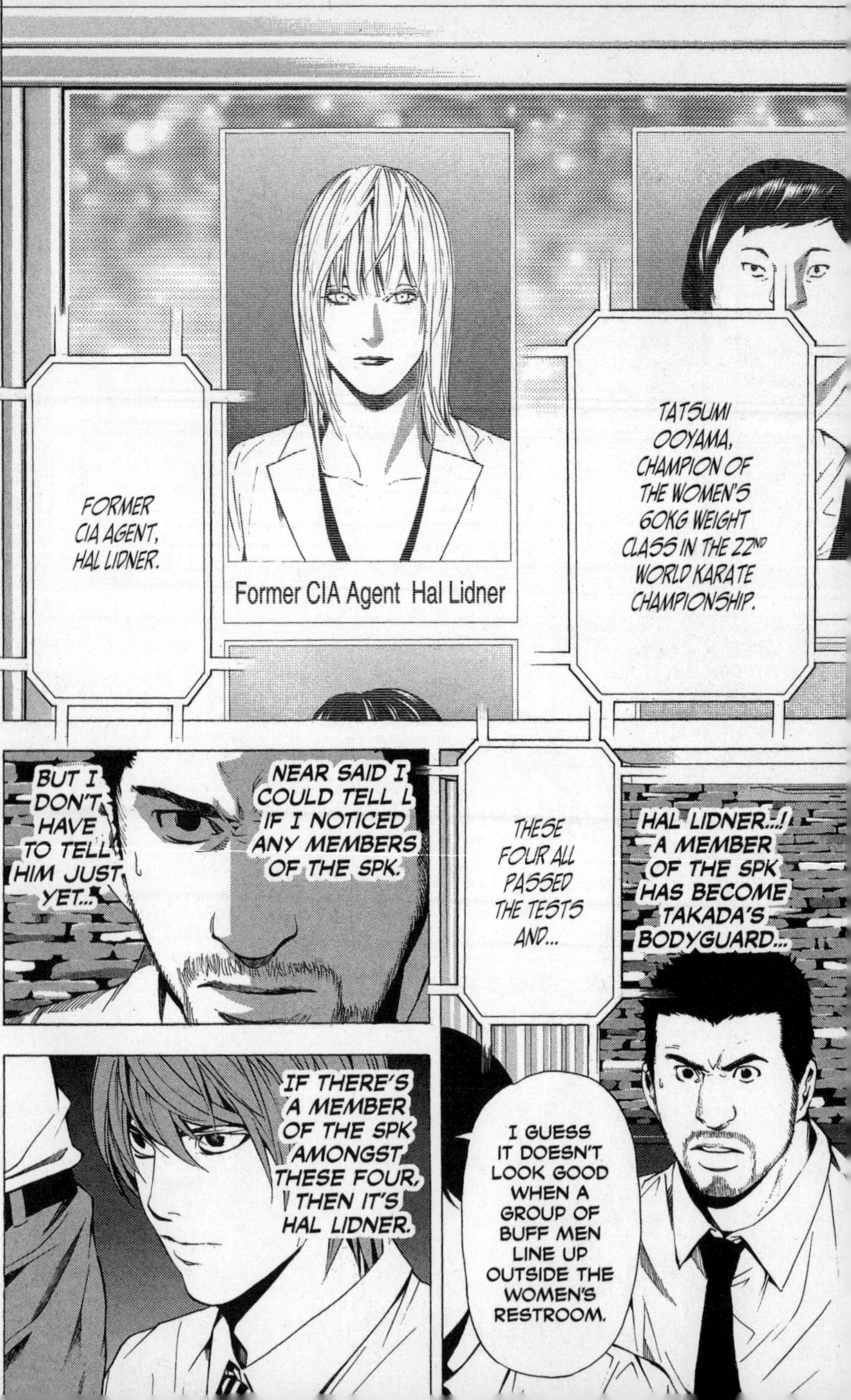
TATSUMI OOYAMA, CHAMPION OF THE WOMEN'S 60KG WEIGHT CLASS IN THE 22ND WORLD KARATE CHAMPIONSHIP.
Former CIA Agent Hal Lidner
FORMER CIA AGENT, HAL LIDNER.
THESE FOUR ALL PASSED THE TESTS AND...
HAL LIDNER...! A MEMBER OF THE SPK HAS BECOME TAKADA'S BODYGUARD...
NEAR SAID I COULD TELL L IF I NOTICED ANY MEMBERS OF THE SPK.
BUT I DON'T HAVE TO TELL HIM JUST YET...
I GUESS IT DOESN'T LOOK GOOD WHEN A GROUP OF BUFF MEN LINE UP OUTSIDE THE WOMEN'S RESTROOM.
IF THERE'S A MEMBER OF THE SPK AMONGST THESE FOUR, THEN IT'S HAL LIDNER.

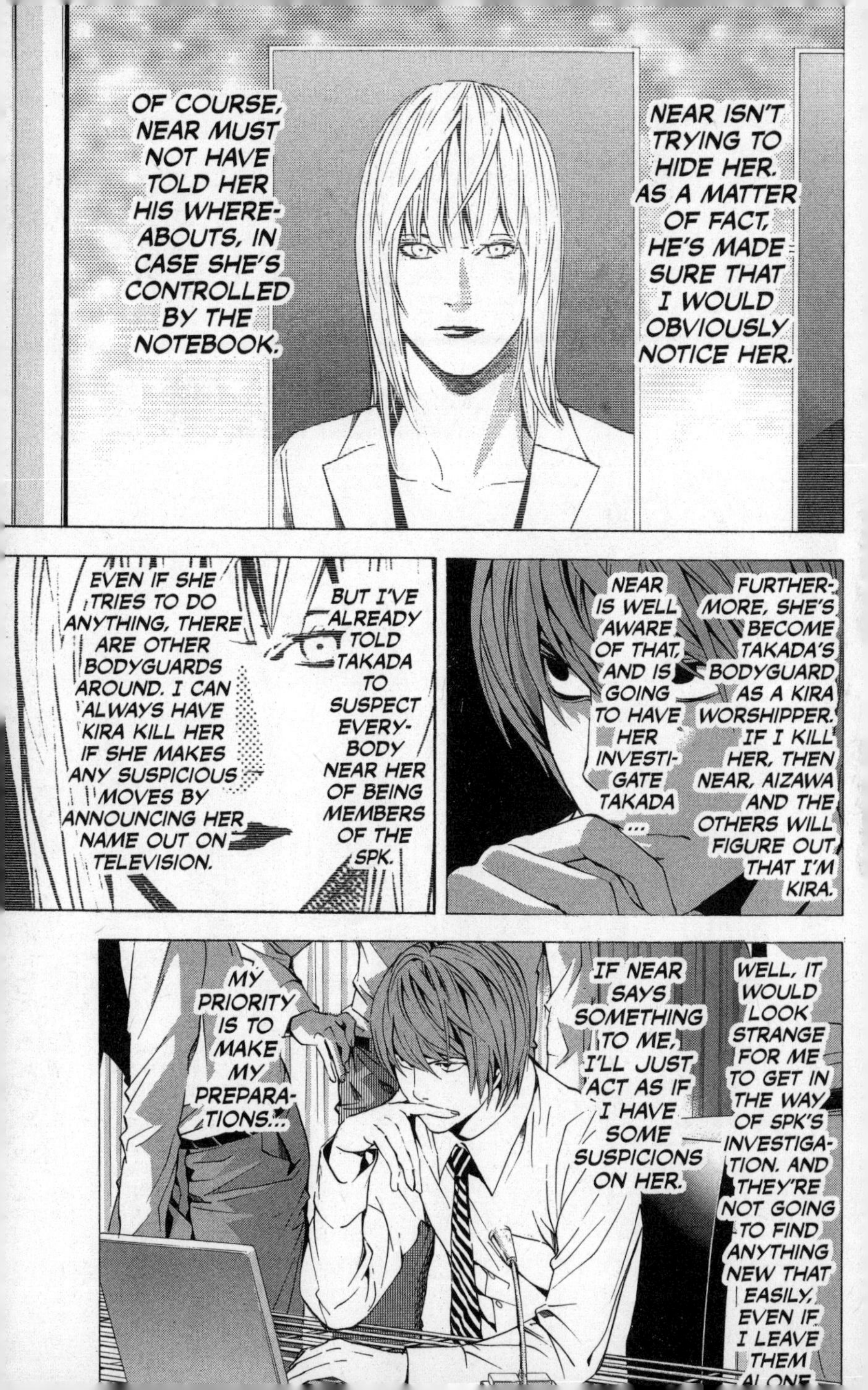
NEAR ISN'T TRYING TO HIDE HER. AS A MATTER OF FACT, HE'S MADE SURE THAT I WOULD OBVIOUSLY NOTICE HER.
OF COURSE, NEAR MUST NOT HAVE TOLD HER HIS WHEREABOUTS, IN CASE SHE'S CONTROLLED BY THE NOTEBOOK.
FURTHERMORE, SHE'S BECOME TAKADA'S BODYGUARD AS A KIRA WORSHIPPER. IF I KILL HER, THEN NEAR, AIZAWA AND THE OTHERS WILL FIGURE OUT THAT I'M KIRA.
NEAR IS WELL AWARE OF THAT, AND IS GOING TO HAVE HER INVESTIGATE TAKADA...
BUT I'VE ALREADY TOLD TAKADA TO SUSPECT EVERYBODY NEAR HER OF BEING MEMBERS OF THE SPK.
EVEN IF SHE TRIES TO DO ANYTHING, THERE ARE OTHER BODYGUARDS AROUND. I CAN ALWAYS HAVE KIRA KILL HER IF SHE MAKES ANY SUSPICIOUS MOVES BY ANNOUNCING HER NAME OUT ON TELEVISION.
WELL, IT WOULD LOOK STRANGE FOR ME TO GET IN THE WAY OF SPK'S INVESTIGATION. AND THEY'RE NOT GOING TO FIND ANYTHING NEW THAT EASILY, EVEN IF I LEAVE THEM ALONE.
IF NEAR SAYS SOMETHING TO ME, I'LL JUST ACT AS IF I HAVE SOME SUSPICIONS ON HER.
MY PRIORITY IS TO MAKE MY PREPARATIONS...

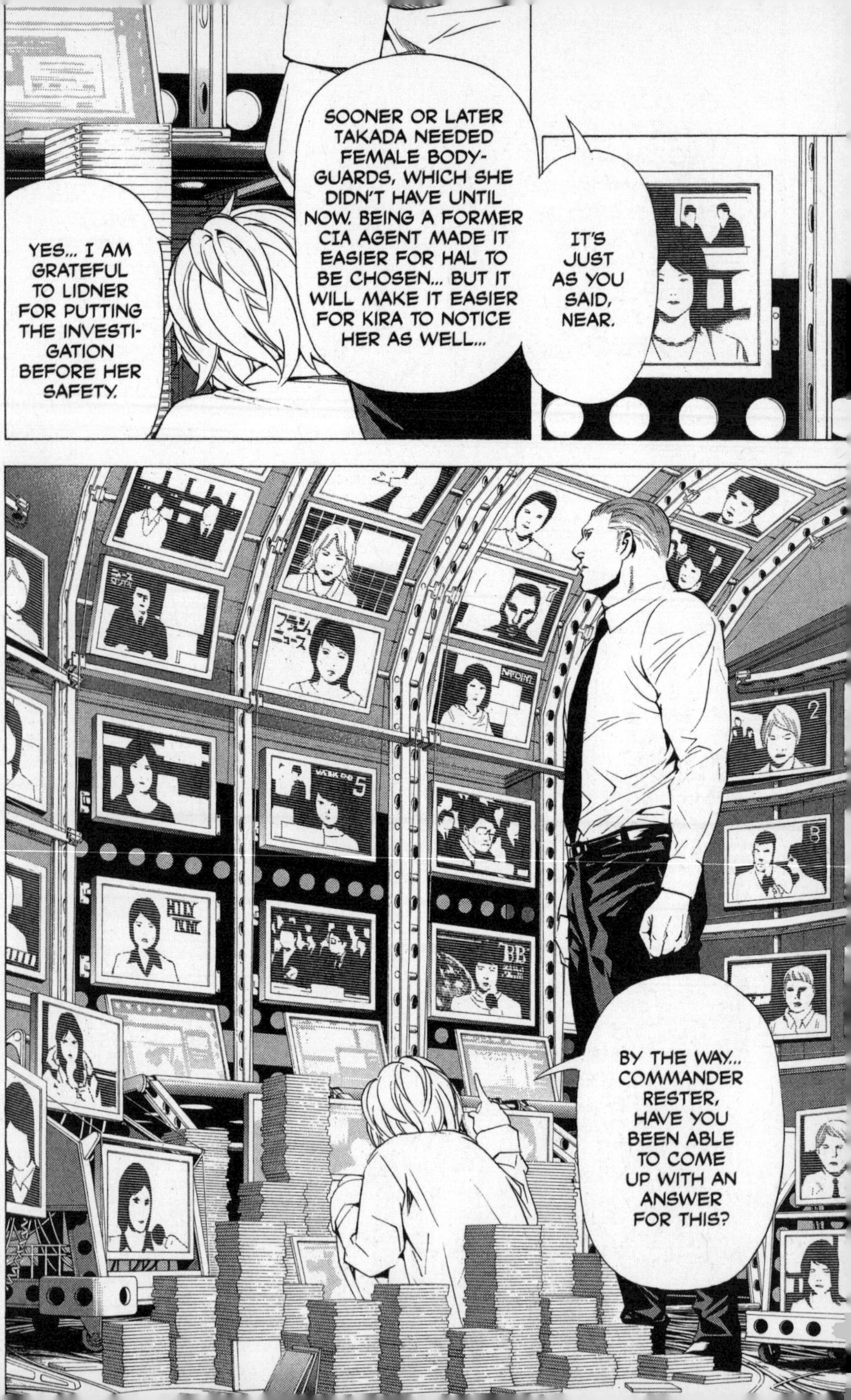
IT'S JUST AS YOU SAID, NEAR.
SOONER OR LATER TAKADA NEEDED FEMALE BODY-GUARDS, WHICH SHE DIDN'T HAVE UNTIL NOW. BEING A FORMER CIA AGENT MADE IT EASIER FOR HAL TO BE CHOSEN... BUT IT WILL MAKE IT EASIER FOR KIRA TO NOTICE HER AS WELL...
YES... I AM GRATEFUL TO LIDNER FOR PUTTING THE INVESTI-GATION BEFORE HER SAFETY.
BY THE WAY... COMMANDER RESTER, HAVE YOU BEEN ABLE TO COME UP WITH AN ANSWER FOR THIS?

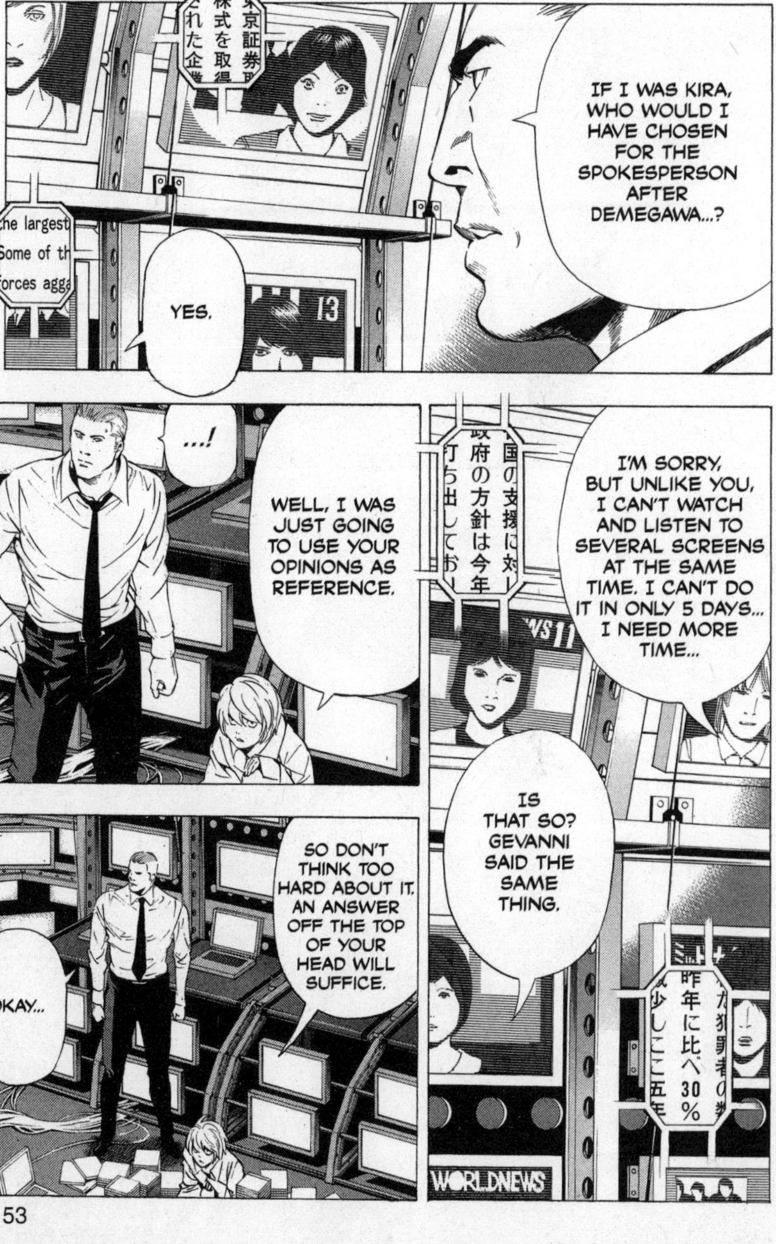
IF I WAS KIRA, WHO WOULD I HAVE CHOSEN FOR THE SPOKESPERSON AFTER DEMEGAWA...?
YES.
I'M SORRY, BUT UNLIKE YOU, I CAN'T WATCH AND LISTEN TO SEVERAL SCREENS AT THE SAME TIME. I CAN'T DO IT IN ONLY 5 DAYS... I NEED MORE TIME...
IS THAT SO? GEVANNI SAID THE SAME THING.
WELL, I WAS JUST GOING TO USE YOUR OPINIONS AS REFERENCE.
...!
SO DON'T THINK TOO HARD ABOUT IT. AN ANSWER OFF THE TOP OF YOUR HEAD WILL SUFFICE.
OKAY...
WORLDNEWS

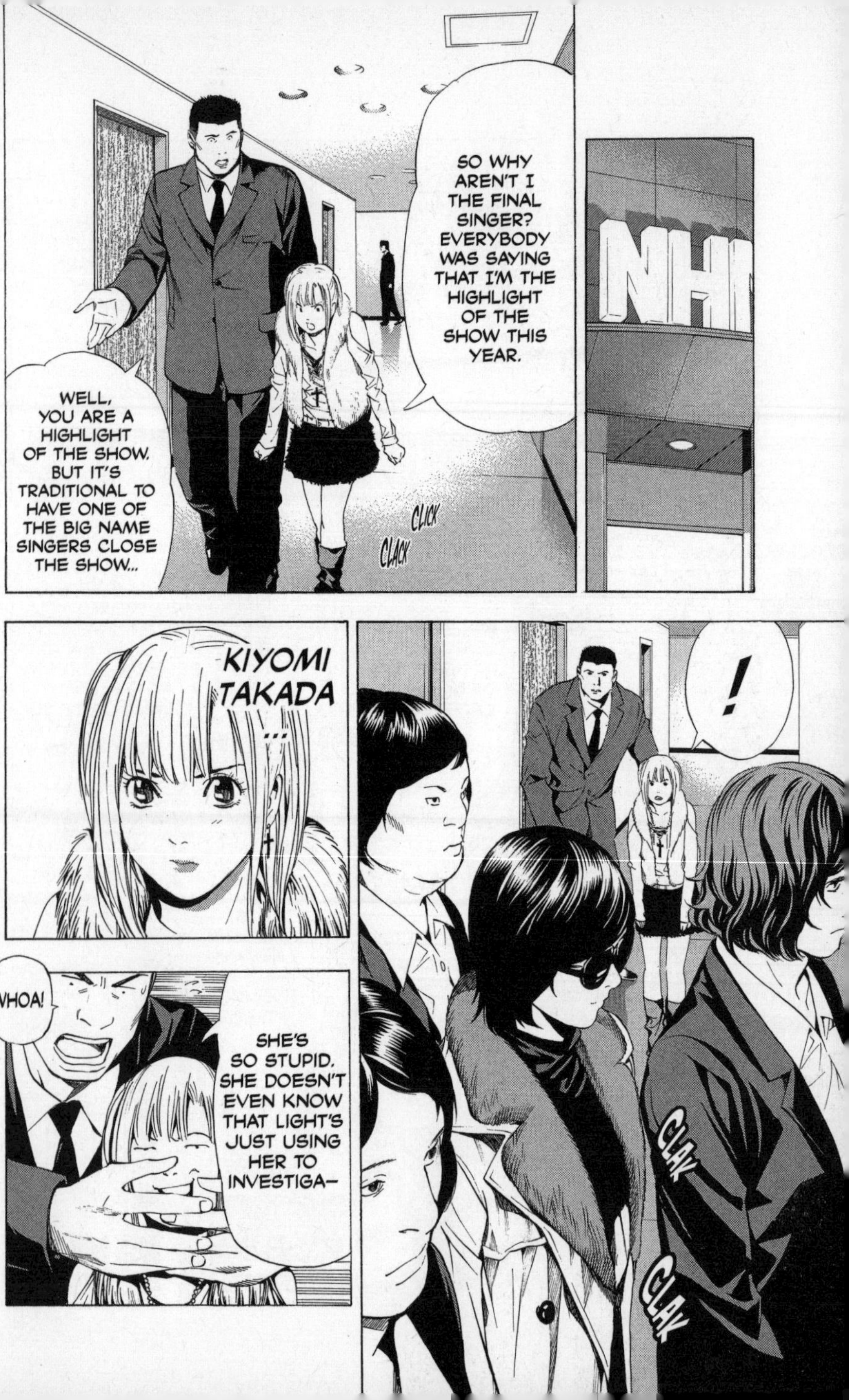
SO WHY AREN'T I THE FINAL SINGER? EVERYBODY WAS SAYING THAT I'M THE HIGHLIGHT OF THE SHOW THIS YEAR.
WELL, YOU ARE A HIGHLIGHT OF THE SHOW. BUT IT'S TRADITIONAL TO HAVE ONE OF THE BIG NAME SINGERS CLOSE THE SHOW...
CLICK
CLACK
!
CLAK
CLAK
KIYOMI TAKADA ...
SHE'S SO STUPID. SHE DOESN'T EVEN KNOW THAT LIGHT'S JUST USING HER TO INVESTIGA—
WHOA!

READ THIS WAY

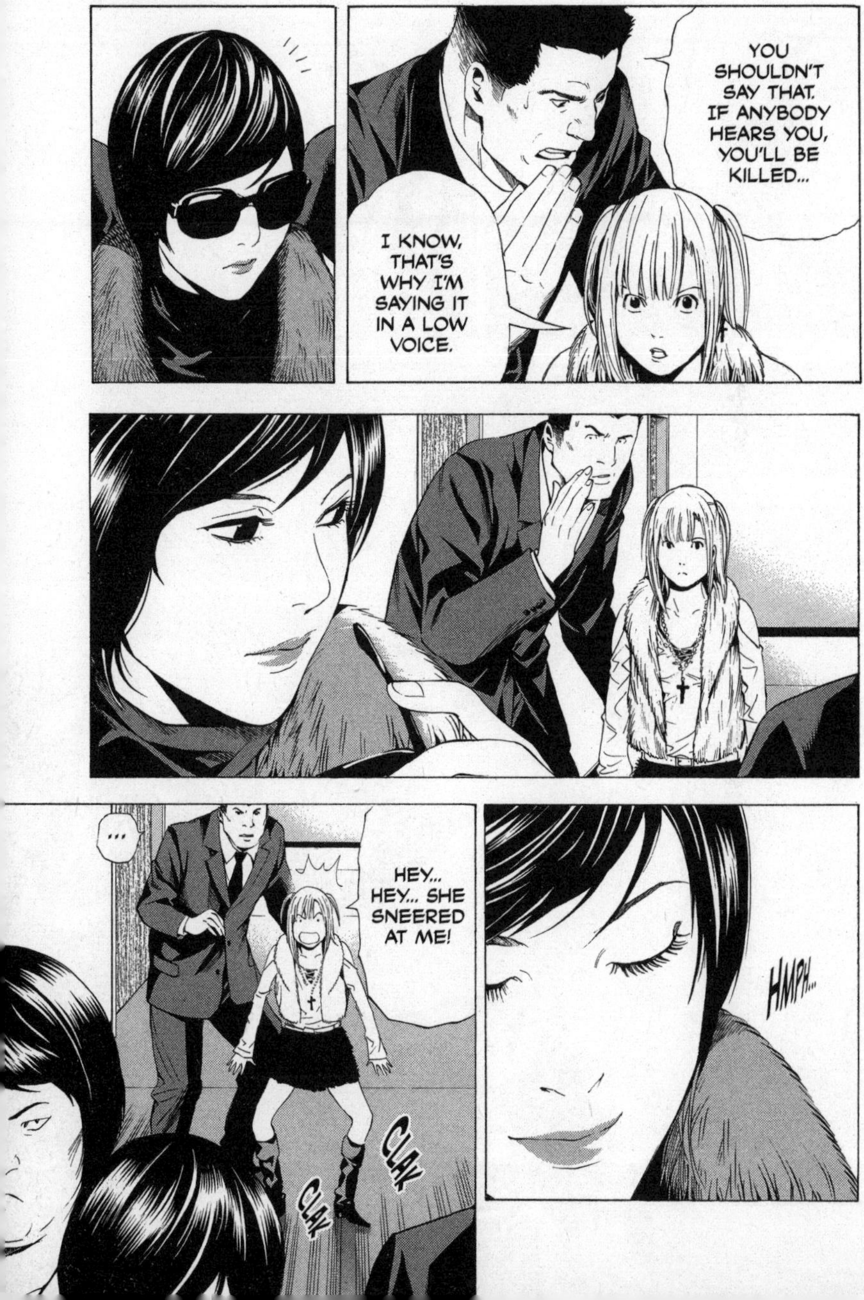
YOU SHOULDN'T SAY THAT. IF ANYBODY HEARS YOU, YOU'LL BE KILLED...
I KNOW, THAT'S WHY I'M SAYING IT IN A LOW VOICE.
HMPH...
...
HEY... HEY... SHE SNEERED AT ME!
CLAK
CLAK

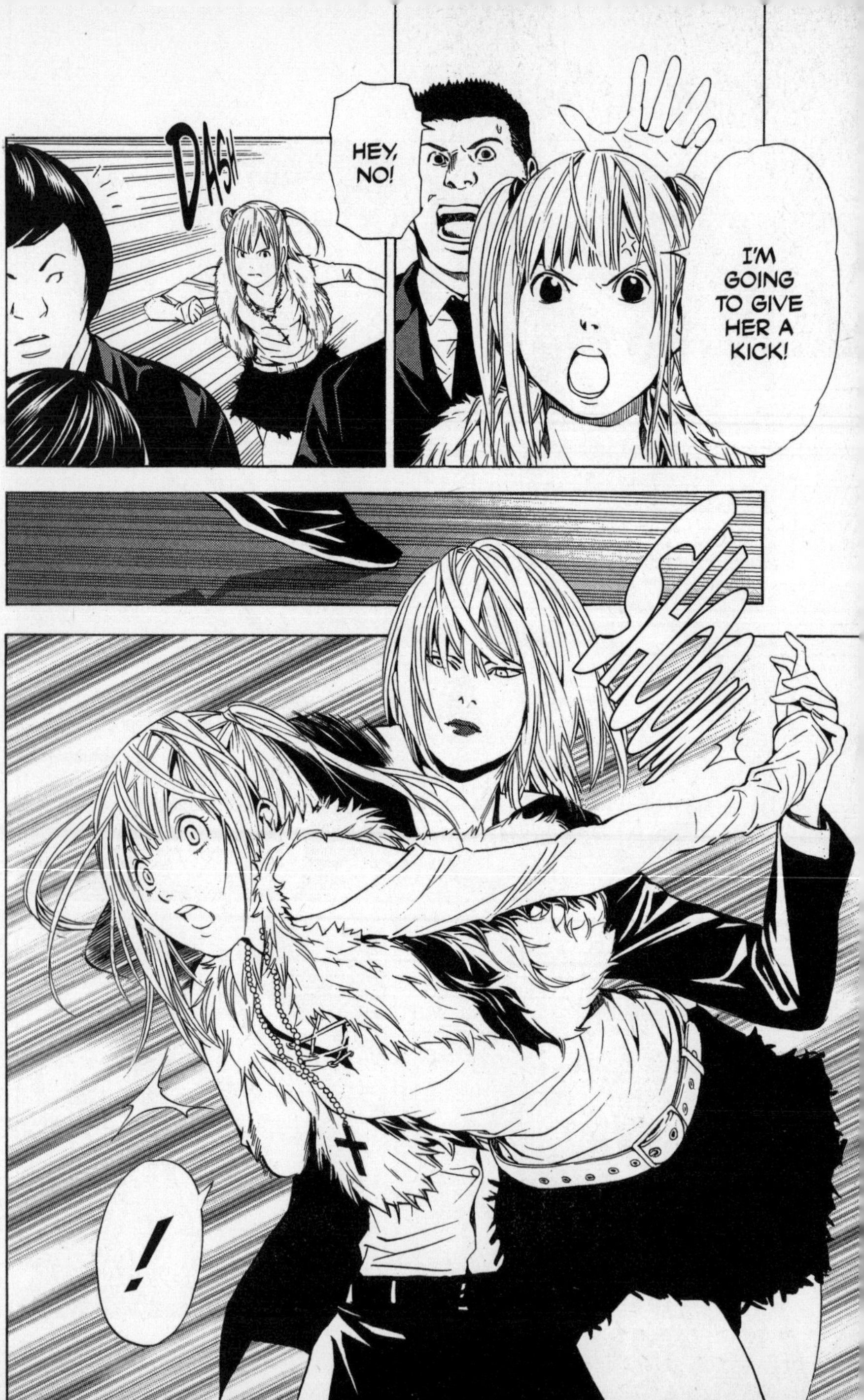
I'M GOING TO GIVE HER A KICK!
HEY, NO!
DASH
!

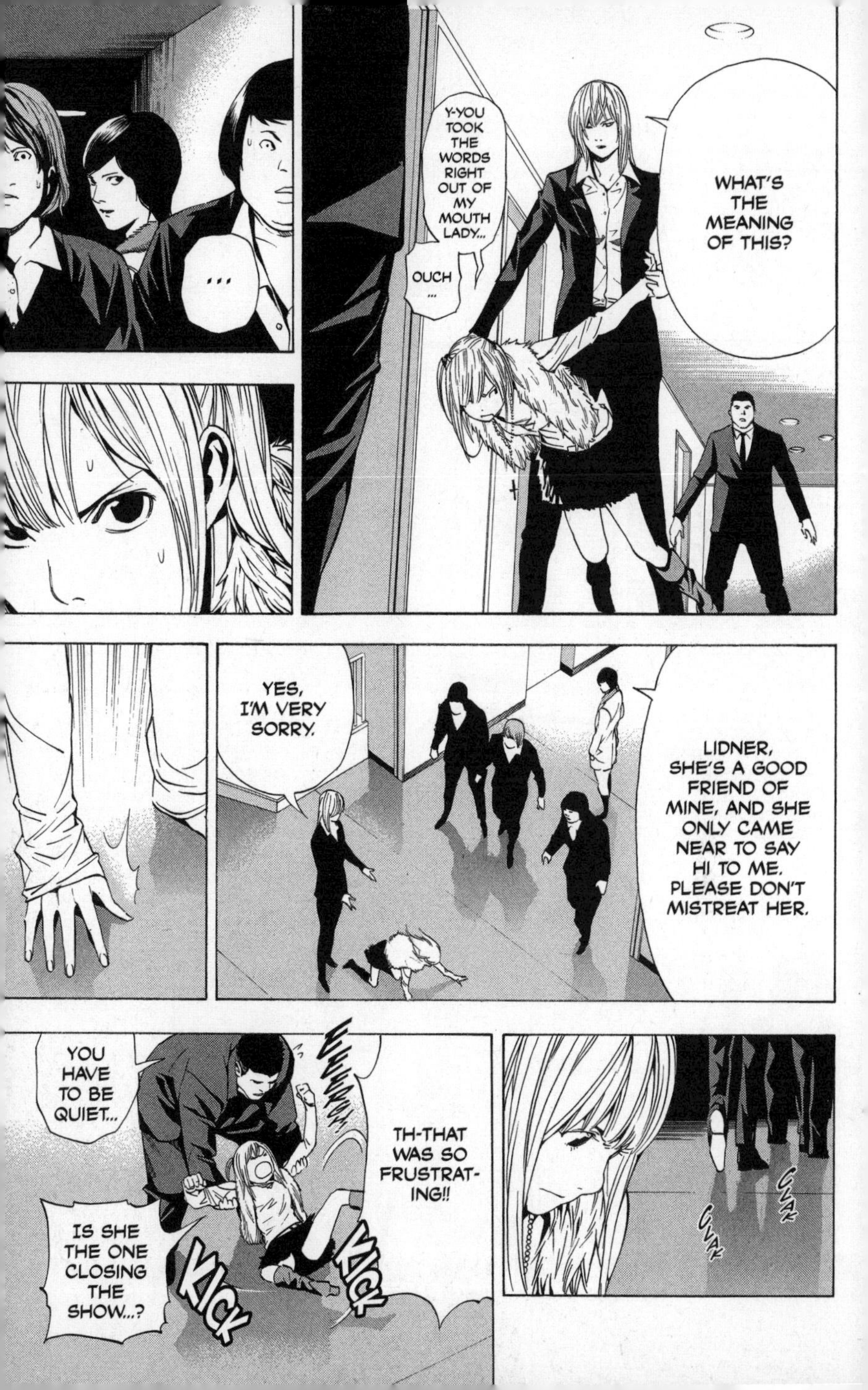
WHAT'S THE MEANING OF THIS?
Y-YOU TOOK THE WORDS RIGHT OUT OF MY MOUTH LADY...
OUCH ...
...
LIDNER, SHE'S A GOOD FRIEND OF MINE, AND SHE ONLY CAME NEAR TO SAY HI TO ME. PLEASE DON'T MISTREAT HER.
YES, I'M VERY SORRY.
CLAK
CLAK
TH-THAT WAS SO FRUSTRAT-ING!!
YOU HAVE TO BE QUIET...
KICK
IS SHE THE ONE CLOSING THE SHOW...?
KICK

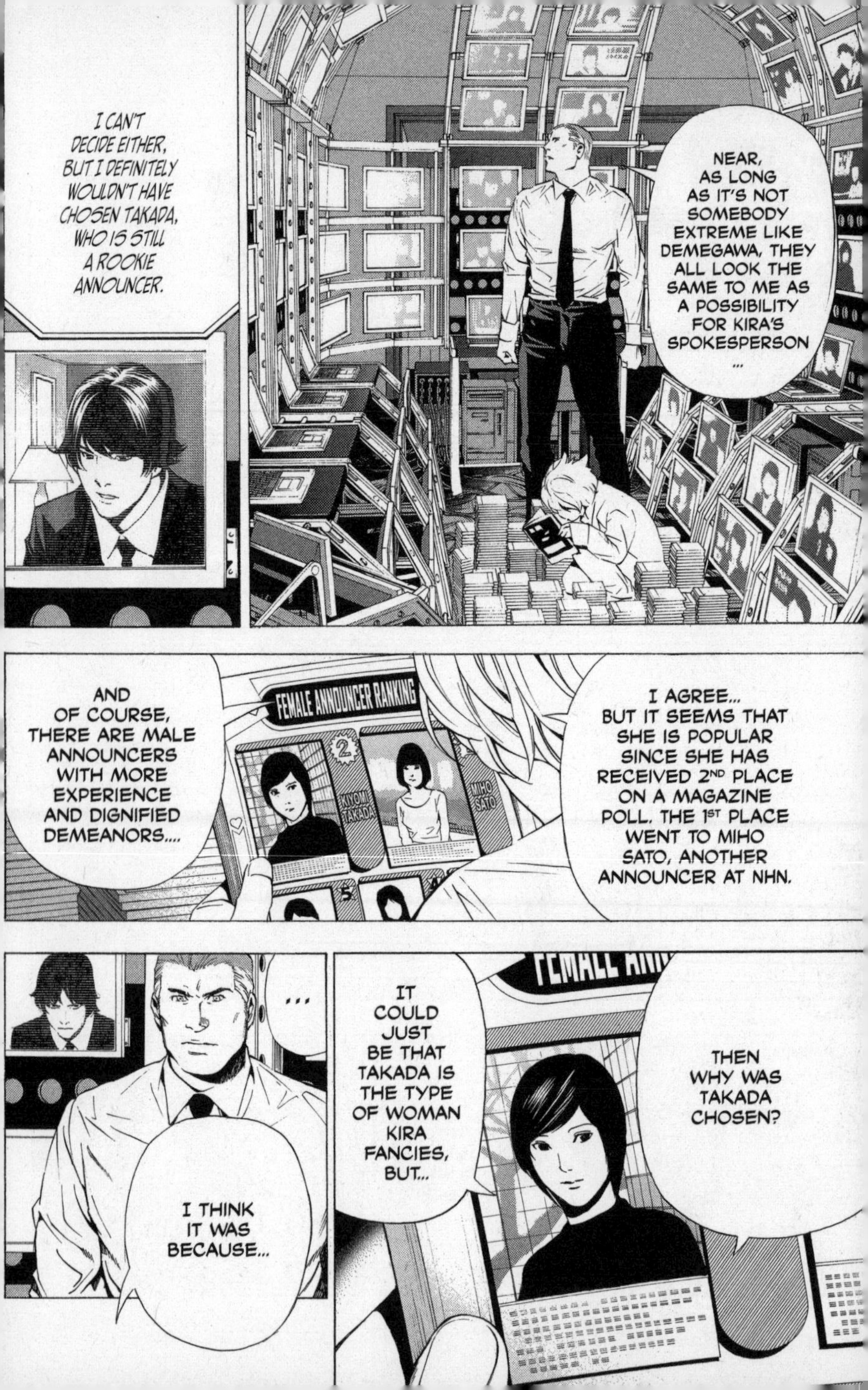
NEAR, AS LONG AS IT'S NOT SOMEBODY EXTREME LIKE DEMEGAWA, THEY ALL LOOK THE SAME TO ME AS A POSSIBILITY FOR KIRA'S SPOKESPERSON ...
I CAN'T DECIDE EITHER, BUT I DEFINITELY WOULDN'T HAVE CHOSEN TAKADA, WHO IS STILL A ROOKIE ANNOUNCER.
I AGREE... BUT IT SEEMS THAT SHE IS POPULAR SINCE SHE HAS RECEIVED 2ND PLACE ON A MAGAZINE POLL. THE 1ST PLACE WENT TO MIHO SATO, ANOTHER ANNOUNCER AT NHN.
FEMALE ANNOUNCER RANKING
2
MIHO SATO
KIYOMI TAKADA
AND OF COURSE, THERE ARE MALE ANNOUNCERS WITH MORE EXPERIENCE AND DIGNIFIED DEMEANORS....
THEN WHY WAS TAKADA CHOSEN?
IT COULD JUST BE THAT TAKADA IS THE TYPE OF WOMAN KIRA FANCIES, BUT...
...
I THINK IT WAS BECAUSE...

READ THIS WAY

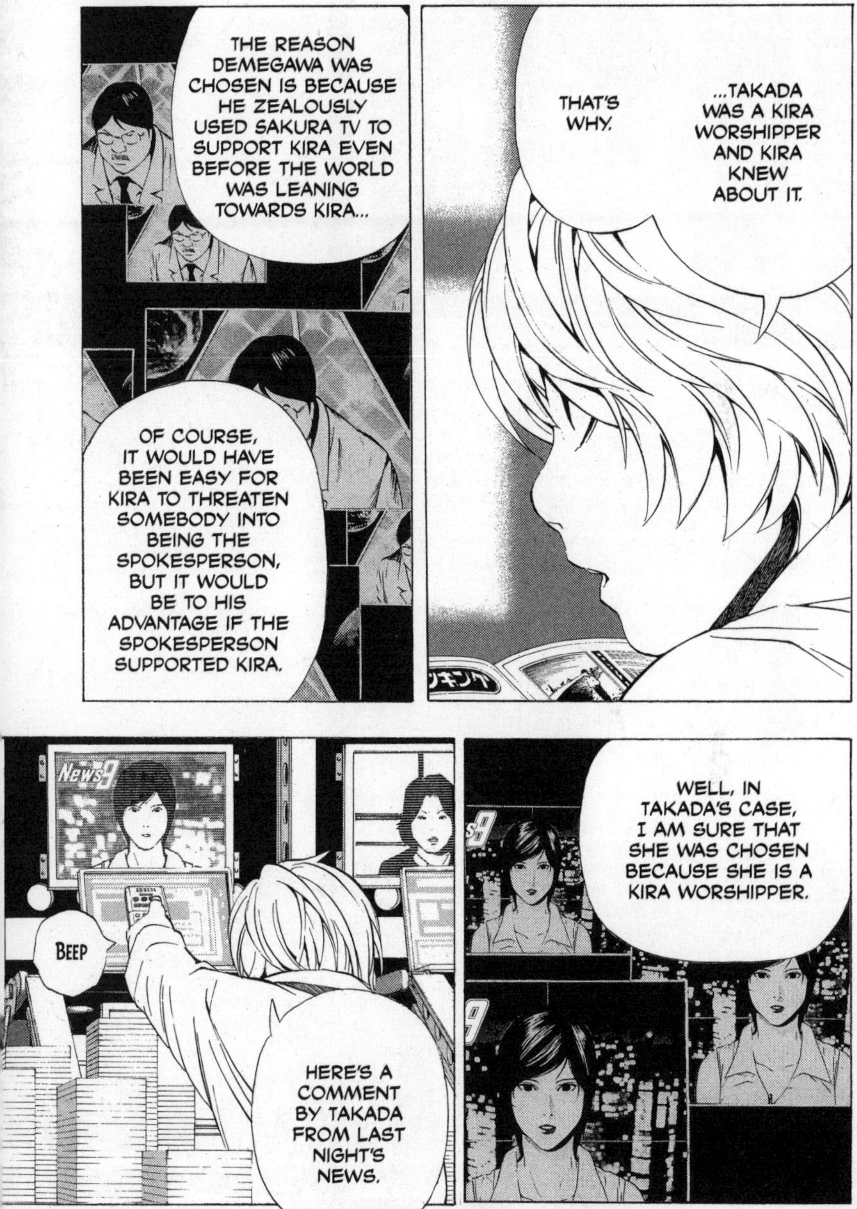

...TAKADA WAS A KIRA WORSHIPPER AND KIRA KNEW ABOUT IT.
THAT'S WHY.
THE REASON DEMEGAWA WAS CHOSEN IS BECAUSE HE ZEALOUSLY USED SAKURA TV TO SUPPORT KIRA EVEN BEFORE THE WORLD WAS LEANING TOWARDS KIRA...
OF COURSE, IT WOULD HAVE BEEN EASY FOR KIRA TO THREATEN SOMEBODY INTO BEING THE SPOKESPERSON, BUT IT WOULD BE TO HIS ADVANTAGE IF THE SPOKESPERSON SUPPORTED KIRA.
WELL, IN TAKADA'S CASE, I AM SURE THAT SHE WAS CHOSEN BECAUSE SHE IS A KIRA WORSHIPPER.
BEEP
HERE'S A COMMENT BY TAKADA FROM LAST NIGHT'S NEWS.

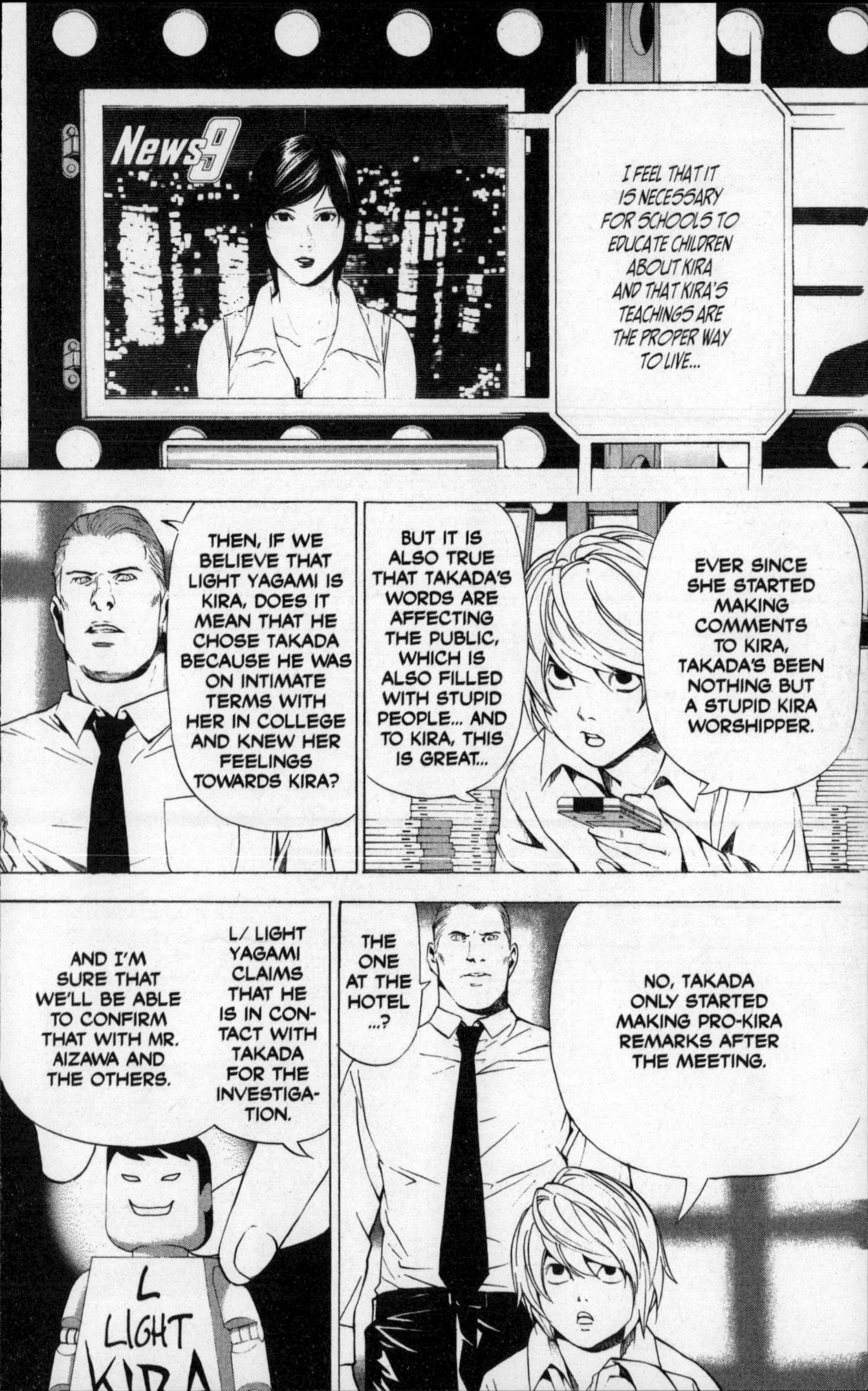
News 9
I FEEL THAT IT IS NECESSARY FOR SCHOOLS TO EDUCATE CHILDREN ABOUT KIRA AND THAT KIRA'S TEACHINGS ARE THE PROPER WAY TO LIVE...
EVER SINCE SHE STARTED MAKING COMMENTS TO KIRA, TAKADA'S BEEN NOTHING BUT A STUPID KIRA WORSHIPPER.
BUT IT IS ALSO TRUE THAT TAKADA'S WORDS ARE AFFECTING THE PUBLIC, WHICH IS ALSO FILLED WITH STUPID PEOPLE... AND TO KIRA, THIS IS GREAT...
THEN, IF WE BELIEVE THAT LIGHT YAGAMI IS KIRA, DOES IT MEAN THAT HE CHOSE TAKADA BECAUSE HE WAS ON INTIMATE TERMS WITH HER IN COLLEGE AND KNEW HER FEELINGS TOWARDS KIRA?
NO, TAKADA ONLY STARTED MAKING PRO-KIRA REMARKS AFTER THE MEETING.
THE ONE AT THE HOTEL ...?
L/ LIGHT YAGAMI CLAIMS THAT HE IS IN CONTACT WITH TAKADA FOR THE INVESTIGATION.
AND I'M SURE THAT WE'LL BE ABLE TO CONFIRM THAT WITH MR. AIZAWA AND THE OTHERS.
L
LIGHT

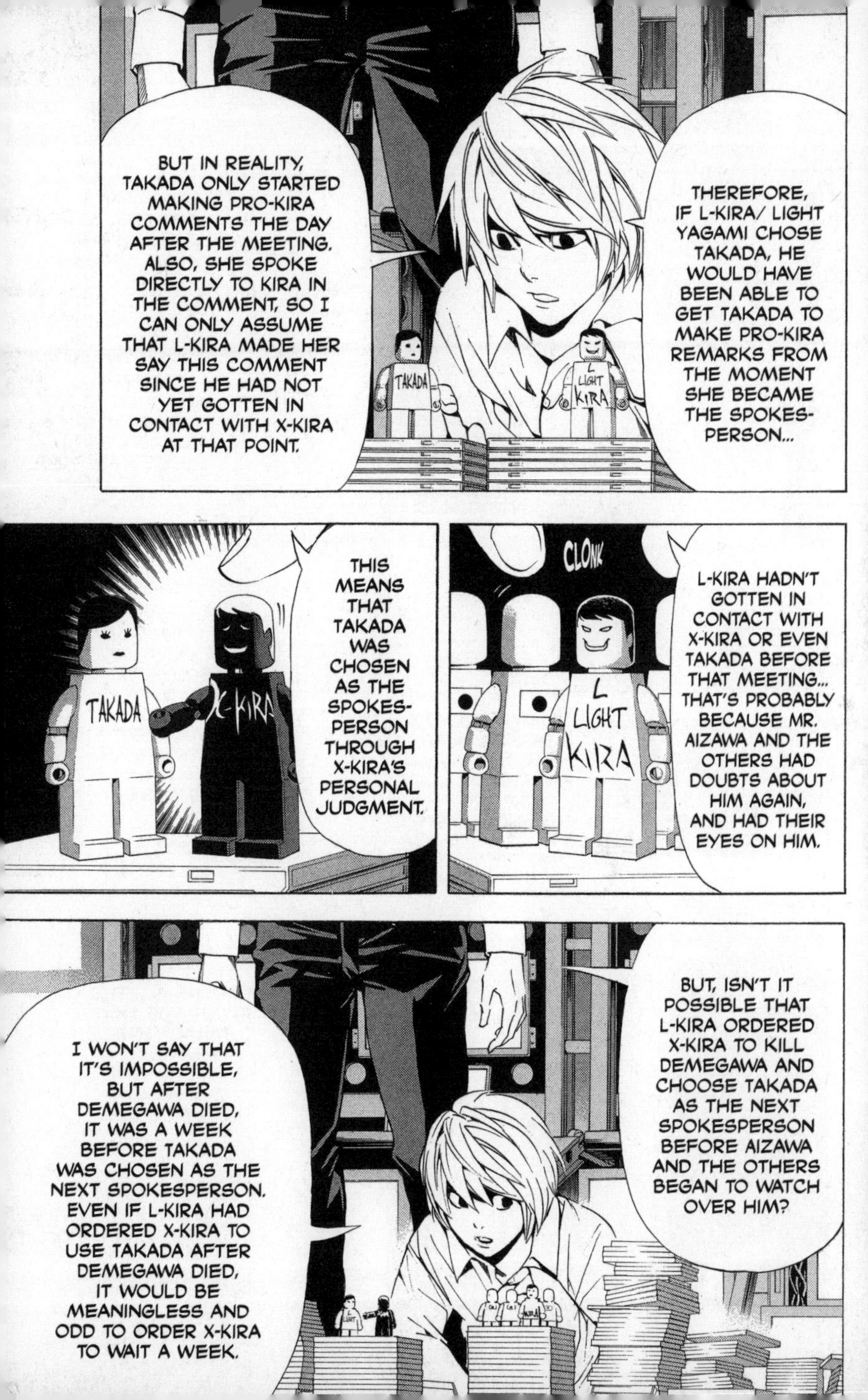
THEREFORE, IF L-KIRA/ LIGHT YAGAMI CHOSE TAKADA, HE WOULD HAVE BEEN ABLE TO GET TAKADA TO MAKE PRO-KIRA REMARKS FROM THE MOMENT SHE BECAME THE SPOKES-PERSON...
L LIGHT KIRA
TAKADA
BUT IN REALITY, TAKADA ONLY STARTED MAKING PRO-KIRA COMMENTS THE DAY AFTER THE MEETING. ALSO, SHE SPOKE DIRECTLY TO KIRA IN THE COMMENT, SO I CAN ONLY ASSUME THAT L-KIRA MADE HER SAY THIS COMMENT SINCE HE HAD NOT YET GOTTEN IN CONTACT WITH X-KIRA AT THAT POINT.
CLONK
L-KIRA HADN'T GOTTEN IN CONTACT WITH X-KIRA OR EVEN TAKADA BEFORE THAT MEETING... THAT'S PROBABLY BECAUSE MR. AIZAWA AND THE OTHERS HAD DOUBTS ABOUT HIM AGAIN, AND HAD THEIR EYES ON HIM.
L LIGHT KIRA
THIS MEANS THAT TAKADA WAS CHOSEN AS THE SPOKES-PERSON THROUGH X-KIRA'S PERSONAL JUDGMENT.
TAKADA
X-KIRA
BUT, ISN'T IT POSSIBLE THAT L-KIRA ORDERED X-KIRA TO KILL DEMEGAWA AND CHOOSE TAKADA AS THE NEXT SPOKESPERSON BEFORE AIZAWA AND THE OTHERS BEGAN TO WATCH OVER HIM?
I WON'T SAY THAT IT'S IMPOSSIBLE, BUT AFTER DEMEGAWA DIED, IT WAS A WEEK BEFORE TAKADA WAS CHOSEN AS THE NEXT SPOKESPERSON. EVEN IF L-KIRA HAD ORDERED X-KIRA TO USE TAKADA AFTER DEMEGAWA DIED, IT WOULD BE MEANINGLESS AND ODD TO ORDER X-KIRA TO WAIT A WEEK.

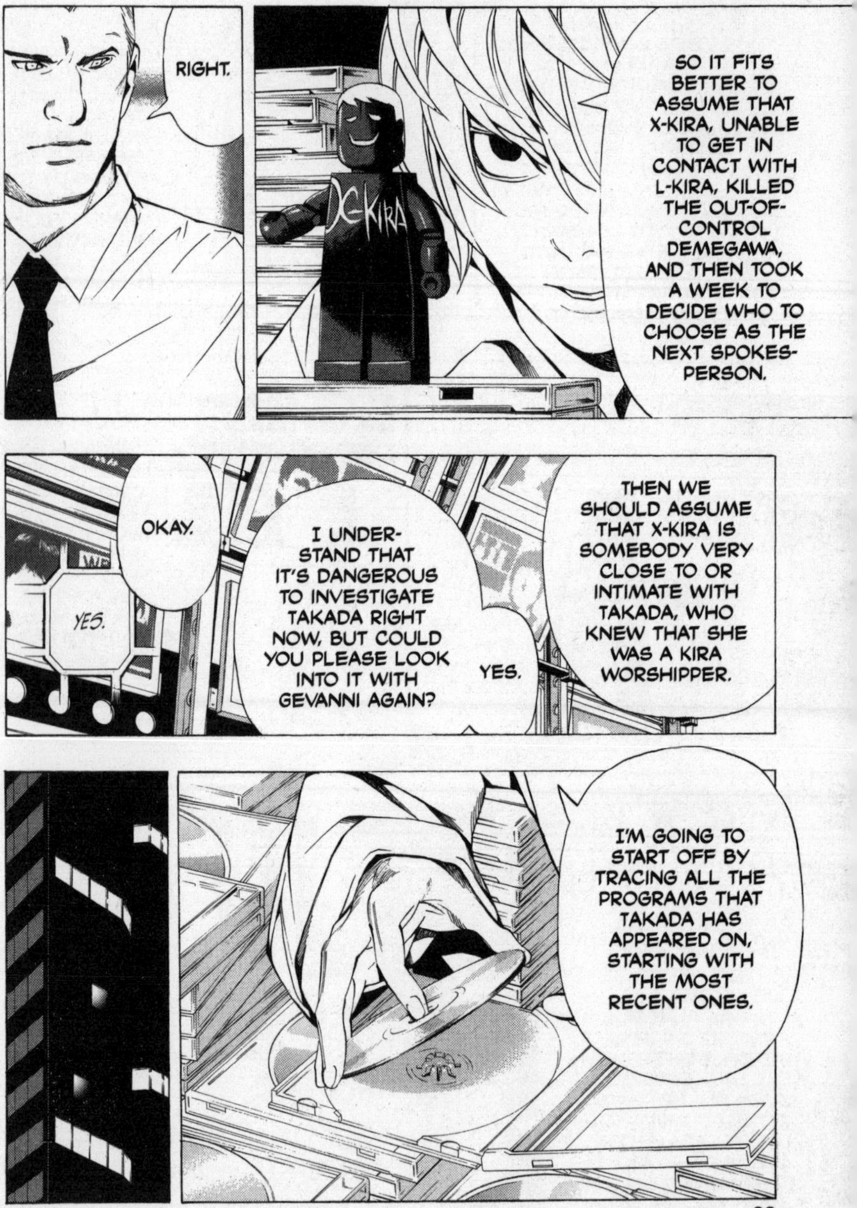
SO IT FITS BETTER TO ASSUME THAT X-KIRA, UNABLE TO GET IN CONTACT WITH L-KIRA, KILLED THE OUT-OF-CONTROL DEMEGAWA, AND THEN TOOK A WEEK TO DECIDE WHO TO CHOOSE AS THE NEXT SPOKES-PERSON.
RIGHT.
THEN WE SHOULD ASSUME THAT X-KIRA IS SOMEBODY VERY CLOSE TO OR INTIMATE WITH TAKADA, WHO KNEW THAT SHE WAS A KIRA WORSHIPPER.
YES.
I UNDER-STAND THAT IT'S DANGEROUS TO INVESTIGATE TAKADA RIGHT NOW, BUT COULD YOU PLEASE LOOK INTO IT WITH GEVANNI AGAIN?
OKAY.
YES.
I'M GOING TO START OFF BY TRACING ALL THE PROGRAMS THAT TAKADA HAS APPEARED ON, STARTING WITH THE MOST RECENT ONES.

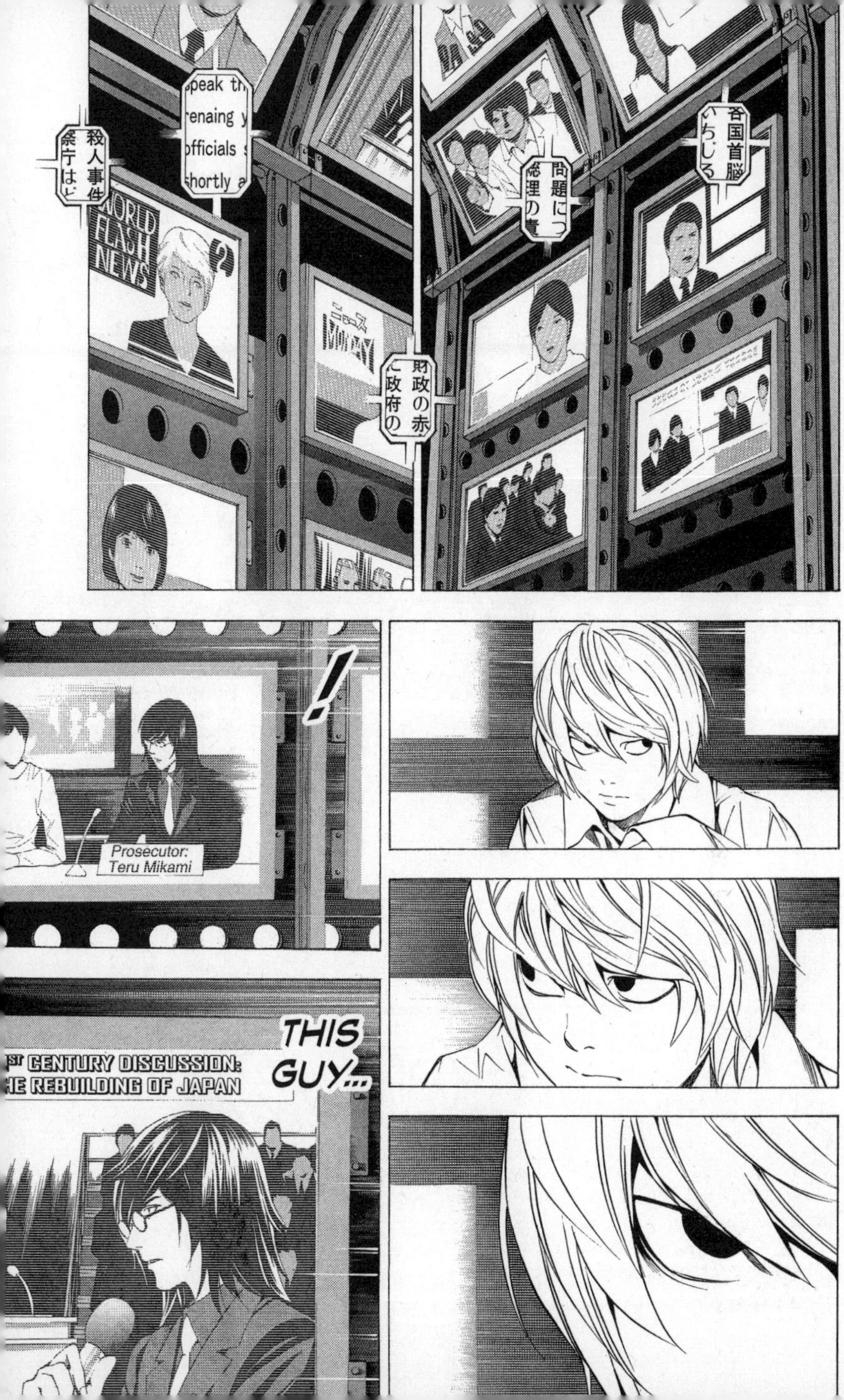
各国首脳
いちじる
問題につ
処理の責
財政の赤
に政府の
WORLD FLASH NEWS
ニュース
MONDAY
speak th
renaing y
officials s
shortly a
殺人事件
察庁はど
!
Prosecutor:
Teru Mikami
THIS GUY...
ST CENTURY DISCUSSION:
HE REBUILDING OF JAPAN

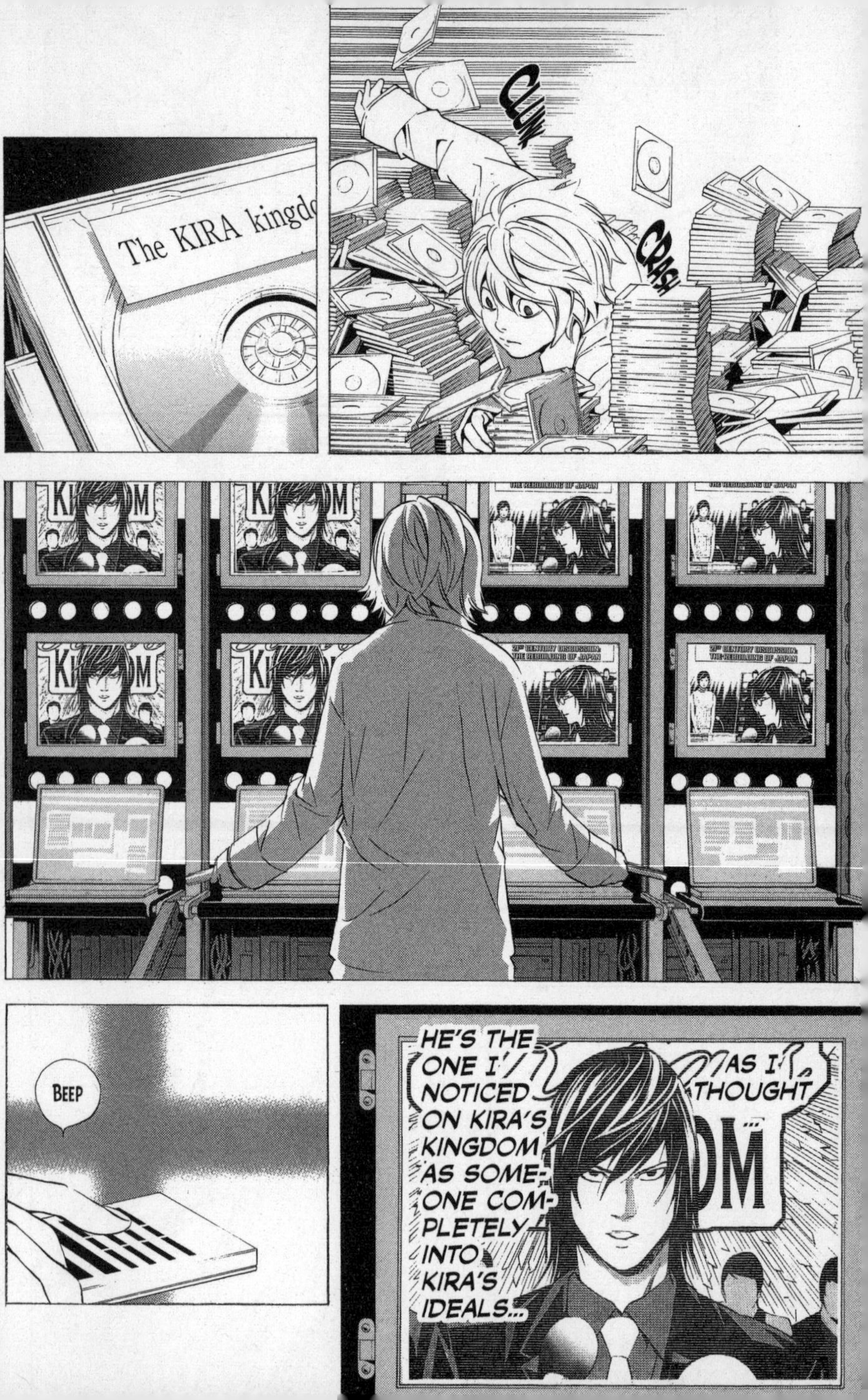
CLINK
CRASH
The KIRA kingdo
21st CENTURY DISCUSSION: THE REBUILDING OF JAPAN
AS I THOUGHT...
HE'S THE ONE I NOTICED ON KIRA'S KINGDOM AS SOMEONE COMPLETELY INTO KIRA'S IDEALS...
BEEP

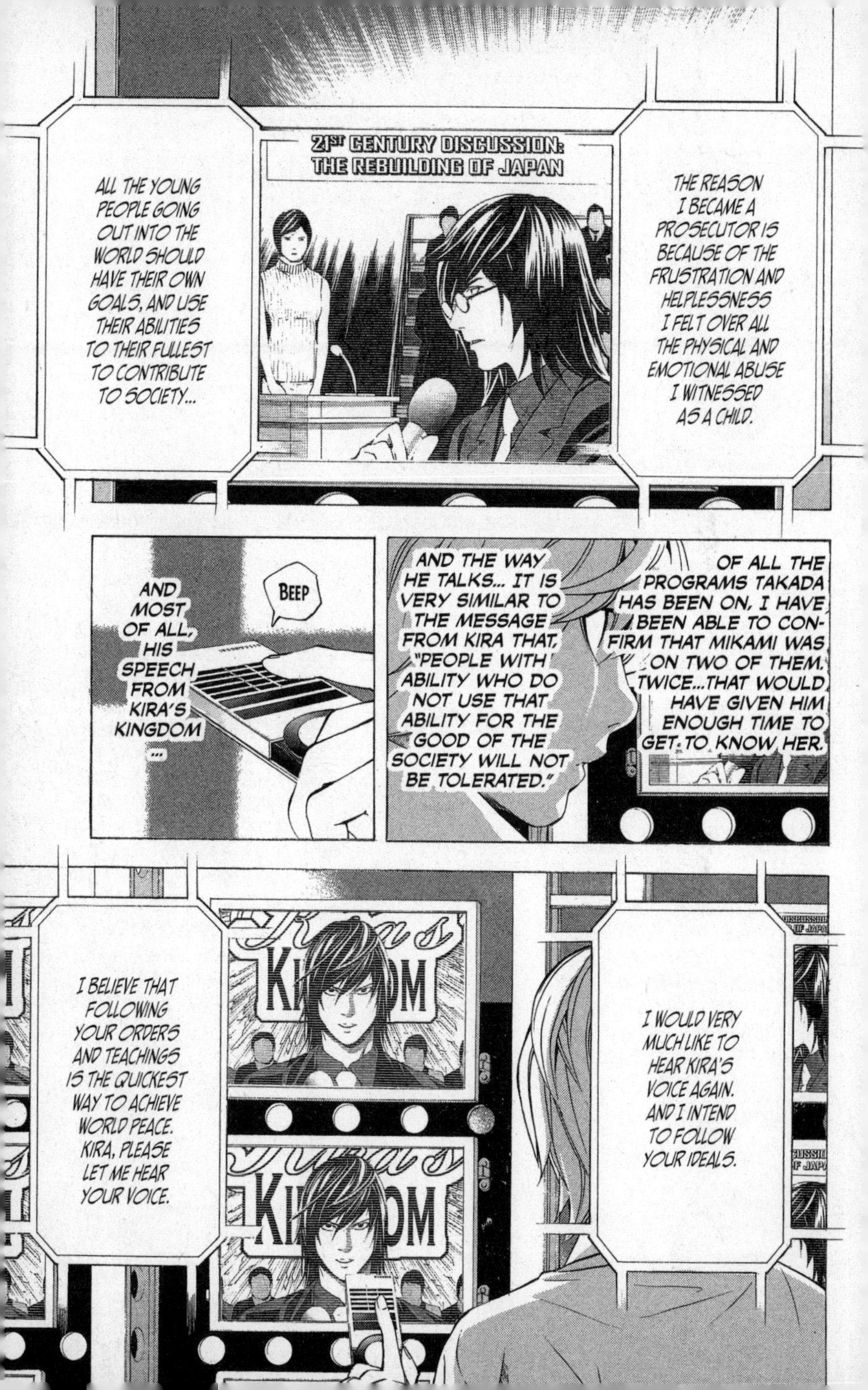
21ST CENTURY DISCUSSION: THE REBUILDING OF JAPAN
THE REASON I BECAME A PROSECUTOR IS BECAUSE OF THE FRUSTRATION AND HELPLESSNESS I FELT OVER ALL THE PHYSICAL AND EMOTIONAL ABUSE I WITNESSED AS A CHILD.
ALL THE YOUNG PEOPLE GOING OUT INTO THE WORLD SHOULD HAVE THEIR OWN GOALS, AND USE THEIR ABILITIES TO THEIR FULLEST TO CONTRIBUTE TO SOCIETY...
OF ALL THE PROGRAMS TAKADA HAS BEEN ON, I HAVE BEEN ABLE TO CONFIRM THAT MIKAMI WAS ON TWO OF THEM. TWICE...THAT WOULD HAVE GIVEN HIM ENOUGH TIME TO GET TO KNOW HER.
AND THE WAY HE TALKS... IT IS VERY SIMILAR TO THE MESSAGE FROM KIRA THAT, "PEOPLE WITH ABILITY WHO DO NOT USE THAT ABILITY FOR THE GOOD OF THE SOCIETY WILL NOT BE TOLERATED."
BEEP
AND MOST OF ALL, HIS SPEECH FROM KIRA'S KINGDOM ...
I WOULD VERY MUCH LIKE TO HEAR KIRA'S VOICE AGAIN. AND I INTEND TO FOLLOW YOUR IDEALS.
I BELIEVE THAT FOLLOWING YOUR ORDERS AND TEACHINGS IS THE QUICKEST WAY TO ACHIEVE WORLD PEACE. KIRA, PLEASE LET ME HEAR YOUR VOICE.

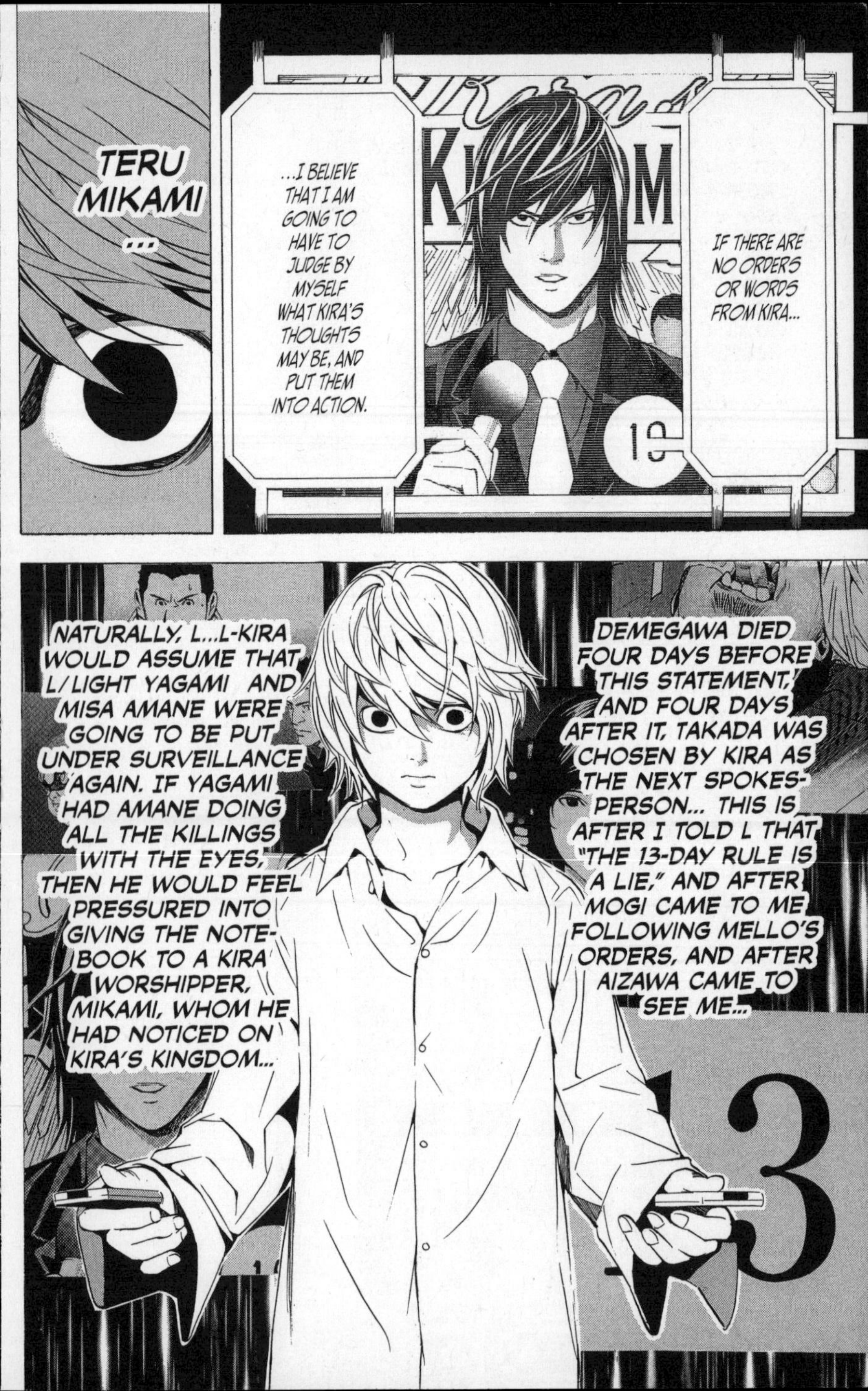
IF THERE ARE NO ORDERS OR WORDS FROM KIRA...
...I BELIEVE THAT I AM GOING TO HAVE TO JUDGE BY MYSELF WHAT KIRA'S THOUGHTS MAY BE, AND PUT THEM INTO ACTION.
TERU MIKAMI ...
DEMEGAWA DIED FOUR DAYS BEFORE THIS STATEMENT, AND FOUR DAYS AFTER IT, TAKADA WAS CHOSEN BY KIRA AS THE NEXT SPOKES-PERSON... THIS IS AFTER I TOLD L THAT "THE 13-DAY RULE IS A LIE," AND AFTER MOGI CAME TO ME FOLLOWING MELLO'S ORDERS, AND AFTER AIZAWA CAME TO SEE ME...
NATURALLY, L...L-KIRA WOULD ASSUME THAT L/LIGHT YAGAMI AND MISA AMANE WERE GOING TO BE PUT UNDER SURVEILLANCE AGAIN. IF YAGAMI HAD AMANE DOING ALL THE KILLINGS WITH THE EYES, THEN HE WOULD FEEL PRESSURED INTO GIVING THE NOTE-BOOK TO A KIRA WORSHIPPER, MIKAMI, WHOM HE HAD NOTICED ON KIRA'S KINGDOM...

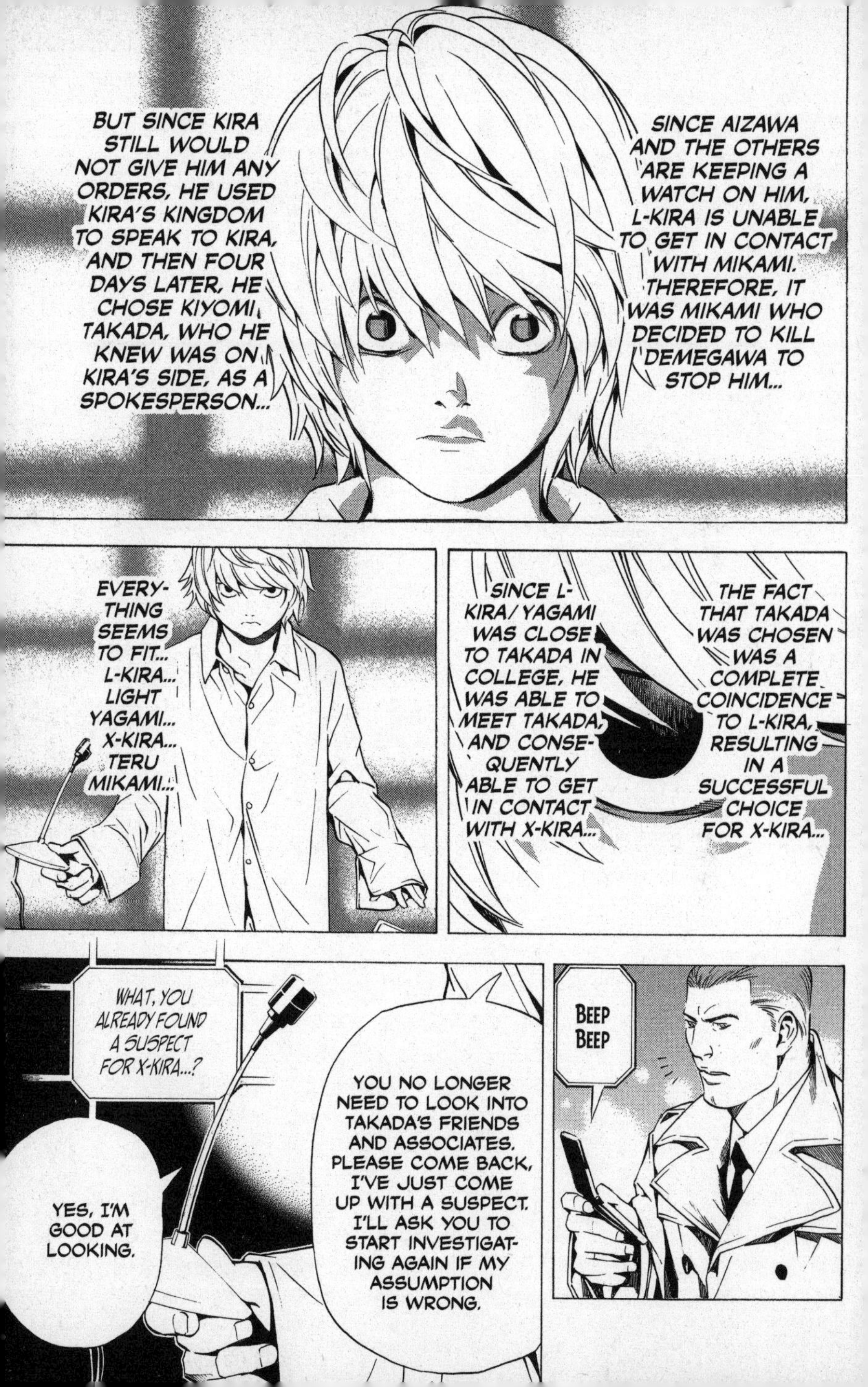
SINCE AIZAWA AND THE OTHERS ARE KEEPING A WATCH ON HIM, L-KIRA IS UNABLE TO GET IN CONTACT WITH MIKAMI. THEREFORE, IT WAS MIKAMI WHO DECIDED TO KILL DEMEGAWA TO STOP HIM...
BUT SINCE KIRA STILL WOULD NOT GIVE HIM ANY ORDERS, HE USED KIRA'S KINGDOM TO SPEAK TO KIRA, AND THEN FOUR DAYS LATER, HE CHOSE KIYOMI TAKADA, WHO HE KNEW WAS ON KIRA'S SIDE, AS A SPOKESPERSON...
THE FACT THAT TAKADA WAS CHOSEN WAS A COMPLETE COINCIDENCE TO L-KIRA, RESULTING IN A SUCCESSFUL CHOICE FOR X-KIRA...
SINCE L-KIRA/YAGAMI WAS CLOSE TO TAKADA IN COLLEGE, HE WAS ABLE TO MEET TAKADA, AND CONSEQUENTLY ABLE TO GET IN CONTACT WITH X-KIRA...
EVERYTHING SEEMS TO FIT... L-KIRA... LIGHT YAGAMI... X-KIRA... TERU MIKAMI...
BEEP BEEP
YOU NO LONGER NEED TO LOOK INTO TAKADA'S FRIENDS AND ASSOCIATES. PLEASE COME BACK, I'VE JUST COME UP WITH A SUSPECT. I'LL ASK YOU TO START INVESTIGATING AGAIN IF MY ASSUMPTION IS WRONG.
WHAT, YOU ALREADY FOUND A SUSPECT FOR X-KIRA...?
YES, I'M GOOD AT LOOKING.

DEATH NOTE
How to use it
LXII

○ Once the victim's name, cause of death and situation of death have been written down in the DEATH NOTE, this death will still take place even if that DEATH NOTE or the part of the Note in which it has been written is destroyed, for example, burned into ashes, before the stated time of death.

一度、名前・死因・死の状況が書き込まれれば、
万が一、その設定した死の時間の前にノートや書き込んだその部分が
燃える等しても書き込まれた内容に影響はない。

○ If the victim's name has been written and then the DEATH NOTE is destroyed in the middle of writing the cause of death, the victim will be killed by heart attack in 40 seconds after writing the name.

名を記し死因を書いている途中で燃える等した場合は
名を記してから40秒で心臓麻痺となる。

○ If the victim's name and cause of death have been written and the DEATH NOTE is destroyed, like burned, in the middle of writing the situation of death, then the victim will be killed within 6 minutes and 40 seconds via the stated cause of death if the cause is possible within that period of time, but otherwise, the victim will die by heart attack.

名前・死因を書き、死の状況を書いている途中で燃える等した場合は
6分40秒以内で可能な死因ならば死因は有効、
不可能であれば心臓麻痺となる。

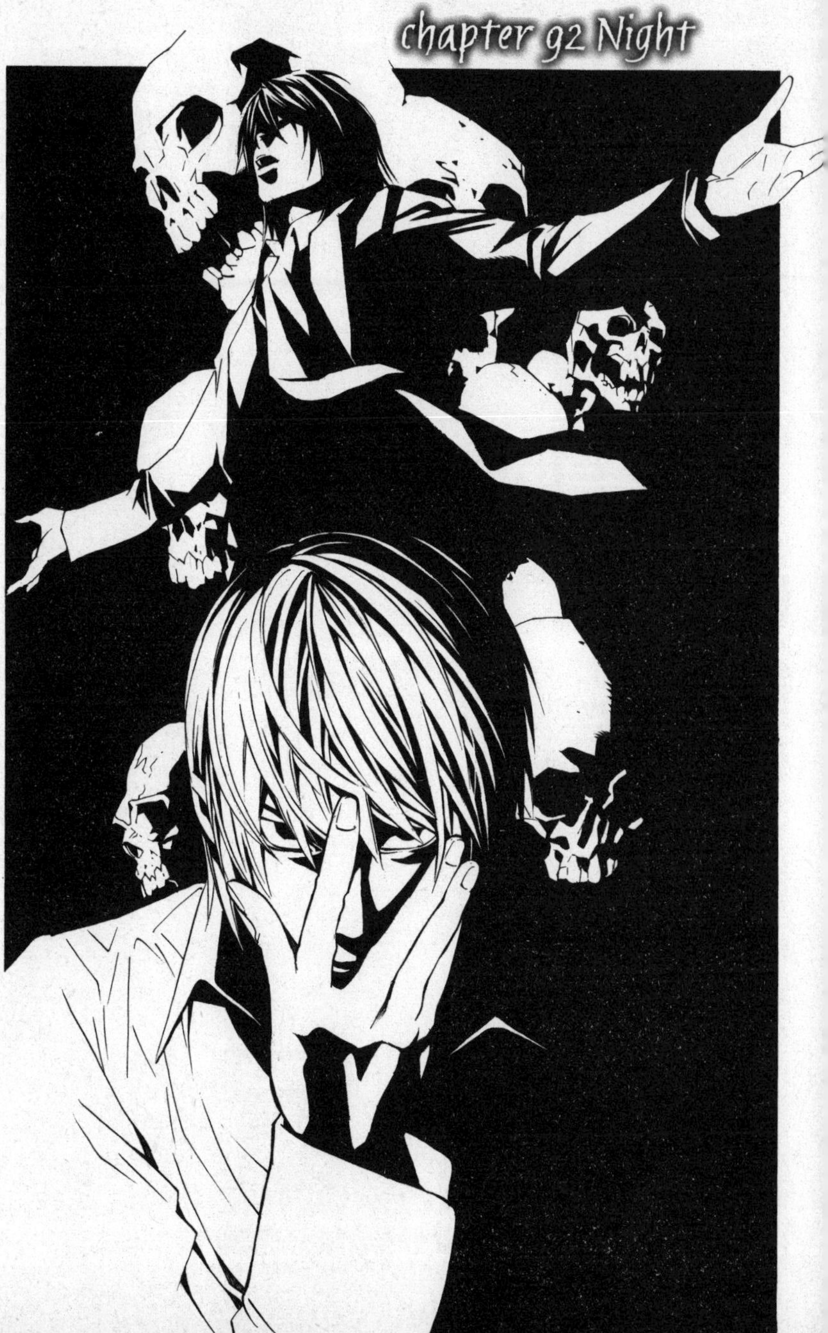
chapter 92 Night

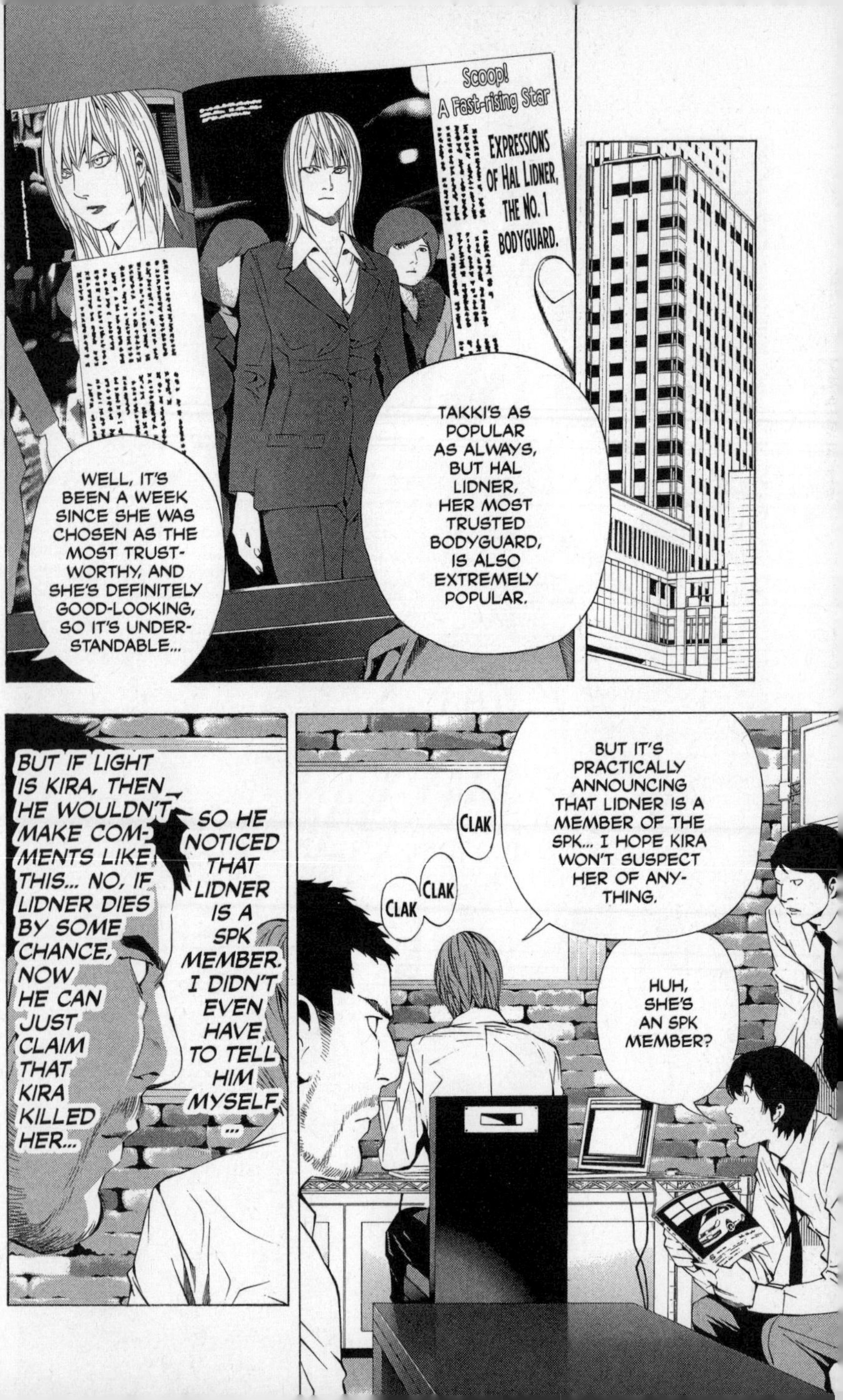
Scoop! A Fast-rising Star
EXPRESSIONS OF HAL LIDNER, THE NO. 1 BODYGUARD.
TAKKI'S AS POPULAR AS ALWAYS, BUT HAL LIDNER, HER MOST TRUSTED BODYGUARD, IS ALSO EXTREMELY POPULAR.
WELL, IT'S BEEN A WEEK SINCE SHE WAS CHOSEN AS THE MOST TRUST-WORTHY, AND SHE'S DEFINITELY GOOD-LOOKING, SO IT'S UNDER-STANDABLE...
BUT IT'S PRACTICALLY ANNOUNCING THAT LIDNER IS A MEMBER OF THE SPK... I HOPE KIRA WON'T SUSPECT HER OF ANY-THING.
CLAK
CLAK
CLAK
HUH, SHE'S AN SPK MEMBER?
SO HE NOTICED THAT LIDNER IS A SPK MEMBER. I DIDN'T EVEN HAVE TO TELL HIM MYSELF...
BUT IF LIGHT IS KIRA, THEN HE WOULDN'T MAKE COM-MENTS LIKE THIS... NO, IF LIDNER DIES BY SOME CHANCE, NOW HE CAN JUST CLAIM THAT KIRA KILLED HER...

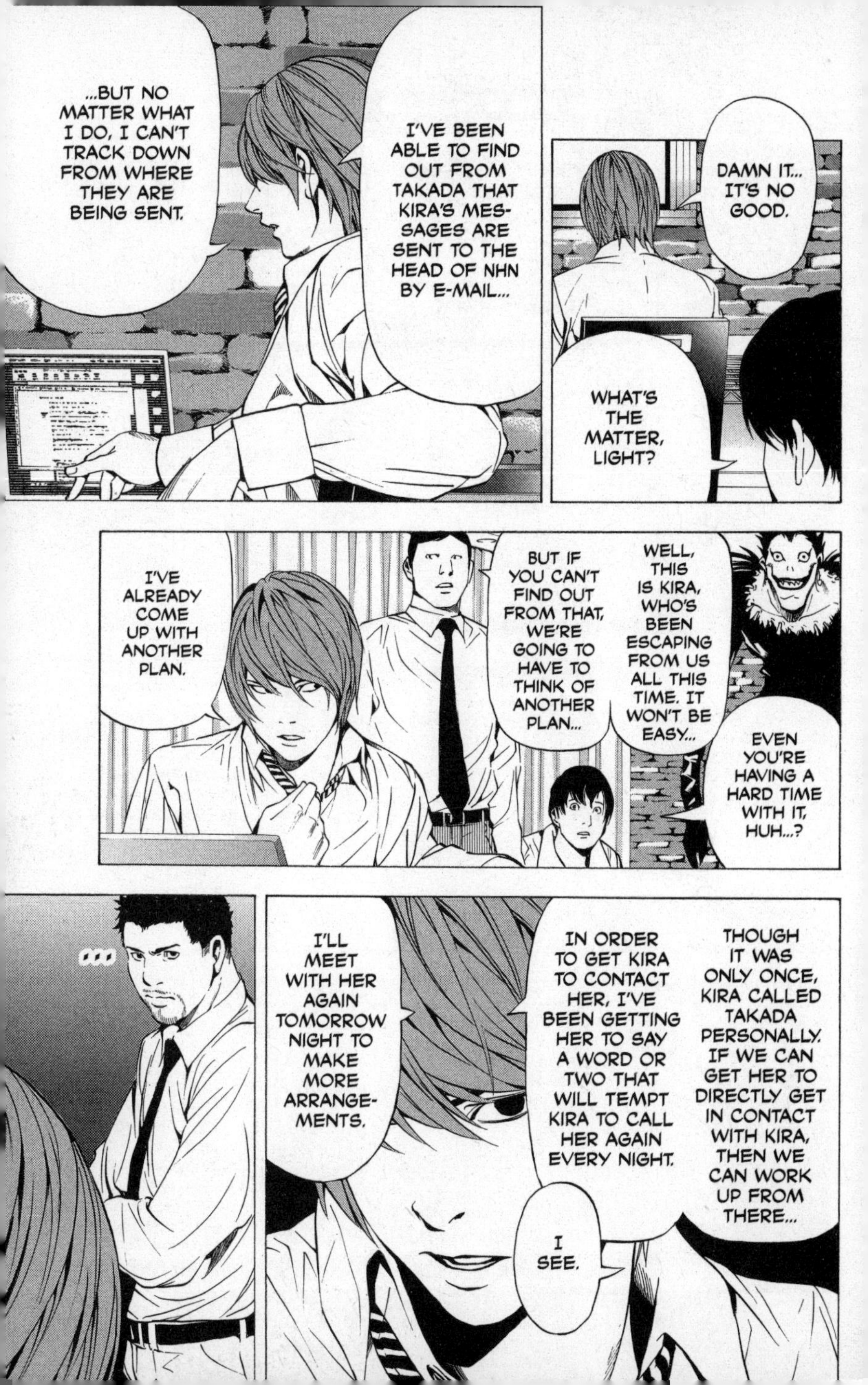
DAMN IT... IT'S NO GOOD.
WHAT'S THE MATTER, LIGHT?
I'VE BEEN ABLE TO FIND OUT FROM TAKADA THAT KIRA'S MES-SAGES ARE SENT TO THE HEAD OF NHN BY E-MAIL...
...BUT NO MATTER WHAT I DO, I CAN'T TRACK DOWN FROM WHERE THEY ARE BEING SENT.
WELL, THIS IS KIRA, WHO'S BEEN ESCAPING FROM US ALL THIS TIME. IT WON'T BE EASY...
EVEN YOU'RE HAVING A HARD TIME WITH IT, HUH...?
BUT IF YOU CAN'T FIND OUT FROM THAT, WE'RE GOING TO HAVE TO THINK OF ANOTHER PLAN...
I'VE ALREADY COME UP WITH ANOTHER PLAN.
THOUGH IT WAS ONLY ONCE, KIRA CALLED TAKADA PERSONALLY. IF WE CAN GET HER TO DIRECTLY GET IN CONTACT WITH KIRA, THEN WE CAN WORK UP FROM THERE...
IN ORDER TO GET KIRA TO CONTACT HER, I'VE BEEN GETTING HER TO SAY A WORD OR TWO THAT WILL TEMPT KIRA TO CALL HER AGAIN EVERY NIGHT.
I'LL MEET WITH HER AGAIN TOMORROW NIGHT TO MAKE MORE ARRANGE-MENTS.
I SEE.
...

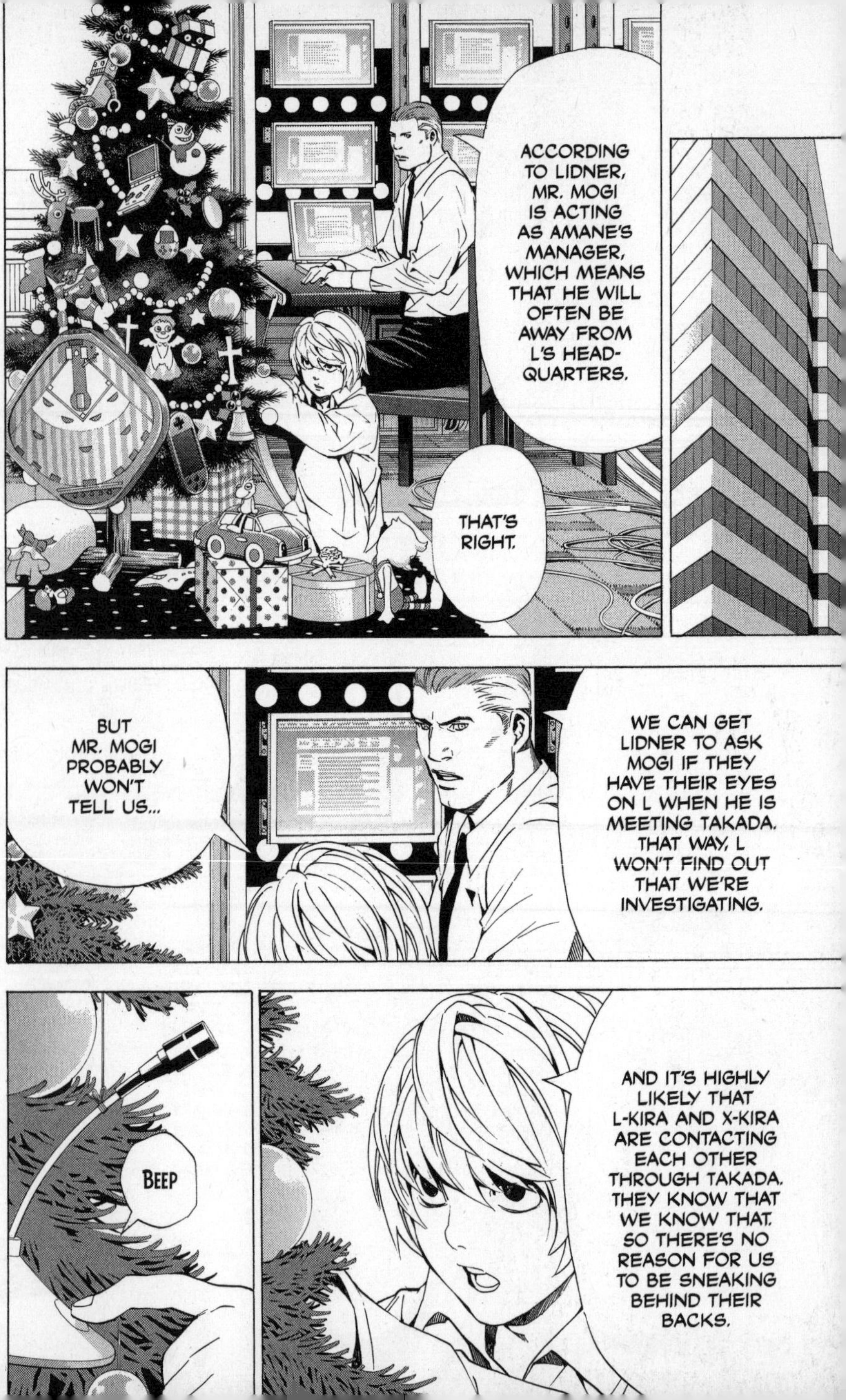
ACCORDING TO LIDNER, MR. MOGI IS ACTING AS AMANE'S MANAGER, WHICH MEANS THAT HE WILL OFTEN BE AWAY FROM L'S HEAD-QUARTERS.
THAT'S RIGHT.
WE CAN GET LIDNER TO ASK MOGI IF THEY HAVE THEIR EYES ON L WHEN HE IS MEETING TAKADA. THAT WAY, L WON'T FIND OUT THAT WE'RE INVESTIGATING.
BUT MR. MOGI PROBABLY WON'T TELL US...
AND IT'S HIGHLY LIKELY THAT L-KIRA AND X-KIRA ARE CONTACTING EACH OTHER THROUGH TAKADA. THEY KNOW THAT WE KNOW THAT. SO THERE'S NO REASON FOR US TO BE SNEAKING BEHIND THEIR BACKS.
BEEP

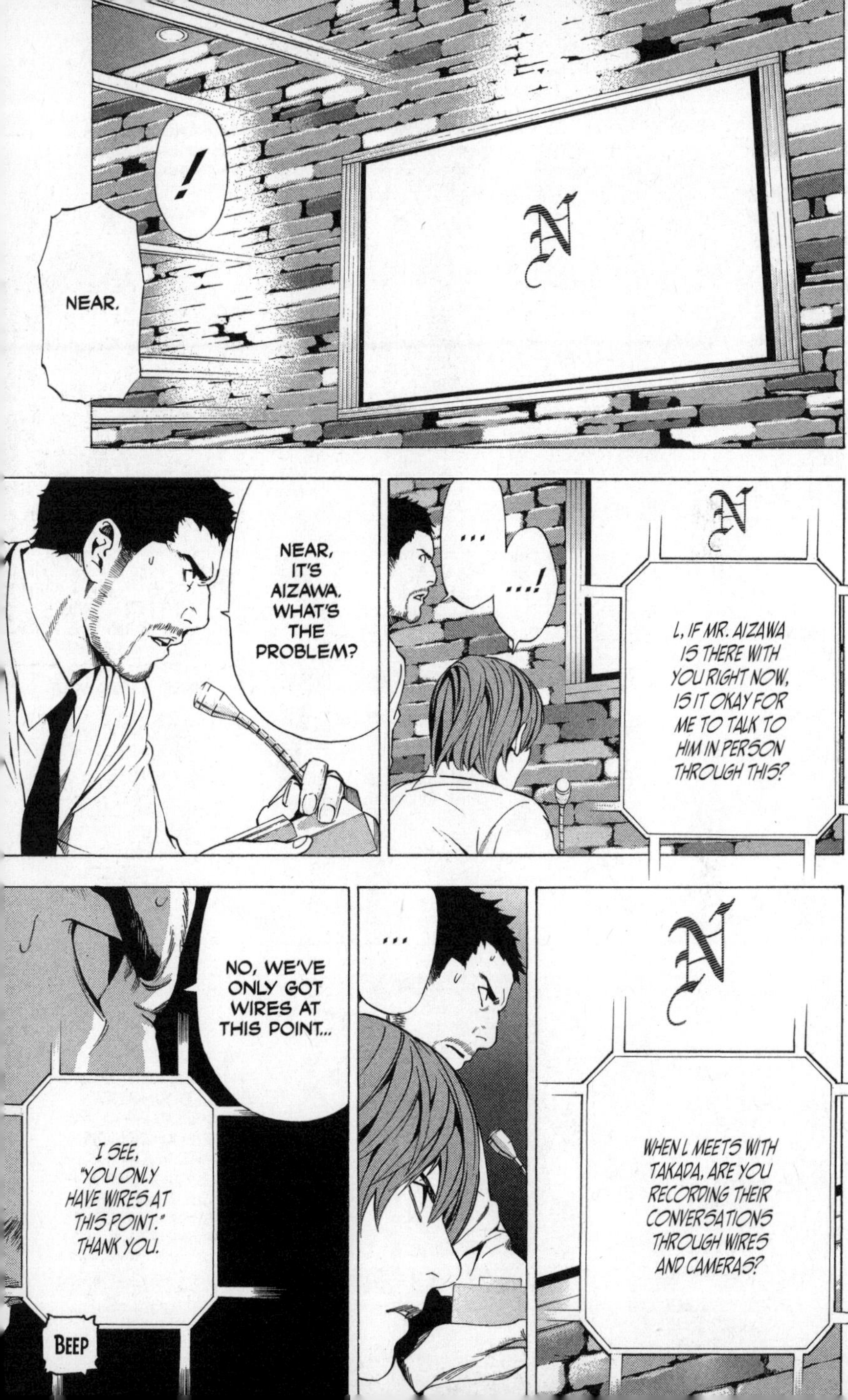
!
NEAR.
L, IF MR. AIZAWA IS THERE WITH YOU RIGHT NOW, IS IT OKAY FOR ME TO TALK TO HIM IN PERSON THROUGH THIS?
...
...!
NEAR, IT'S AIZAWA. WHAT'S THE PROBLEM?
WHEN L MEETS WITH TAKADA, ARE YOU RECORDING THEIR CONVERSATIONS THROUGH WIRES AND CAMERAS?
...
NO, WE'VE ONLY GOT WIRES AT THIS POINT...
I SEE, "YOU ONLY HAVE WIRES AT THIS POINT." THANK YOU.
BEEP

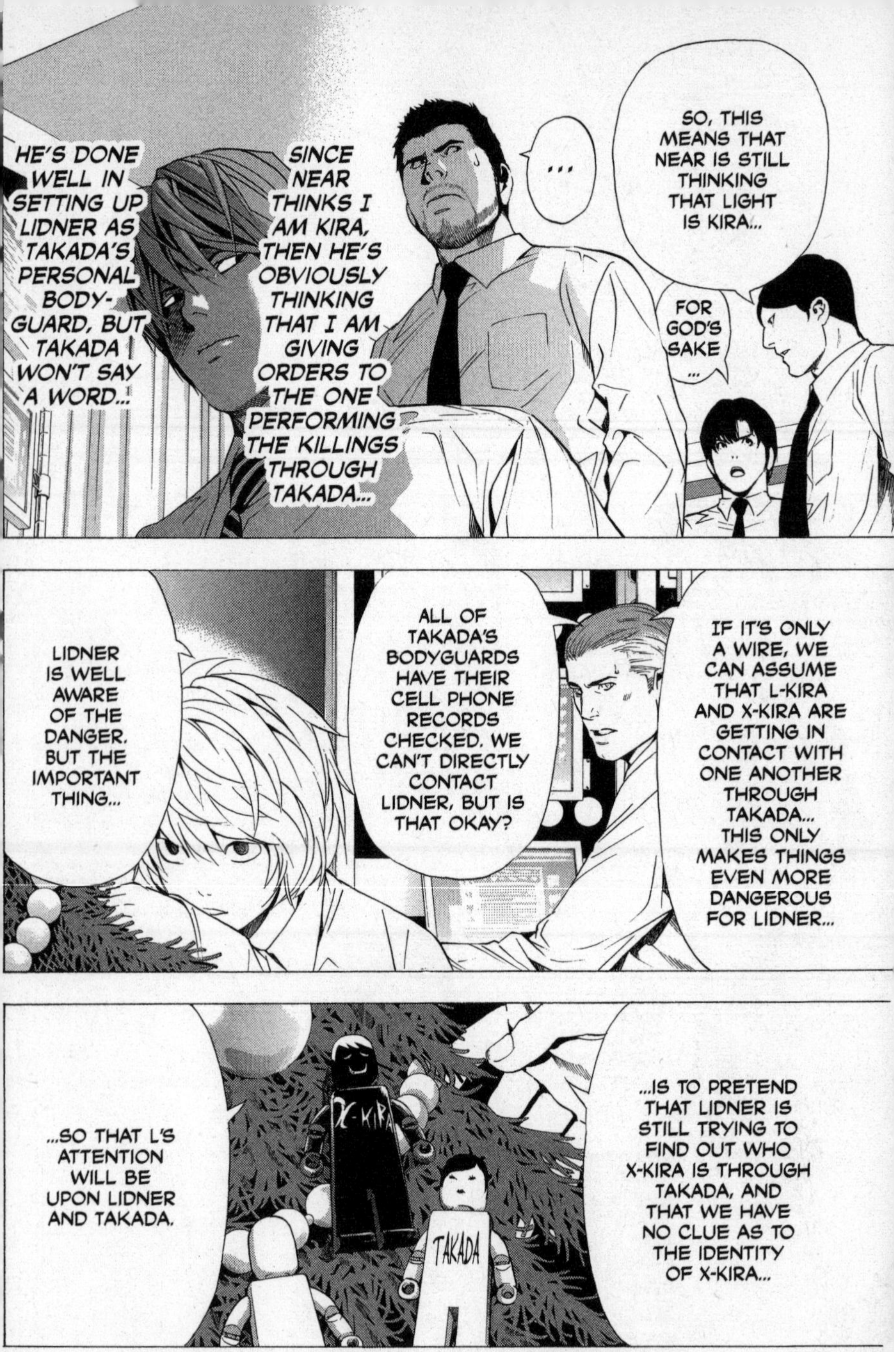
SO, THIS MEANS THAT NEAR IS STILL THINKING THAT LIGHT IS KIRA...
FOR GOD'S SAKE ...
...
SINCE NEAR THINKS I AM KIRA, THEN HE'S OBVIOUSLY THINKING THAT I AM GIVING ORDERS TO THE ONE PERFORMING THE KILLINGS THROUGH TAKADA...
HE'S DONE WELL IN SETTING UP LIDNER AS TAKADA'S PERSONAL BODY-GUARD, BUT TAKADA WON'T SAY A WORD...
IF IT'S ONLY A WIRE, WE CAN ASSUME THAT L-KIRA AND X-KIRA ARE GETTING IN CONTACT WITH ONE ANOTHER THROUGH TAKADA... THIS ONLY MAKES THINGS EVEN MORE DANGEROUS FOR LIDNER...
ALL OF TAKADA'S BODYGUARDS HAVE THEIR CELL PHONE RECORDS CHECKED. WE CAN'T DIRECTLY CONTACT LIDNER, BUT IS THAT OKAY?
LIDNER IS WELL AWARE OF THE DANGER. BUT THE IMPORTANT THING...
...IS TO PRETEND THAT LIDNER IS STILL TRYING TO FIND OUT WHO X-KIRA IS THROUGH TAKADA, AND THAT WE HAVE NO CLUE AS TO THE IDENTITY OF X-KIRA...
...SO THAT L'S ATTENTION WILL BE UPON LIDNER AND TAKADA.
TAKADA

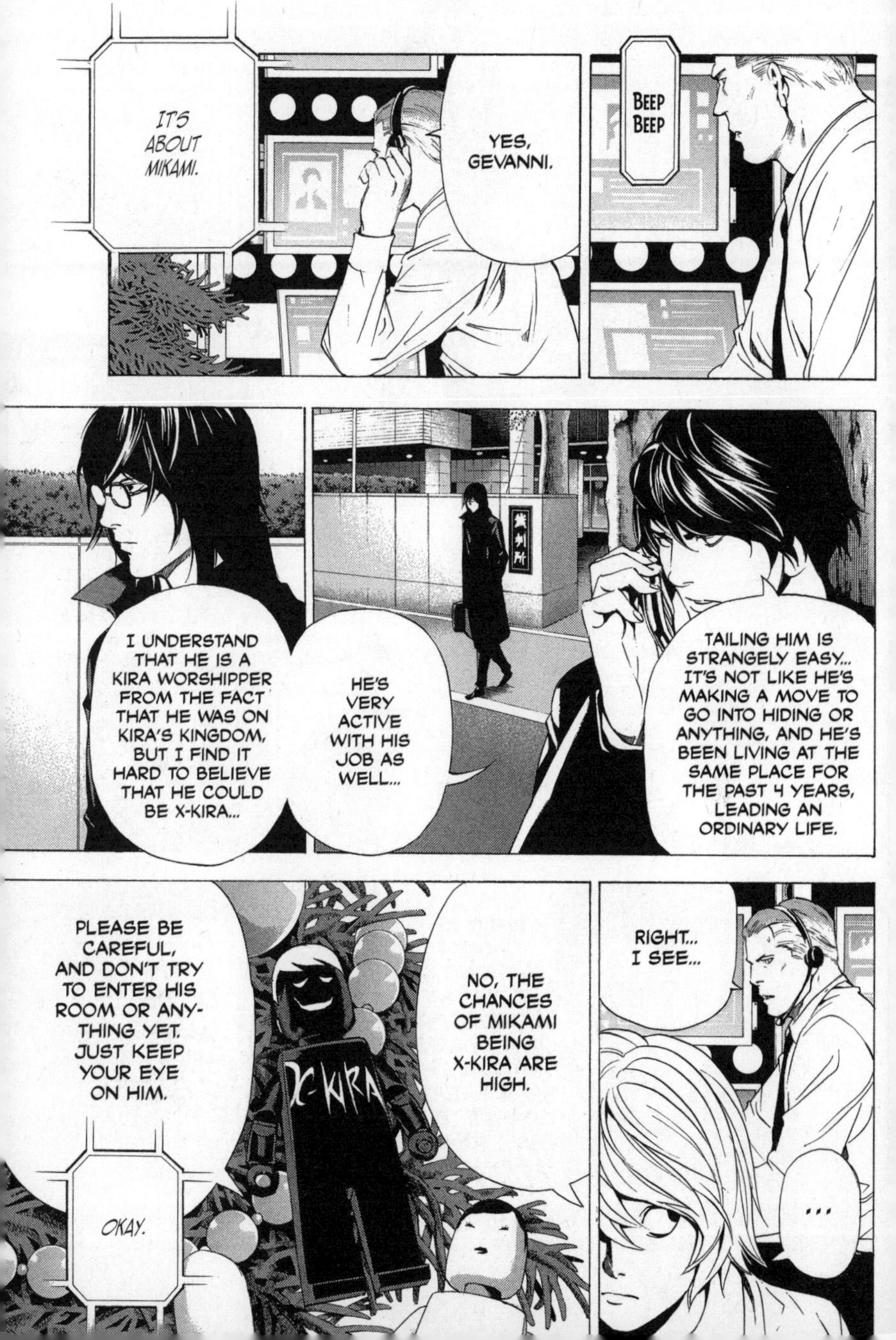
BEEP BEEP
YES, GEVANNI.
IT'S ABOUT MIKAMI.
TAILING HIM IS STRANGELY EASY... IT'S NOT LIKE HE'S MAKING A MOVE TO GO INTO HIDING OR ANYTHING, AND HE'S BEEN LIVING AT THE SAME PLACE FOR THE PAST 4 YEARS, LEADING AN ORDINARY LIFE.
HE'S VERY ACTIVE WITH HIS JOB AS WELL...
I UNDERSTAND THAT HE IS A KIRA WORSHIPPER FROM THE FACT THAT HE WAS ON KIRA'S KINGDOM, BUT I FIND IT HARD TO BELIEVE THAT HE COULD BE X-KIRA...
RIGHT... I SEE...
...
NO, THE CHANCES OF MIKAMI BEING X-KIRA ARE HIGH.
PLEASE BE CAREFUL, AND DON'T TRY TO ENTER HIS ROOM OR ANY-THING YET. JUST KEEP YOUR EYE ON HIM.
OKAY.

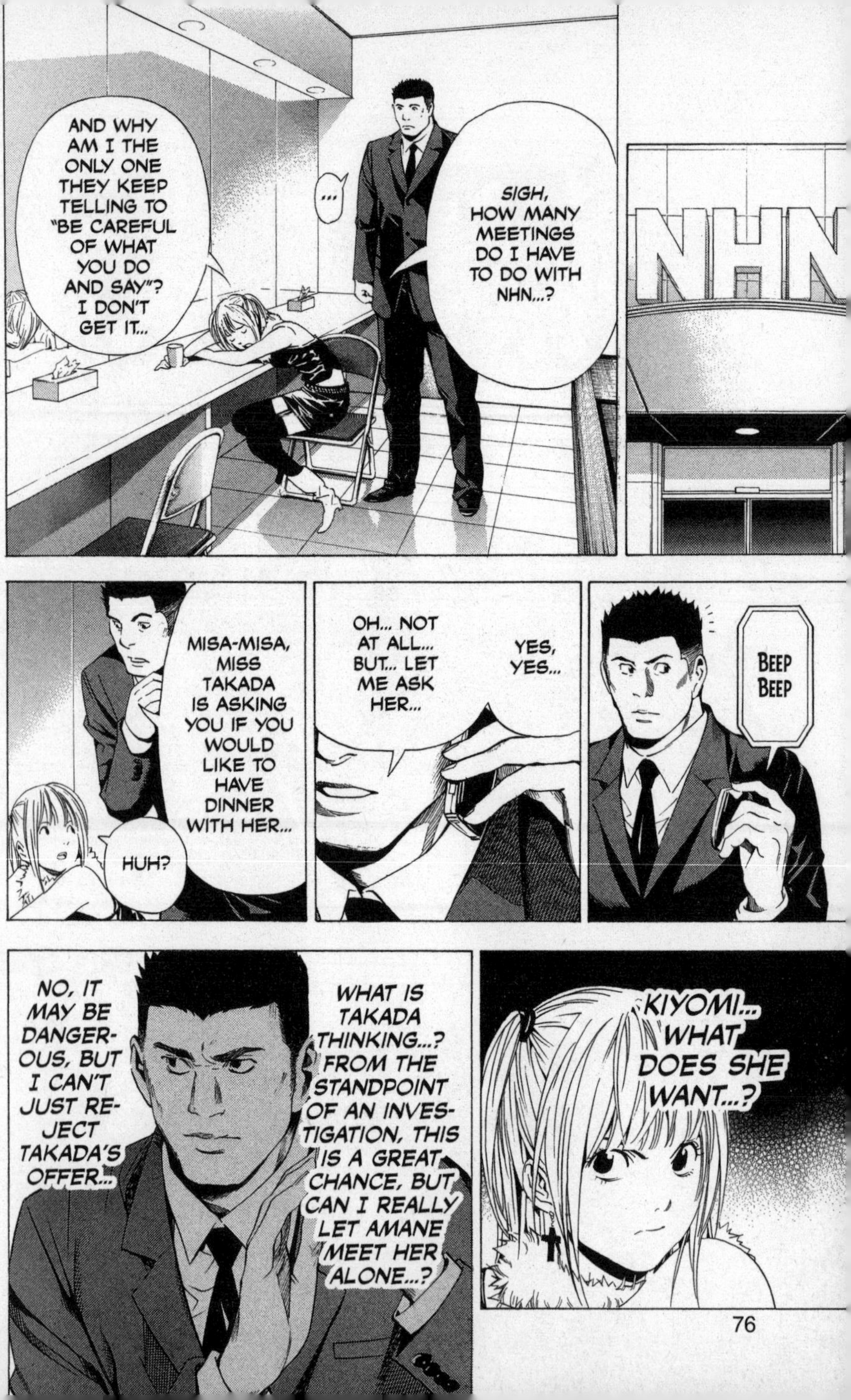

NHN
SIGH, HOW MANY MEETINGS DO I HAVE TO DO WITH NHN...?
...
AND WHY AM I THE ONLY ONE THEY KEEP TELLING TO "BE CAREFUL OF WHAT YOU DO AND SAY"? I DON'T GET IT...
BEEP BEEP
YES, YES...
OH... NOT AT ALL... BUT... LET ME ASK HER...
MISA-MISA, MISS TAKADA IS ASKING YOU IF YOU WOULD LIKE TO HAVE DINNER WITH HER...
HUH?
KIYOMI... WHAT DOES SHE WANT...?
WHAT IS TAKADA THINKING...? FROM THE STANDPOINT OF AN INVESTIGATION, THIS IS A GREAT CHANCE, BUT CAN I REALLY LET AMANE MEET HER ALONE...?
NO, IT MAY BE DANGEROUS, BUT I CAN'T JUST REJECT TAKADA'S OFFER...

READ THIS WAY

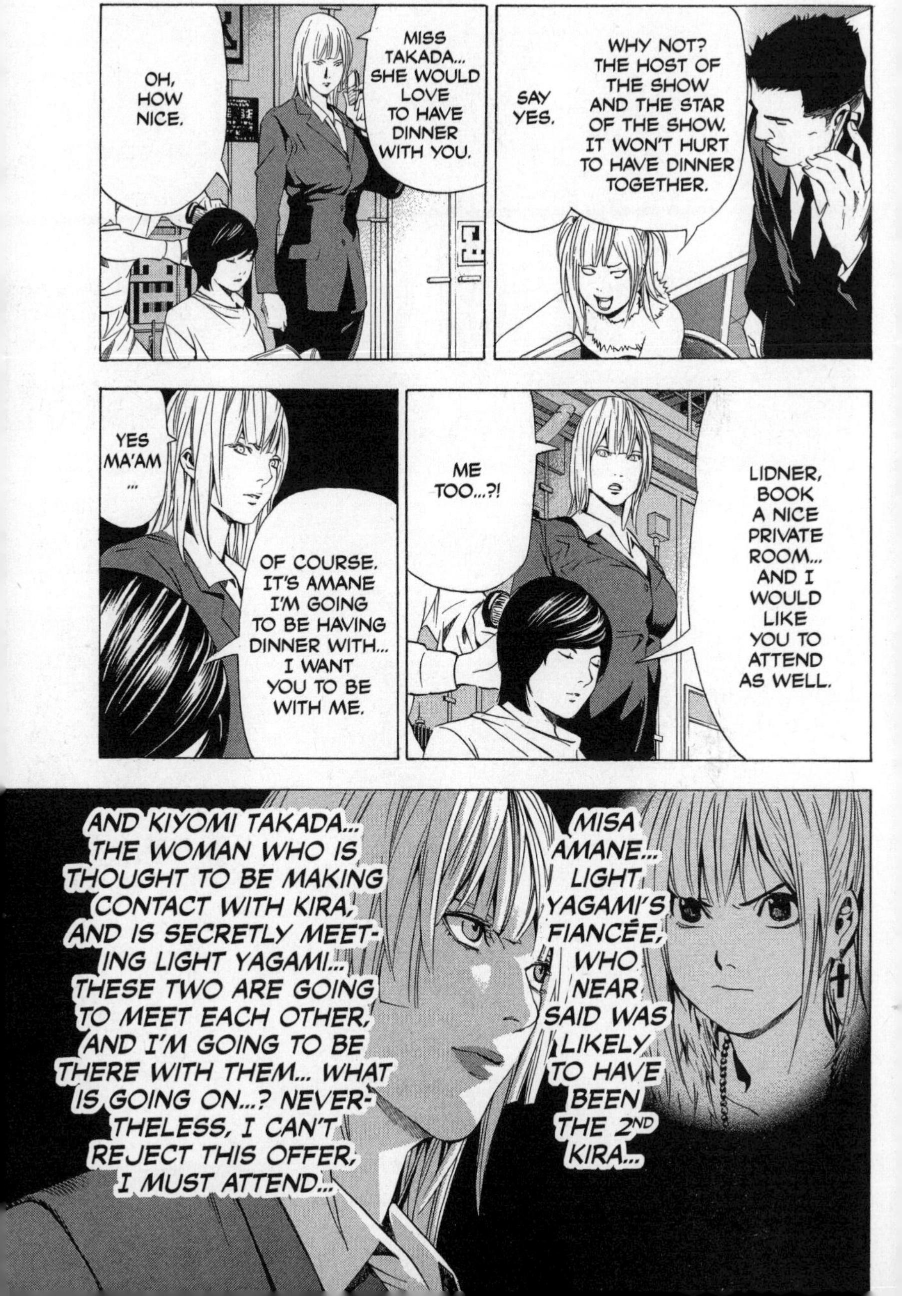
WHY NOT? THE HOST OF THE SHOW AND THE STAR OF THE SHOW. IT WON'T HURT TO HAVE DINNER TOGETHER.
SAY YES.
MISS TAKADA... SHE WOULD LOVE TO HAVE DINNER WITH YOU.
OH, HOW NICE.
LIDNER, BOOK A NICE PRIVATE ROOM... AND I WOULD LIKE YOU TO ATTEND AS WELL.
ME TOO...?!
OF COURSE. IT'S AMANE I'M GOING TO BE HAVING DINNER WITH... I WANT YOU TO BE WITH ME.
YES MA'AM ...
MISA AMANE... LIGHT YAGAMI'S FIANCÉE, WHO NEAR SAID WAS LIKELY TO HAVE BEEN THE 2ND KIRA...
AND KIYOMI TAKADA... THE WOMAN WHO IS THOUGHT TO BE MAKING CONTACT WITH KIRA, AND IS SECRETLY MEETING LIGHT YAGAMI... THESE TWO ARE GOING TO MEET EACH OTHER, AND I'M GOING TO BE THERE WITH THEM... WHAT IS GOING ON...? NEVERTHELESS, I CAN'T REJECT THIS OFFER, I MUST ATTEND...

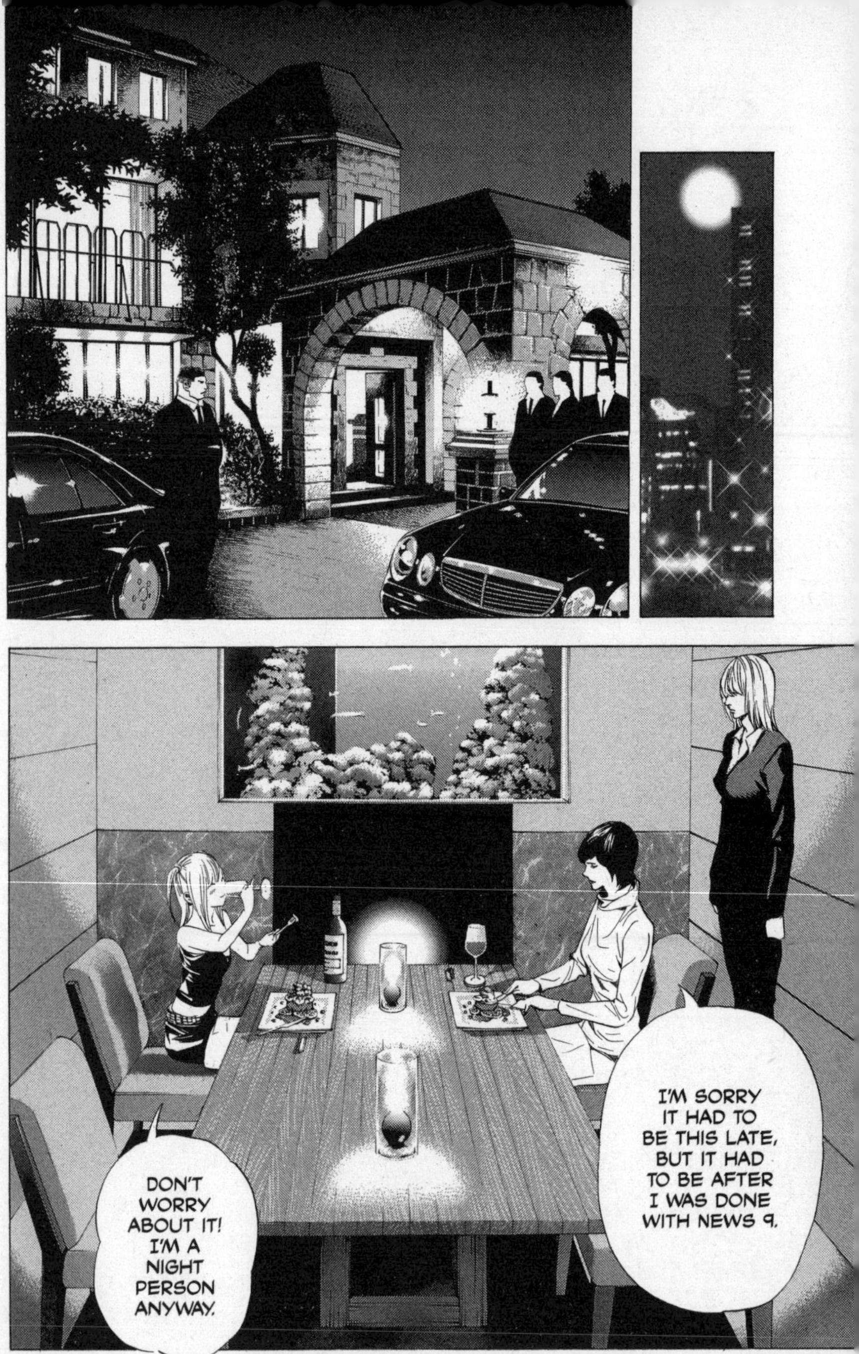
I'M SORRY IT HAD TO BE THIS LATE, BUT IT HAD TO BE AFTER I WAS DONE WITH NEWS 9.
DON'T WORRY ABOUT IT! I'M A NIGHT PERSON ANYWAY.

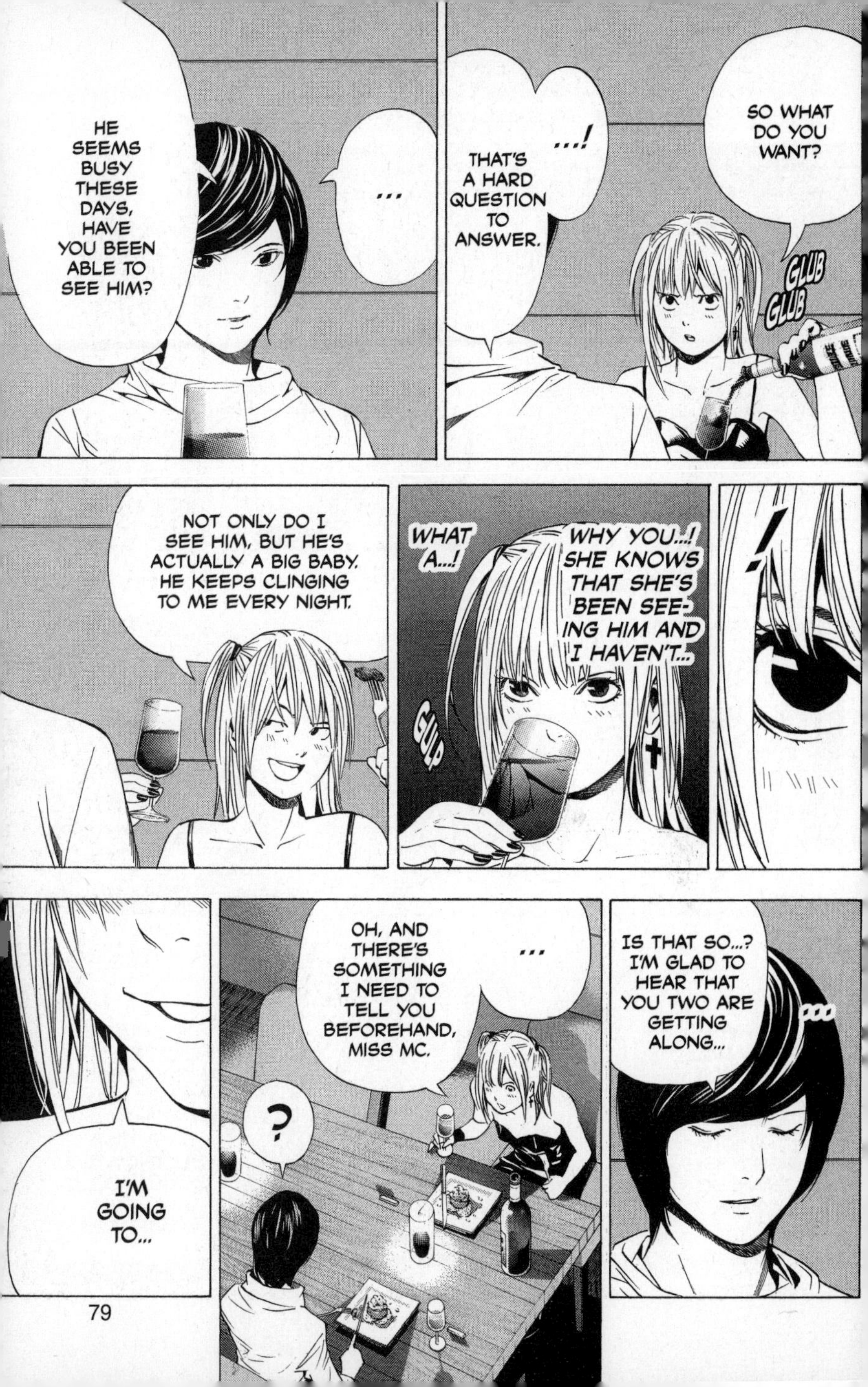
SO WHAT DO YOU WANT?
...!
THAT'S A HARD QUESTION TO ANSWER.
GLUB GLUB
...
HE SEEMS BUSY THESE DAYS, HAVE YOU BEEN ABLE TO SEE HIM?
!
WHY YOU...! SHE KNOWS THAT SHE'S BEEN SEE-ING HIM AND I HAVEN'T...
WHAT A...!
GULP
NOT ONLY DO I SEE HIM, BUT HE'S ACTUALLY A BIG BABY. HE KEEPS CLINGING TO ME EVERY NIGHT.
IS THAT SO...? I'M GLAD TO HEAR THAT YOU TWO ARE GETTING ALONG...
...
...
OH, AND THERE'S SOMETHING I NEED TO TELL YOU BEFOREHAND, MISS MC.
?
I'M GOING TO...

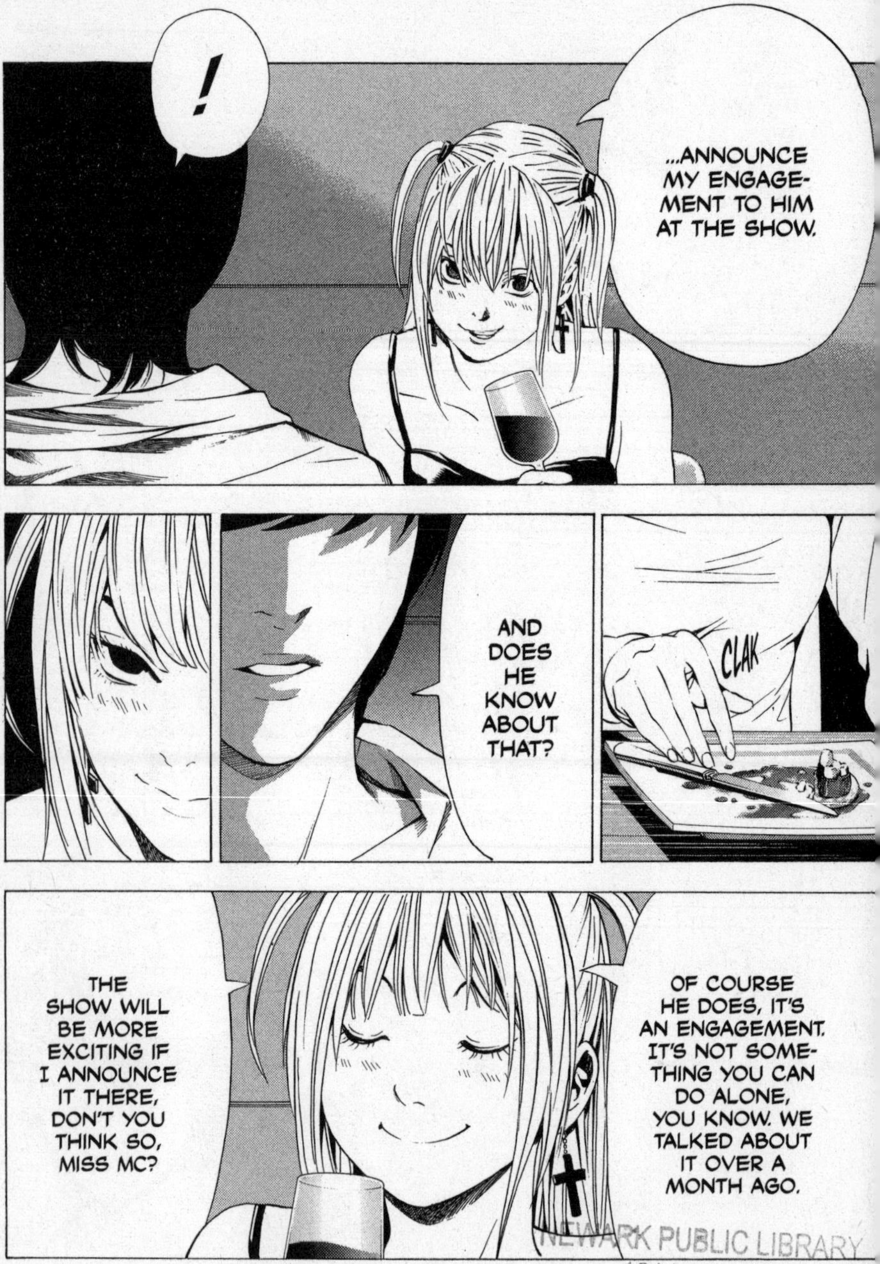
...ANNOUNCE MY ENGAGEMENT TO HIM AT THE SHOW.
!
CLAK
AND DOES HE KNOW ABOUT THAT?
OF COURSE HE DOES, IT'S AN ENGAGEMENT. IT'S NOT SOMETHING YOU CAN DO ALONE, YOU KNOW. WE TALKED ABOUT IT OVER A MONTH AGO.
THE SHOW WILL BE MORE EXCITING IF I ANNOUNCE IT THERE, DON'T YOU THINK SO, MISS MC?

READ THIS WAY

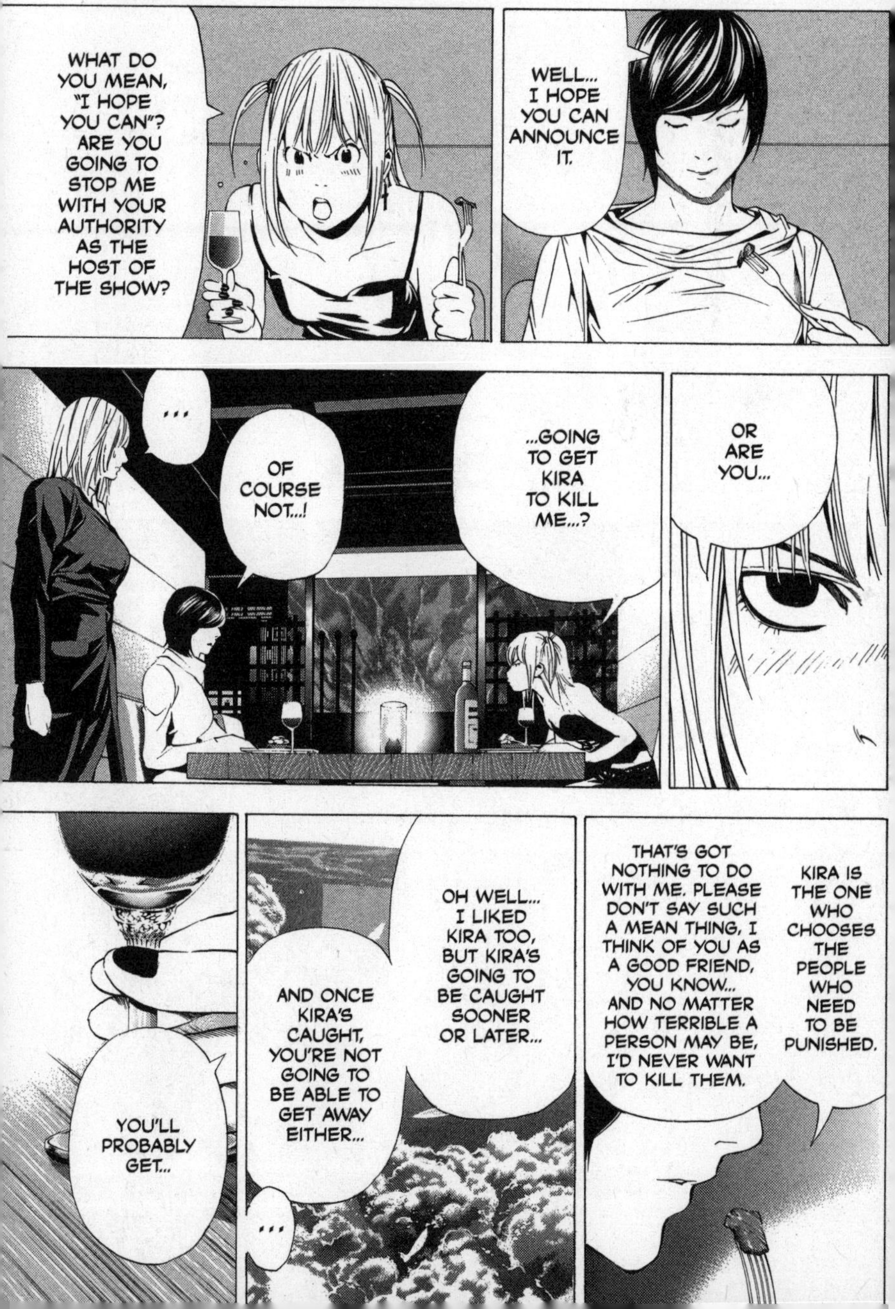

WELL... I HOPE YOU CAN ANNOUNCE IT.
WHAT DO YOU MEAN, "I HOPE YOU CAN"? ARE YOU GOING TO STOP ME WITH YOUR AUTHORITY AS THE HOST OF THE SHOW?
OR ARE YOU...
...GOING TO GET KIRA TO KILL ME...?
OF COURSE NOT...!
...
KIRA IS THE ONE WHO CHOOSES THE PEOPLE WHO NEED TO BE PUNISHED.
THAT'S GOT NOTHING TO DO WITH ME. PLEASE DON'T SAY SUCH A MEAN THING, I THINK OF YOU AS A GOOD FRIEND, YOU KNOW... AND NO MATTER HOW TERRIBLE A PERSON MAY BE, I'D NEVER WANT TO KILL THEM.
OH WELL... I LIKED KIRA TOO, BUT KIRA'S GOING TO BE CAUGHT SOONER OR LATER...
AND ONCE KIRA'S CAUGHT, YOU'RE NOT GOING TO BE ABLE TO GET AWAY EITHER...
...
YOU'LL PROBABLY GET...

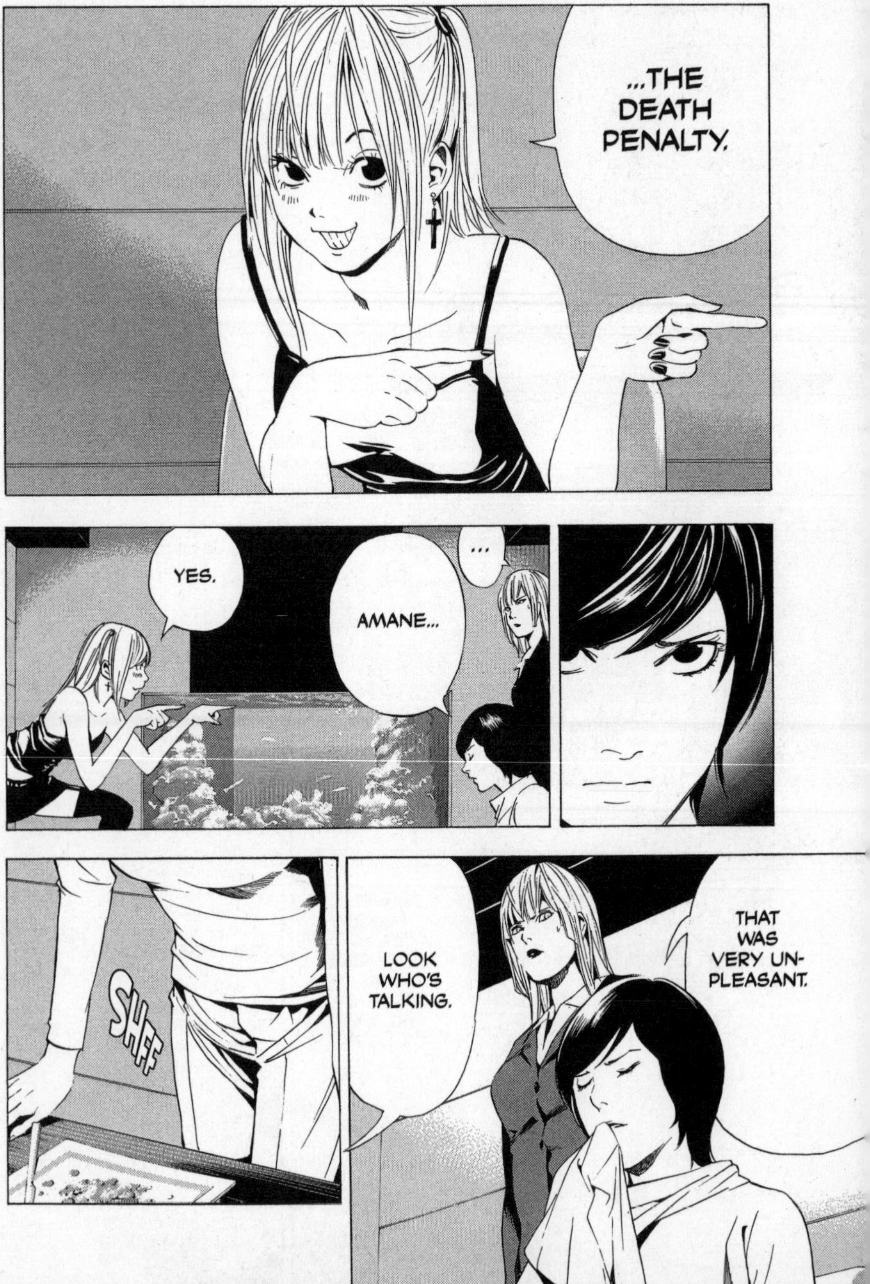
...THE DEATH PENALTY.
...
AMANE...
YES.
THAT WAS VERY UN-PLEASANT.
LOOK WHO'S TALKING.
SHFF

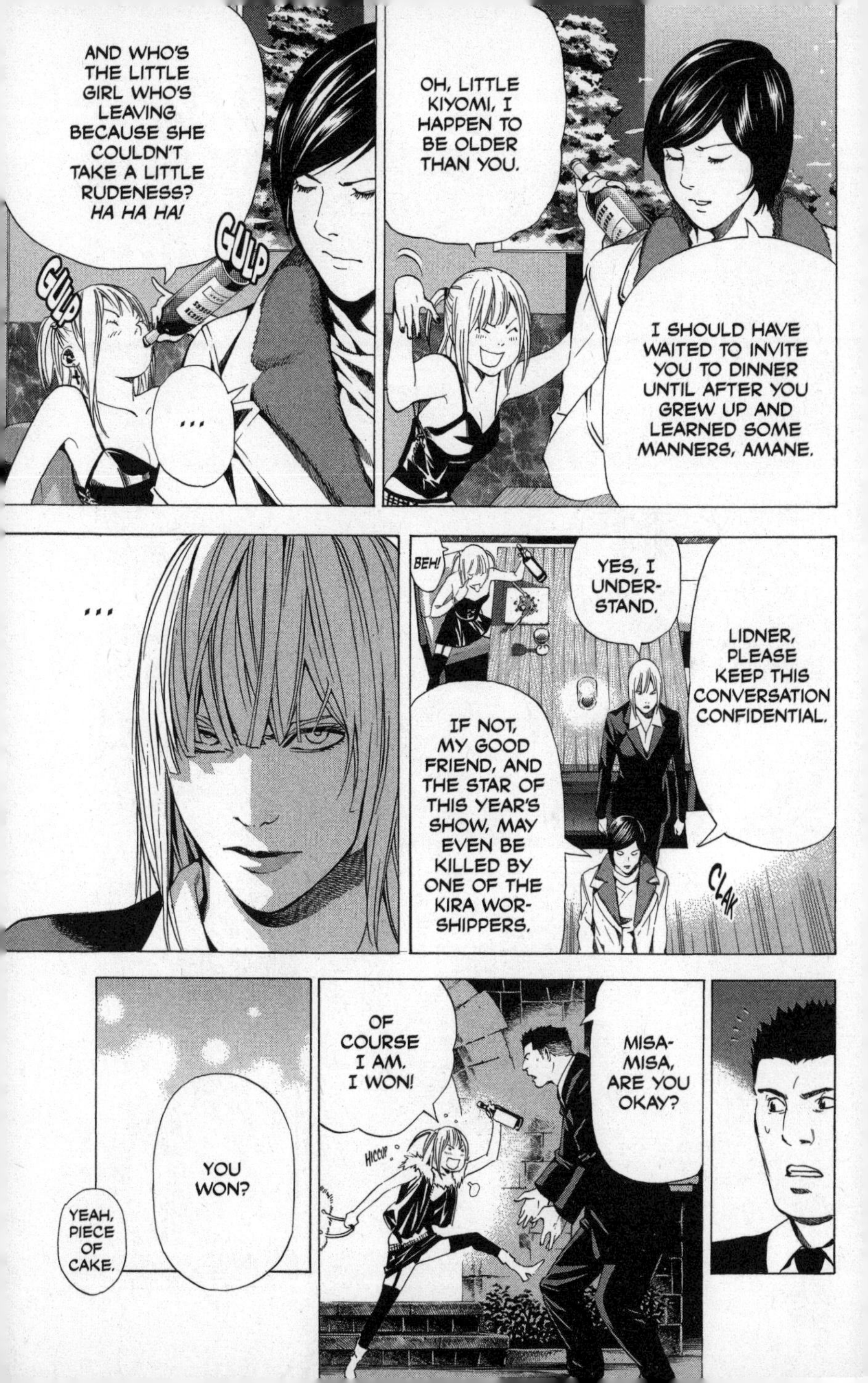

I SHOULD HAVE WAITED TO INVITE YOU TO DINNER UNTIL AFTER YOU GREW UP AND LEARNED SOME MANNERS, AMANE.
OH, LITTLE KIYOMI, I HAPPEN TO BE OLDER THAN YOU.
AND WHO'S THE LITTLE GIRL WHO'S LEAVING BECAUSE SHE COULDN'T TAKE A LITTLE RUDENESS? *HA HA HA!*
GULP
GULP
...
LIDNER, PLEASE KEEP THIS CONVERSATION CONFIDENTIAL.
YES, I UNDER-STAND.
IF NOT, MY GOOD FRIEND, AND THE STAR OF THIS YEAR'S SHOW, MAY EVEN BE KILLED BY ONE OF THE KIRA WOR-SHIPPERS.
BEH!
CLAK
...
MISA-MISA, ARE YOU OKAY?
OF COURSE I AM. I WON!
HICCUP
YOU WON?
YEAH, PIECE OF CAKE.

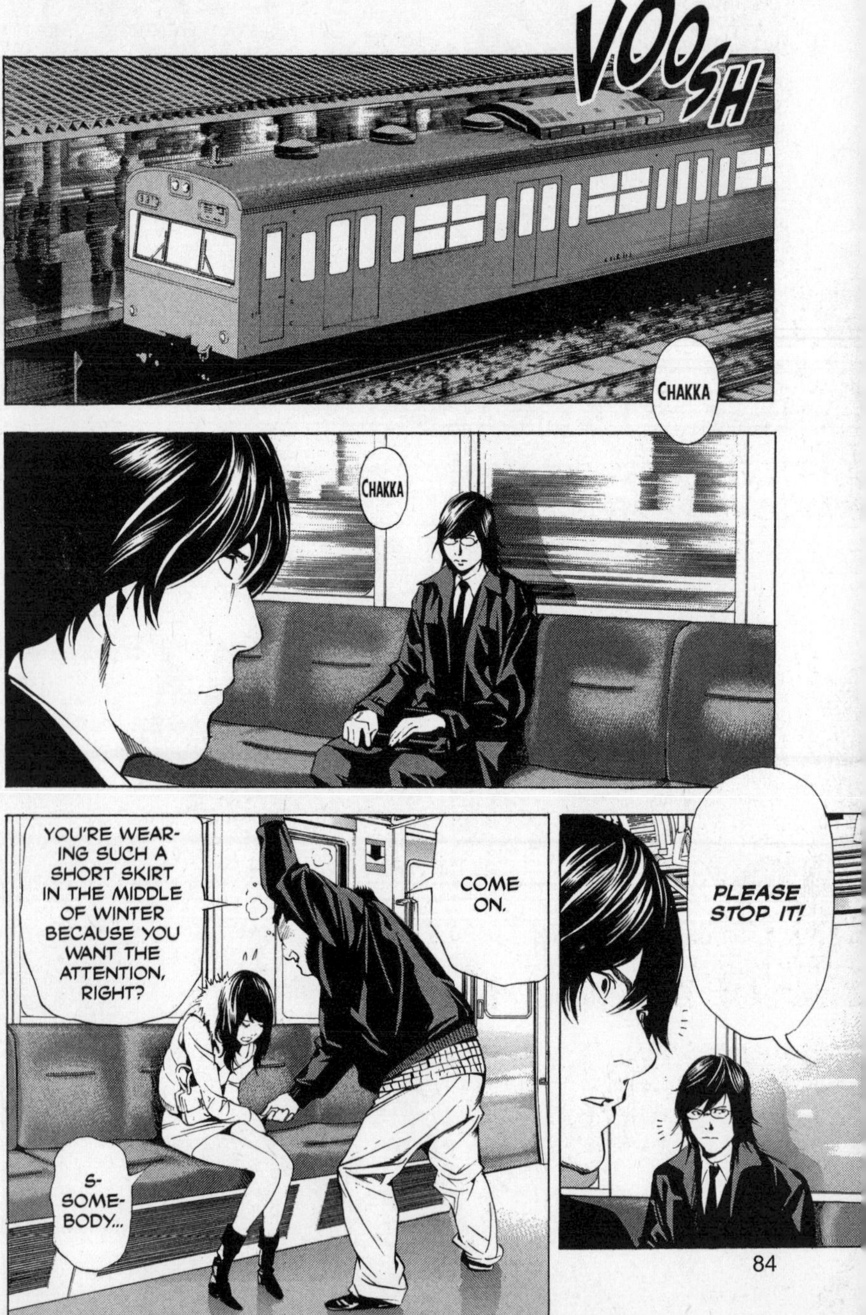
VOOSH
CHAKKA
CHAKKA
YOU'RE WEARING SUCH A SHORT SKIRT IN THE MIDDLE OF WINTER BECAUSE YOU WANT THE ATTENTION, RIGHT?
COME ON.
S-SOMEBODY...
PLEASE STOP IT!

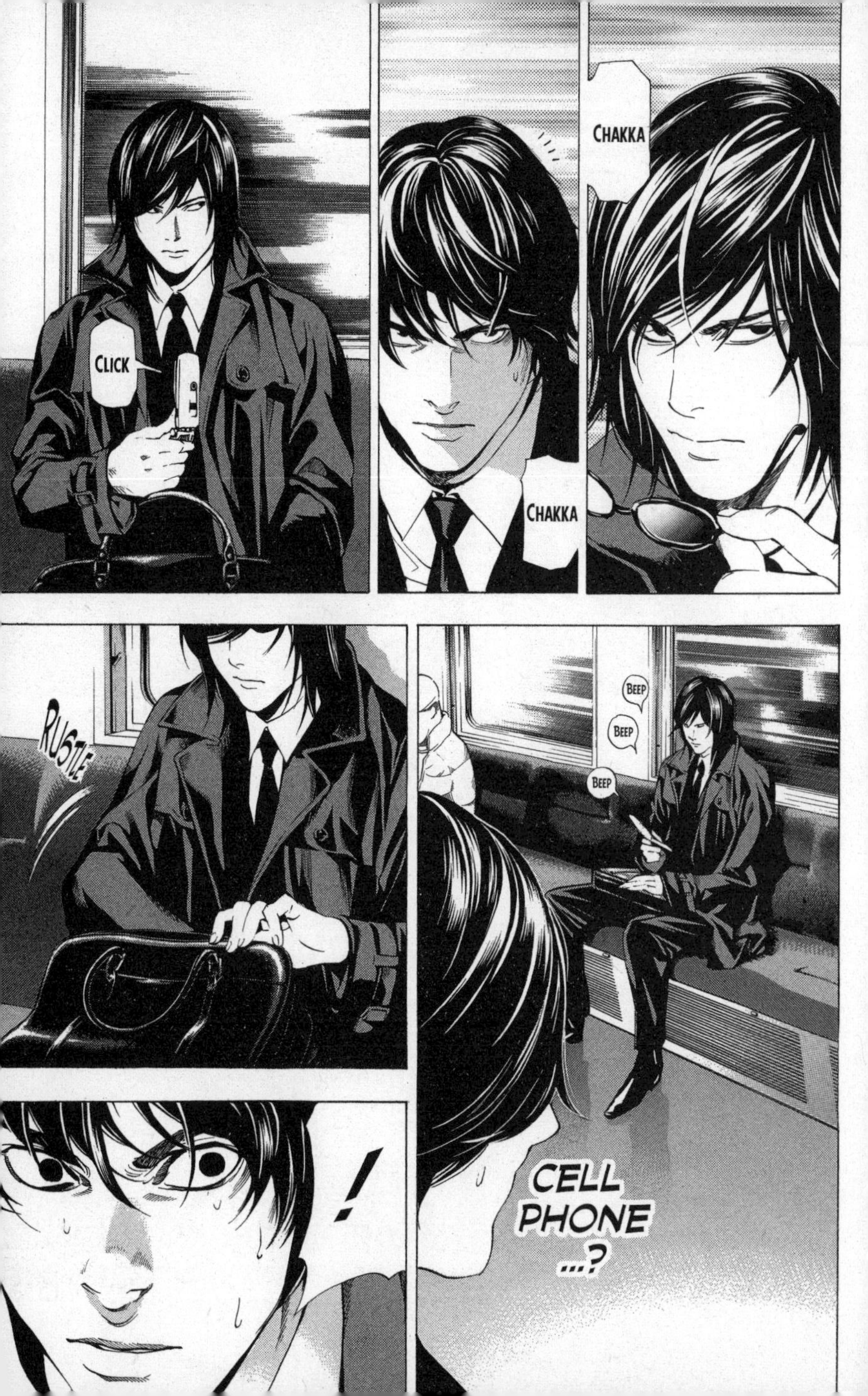
CHAKKA
CHAKKA
CLICK
BEEP
BEEP
BEEP
CELL PHONE ...?
RUSTLE
!

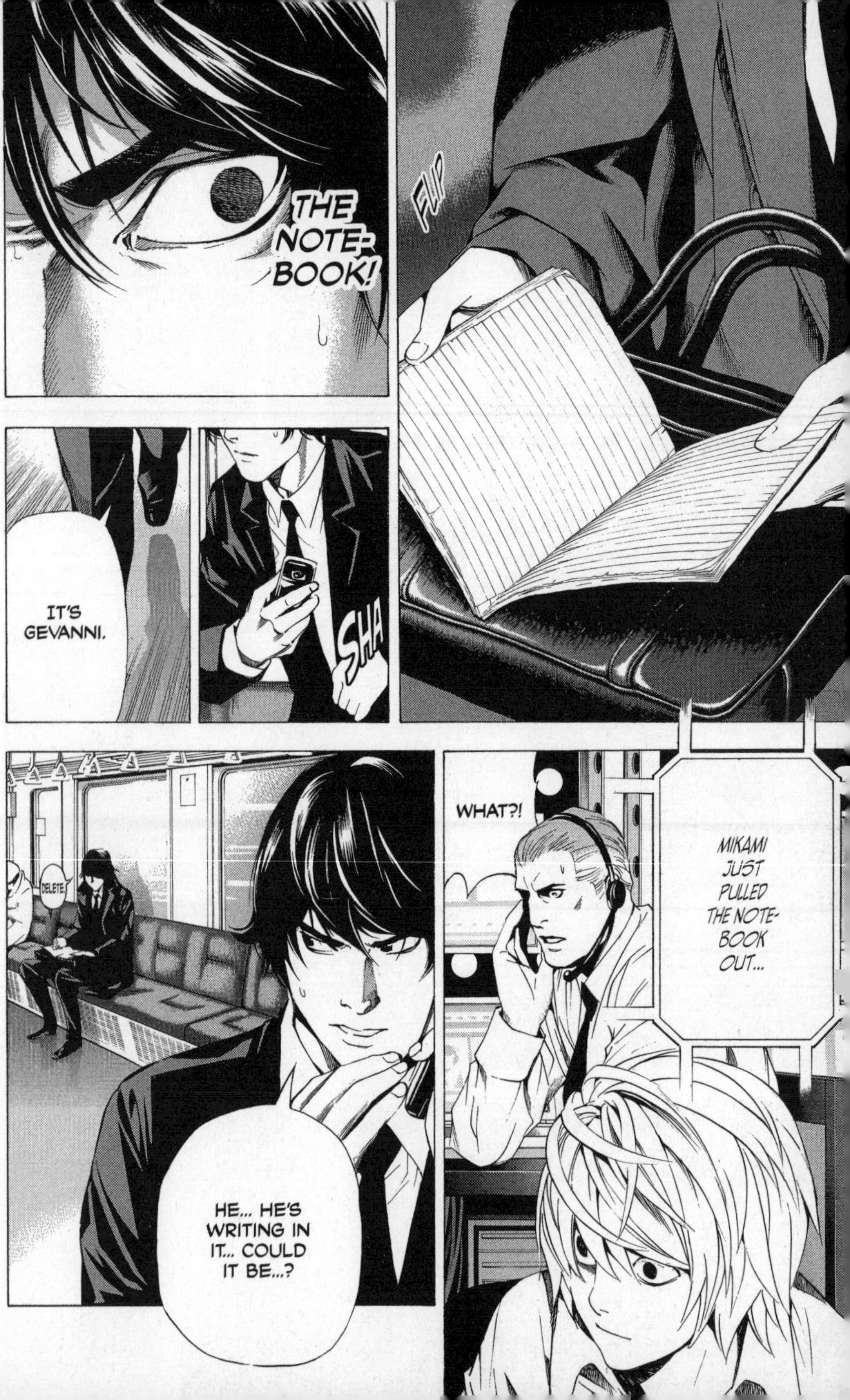
FLIP
THE NOTE-BOOK!
SHA
IT'S GEVANNI.
MIKAMI JUST PULLED THE NOTE-BOOK OUT...
WHAT?!
DELETE
HE... HE'S WRITING IN IT... COULD IT BE...?

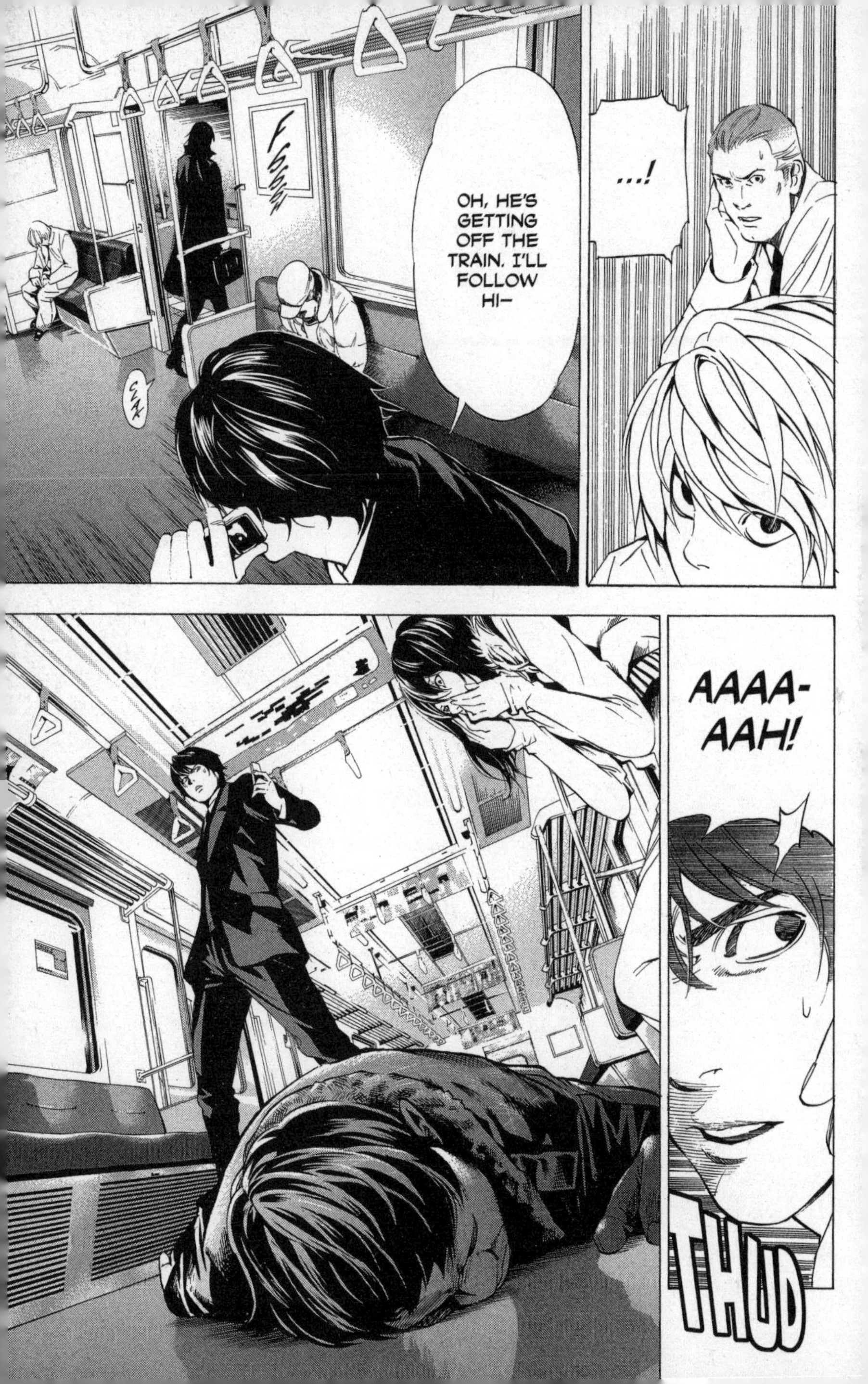
...!
OH, HE'S GETTING OFF THE TRAIN. I'LL FOLLOW HI—
AAAA-AAH!
THUD

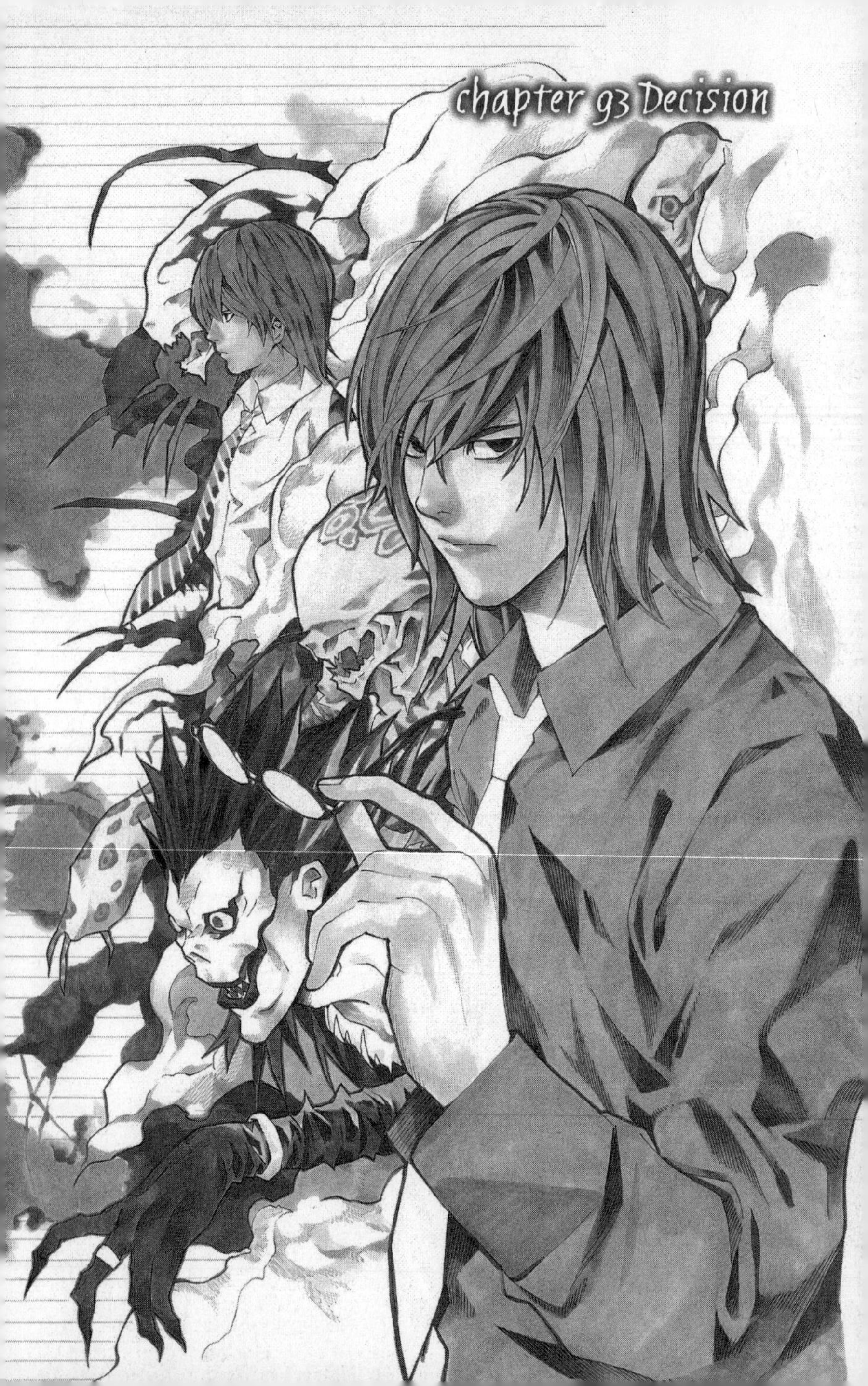
chapter 93 Decision

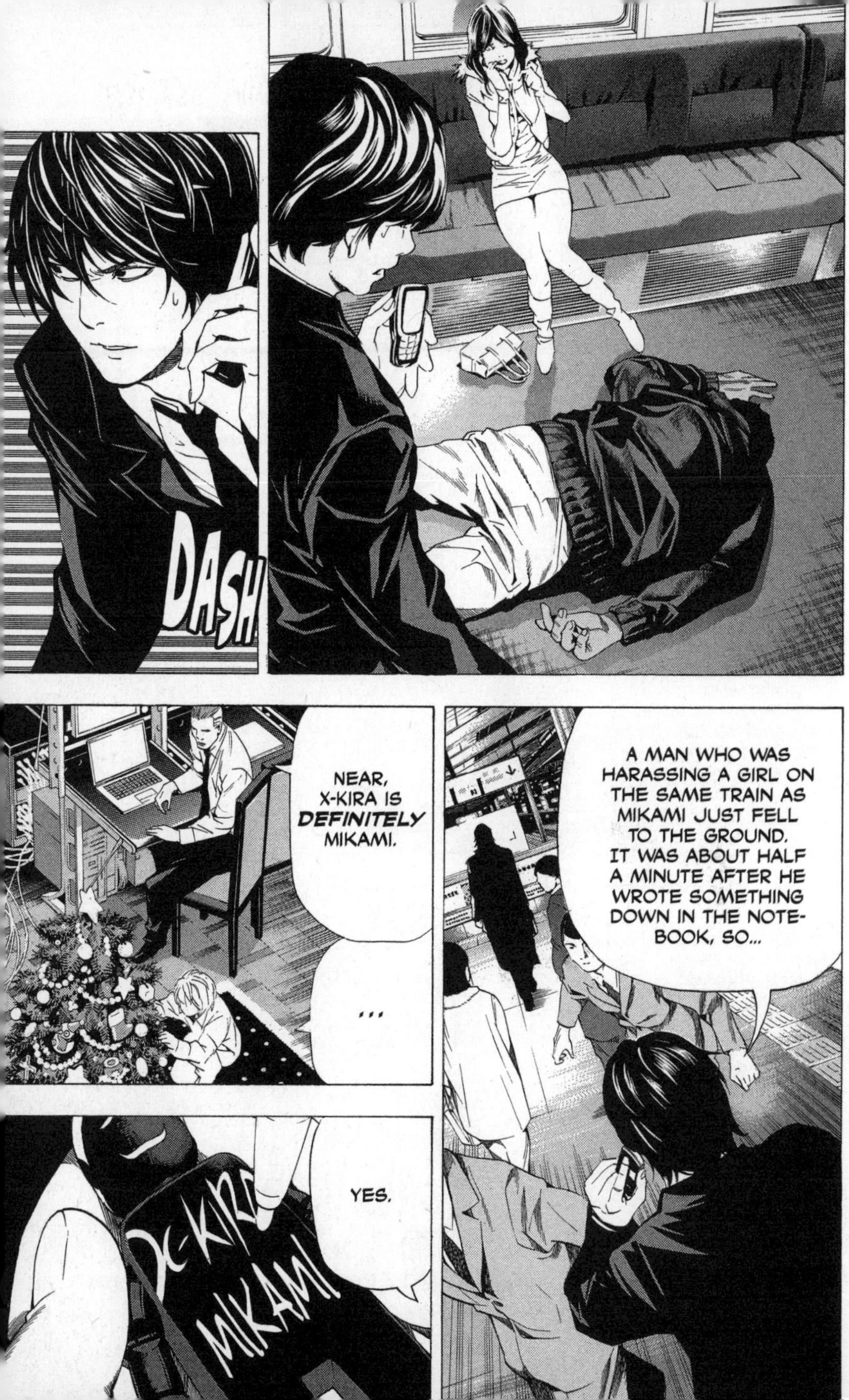
DASH
A MAN WHO WAS HARASSING A GIRL ON THE SAME TRAIN AS MIKAMI JUST FELL TO THE GROUND. IT WAS ABOUT HALF A MINUTE AFTER HE WROTE SOMETHING DOWN IN THE NOTE-BOOK, SO...
NEAR, X-KIRA IS **DEFINITELY** MIKAMI.
...
YES.
X-KIRA
MIKAMI

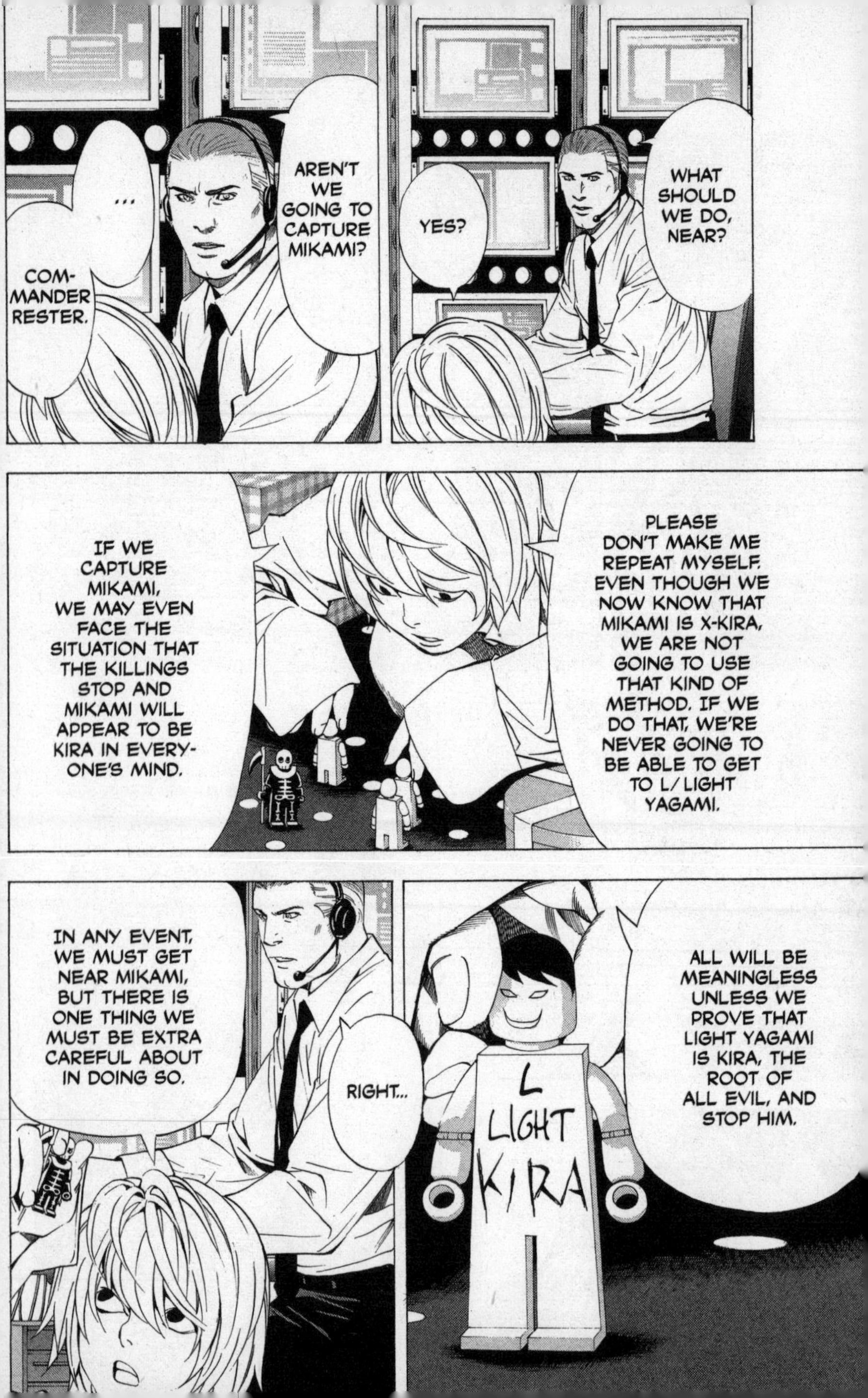
WHAT SHOULD WE DO, NEAR?
YES?
AREN'T WE GOING TO CAPTURE MIKAMI?
...
COM-MANDER RESTER.
PLEASE DON'T MAKE ME REPEAT MYSELF. EVEN THOUGH WE NOW KNOW THAT MIKAMI IS X-KIRA, WE ARE NOT GOING TO USE THAT KIND OF METHOD. IF WE DO THAT, WE'RE NEVER GOING TO BE ABLE TO GET TO L/LIGHT YAGAMI.
IF WE CAPTURE MIKAMI, WE MAY EVEN FACE THE SITUATION THAT THE KILLINGS STOP AND MIKAMI WILL APPEAR TO BE KIRA IN EVERY-ONE'S MIND.
ALL WILL BE MEANINGLESS UNLESS WE PROVE THAT LIGHT YAGAMI IS KIRA, THE ROOT OF ALL EVIL, AND STOP HIM.
L
LIGHT
KIRA
IN ANY EVENT, WE MUST GET NEAR MIKAMI, BUT THERE IS ONE THING WE MUST BE EXTRA CAREFUL ABOUT IN DOING SO.
RIGHT...

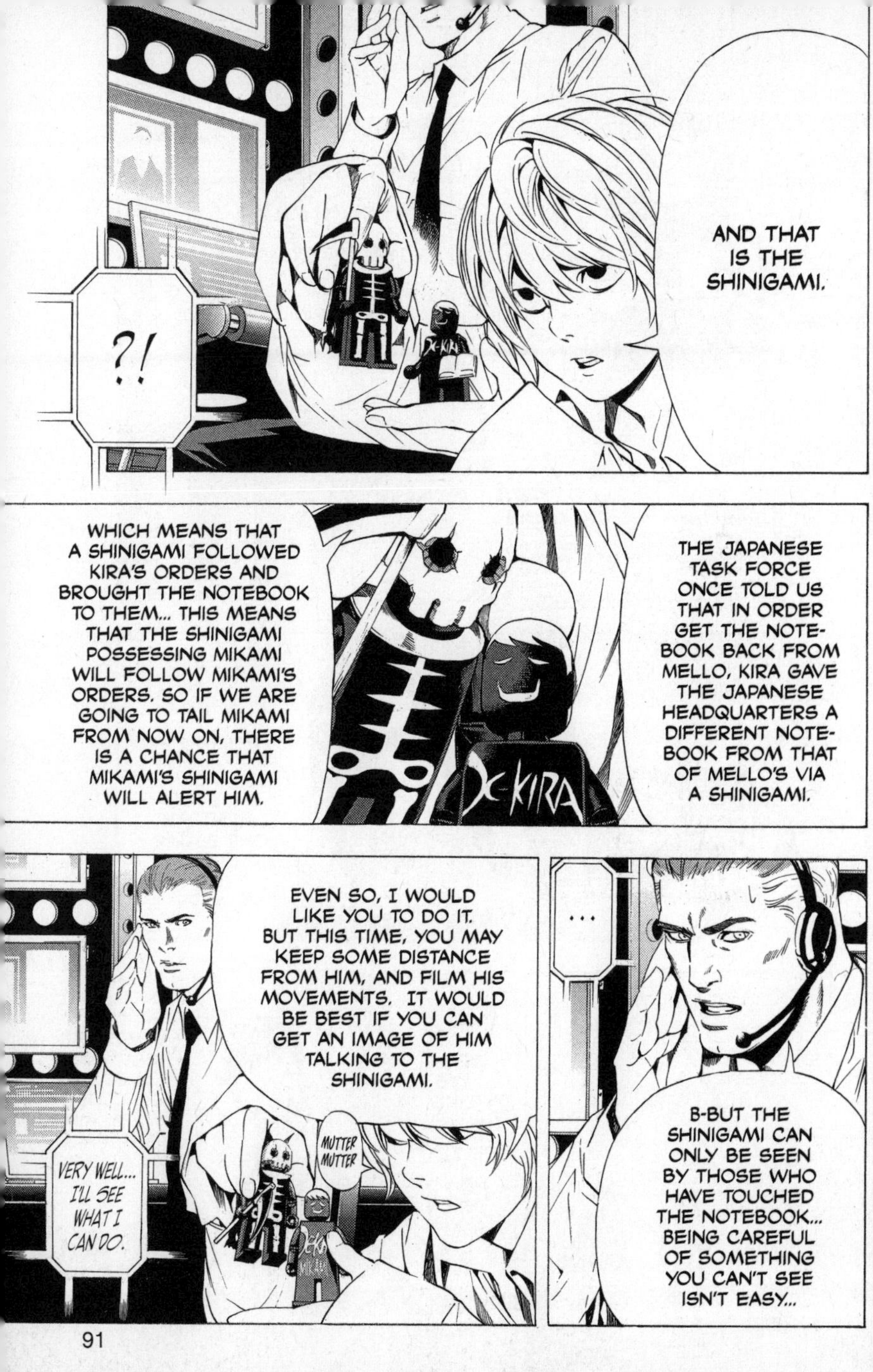
AND THAT IS THE SHINIGAMI.
?!
THE JAPANESE TASK FORCE ONCE TOLD US THAT IN ORDER GET THE NOTE-BOOK BACK FROM MELLO, KIRA GAVE THE JAPANESE HEADQUARTERS A DIFFERENT NOTE-BOOK FROM THAT OF MELLO'S VIA A SHINIGAMI.
WHICH MEANS THAT A SHINIGAMI FOLLOWED KIRA'S ORDERS AND BROUGHT THE NOTEBOOK TO THEM... THIS MEANS THAT THE SHINIGAMI POSSESSING MIKAMI WILL FOLLOW MIKAMI'S ORDERS. SO IF WE ARE GOING TO TAIL MIKAMI FROM NOW ON, THERE IS A CHANCE THAT MIKAMI'S SHINIGAMI WILL ALERT HIM.
KIRA
...
B-BUT THE SHINIGAMI CAN ONLY BE SEEN BY THOSE WHO HAVE TOUCHED THE NOTEBOOK... BEING CAREFUL OF SOMETHING YOU CAN'T SEE ISN'T EASY...
EVEN SO, I WOULD LIKE YOU TO DO IT. BUT THIS TIME, YOU MAY KEEP SOME DISTANCE FROM HIM, AND FILM HIS MOVEMENTS. IT WOULD BE BEST IF YOU CAN GET AN IMAGE OF HIM TALKING TO THE SHINIGAMI.
MUTTER MUTTER
VERY WELL... I'LL SEE WHAT I CAN DO.

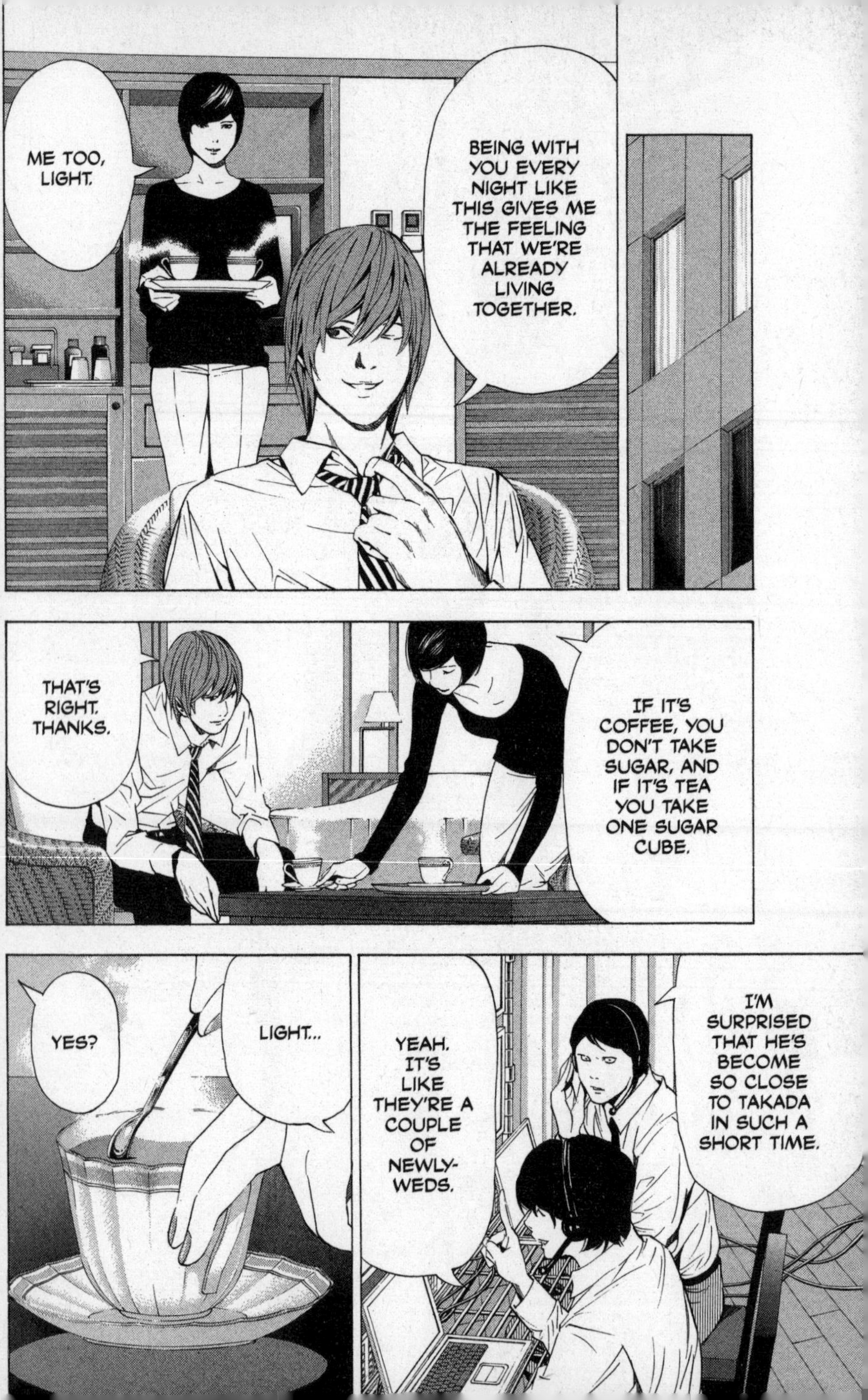
BEING WITH YOU EVERY NIGHT LIKE THIS GIVES ME THE FEELING THAT WE'RE ALREADY LIVING TOGETHER.
ME TOO, LIGHT.
IF IT'S COFFEE, YOU DON'T TAKE SUGAR, AND IF IT'S TEA YOU TAKE ONE SUGAR CUBE.
THAT'S RIGHT. THANKS.
I'M SURPRISED THAT HE'S BECOME SO CLOSE TO TAKADA IN SUCH A SHORT TIME.
YEAH. IT'S LIKE THEY'RE A COUPLE OF NEWLY-WEDS.
LIGHT...
YES?

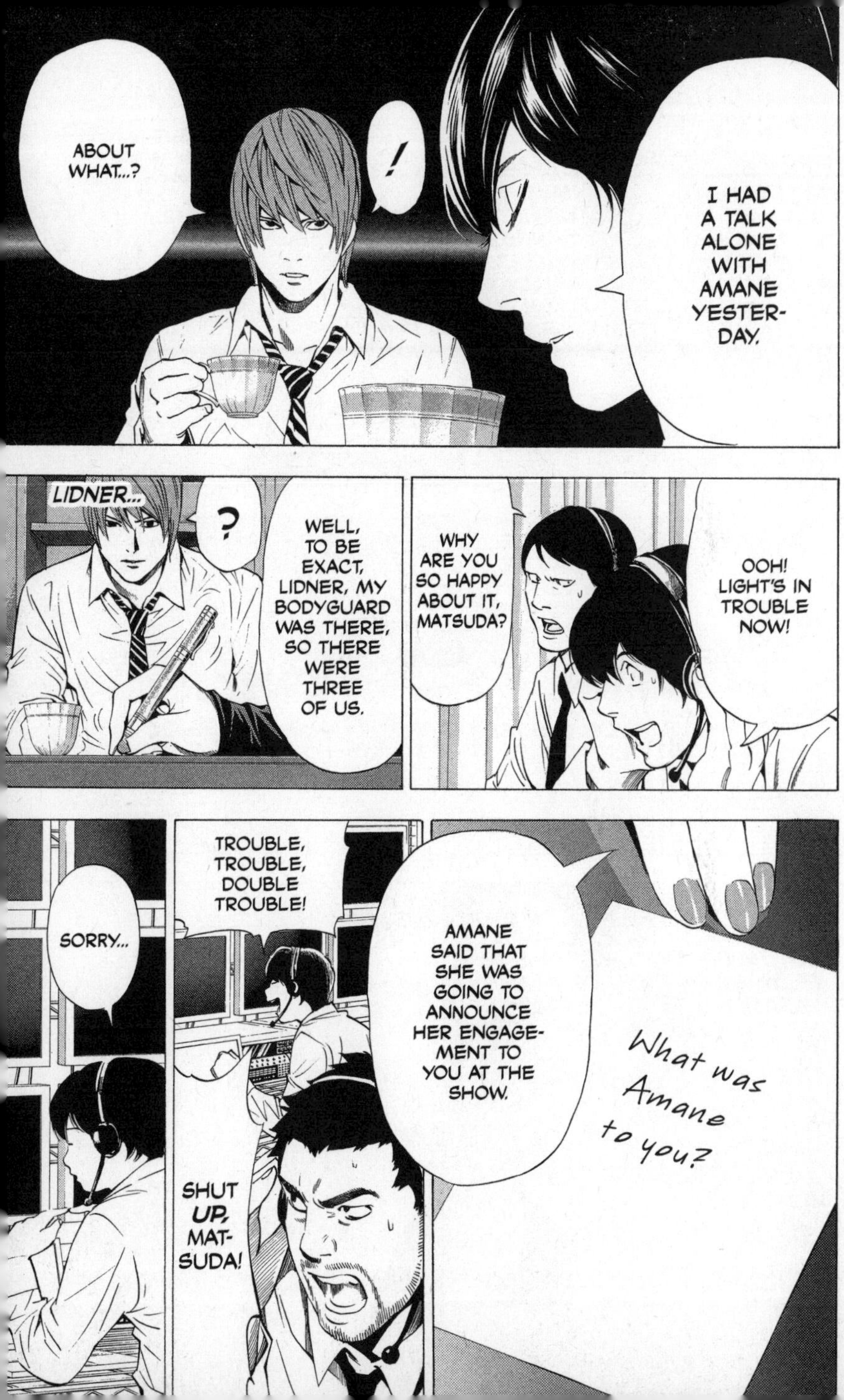
I HAD A TALK ALONE WITH AMANE YESTERDAY.
!
ABOUT WHAT...?
OOH! LIGHT'S IN TROUBLE NOW!
WHY ARE YOU SO HAPPY ABOUT IT, MATSUDA?
WELL, TO BE EXACT, LIDNER, MY BODYGUARD WAS THERE, SO THERE WERE THREE OF US.
?
LIDNER...
AMANE SAID THAT SHE WAS GOING TO ANNOUNCE HER ENGAGEMENT TO YOU AT THE SHOW.
What was Amane to you?
TROUBLE, TROUBLE, DOUBLE TROUBLE!
SHUT UP, MATSUDA!
SORRY...

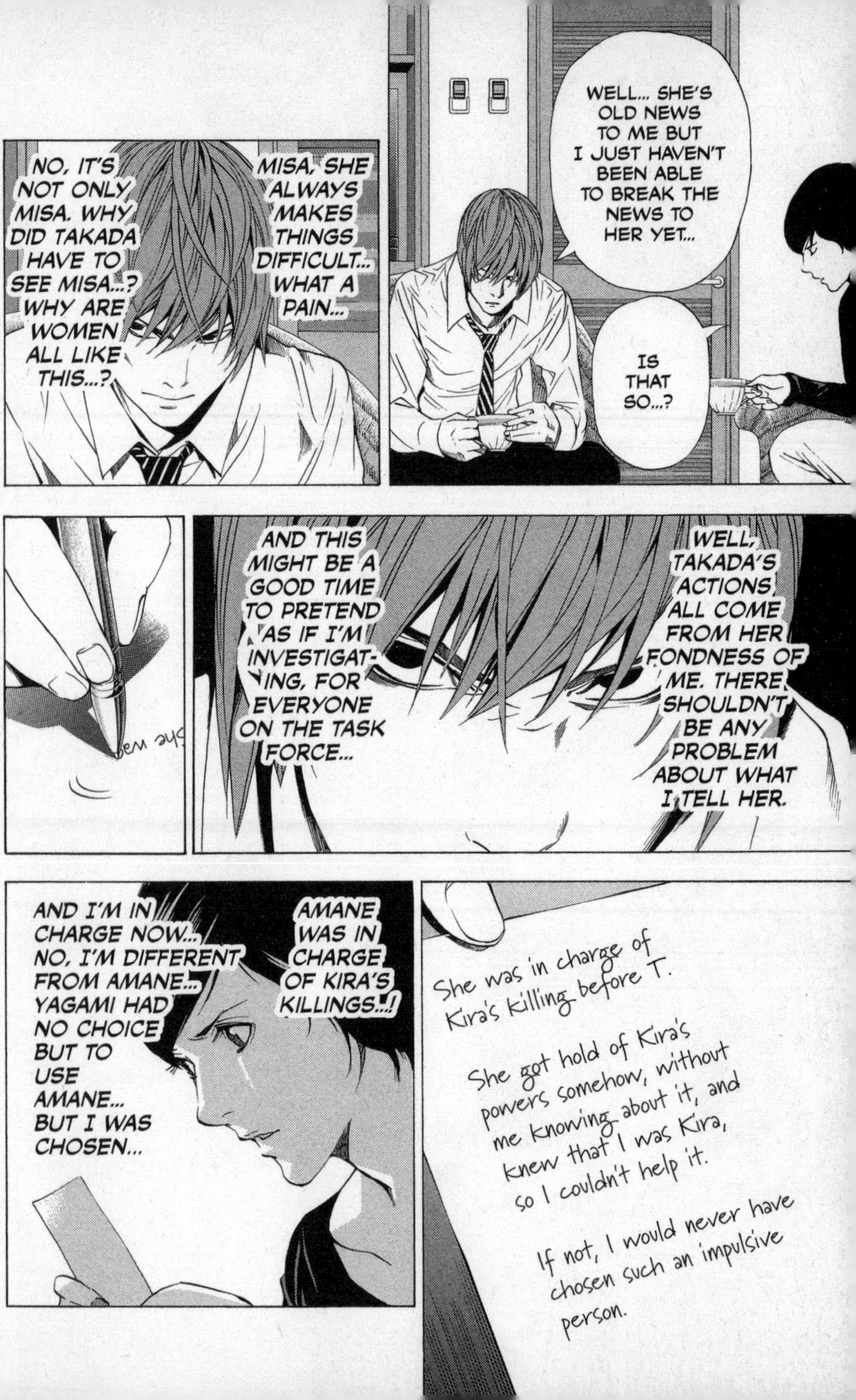
WELL... SHE'S OLD NEWS TO ME BUT I JUST HAVEN'T BEEN ABLE TO BREAK THE NEWS TO HER YET...
IS THAT SO...?
MISA, SHE ALWAYS MAKES THINGS DIFFICULT... WHAT A PAIN...
NO, IT'S NOT ONLY MISA. WHY DID TAKADA HAVE TO SEE MISA...? WHY ARE WOMEN ALL LIKE THIS...?
WELL, TAKADA'S ACTIONS ALL COME FROM HER FONDNESS OF ME. THERE SHOULDN'T BE ANY PROBLEM ABOUT WHAT I TELL HER.
AND THIS MIGHT BE A GOOD TIME TO PRETEND AS IF I'M INVESTIGATING, FOR EVERYONE ON THE TASK FORCE...
She was in charge of Kira's killing before T.
She got hold of Kira's powers somehow, without me knowing about it, and knew that I was Kira, so I couldn't help it.
If not, I would never have chosen such an impulsive person.
AMANE WAS IN CHARGE OF KIRA'S KILLINGS...!
AND I'M IN CHARGE NOW... NO, I'M DIFFERENT FROM AMANE... YAGAMI HAD NO CHOICE BUT TO USE AMANE... BUT I WAS CHOSEN...

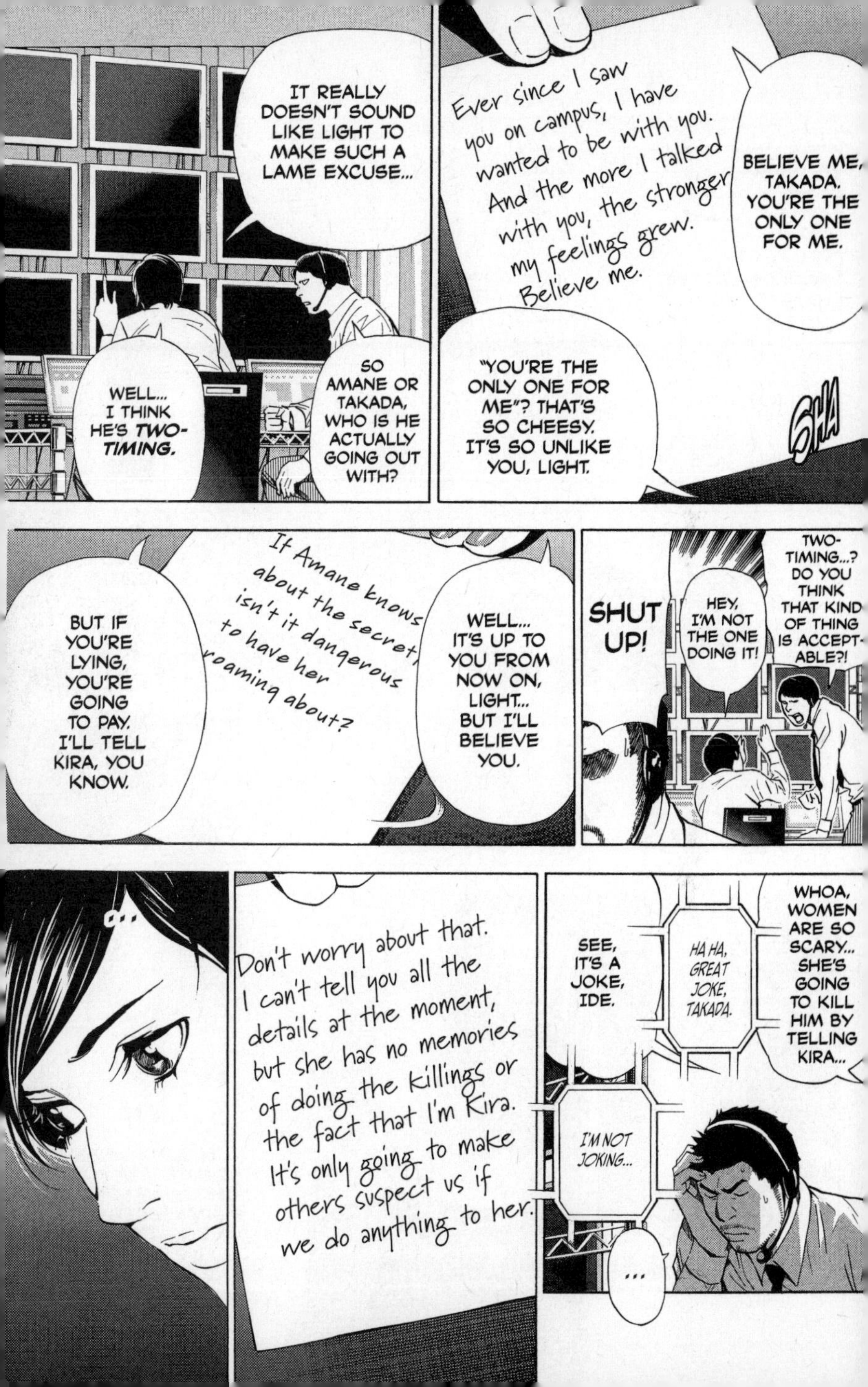
Ever since I saw you on campus, I have wanted to be with you. And the more I talked with you, the stronger my feelings grew. Believe me.
BELIEVE ME, TAKADA. YOU'RE THE ONLY ONE FOR ME.
SHA
"YOU'RE THE ONLY ONE FOR ME"? THAT'S SO CHEESY. IT'S SO UNLIKE YOU, LIGHT.
IT REALLY DOESN'T SOUND LIKE LIGHT TO MAKE SUCH A LAME EXCUSE...
SO AMANE OR TAKADA, WHO IS HE ACTUALLY GOING OUT WITH?
WELL... I THINK HE'S *TWO-TIMING.*
TWO-TIMING...? DO YOU THINK THAT KIND OF THING IS ACCEPTABLE?!
HEY, I'M NOT THE ONE DOING IT!
SHUT UP!
WELL... IT'S UP TO YOU FROM NOW ON, LIGHT... BUT I'LL BELIEVE YOU.
If Amane knows about the secret, isn't it dangerous to have her roaming about?
BUT IF YOU'RE LYING, YOU'RE GOING TO PAY. I'LL TELL KIRA, YOU KNOW.
WHOA, WOMEN ARE SO SCARY... SHE'S GOING TO KILL HIM BY TELLING KIRA...
HA HA, GREAT JOKE, TAKADA.
SEE, IT'S A JOKE, IDE.
I'M NOT JOKING...
...
Don't worry about that. I can't tell you all the details at the moment, but she has no memories of doing the killings or the fact that I'm Kira. It's only going to make others suspect us if we do anything to her.
..

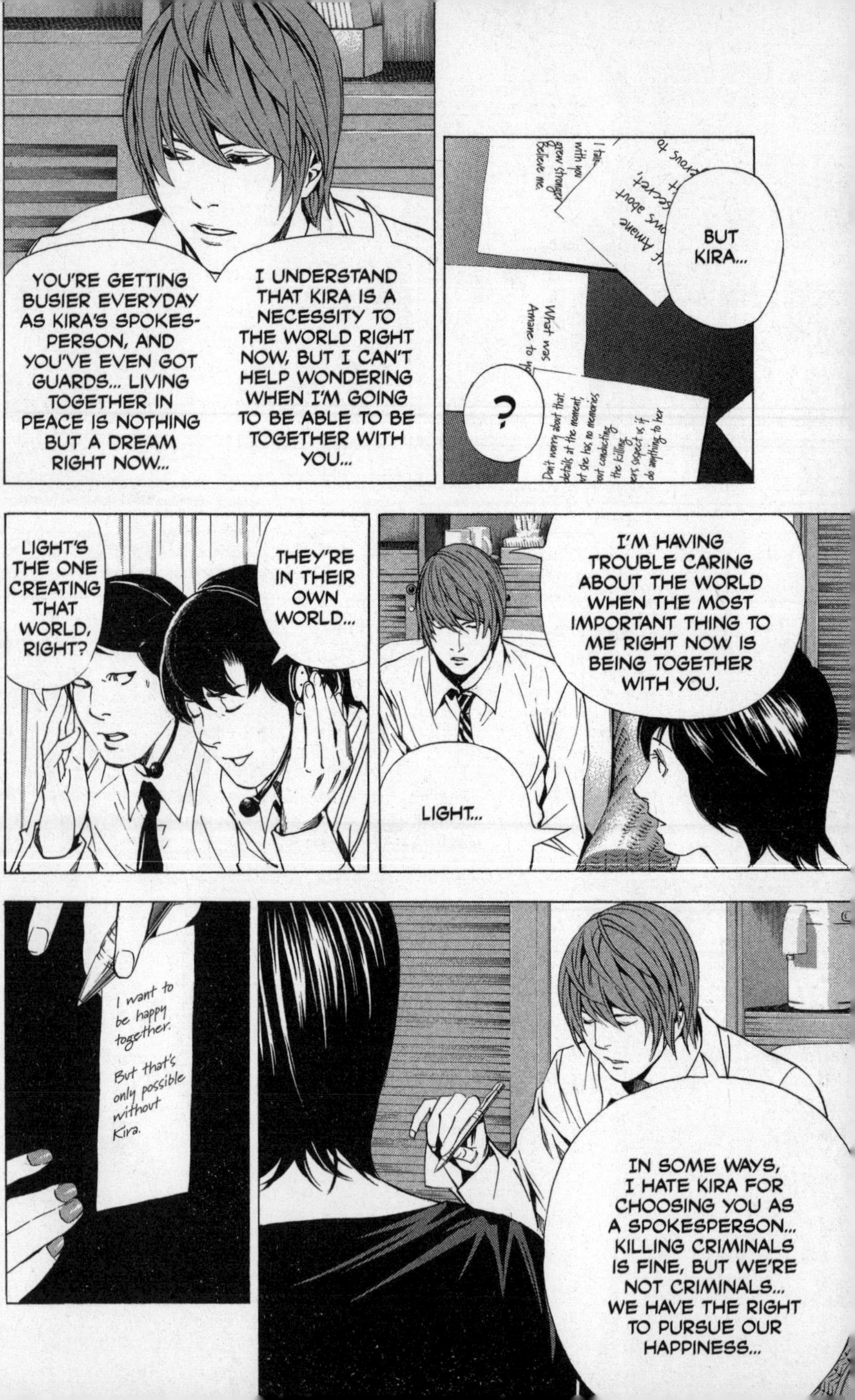
BUT KIRA...
?
I UNDERSTAND THAT KIRA IS A NECESSITY TO THE WORLD RIGHT NOW, BUT I CAN'T HELP WONDERING WHEN I'M GOING TO BE ABLE TO BE TOGETHER WITH YOU...
YOU'RE GETTING BUSIER EVERYDAY AS KIRA'S SPOKES-PERSON, AND YOU'VE EVEN GOT GUARDS... LIVING TOGETHER IN PEACE IS NOTHING BUT A DREAM RIGHT NOW...
I'M HAVING TROUBLE CARING ABOUT THE WORLD WHEN THE MOST IMPORTANT THING TO ME RIGHT NOW IS BEING TOGETHER WITH YOU.
LIGHT...
THEY'RE IN THEIR OWN WORLD...
LIGHT'S THE ONE CREATING THAT WORLD, RIGHT?
IN SOME WAYS, I HATE KIRA FOR CHOOSING YOU AS A SPOKESPERSON... KILLING CRIMINALS IS FINE, BUT WE'RE NOT CRIMINALS... WE HAVE THE RIGHT TO PURSUE OUR HAPPINESS...
I want to be happy together.
But that's only possible without Kira.

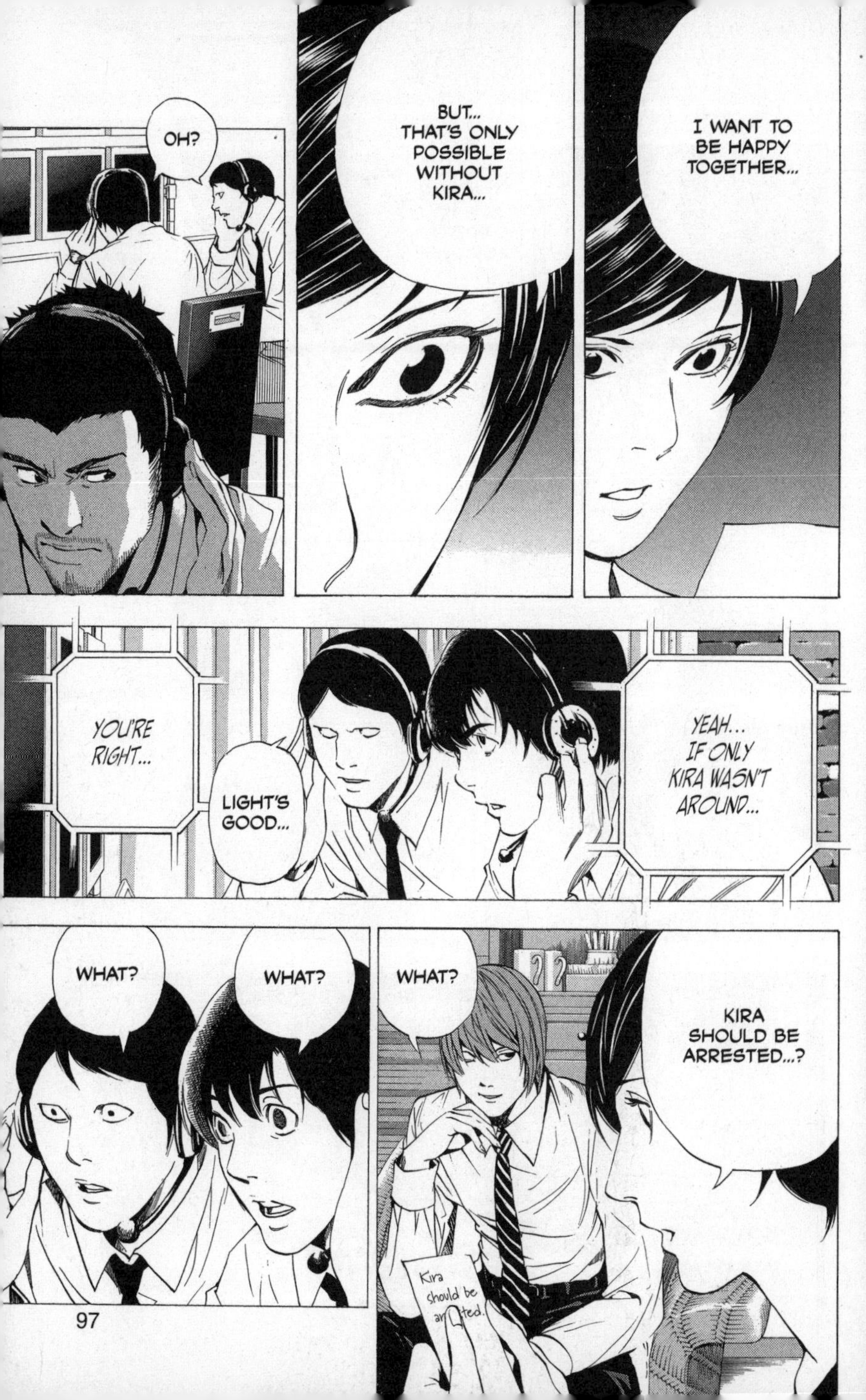
I WANT TO BE HAPPY TOGETHER...
BUT... THAT'S ONLY POSSIBLE WITHOUT KIRA...
OH?
YEAH... IF ONLY KIRA WASN'T AROUND...
LIGHT'S GOOD...
YOU'RE RIGHT...
KIRA SHOULD BE ARRESTED...?
WHAT?
Kira should be arrested.
WHAT?
WHAT?

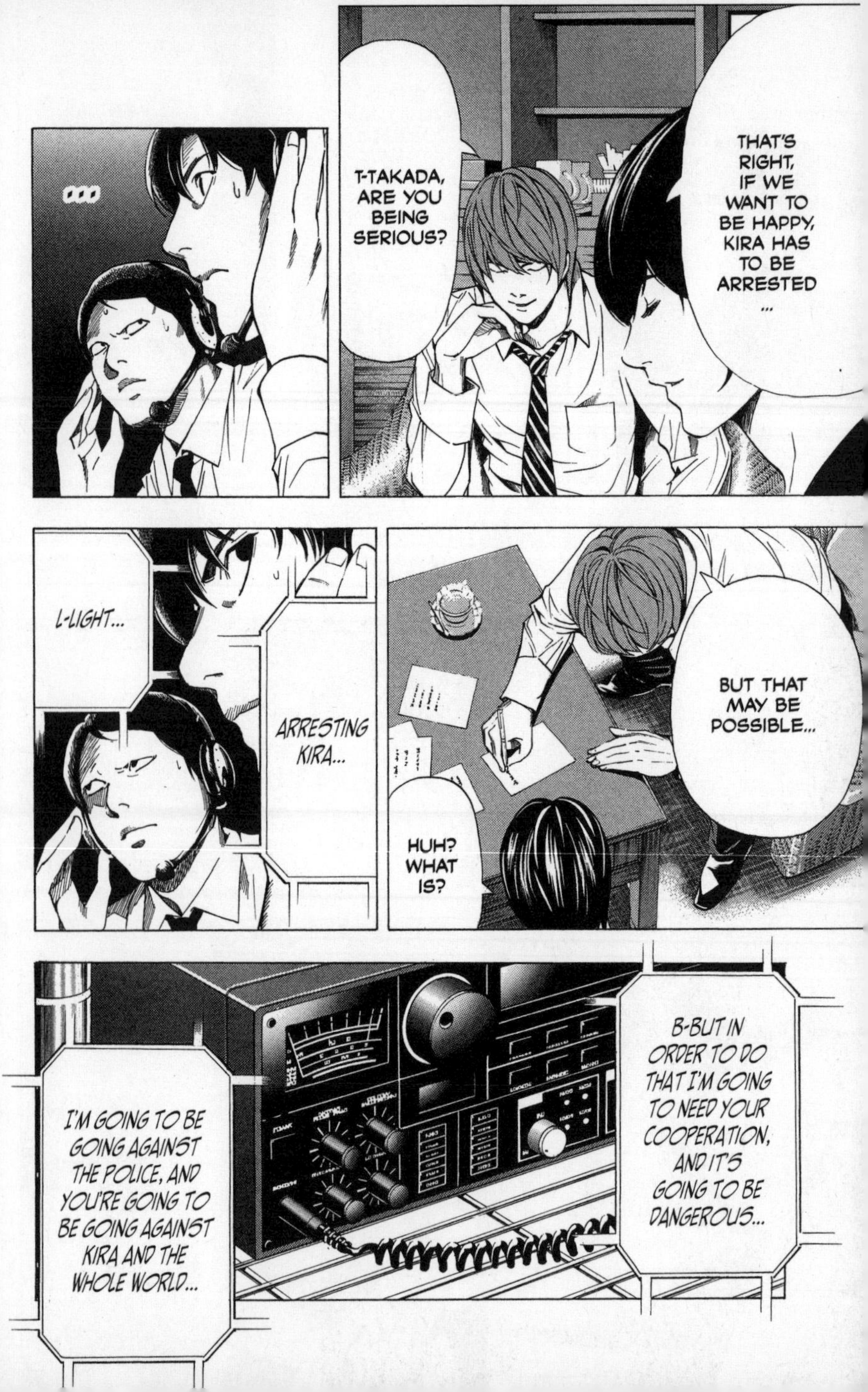
THAT'S RIGHT, IF WE WANT TO BE HAPPY, KIRA HAS TO BE ARRESTED ...
T-TAKADA, ARE YOU BEING SERIOUS?
...
BUT THAT MAY BE POSSIBLE...
HUH? WHAT IS?
L-LIGHT...
ARRESTING KIRA...
B-BUT IN ORDER TO DO THAT I'M GOING TO NEED YOUR COOPERATION, AND IT'S GOING TO BE DANGEROUS...
I'M GOING TO BE GOING AGAINST THE POLICE, AND YOU'RE GOING TO BE GOING AGAINST KIRA AND THE WHOLE WORLD...

READ THIS WAY

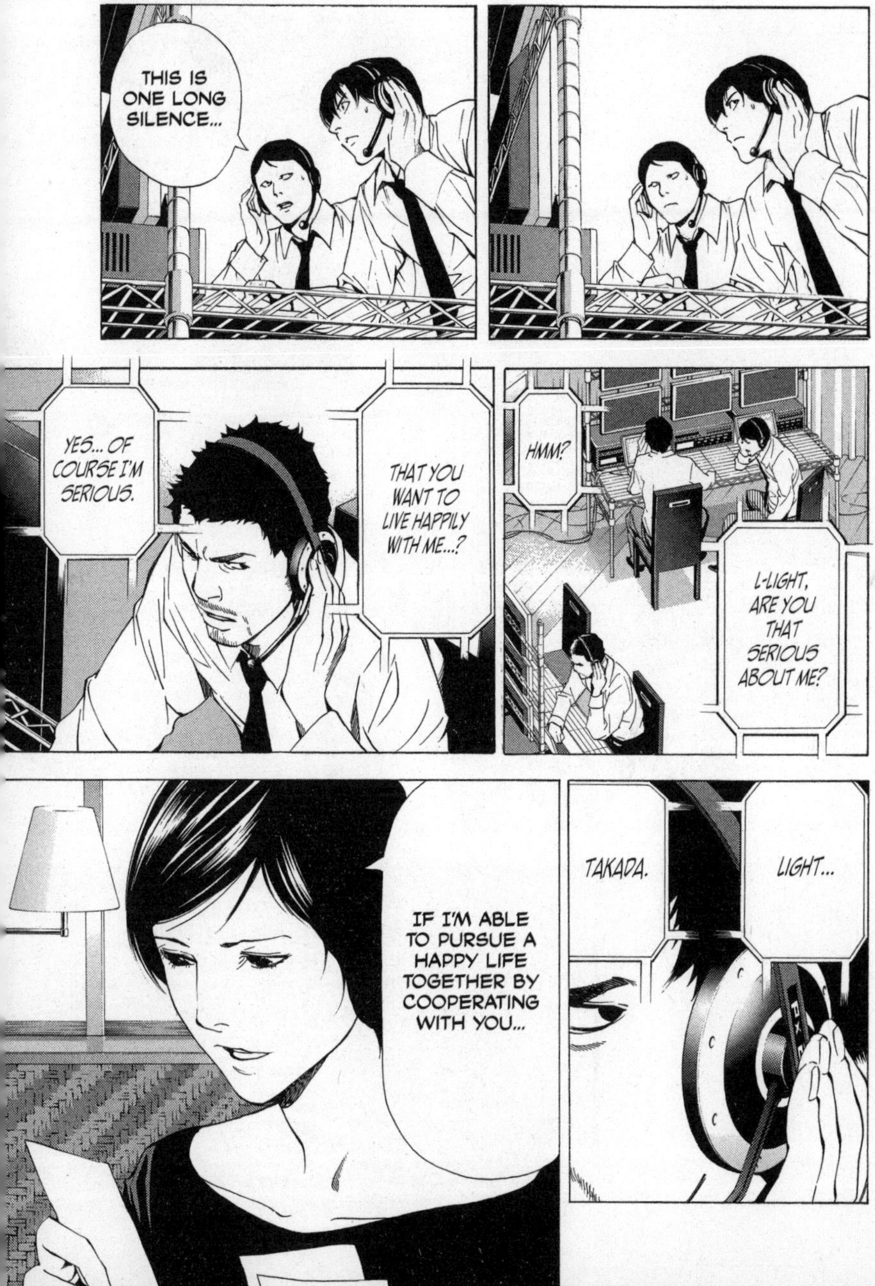
THIS IS ONE LONG SILENCE...
HMM?
L-LIGHT, ARE YOU THAT SERIOUS ABOUT ME?
THAT YOU WANT TO LIVE HAPPILY WITH ME...?
YES... OF COURSE I'M SERIOUS.
LIGHT...
TAKADA.
IF I'M ABLE TO PURSUE A HAPPY LIFE TOGETHER BY COOPERATING WITH YOU...

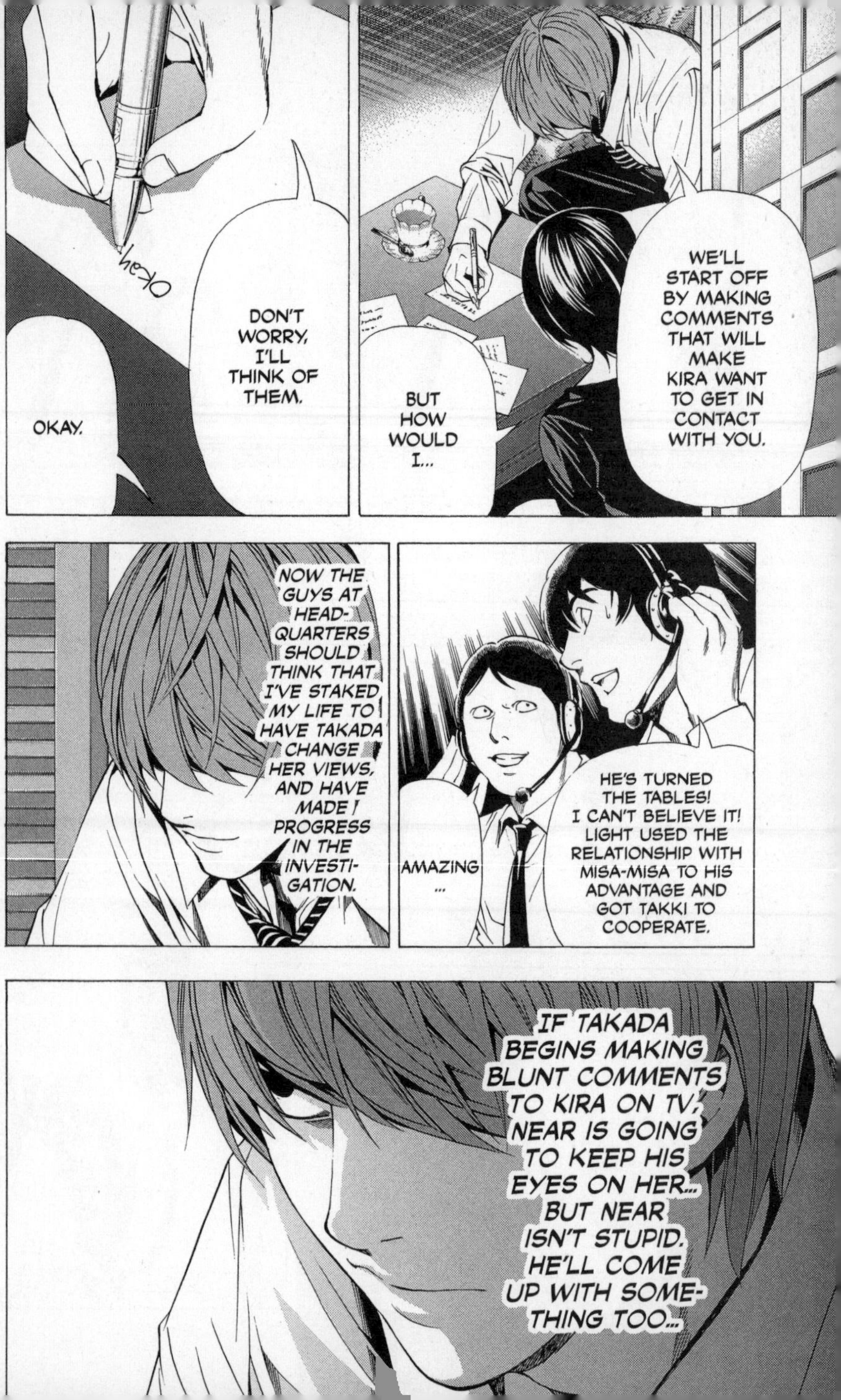
WE'LL START OFF BY MAKING COMMENTS THAT WILL MAKE KIRA WANT TO GET IN CONTACT WITH YOU.
BUT HOW WOULD I...
DON'T WORRY, I'LL THINK OF THEM.
OKAY.
HE'S TURNED THE TABLES! I CAN'T BELIEVE IT! LIGHT USED THE RELATIONSHIP WITH MISA-MISA TO HIS ADVANTAGE AND GOT TAKKI TO COOPERATE.
AMAZING...
NOW THE GUYS AT HEAD-QUARTERS SHOULD THINK THAT I'VE STAKED MY LIFE TO HAVE TAKADA CHANGE HER VIEWS, AND HAVE MADE PROGRESS IN THE INVESTI-GATION.
IF TAKADA BEGINS MAKING BLUNT COMMENTS TO KIRA ON TV, NEAR IS GOING TO KEEP HIS EYES ON HER... BUT NEAR ISN'T STUPID. HE'LL COME UP WITH SOME-THING TOO...

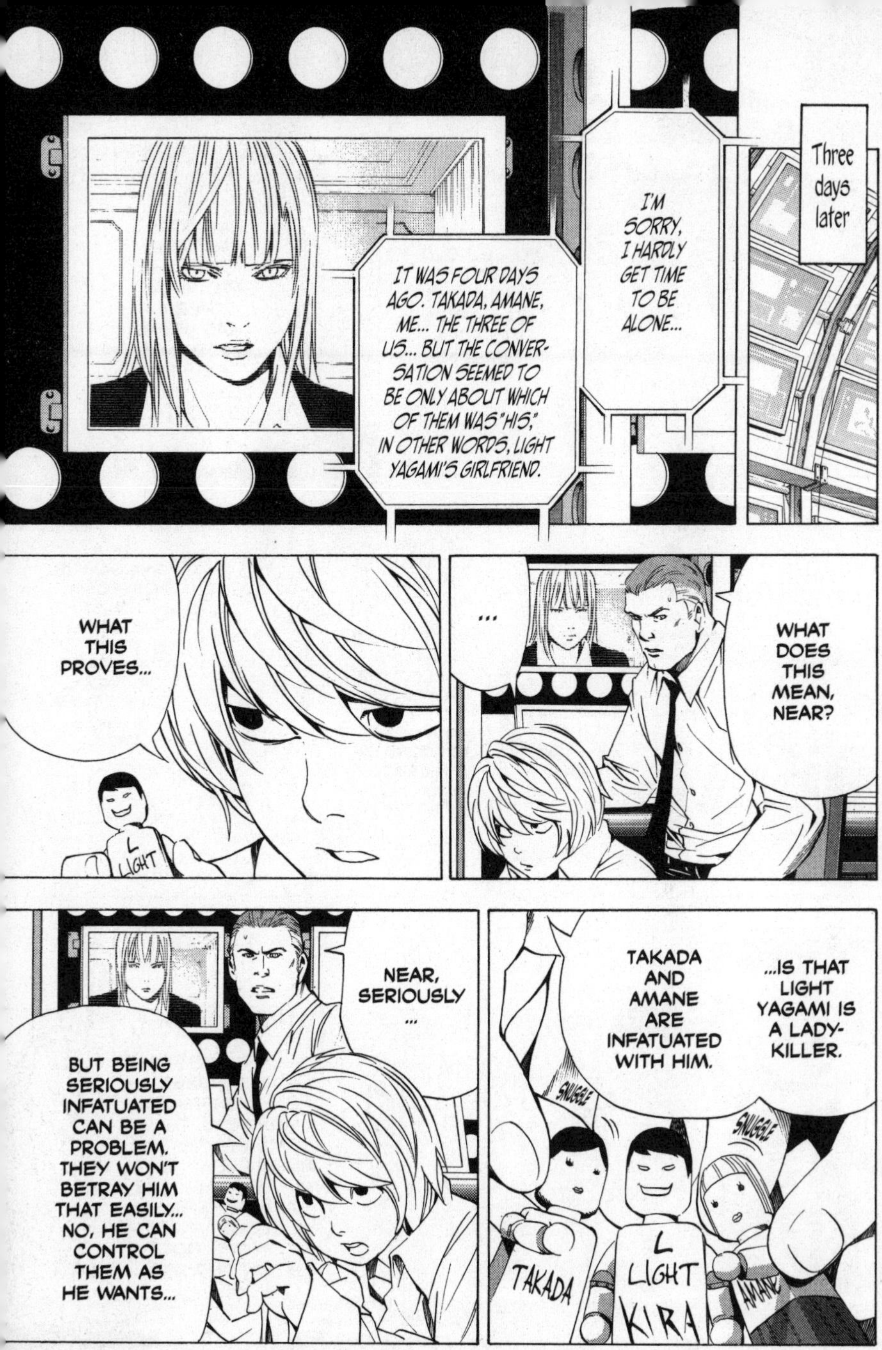
Three days later
I'M SORRY, I HARDLY GET TIME TO BE ALONE...
IT WAS FOUR DAYS AGO. TAKADA, AMANE, ME... THE THREE OF US... BUT THE CONVERSATION SEEMED TO BE ONLY ABOUT WHICH OF THEM WAS "HIS," IN OTHER WORDS, LIGHT YAGAMI'S GIRLFRIEND.
WHAT DOES THIS MEAN, NEAR?
...
WHAT THIS PROVES...
L
LIGHT
...IS THAT LIGHT YAGAMI IS A LADY-KILLER.
TAKADA AND AMANE ARE INFATUATED WITH HIM.
SNUGGLE
SNUGGLE
L
LIGHT
KIRA
TAKADA
AMANE
NEAR, SERIOUSLY ...
BUT BEING SERIOUSLY INFATUATED CAN BE A PROBLEM. THEY WON'T BETRAY HIM THAT EASILY... NO, HE CAN CONTROL THEM AS HE WANTS...

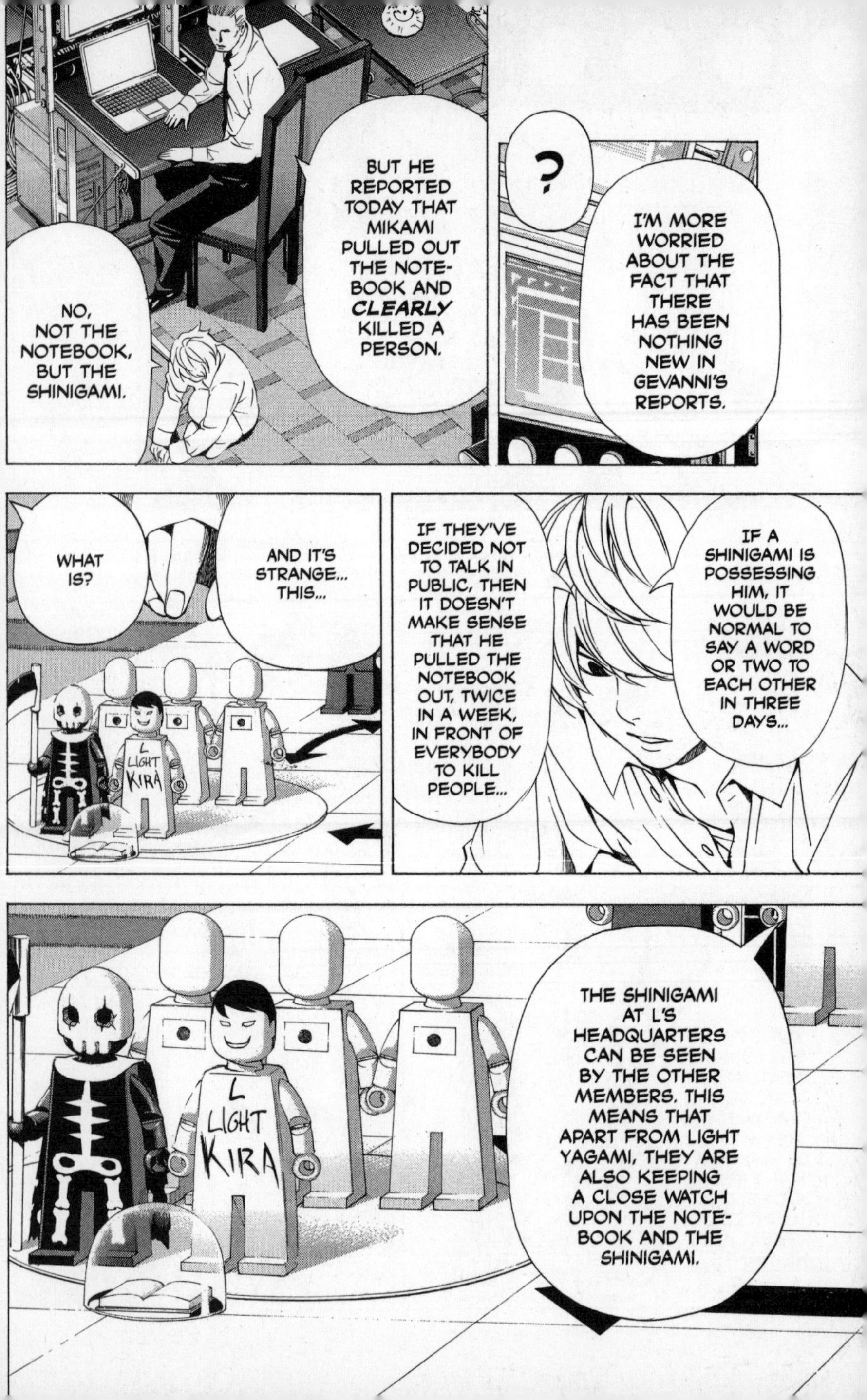
I'M MORE WORRIED ABOUT THE FACT THAT THERE HAS BEEN NOTHING NEW IN GEVANNI'S REPORTS.
?
BUT HE REPORTED TODAY THAT MIKAMI PULLED OUT THE NOTE-BOOK AND *CLEARLY* KILLED A PERSON.
NO, NOT THE NOTEBOOK, BUT THE SHINIGAMI.
IF A SHINIGAMI IS POSSESSING HIM, IT WOULD BE NORMAL TO SAY A WORD OR TWO TO EACH OTHER IN THREE DAYS...
IF THEY'VE DECIDED NOT TO TALK IN PUBLIC, THEN IT DOESN'T MAKE SENSE THAT HE PULLED THE NOTEBOOK OUT, TWICE IN A WEEK, IN FRONT OF EVERYBODY TO KILL PEOPLE...
AND IT'S STRANGE... THIS...
WHAT IS?
L
LIGHT
KIRA
THE SHINIGAMI AT L'S HEADQUARTERS CAN BE SEEN BY THE OTHER MEMBERS. THIS MEANS THAT APART FROM LIGHT YAGAMI, THEY ARE ALSO KEEPING A CLOSE WATCH UPON THE NOTE-BOOK AND THE SHINIGAMI.

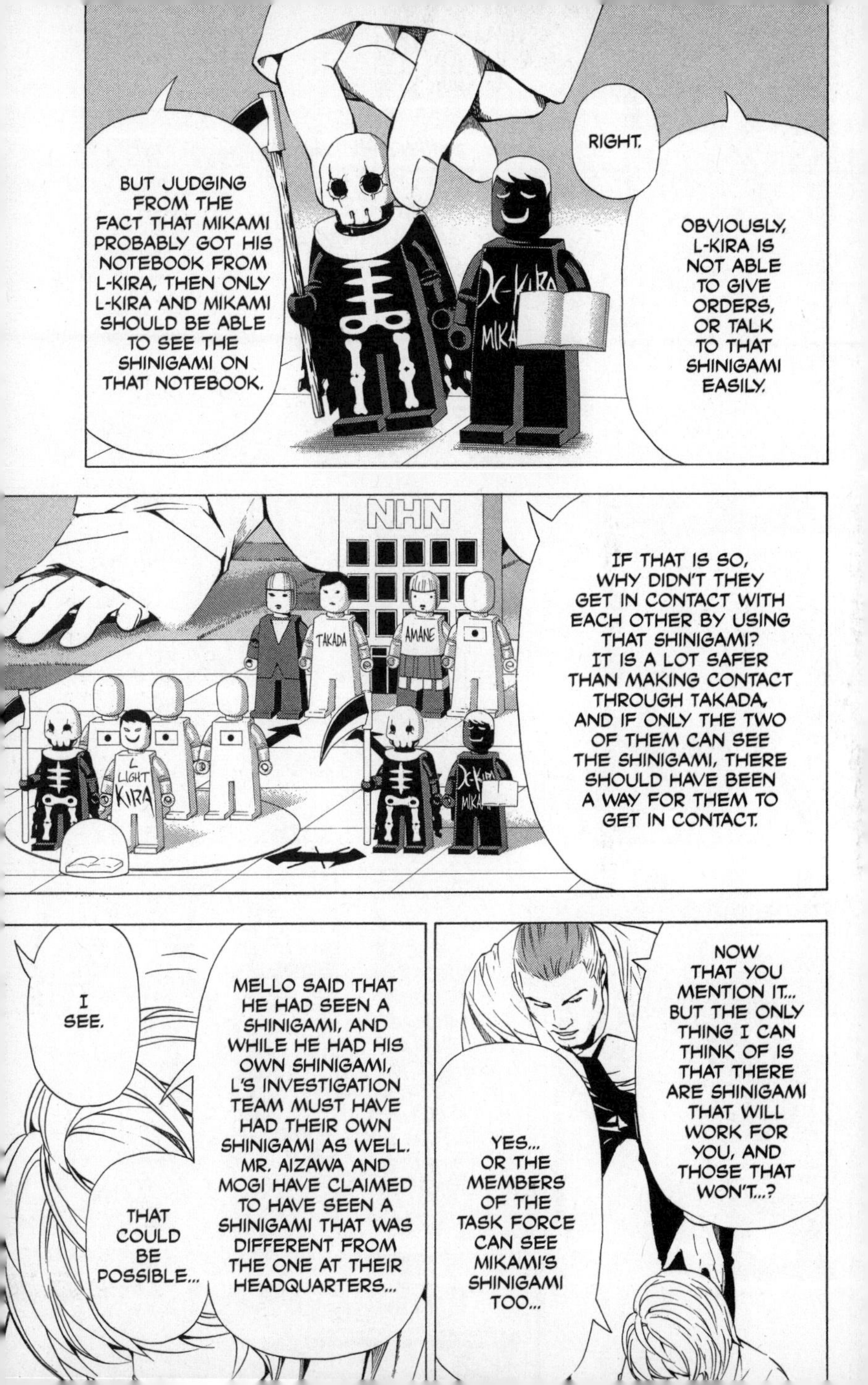
RIGHT.
OBVIOUSLY, L-KIRA IS NOT ABLE TO GIVE ORDERS, OR TALK TO THAT SHINIGAMI EASILY.
BUT JUDGING FROM THE FACT THAT MIKAMI PROBABLY GOT HIS NOTEBOOK FROM L-KIRA, THEN ONLY L-KIRA AND MIKAMI SHOULD BE ABLE TO SEE THE SHINIGAMI ON THAT NOTEBOOK.
IF THAT IS SO, WHY DIDN'T THEY GET IN CONTACT WITH EACH OTHER BY USING THAT SHINIGAMI? IT IS A LOT SAFER THAN MAKING CONTACT THROUGH TAKADA, AND IF ONLY THE TWO OF THEM CAN SEE THE SHINIGAMI, THERE SHOULD HAVE BEEN A WAY FOR THEM TO GET IN CONTACT.
NHN
TAKADA
AMANE
L LIGHT KIRA
NOW THAT YOU MENTION IT... BUT THE ONLY THING I CAN THINK OF IS THAT THERE ARE SHINIGAMI THAT WILL WORK FOR YOU, AND THOSE THAT WON'T...?
YES... OR THE MEMBERS OF THE TASK FORCE CAN SEE MIKAMI'S SHINIGAMI TOO...
MELLO SAID THAT HE HAD SEEN A SHINIGAMI, AND WHILE HE HAD HIS OWN SHINIGAMI, L'S INVESTIGATION TEAM MUST HAVE HAD THEIR OWN SHINIGAMI AS WELL. MR. AIZAWA AND MOGI HAVE CLAIMED TO HAVE SEEN A SHINIGAMI THAT WAS DIFFERENT FROM THE ONE AT THEIR HEADQUARTERS...
I SEE.
THAT COULD BE POSSIBLE...

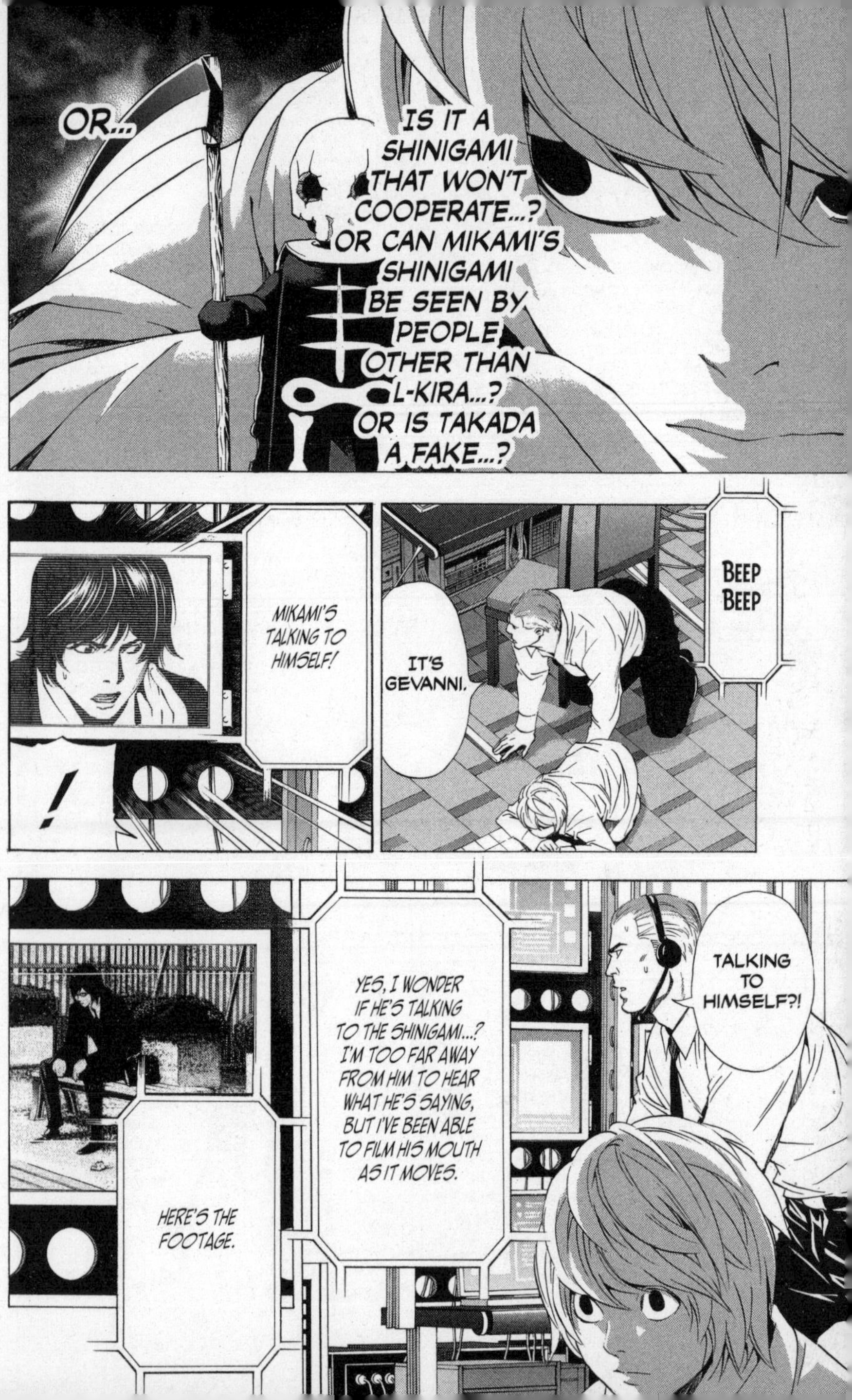
IS IT A SHINIGAMI THAT WON'T COOPERATE...? OR CAN MIKAMI'S SHINIGAMI BE SEEN BY PEOPLE OTHER THAN L-KIRA...? OR IS TAKADA A FAKE...?
OR...
BEEP BEEP
IT'S GEVANNI.
MIKAMI'S TALKING TO HIMSELF!
!
TALKING TO HIMSELF?!
YES, I WONDER IF HE'S TALKING TO THE SHINIGAMI...? I'M TOO FAR AWAY FROM HIM TO HEAR WHAT HE'S SAYING, BUT I'VE BEEN ABLE TO FILM HIS MOUTH AS IT MOVES.
HERE'S THE FOOTAGE.

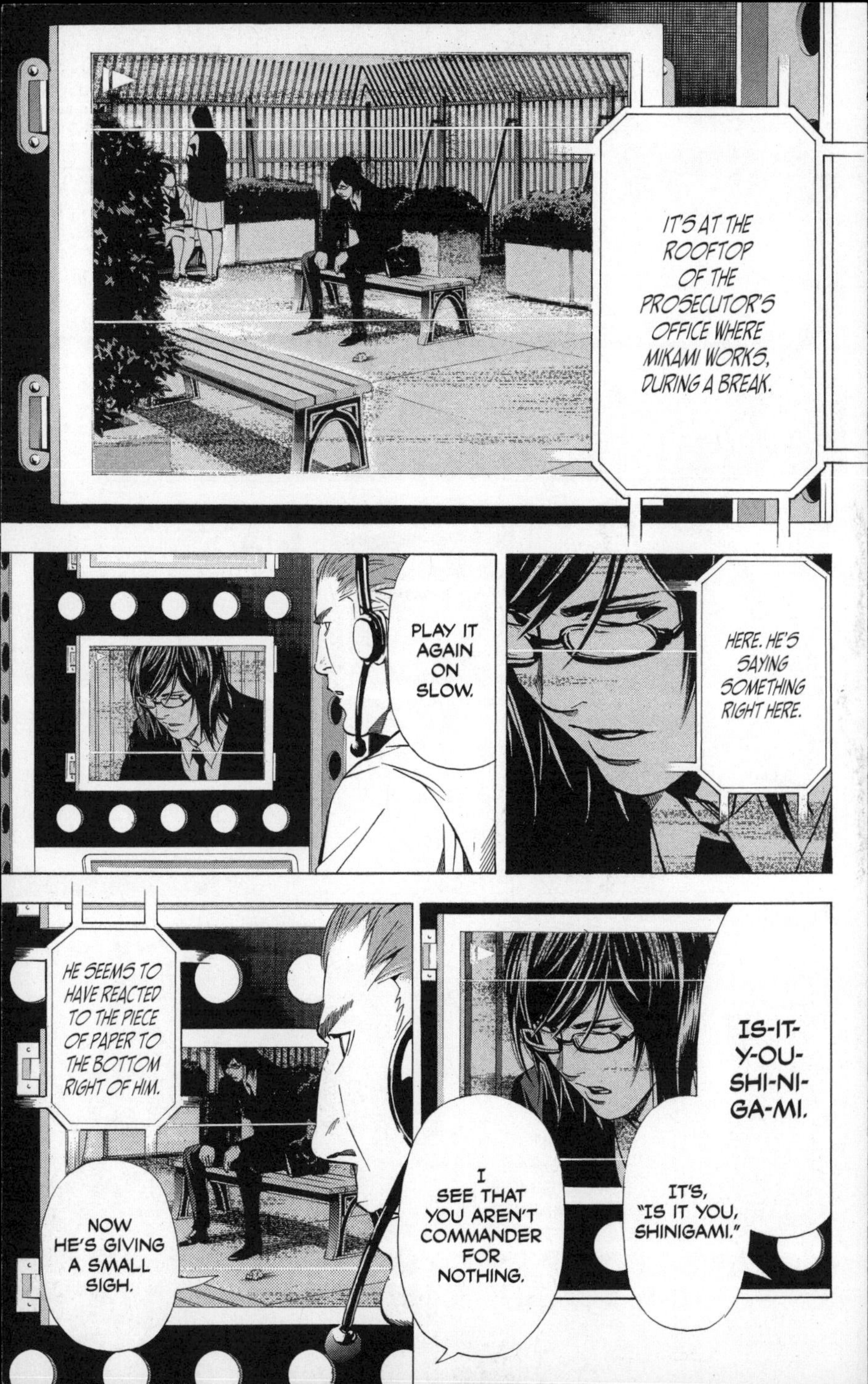
IT'S AT THE ROOFTOP OF THE PROSECUTOR'S OFFICE WHERE MIKAMI WORKS, DURING A BREAK.
HERE. HE'S SAYING SOMETHING RIGHT HERE.
PLAY IT AGAIN ON SLOW.
IS-IT-Y-OU-SHI-NI-GA-MI.
IT'S, "IS IT YOU, SHINIGAMI."
I SEE THAT YOU AREN'T COMMANDER FOR NOTHING.
HE SEEMS TO HAVE REACTED TO THE PIECE OF PAPER TO THE BOTTOM RIGHT OF HIM.
NOW HE'S GIVING A SMALL SIGH.

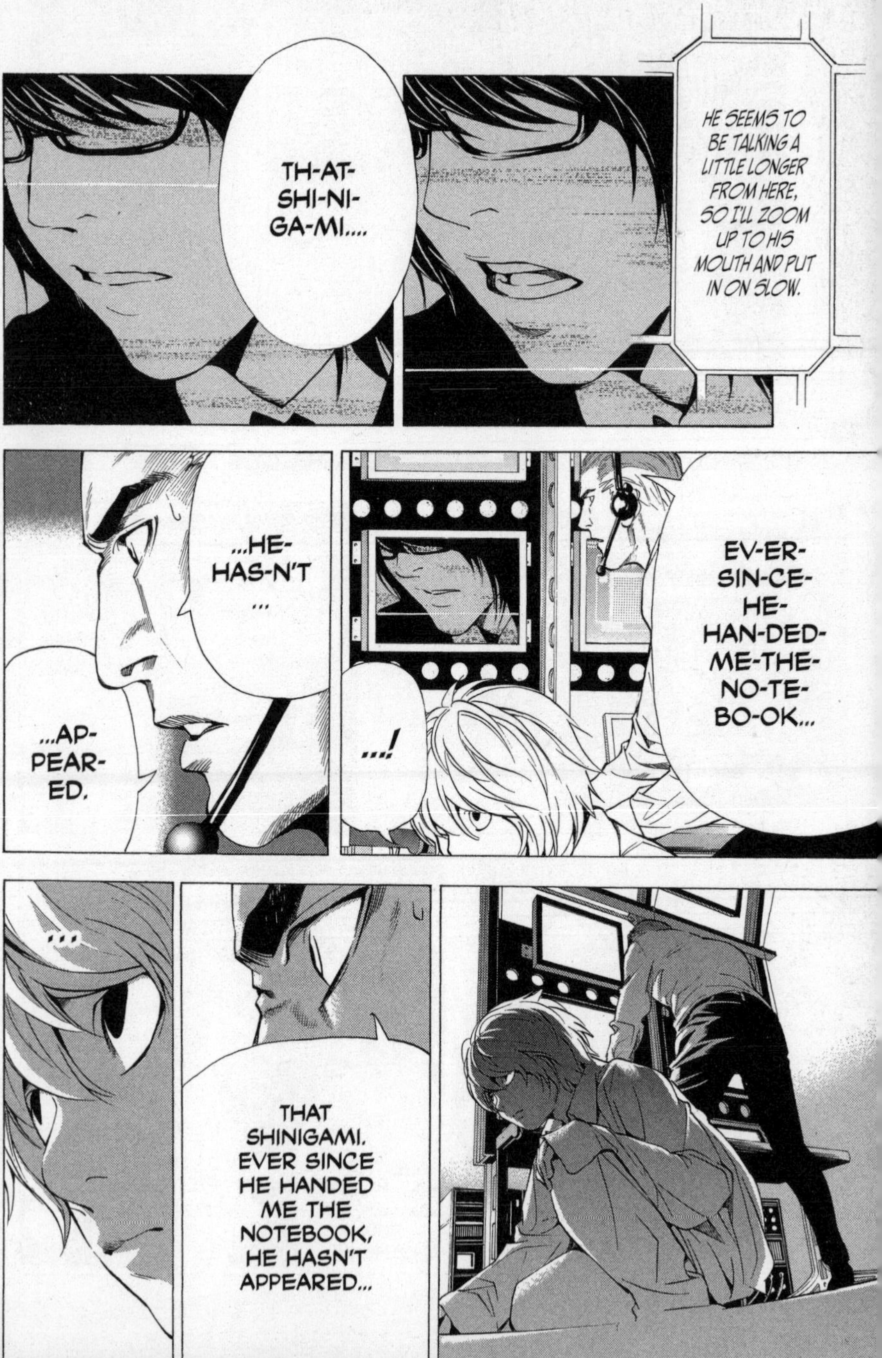
HE SEEMS TO BE TALKING A LITTLE LONGER FROM HERE, SO I'LL ZOOM UP TO HIS MOUTH AND PUT IN ON SLOW.
TH-AT-SHI-NI-GA-MI....
EV-ER-SIN-CE-HE-HAN-DED-ME-THE-NO-TE-BO-OK...
...!
...HE-HAS-N'T...
...AP-PEAR-ED.
THAT SHINIGAMI. EVER SINCE HE HANDED ME THE NOTEBOOK, HE HASN'T APPEARED...
...

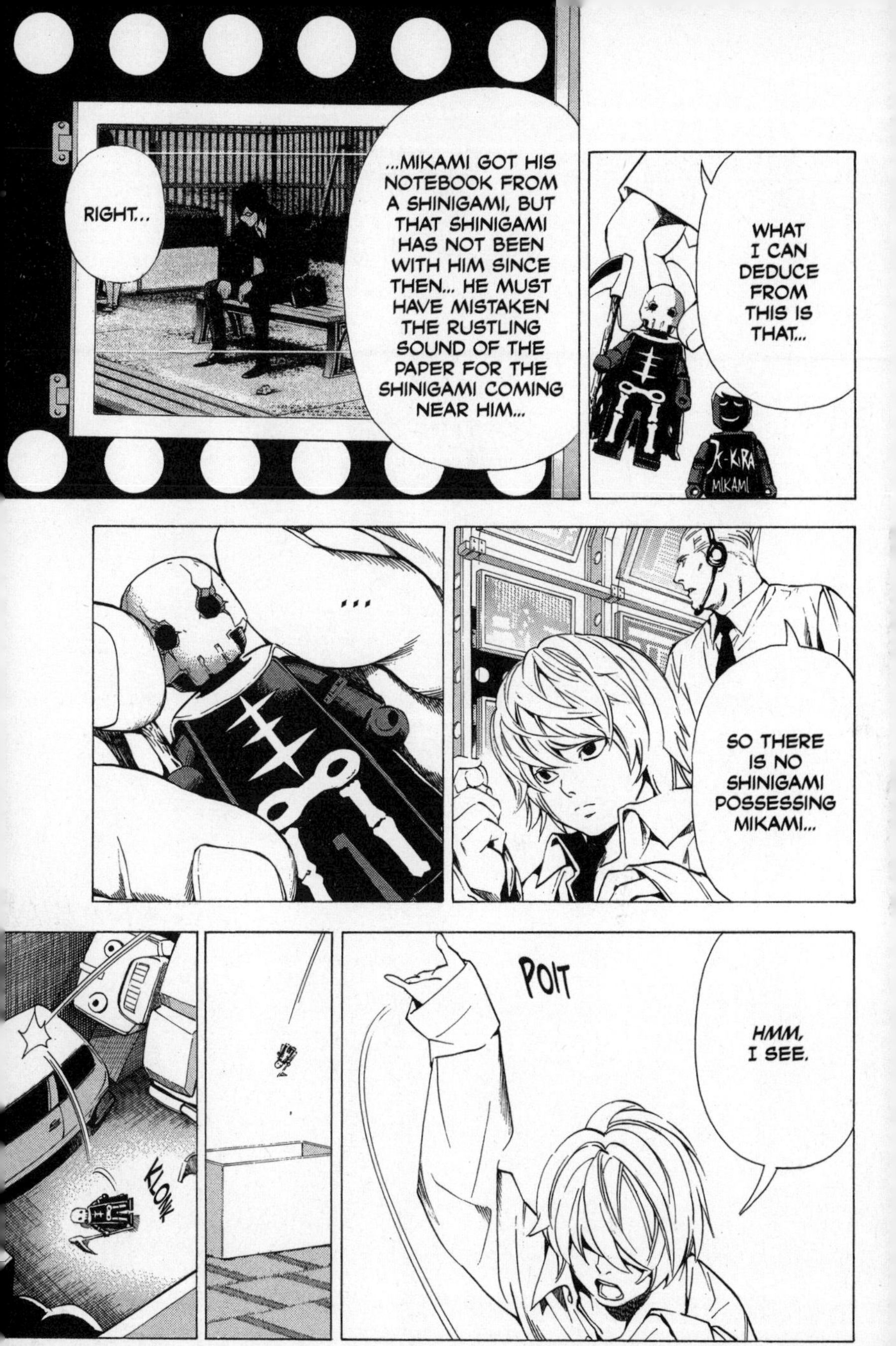
WHAT I CAN DEDUCE FROM THIS IS THAT...
K-KIRA
MIKAMI
...MIKAMI GOT HIS NOTEBOOK FROM A SHINIGAMI, BUT THAT SHINIGAMI HAS NOT BEEN WITH HIM SINCE THEN... HE MUST HAVE MISTAKEN THE RUSTLING SOUND OF THE PAPER FOR THE SHINIGAMI COMING NEAR HIM...
RIGHT...
SO THERE IS NO SHINIGAMI POSSESSING MIKAMI...
...
HMM, I SEE.
POIT
KLONK

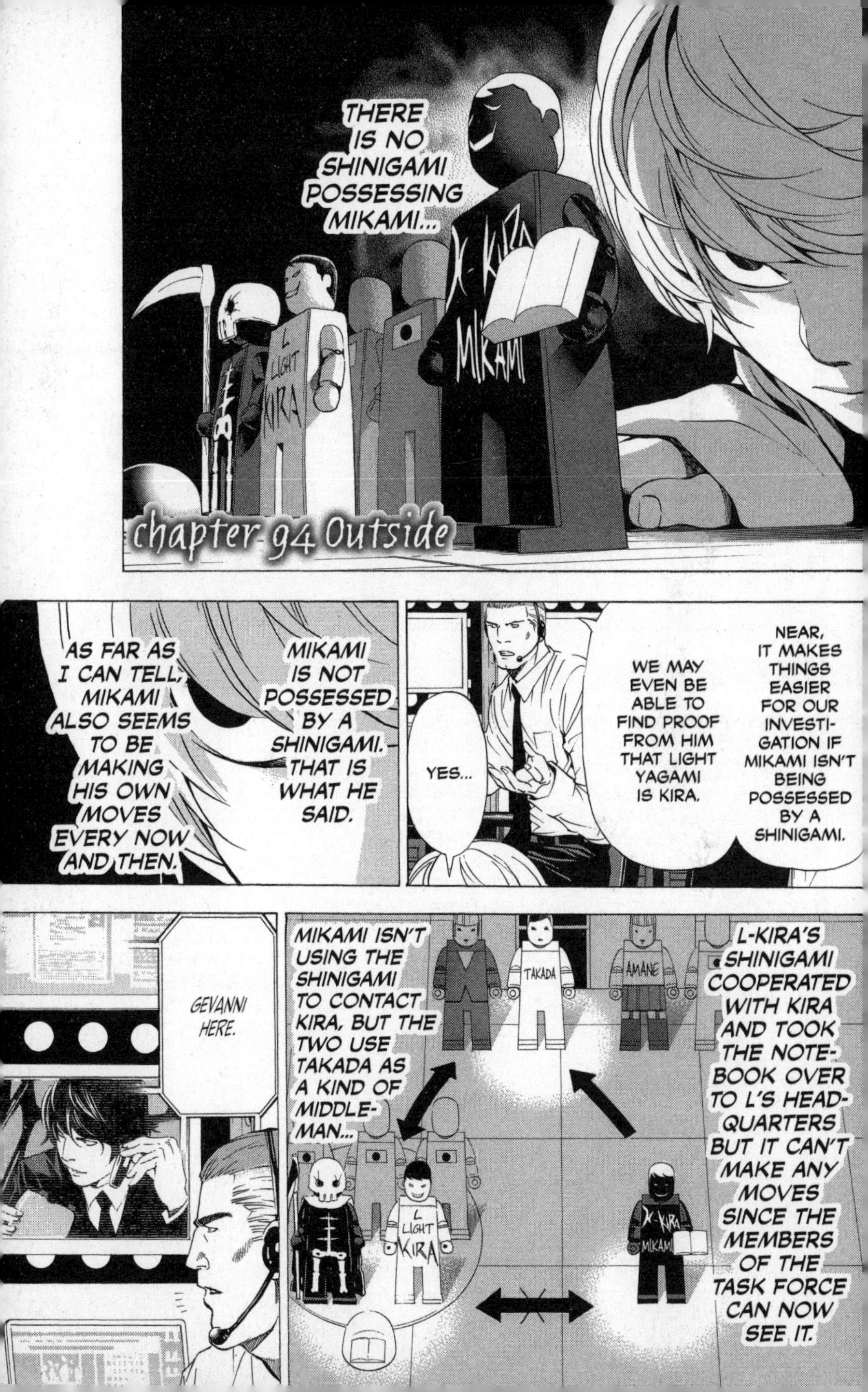
THERE IS NO SHINIGAMI POSSESSING MIKAMI...
chapter 94 Outside
L-KIRA
MIKAMI
L
LIGHT
KIRA
NEAR, IT MAKES THINGS EASIER FOR OUR INVESTIGATION IF MIKAMI ISN'T BEING POSSESSED BY A SHINIGAMI.
WE MAY EVEN BE ABLE TO FIND PROOF FROM HIM THAT LIGHT YAGAMI IS KIRA.
YES...
MIKAMI IS NOT POSSESSED BY A SHINIGAMI. THAT IS WHAT HE SAID.
AS FAR AS I CAN TELL, MIKAMI ALSO SEEMS TO BE MAKING HIS OWN MOVES EVERY NOW AND THEN.
L-KIRA'S SHINIGAMI COOPERATED WITH KIRA AND TOOK THE NOTEBOOK OVER TO L'S HEADQUARTERS BUT IT CAN'T MAKE ANY MOVES SINCE THE MEMBERS OF THE TASK FORCE CAN NOW SEE IT.
MIKAMI ISN'T USING THE SHINIGAMI TO CONTACT KIRA, BUT THE TWO USE TAKADA AS A KIND OF MIDDLEMAN...
TAKADA
AMANE
L
LIGHT
KIRA
L-KIRA
MIKAMI
GEVANNI HERE.

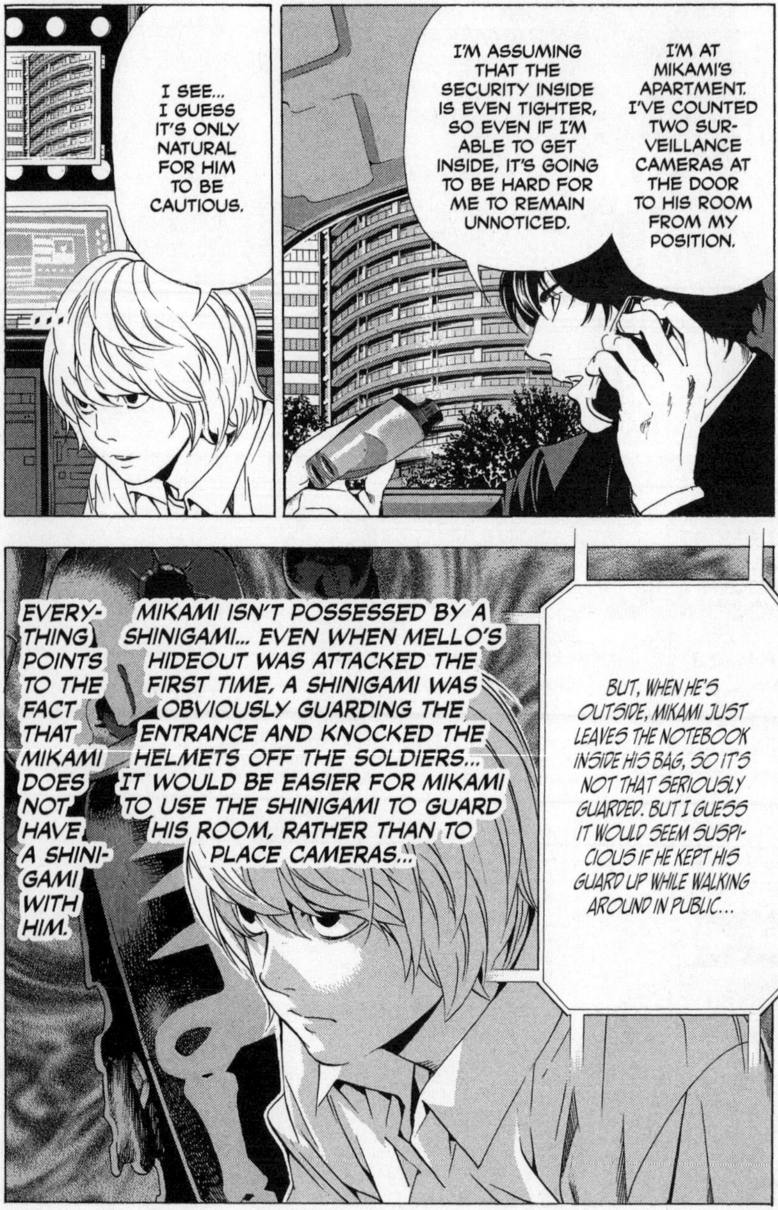
I'M AT MIKAMI'S APARTMENT. I'VE COUNTED TWO SURVEILLANCE CAMERAS AT THE DOOR TO HIS ROOM FROM MY POSITION.
I'M ASSUMING THAT THE SECURITY INSIDE IS EVEN TIGHTER, SO EVEN IF I'M ABLE TO GET INSIDE, IT'S GOING TO BE HARD FOR ME TO REMAIN UNNOTICED.
I SEE... I GUESS IT'S ONLY NATURAL FOR HIM TO BE CAUTIOUS.
....
BUT, WHEN HE'S OUTSIDE, MIKAMI JUST LEAVES THE NOTEBOOK INSIDE HIS BAG, SO IT'S NOT THAT SERIOUSLY GUARDED. BUT I GUESS IT WOULD SEEM SUSPICIOUS IF HE KEPT HIS GUARD UP WHILE WALKING AROUND IN PUBLIC...
MIKAMI ISN'T POSSESSED BY A SHINIGAMI... EVEN WHEN MELLO'S HIDEOUT WAS ATTACKED THE FIRST TIME, A SHINIGAMI WAS OBVIOUSLY GUARDING THE ENTRANCE AND KNOCKED THE HELMETS OFF THE SOLDIERS... IT WOULD BE EASIER FOR MIKAMI TO USE THE SHINIGAMI TO GUARD HIS ROOM, RATHER THAN TO PLACE CAMERAS...
EVERYTHING POINTS TO THE FACT THAT MIKAMI DOES NOT HAVE A SHINIGAMI WITH HIM.

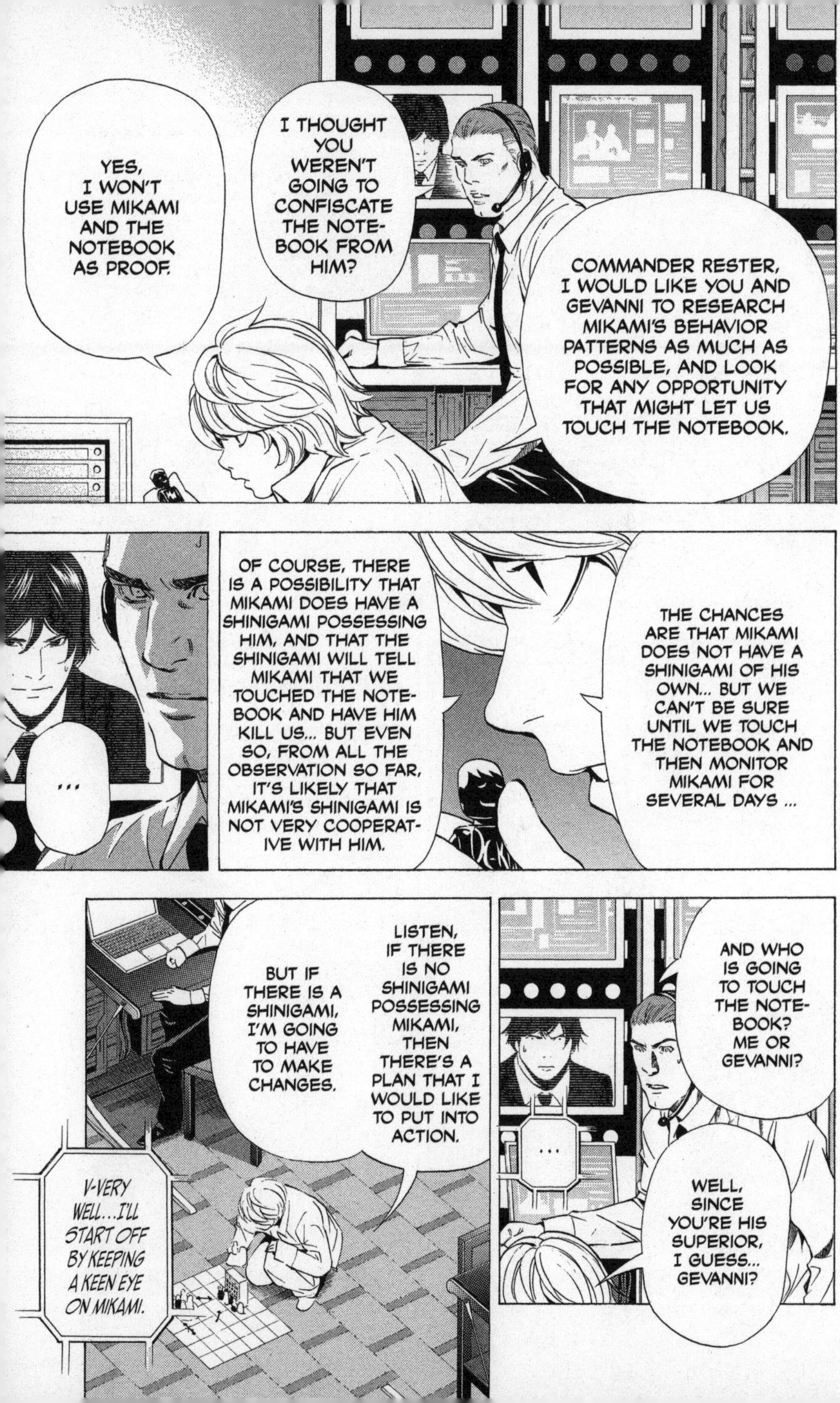
I THOUGHT YOU WEREN'T GOING TO CONFISCATE THE NOTEBOOK FROM HIM?
YES, I WON'T USE MIKAMI AND THE NOTEBOOK AS PROOF.
COMMANDER RESTER, I WOULD LIKE YOU AND GEVANNI TO RESEARCH MIKAMI'S BEHAVIOR PATTERNS AS MUCH AS POSSIBLE, AND LOOK FOR ANY OPPORTUNITY THAT MIGHT LET US TOUCH THE NOTEBOOK.
THE CHANCES ARE THAT MIKAMI DOES NOT HAVE A SHINIGAMI OF HIS OWN... BUT WE CAN'T BE SURE UNTIL WE TOUCH THE NOTEBOOK AND THEN MONITOR MIKAMI FOR SEVERAL DAYS ...
OF COURSE, THERE IS A POSSIBILITY THAT MIKAMI DOES HAVE A SHINIGAMI POSSESSING HIM, AND THAT THE SHINIGAMI WILL TELL MIKAMI THAT WE TOUCHED THE NOTEBOOK AND HAVE HIM KILL US... BUT EVEN SO, FROM ALL THE OBSERVATION SO FAR, IT'S LIKELY THAT MIKAMI'S SHINIGAMI IS NOT VERY COOPERATIVE WITH HIM.
...
AND WHO IS GOING TO TOUCH THE NOTEBOOK? ME OR GEVANNI?
...
WELL, SINCE YOU'RE HIS SUPERIOR, I GUESS... GEVANNI?
LISTEN, IF THERE IS NO SHINIGAMI POSSESSING MIKAMI, THEN THERE'S A PLAN THAT I WOULD LIKE TO PUT INTO ACTION.
BUT IF THERE IS A SHINIGAMI, I'M GOING TO HAVE TO MAKE CHANGES.
V-VERY WELL... I'LL START OFF BY KEEPING A KEEN EYE ON MIKAMI.

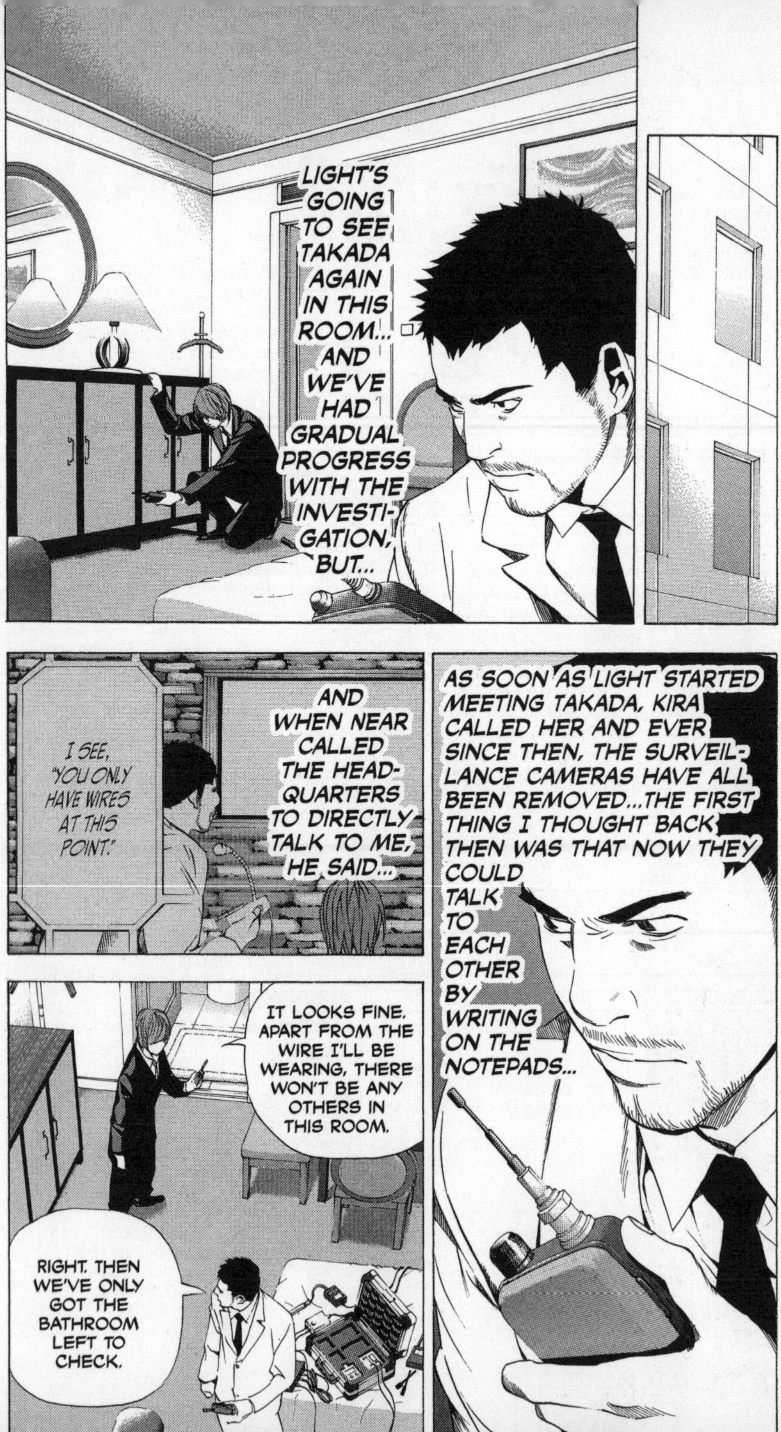
LIGHT'S GOING TO SEE TAKADA AGAIN IN THIS ROOM... AND WE'VE HAD GRADUAL PROGRESS WITH THE INVESTI-GATION, BUT...
AS SOON AS LIGHT STARTED MEETING TAKADA, KIRA CALLED HER AND EVER SINCE THEN, THE SURVEIL-LANCE CAMERAS HAVE ALL BEEN REMOVED...THE FIRST THING I THOUGHT BACK THEN WAS THAT NOW THEY COULD TALK TO EACH OTHER BY WRITING ON THE NOTEPADS...
AND WHEN NEAR CALLED THE HEAD-QUARTERS TO DIRECTLY TALK TO ME, HE SAID...
I SEE, "YOU ONLY HAVE WIRES AT THIS POINT."
IT LOOKS FINE. APART FROM THE WIRE I'LL BE WEARING, THERE WON'T BE ANY OTHERS IN THIS ROOM.
RIGHT. THEN WE'VE ONLY GOT THE BATHROOM LEFT TO CHECK.

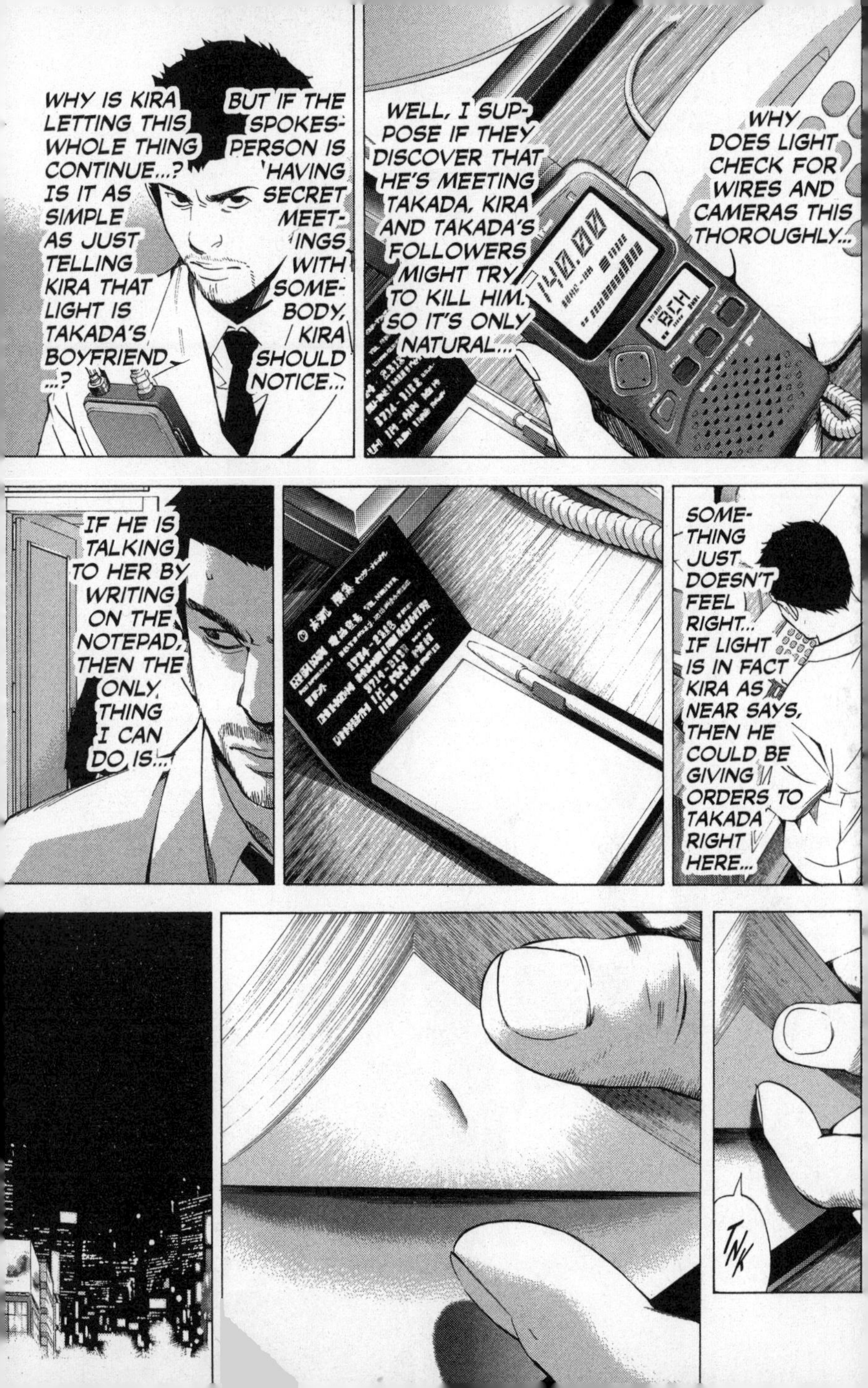
WHY DOES LIGHT CHECK FOR WIRES AND CAMERAS THIS THOROUGHLY...
WELL, I SUPPOSE IF THEY DISCOVER THAT HE'S MEETING TAKADA, KIRA AND TAKADA'S FOLLOWERS MIGHT TRY TO KILL HIM. SO IT'S ONLY NATURAL...
BUT IF THE SPOKESPERSON IS HAVING SECRET MEETINGS WITH SOMEBODY, KIRA SHOULD NOTICE...
WHY IS KIRA LETTING THIS WHOLE THING CONTINUE...? IS IT AS SIMPLE AS JUST TELLING KIRA THAT LIGHT IS TAKADA'S BOYFRIEND...?
SOMETHING JUST DOESN'T FEEL RIGHT... IF LIGHT IS IN FACT KIRA AS NEAR SAYS, THEN HE COULD BE GIVING ORDERS TO TAKADA RIGHT HERE...
IF HE IS TALKING TO HER BY WRITING ON THE NOTEPAD, THEN THE ONLY THING I CAN DO IS...
TNK

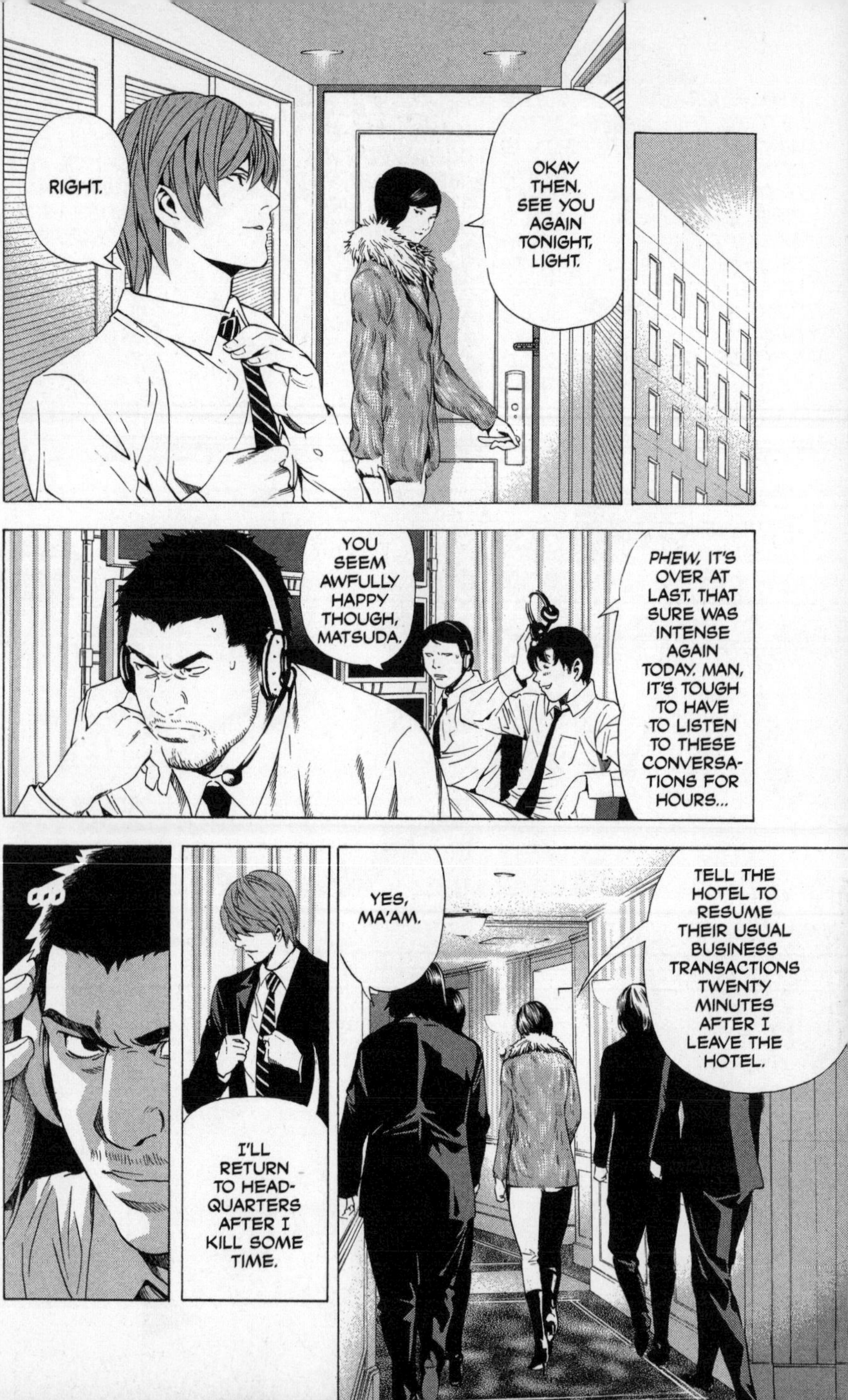
OKAY THEN. SEE YOU AGAIN TONIGHT, LIGHT.
RIGHT.
PHEW, IT'S OVER AT LAST. THAT SURE WAS INTENSE AGAIN TODAY. MAN, IT'S TOUGH TO HAVE TO LISTEN TO THESE CONVERSA-TIONS FOR HOURS...
YOU SEEM AWFULLY HAPPY THOUGH, MATSUDA.
TELL THE HOTEL TO RESUME THEIR USUAL BUSINESS TRANSACTIONS TWENTY MINUTES AFTER I LEAVE THE HOTEL.
YES, MA'AM.
I'LL RETURN TO HEAD-QUARTERS AFTER I KILL SOME TIME.

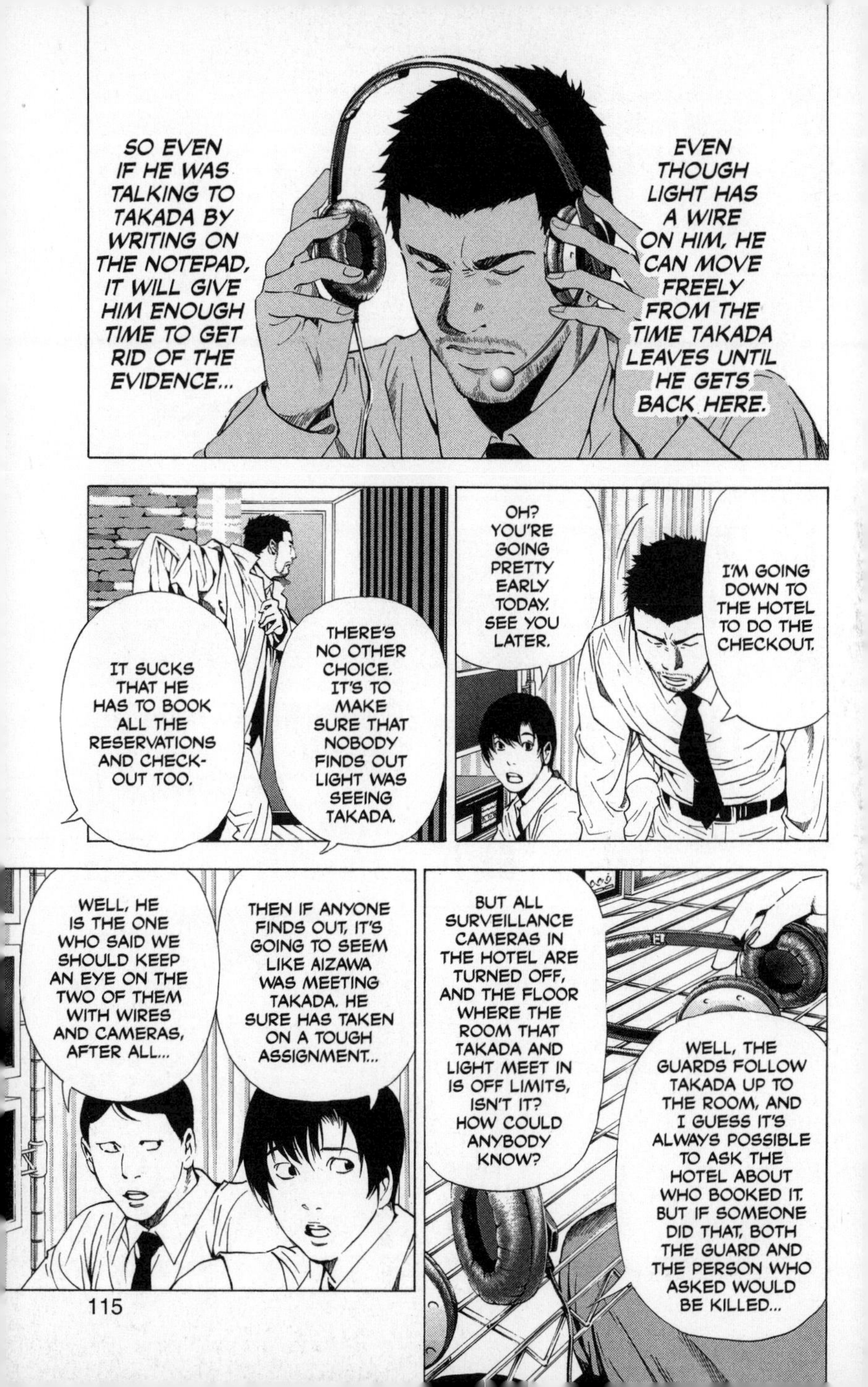
EVEN THOUGH LIGHT HAS A WIRE ON HIM, HE CAN MOVE FREELY FROM THE TIME TAKADA LEAVES UNTIL HE GETS BACK HERE.
SO EVEN IF HE WAS TALKING TO TAKADA BY WRITING ON THE NOTEPAD, IT WILL GIVE HIM ENOUGH TIME TO GET RID OF THE EVIDENCE...
I'M GOING DOWN TO THE HOTEL TO DO THE CHECKOUT.
OH? YOU'RE GOING PRETTY EARLY TODAY. SEE YOU LATER.
THERE'S NO OTHER CHOICE. IT'S TO MAKE SURE THAT NOBODY FINDS OUT LIGHT WAS SEEING TAKADA.
IT SUCKS THAT HE HAS TO BOOK ALL THE RESERVATIONS AND CHECK-OUT TOO.
BUT ALL SURVEILLANCE CAMERAS IN THE HOTEL ARE TURNED OFF, AND THE FLOOR WHERE THE ROOM THAT TAKADA AND LIGHT MEET IN IS OFF LIMITS, ISN'T IT? HOW COULD ANYBODY KNOW?
WELL, THE GUARDS FOLLOW TAKADA UP TO THE ROOM, AND I GUESS IT'S ALWAYS POSSIBLE TO ASK THE HOTEL ABOUT WHO BOOKED IT. BUT IF SOMEONE DID THAT, BOTH THE GUARD AND THE PERSON WHO ASKED WOULD BE KILLED...
THEN IF ANYONE FINDS OUT, IT'S GOING TO SEEM LIKE AIZAWA WAS MEETING TAKADA. HE SURE HAS TAKEN ON A TOUGH ASSIGNMENT...
WELL, HE IS THE ONE WHO SAID WE SHOULD KEEP AN EYE ON THE TWO OF THEM WITH WIRES AND CAMERAS, AFTER ALL...

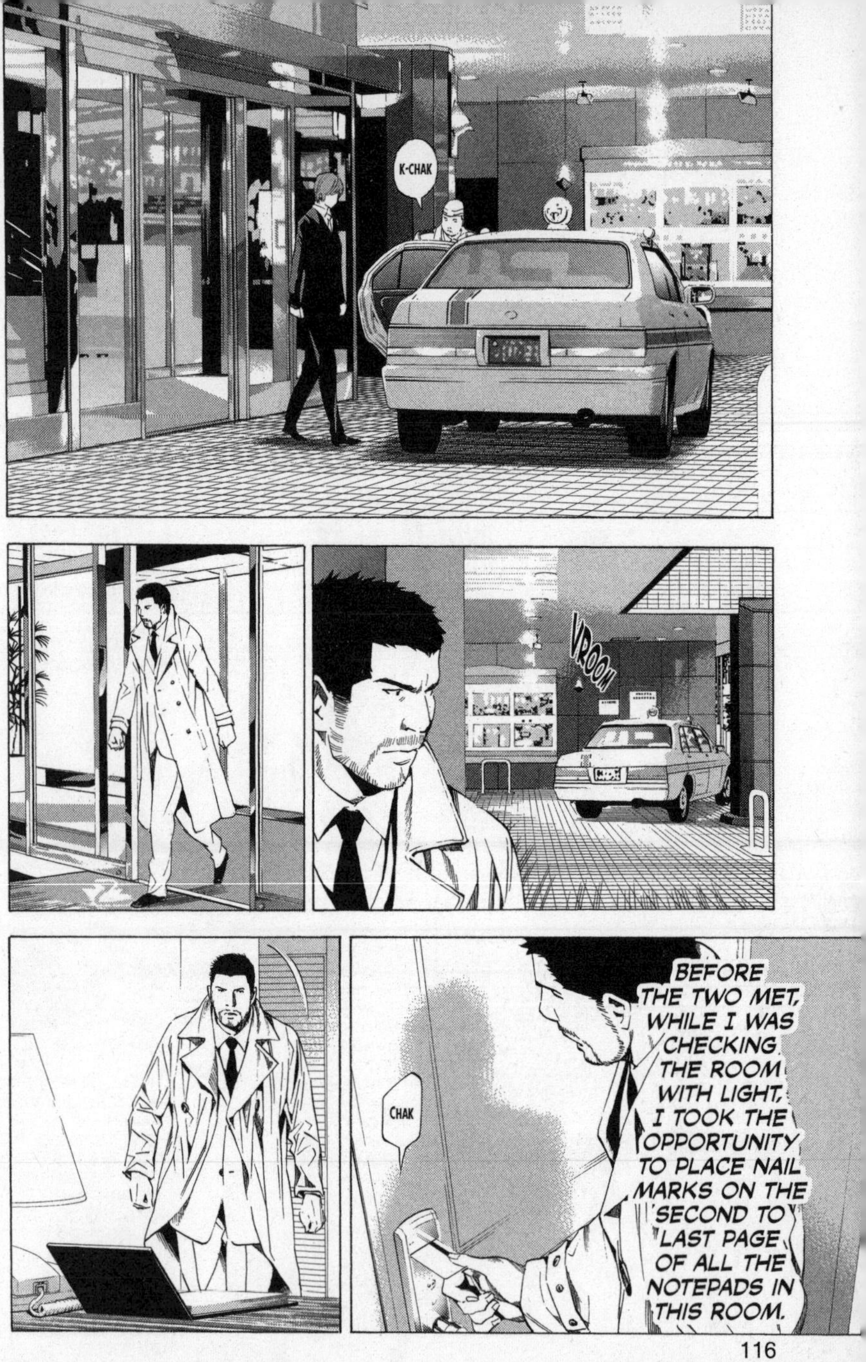
K-CHAK
VROOM
BEFORE THE TWO MET, WHILE I WAS CHECKING THE ROOM WITH LIGHT, I TOOK THE OPPORTUNITY TO PLACE NAIL MARKS ON THE SECOND TO LAST PAGE OF ALL THE NOTEPADS IN THIS ROOM.
CHAK

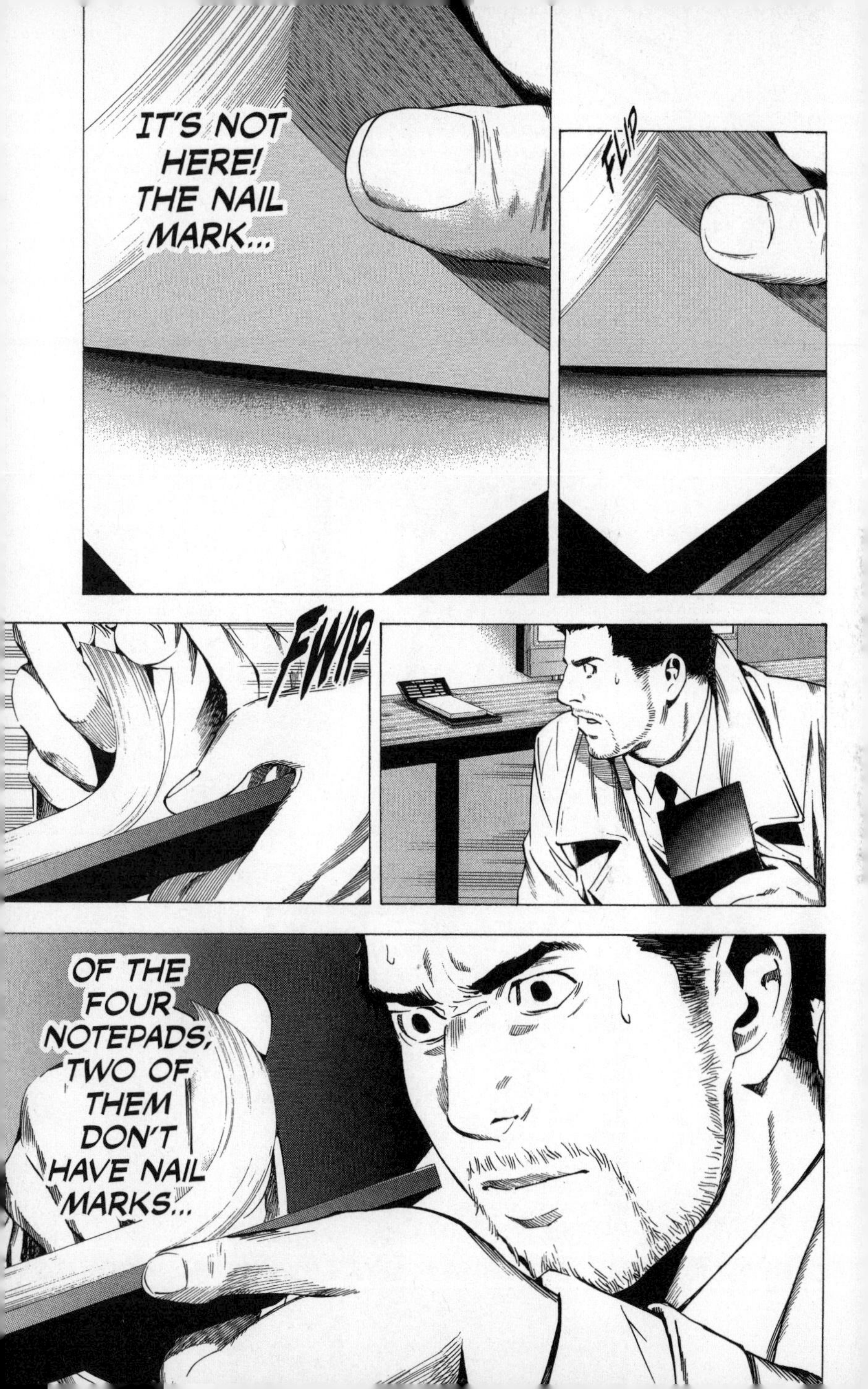
FLIP
IT'S NOT HERE! THE NAIL MARK...
FWIP
OF THE FOUR NOTEPADS, TWO OF THEM DON'T HAVE NAIL MARKS...

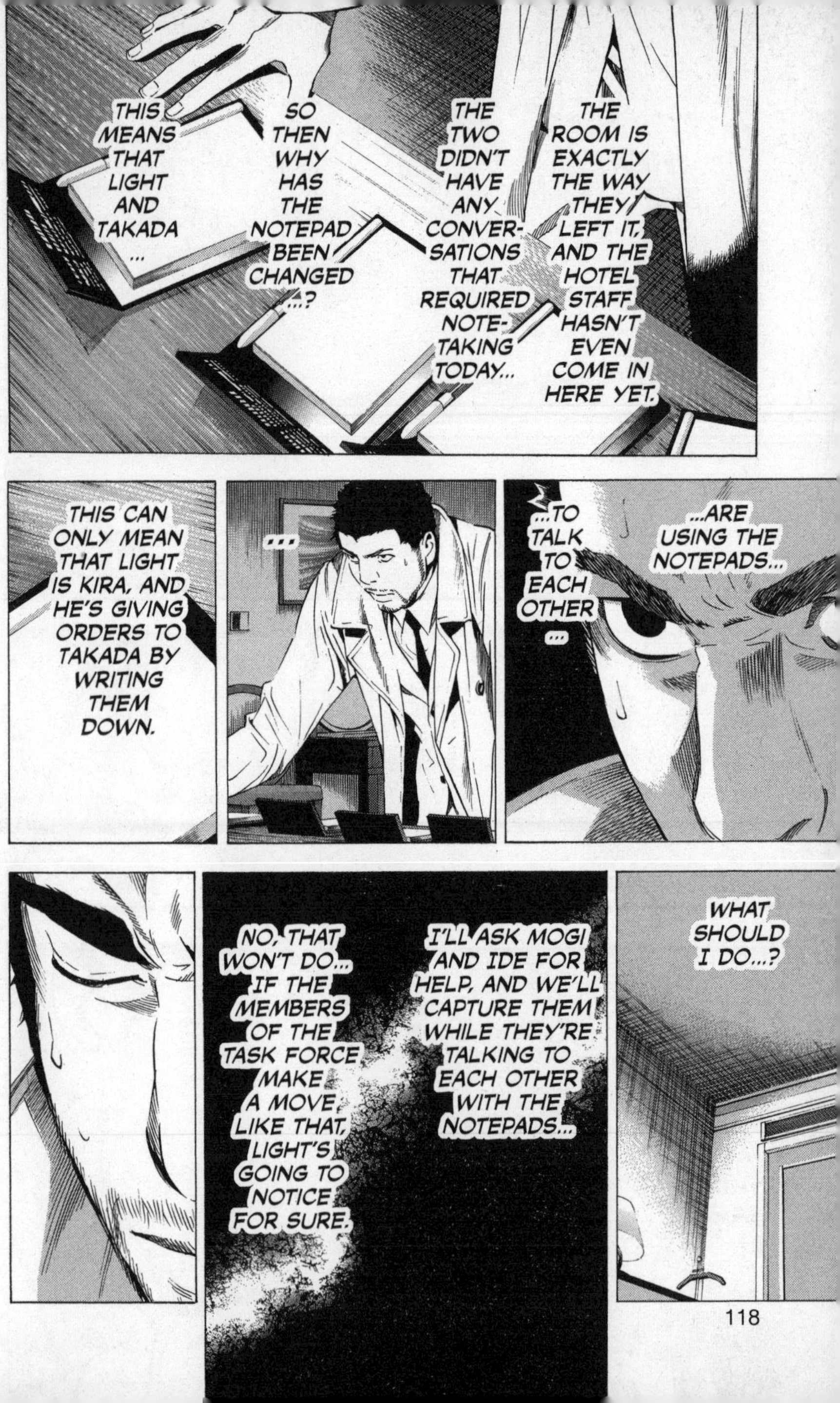
THE ROOM IS EXACTLY THE WAY THEY LEFT IT, AND THE HOTEL STAFF HASN'T EVEN COME IN HERE YET.
THE TWO DIDN'T HAVE ANY CONVERSATIONS THAT REQUIRED NOTE-TAKING TODAY...
SO THEN WHY HAS THE NOTEPAD BEEN CHANGED ...?
THIS MEANS THAT LIGHT AND TAKADA ...
...ARE USING THE NOTEPADS...
...TO TALK TO EACH OTHER ...
...
THIS CAN ONLY MEAN THAT LIGHT IS KIRA, AND HE'S GIVING ORDERS TO TAKADA BY WRITING THEM DOWN.
WHAT SHOULD I DO...?
I'LL ASK MOGI AND IDE FOR HELP, AND WE'LL CAPTURE THEM WHILE THEY'RE TALKING TO EACH OTHER WITH THE NOTEPADS...
NO, THAT WON'T DO... IF THE MEMBERS OF THE TASK FORCE MAKE A MOVE LIKE THAT, LIGHT'S GOING TO NOTICE FOR SURE.

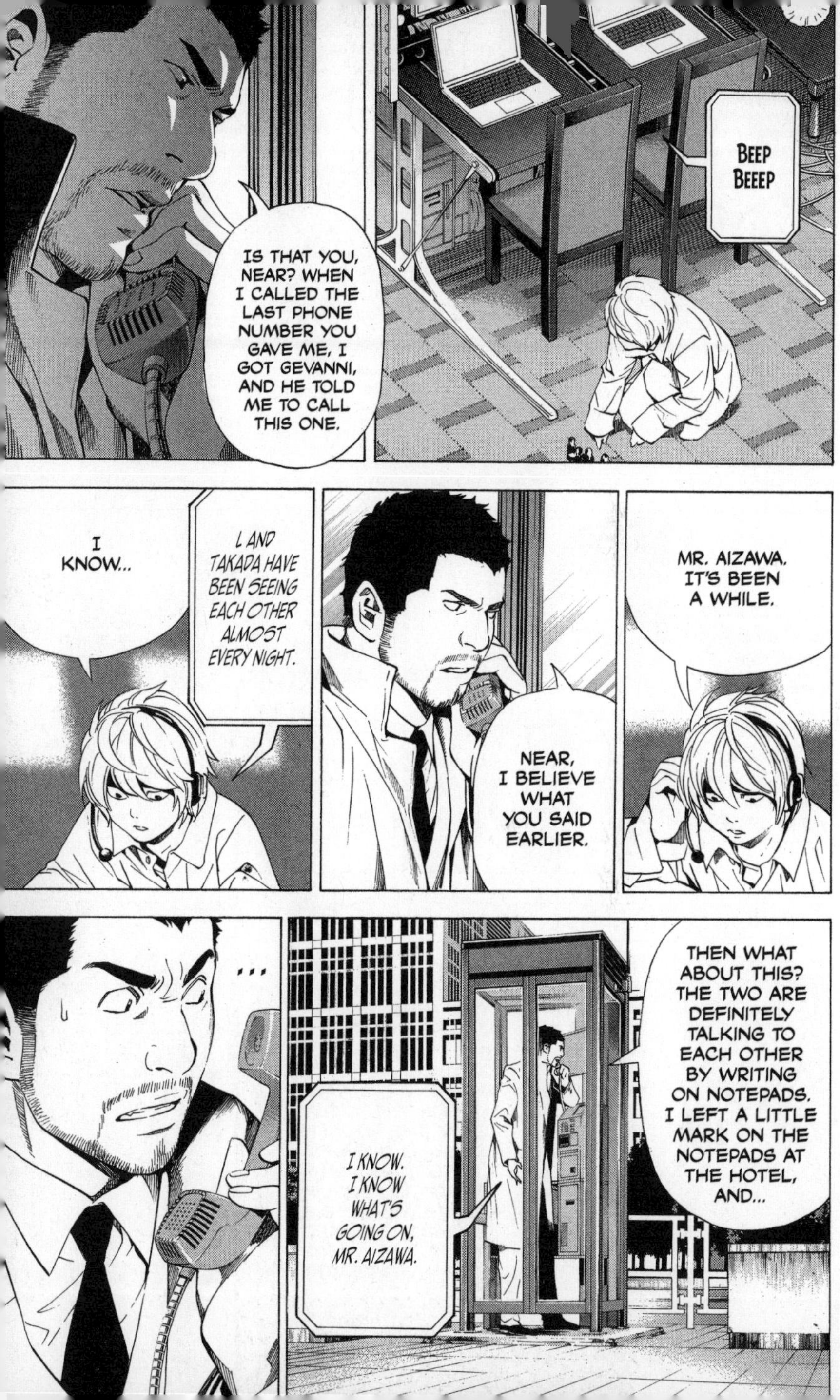
BEEP BEEEP
IS THAT YOU, NEAR? WHEN I CALLED THE LAST PHONE NUMBER YOU GAVE ME, I GOT GEVANNI, AND HE TOLD ME TO CALL THIS ONE.
MR. AIZAWA. IT'S BEEN A WHILE.
NEAR, I BELIEVE WHAT YOU SAID EARLIER.
L AND TAKADA HAVE BEEN SEEING EACH OTHER ALMOST EVERY NIGHT.
I KNOW...
THEN WHAT ABOUT THIS? THE TWO ARE DEFINITELY TALKING TO EACH OTHER BY WRITING ON NOTEPADS. I LEFT A LITTLE MARK ON THE NOTEPADS AT THE HOTEL, AND...
I KNOW. I KNOW WHAT'S GOING ON, MR. AIZAWA.
...

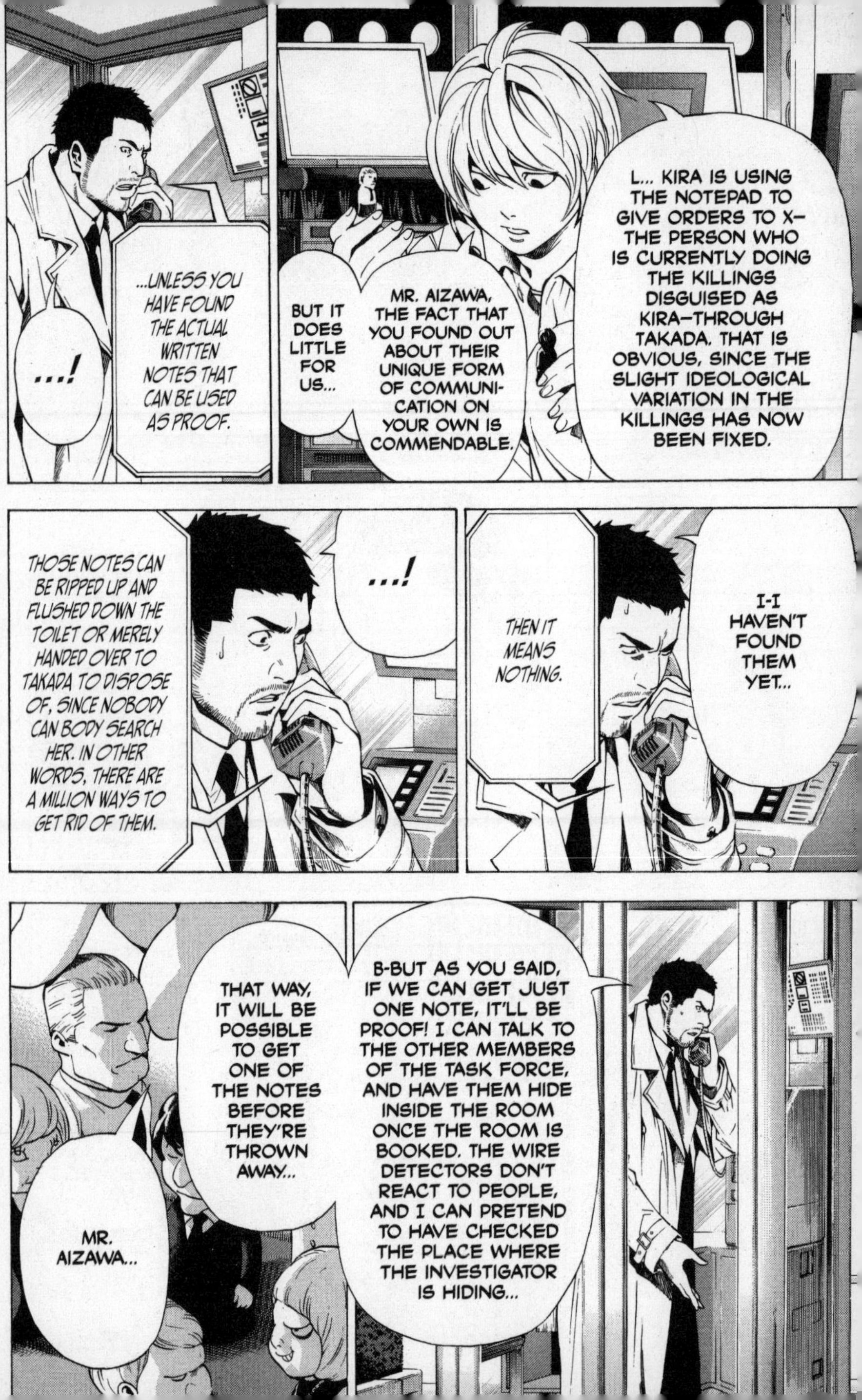
L... KIRA IS USING THE NOTEPAD TO GIVE ORDERS TO X—THE PERSON WHO IS CURRENTLY DOING THE KILLINGS DISGUISED AS KIRA—THROUGH TAKADA. THAT IS OBVIOUS, SINCE THE SLIGHT IDEOLOGICAL VARIATION IN THE KILLINGS HAS NOW BEEN FIXED.
MR. AIZAWA, THE FACT THAT YOU FOUND OUT ABOUT THEIR UNIQUE FORM OF COMMUNICATION ON YOUR OWN IS COMMENDABLE.
BUT IT DOES LITTLE FOR US...
...UNLESS YOU HAVE FOUND THE ACTUAL WRITTEN NOTES THAT CAN BE USED AS PROOF.
...!
I-I HAVEN'T FOUND THEM YET...
THEN IT MEANS NOTHING.
...!
THOSE NOTES CAN BE RIPPED UP AND FLUSHED DOWN THE TOILET OR MERELY HANDED OVER TO TAKADA TO DISPOSE OF, SINCE NOBODY CAN BODY SEARCH HER. IN OTHER WORDS, THERE ARE A MILLION WAYS TO GET RID OF THEM.
B-BUT AS YOU SAID, IF WE CAN GET JUST ONE NOTE, IT'LL BE PROOF! I CAN TALK TO THE OTHER MEMBERS OF THE TASK FORCE, AND HAVE THEM HIDE INSIDE THE ROOM ONCE THE ROOM IS BOOKED. THE WIRE DETECTORS DON'T REACT TO PEOPLE, AND I CAN PRETEND TO HAVE CHECKED THE PLACE WHERE THE INVESTIGATOR IS HIDING...
THAT WAY, IT WILL BE POSSIBLE TO GET ONE OF THE NOTES BEFORE THEY'RE THROWN AWAY...
MR. AIZAWA...

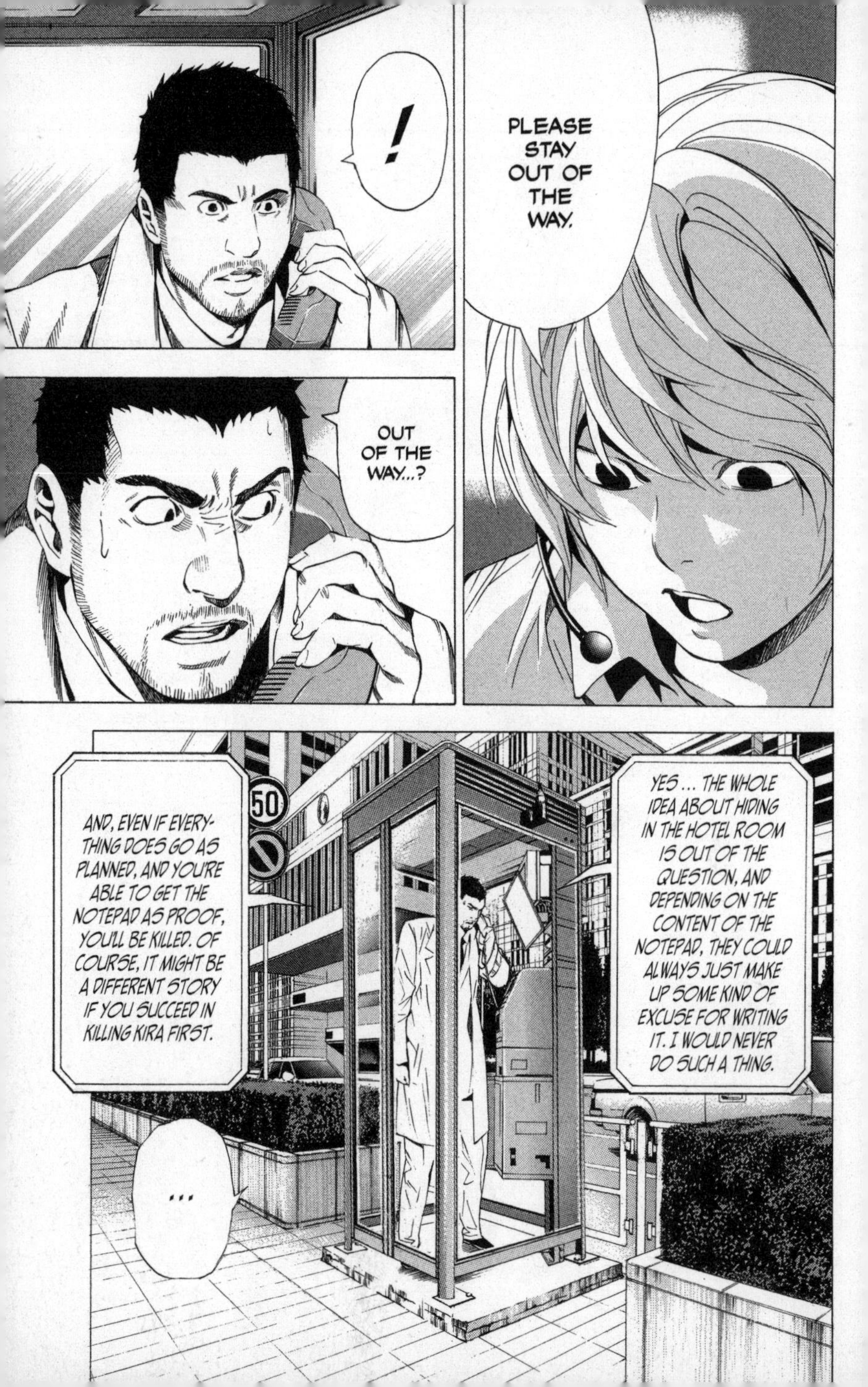
PLEASE STAY OUT OF THE WAY.
!
OUT OF THE WAY...?
YES ... THE WHOLE IDEA ABOUT HIDING IN THE HOTEL ROOM IS OUT OF THE QUESTION, AND DEPENDING ON THE CONTENT OF THE NOTEPAD, THEY COULD ALWAYS JUST MAKE UP SOME KIND OF EXCUSE FOR WRITING IT. I WOULD NEVER DO SUCH A THING.
AND, EVEN IF EVERYTHING DOES GO AS PLANNED, AND YOU'RE ABLE TO GET THE NOTEPAD AS PROOF, YOU'LL BE KILLED. OF COURSE, IT MIGHT BE A DIFFERENT STORY IF YOU SUCCEED IN KILLING KIRA FIRST.
...

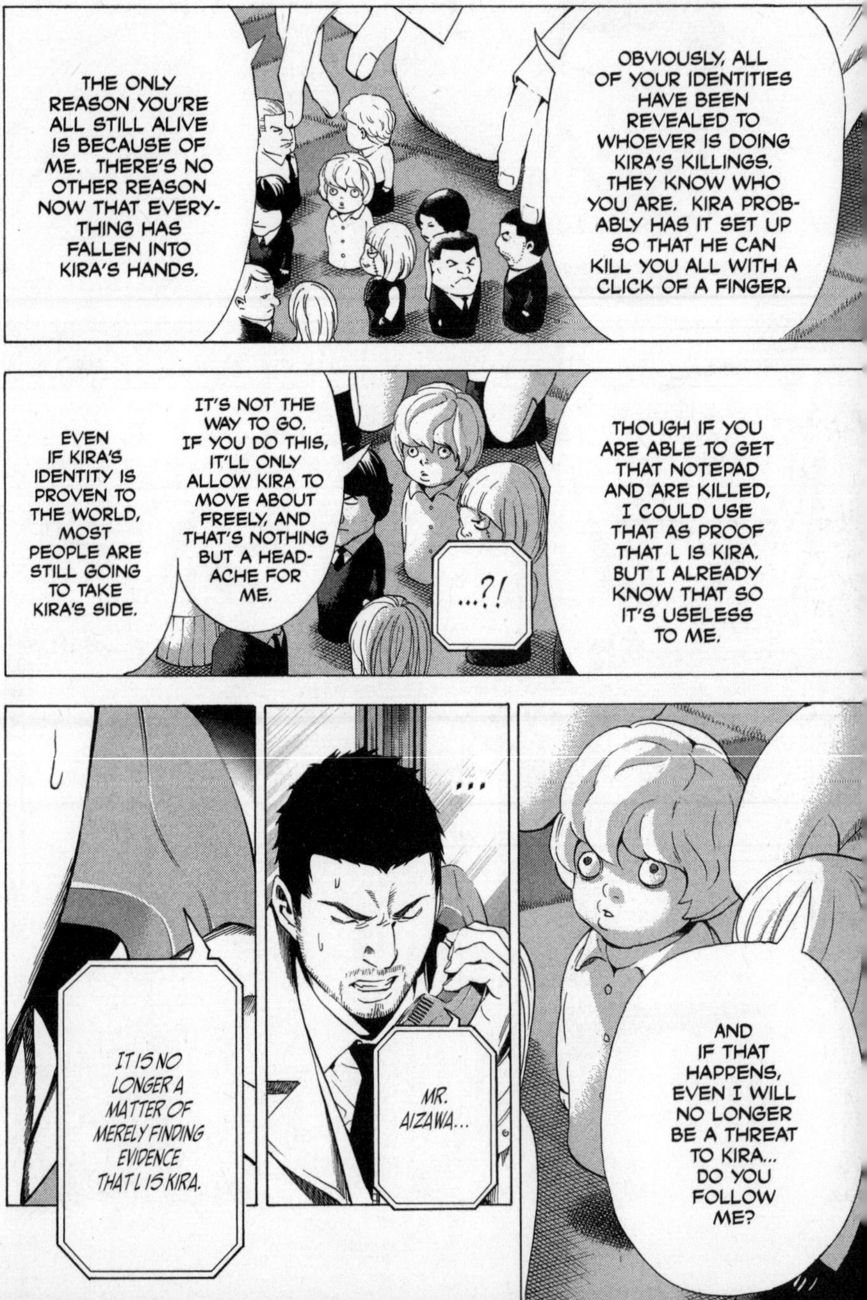
OBVIOUSLY, ALL OF YOUR IDENTITIES HAVE BEEN REVEALED TO WHOEVER IS DOING KIRA'S KILLINGS. THEY KNOW WHO YOU ARE. KIRA PROBABLY HAS IT SET UP SO THAT HE CAN KILL YOU ALL WITH A CLICK OF A FINGER.
THE ONLY REASON YOU'RE ALL STILL ALIVE IS BECAUSE OF ME. THERE'S NO OTHER REASON NOW THAT EVERYTHING HAS FALLEN INTO KIRA'S HANDS.
THOUGH IF YOU ARE ABLE TO GET THAT NOTEPAD AND ARE KILLED, I COULD USE THAT AS PROOF THAT L IS KIRA, BUT I ALREADY KNOW THAT SO IT'S USELESS TO ME.
...?!
IT'S NOT THE WAY TO GO. IF YOU DO THIS, IT'LL ONLY ALLOW KIRA TO MOVE ABOUT FREELY, AND THAT'S NOTHING BUT A HEADACHE FOR ME.
EVEN IF KIRA'S IDENTITY IS PROVEN TO THE WORLD, MOST PEOPLE ARE STILL GOING TO TAKE KIRA'S SIDE.
AND IF THAT HAPPENS, EVEN I WILL NO LONGER BE A THREAT TO KIRA... DO YOU FOLLOW ME?
...
MR. AIZAWA...
IT IS NO LONGER A MATTER OF MERELY FINDING EVIDENCE THAT L IS KIRA.

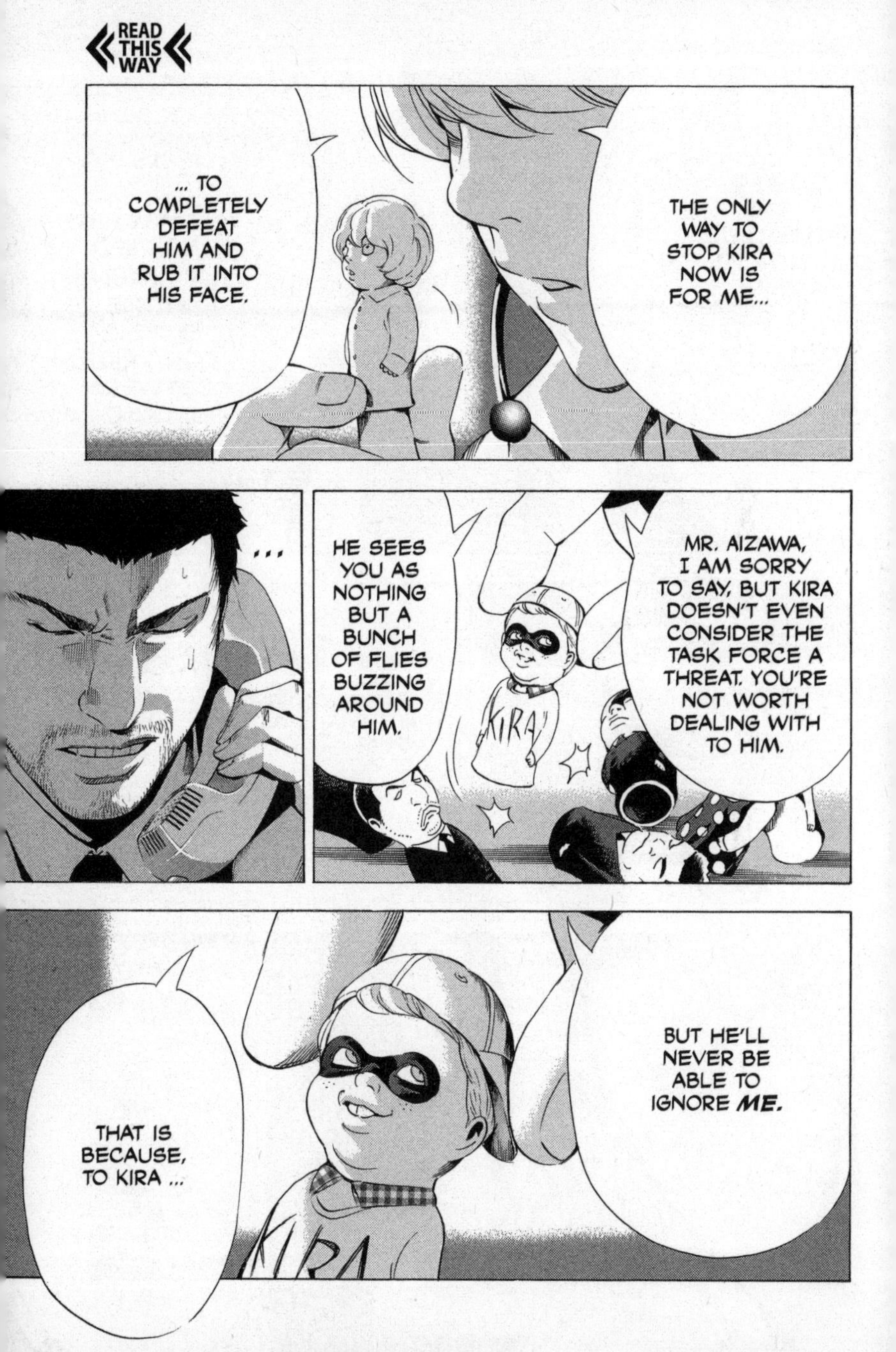
READ THIS WAY
THE ONLY WAY TO STOP KIRA NOW IS FOR ME...
... TO COMPLETELY DEFEAT HIM AND RUB IT INTO HIS FACE.
MR. AIZAWA, I AM SORRY TO SAY, BUT KIRA DOESN'T EVEN CONSIDER THE TASK FORCE A THREAT. YOU'RE NOT WORTH DEALING WITH TO HIM.
HE SEES YOU AS NOTHING BUT A BUNCH OF FLIES BUZZING AROUND HIM.
KIRA
...
BUT HE'LL NEVER BE ABLE TO IGNORE *ME.*
THAT IS BECAUSE, TO KIRA ...

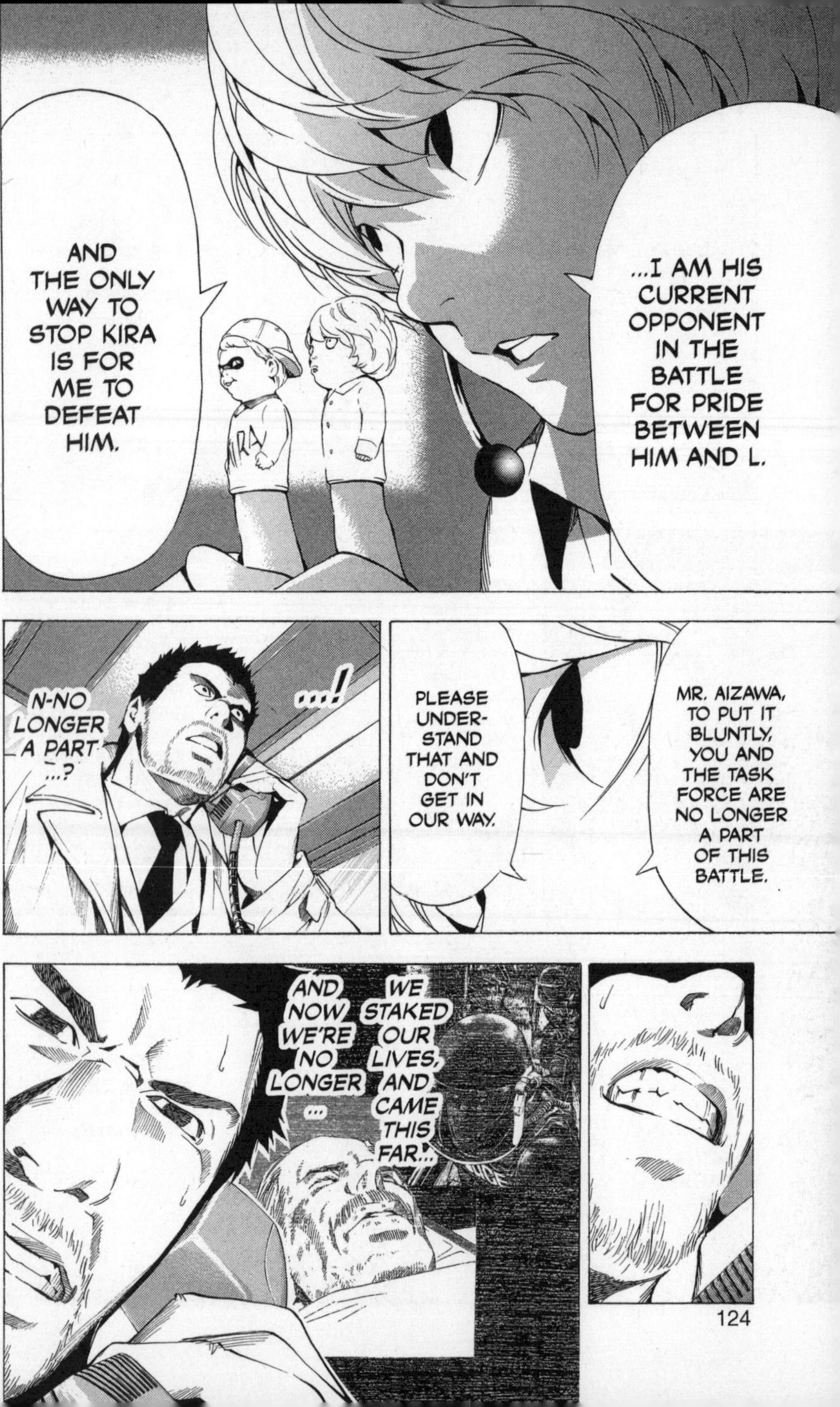
...I AM HIS CURRENT OPPONENT IN THE BATTLE FOR PRIDE BETWEEN HIM AND L.
AND THE ONLY WAY TO STOP KIRA IS FOR ME TO DEFEAT HIM.
MR. AIZAWA, TO PUT IT BLUNTLY, YOU AND THE TASK FORCE ARE NO LONGER A PART OF THIS BATTLE.
PLEASE UNDERSTAND THAT AND DON'T GET IN OUR WAY.
...!
N-NO LONGER A PART ...?
WE STAKED OUR LIVES, AND CAME THIS FAR...
AND NOW WE'RE NO LONGER ...

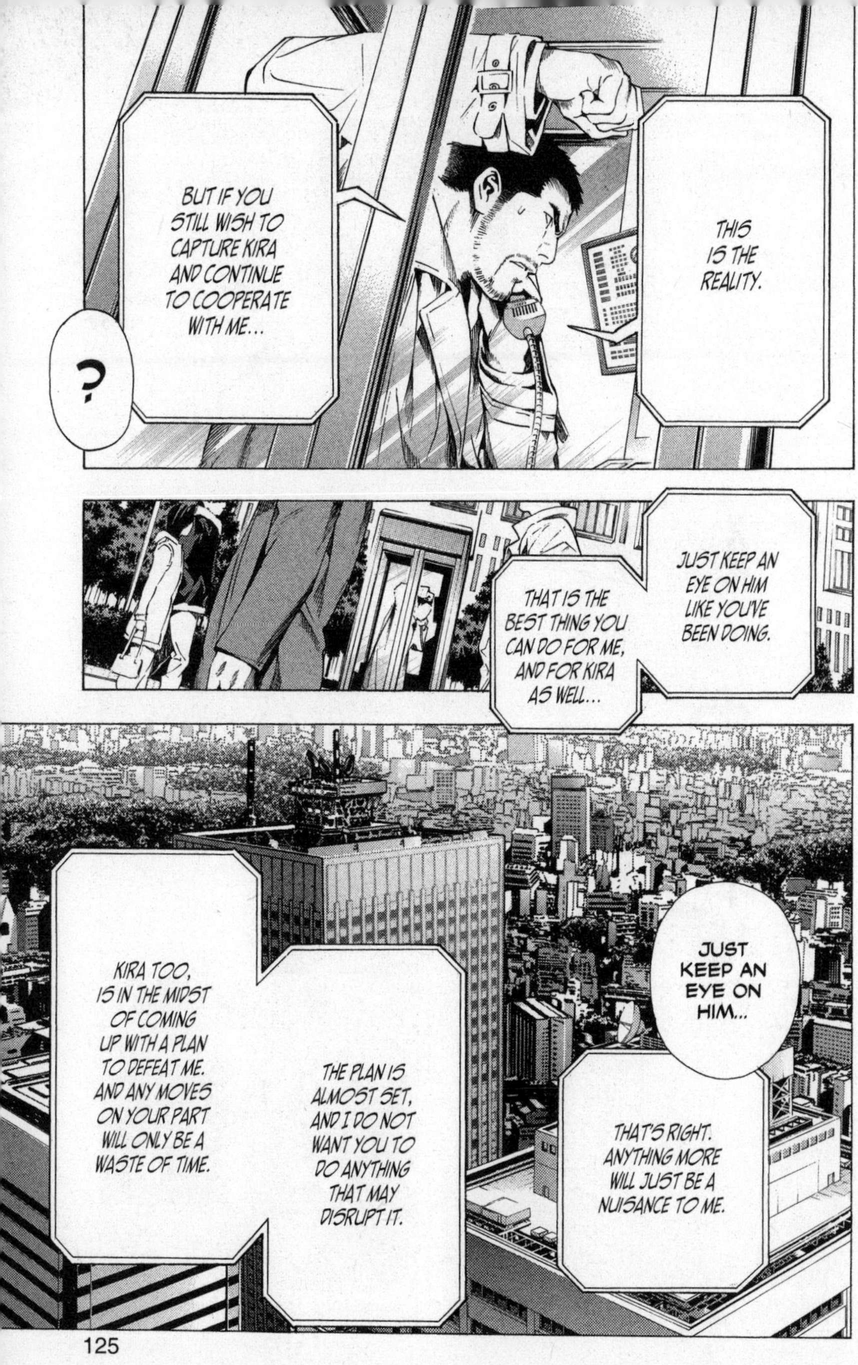
THIS IS THE REALITY.
BUT IF YOU STILL WISH TO CAPTURE KIRA AND CONTINUE TO COOPERATE WITH ME...
?
JUST KEEP AN EYE ON HIM LIKE YOU'VE BEEN DOING.
THAT IS THE BEST THING YOU CAN DO FOR ME, AND FOR KIRA AS WELL...
JUST KEEP AN EYE ON HIM...
THAT'S RIGHT. ANYTHING MORE WILL JUST BE A NUISANCE TO ME.
KIRA TOO, IS IN THE MIDST OF COMING UP WITH A PLAN TO DEFEAT ME. AND ANY MOVES ON YOUR PART WILL ONLY BE A WASTE OF TIME.
THE PLAN IS ALMOST SET, AND I DO NOT WANT YOU TO DO ANYTHING THAT MAY DISRUPT IT.

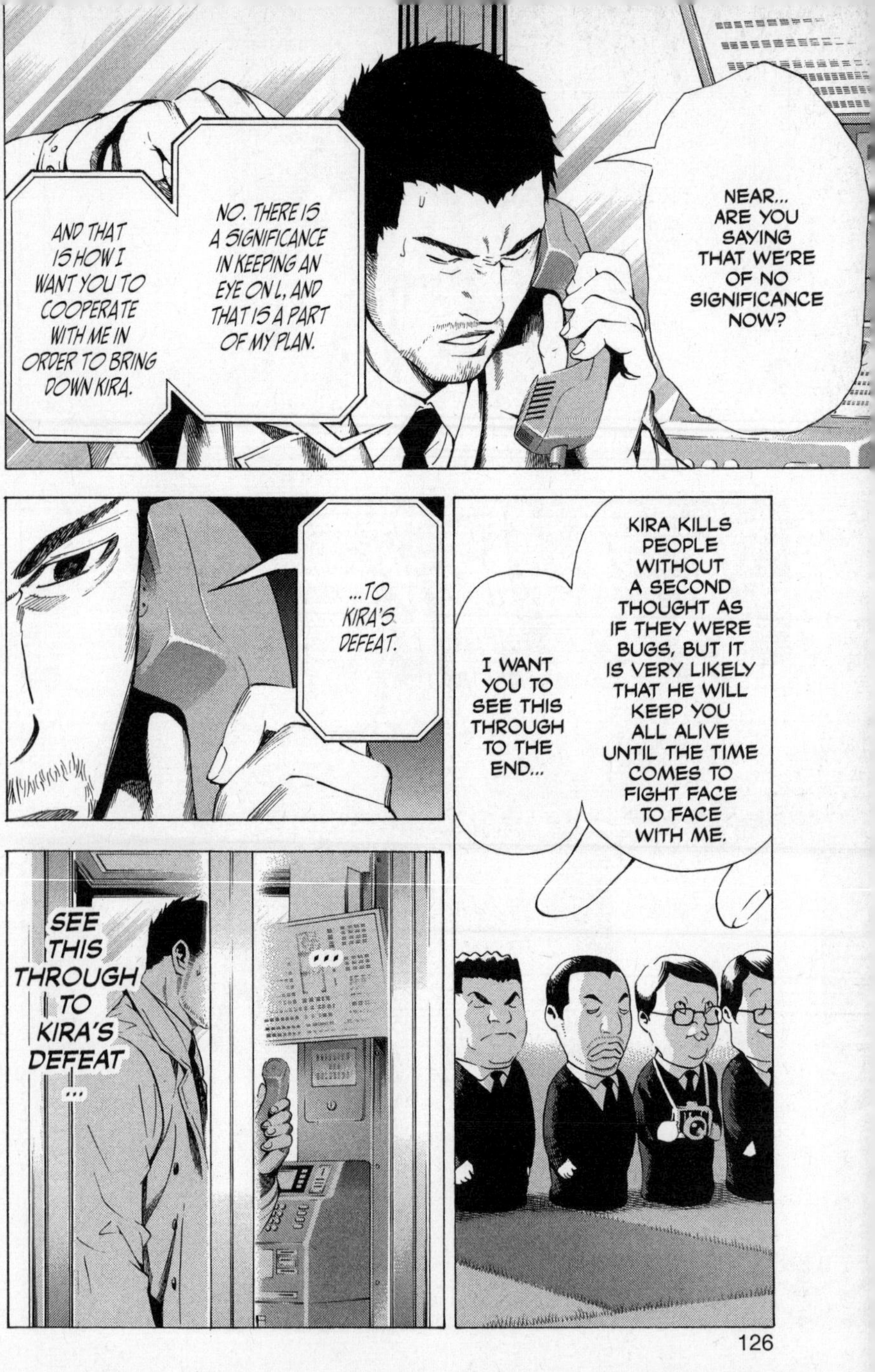
NEAR... ARE YOU SAYING THAT WE'RE OF NO SIGNIFICANCE NOW?
NO. THERE IS A SIGNIFICANCE IN KEEPING AN EYE ON L, AND THAT IS A PART OF MY PLAN.
AND THAT IS HOW I WANT YOU TO COOPERATE WITH ME IN ORDER TO BRING DOWN KIRA.
KIRA KILLS PEOPLE WITHOUT A SECOND THOUGHT AS IF THEY WERE BUGS, BUT IT IS VERY LIKELY THAT HE WILL KEEP YOU ALL ALIVE UNTIL THE TIME COMES TO FIGHT FACE TO FACE WITH ME.
I WANT YOU TO SEE THIS THROUGH TO THE END...
...TO KIRA'S DEFEAT.
...
SEE THIS THROUGH TO KIRA'S DEFEAT...

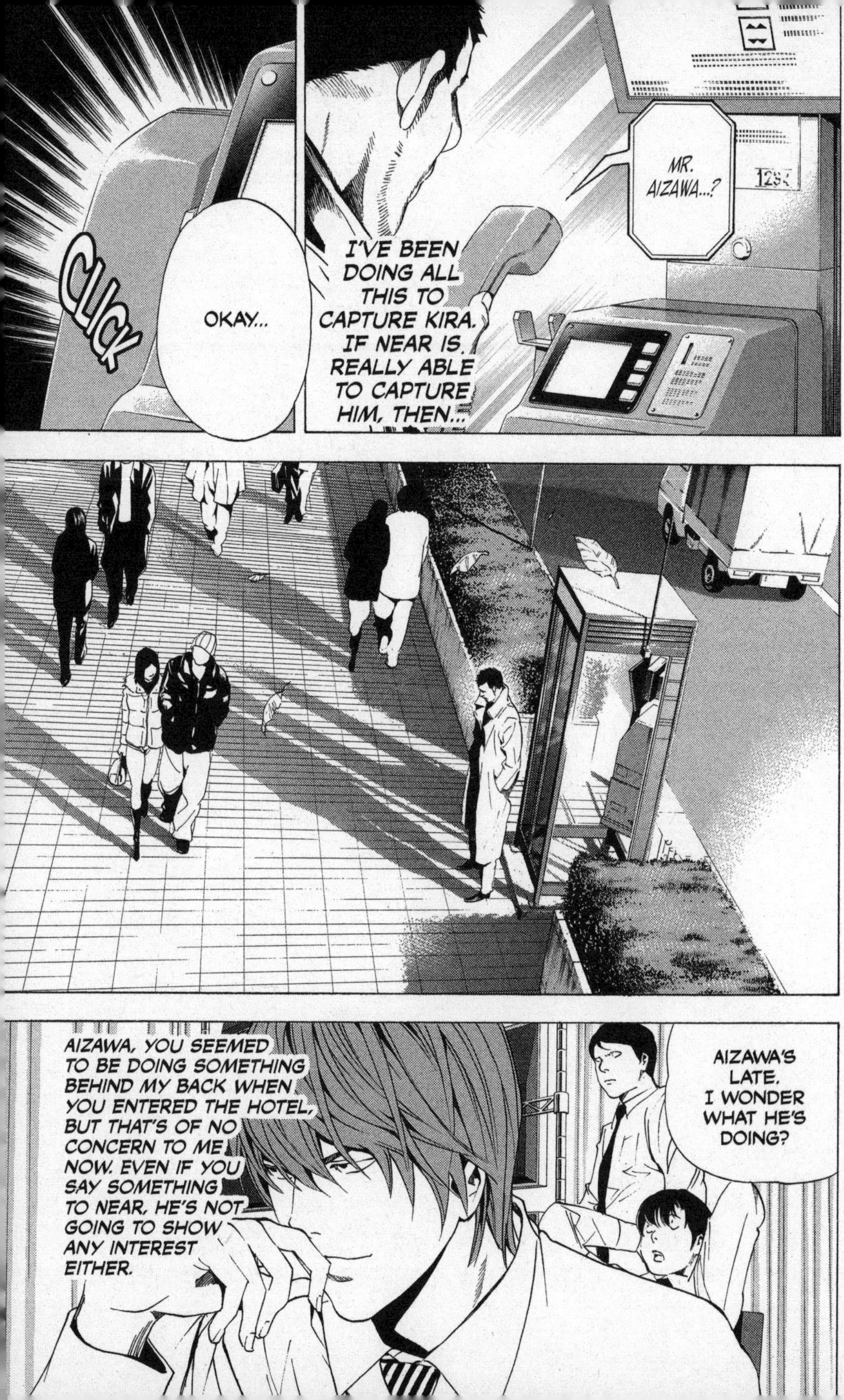
MR. AIZAWA...?
I'VE BEEN DOING ALL THIS TO CAPTURE KIRA. IF NEAR IS REALLY ABLE TO CAPTURE HIM, THEN...
OKAY...
CLICK
AIZAWA'S LATE. I WONDER WHAT HE'S DOING?
AIZAWA, YOU SEEMED TO BE DOING SOMETHING BEHIND MY BACK WHEN YOU ENTERED THE HOTEL, BUT THAT'S OF NO CONCERN TO ME NOW. EVEN IF YOU SAY SOMETHING TO NEAR, HE'S NOT GOING TO SHOW ANY INTEREST EITHER.

DEATH NOTE
How to use it
LXIII

⊙ No matter what medical or scientific method may be employed, it is impossible for humans to distinguish whether or not the human has the eye power of a god of death. Even gods of death cannot distinguish this fact, except for the very god of death that traded his/her eye power with that human.

死神の眼球を持った人間の判別は、
人間界のどんな医学や科学をもってしてもできないし、
死神でもその人間と直接眼球の取引をした死神にしかわからない。

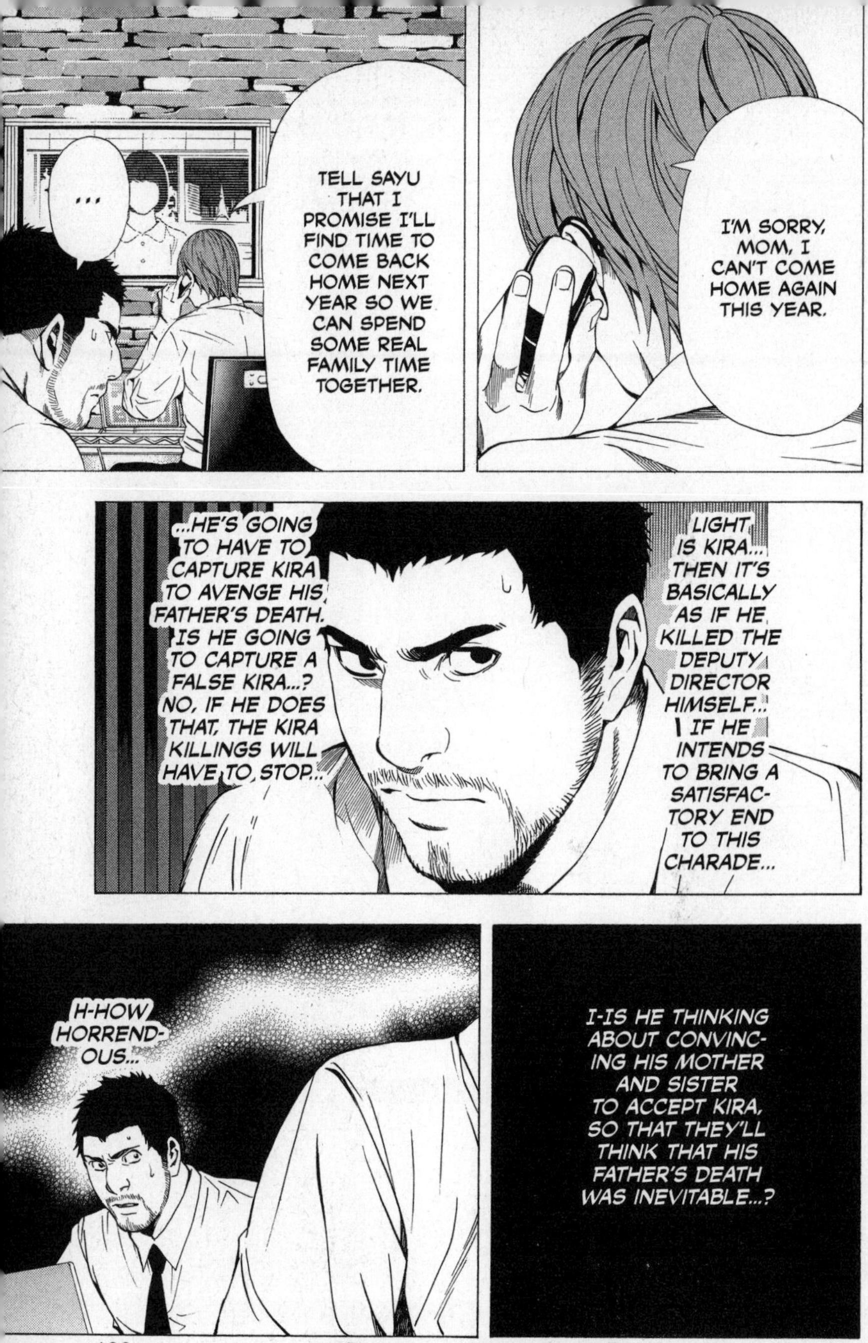
I'M SORRY, MOM, I CAN'T COME HOME AGAIN THIS YEAR.
TELL SAYU THAT I PROMISE I'LL FIND TIME TO COME BACK HOME NEXT YEAR SO WE CAN SPEND SOME REAL FAMILY TIME TOGETHER.
...
LIGHT IS KIRA... THEN IT'S BASICALLY AS IF HE KILLED THE DEPUTY DIRECTOR HIMSELF... IF HE INTENDS TO BRING A SATISFACTORY END TO THIS CHARADE...
...HE'S GOING TO HAVE TO CAPTURE KIRA TO AVENGE HIS FATHER'S DEATH. IS HE GOING TO CAPTURE A FALSE KIRA...? NO, IF HE DOES THAT, THE KIRA KILLINGS WILL HAVE TO STOP...
I-IS HE THINKING ABOUT CONVINCING HIS MOTHER AND SISTER TO ACCEPT KIRA, SO THAT THEY'LL THINK THAT HIS FATHER'S DEATH WAS INEVITABLE...?
H-HOW HORRENDOUS...

chapter 95 Convinced

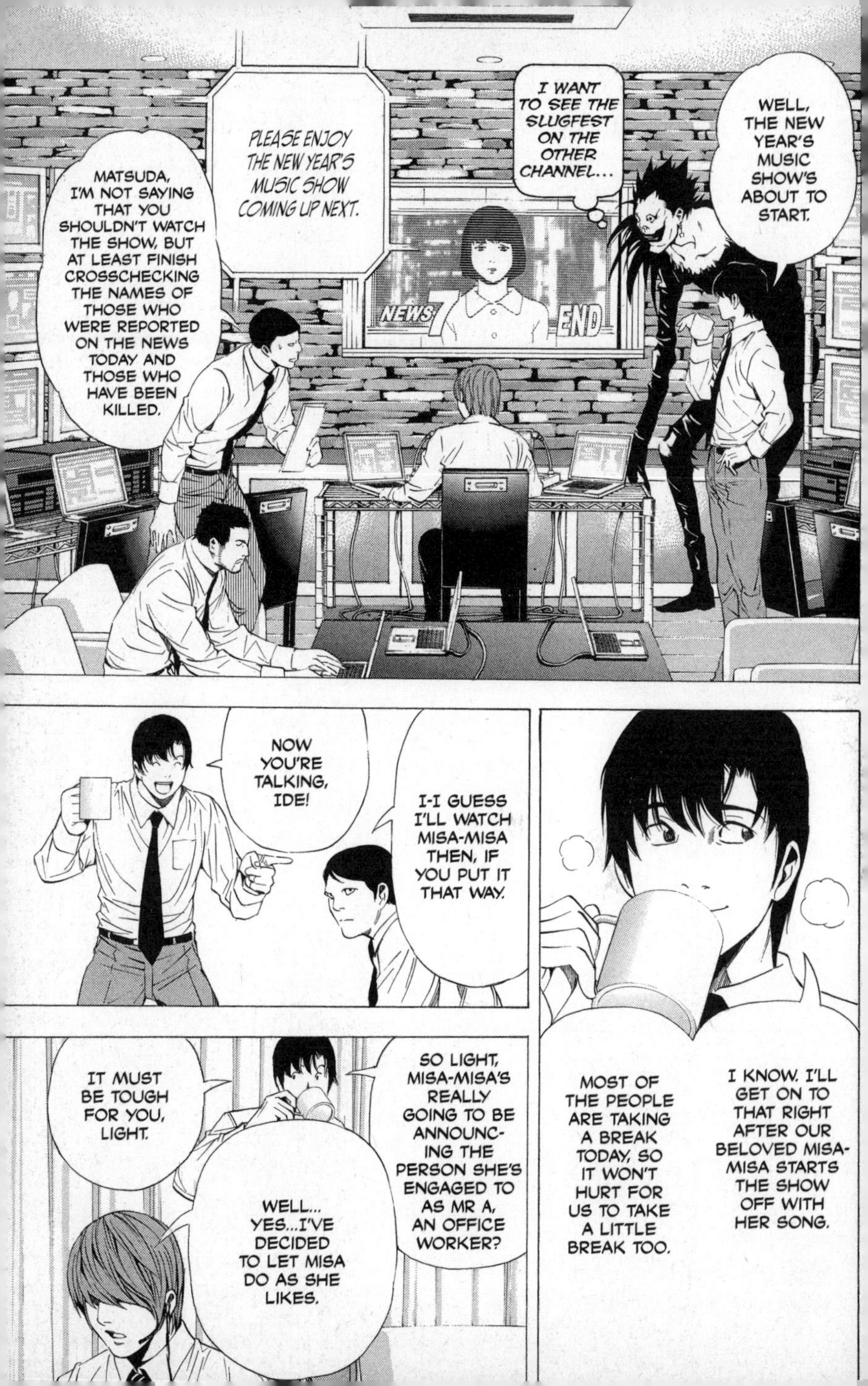
WELL, THE NEW YEAR'S MUSIC SHOW'S ABOUT TO START.
I WANT TO SEE THE SLUGFEST ON THE OTHER CHANNEL...
PLEASE ENJOY THE NEW YEAR'S MUSIC SHOW COMING UP NEXT.
NEWS 7 END
MATSUDA, I'M NOT SAYING THAT YOU SHOULDN'T WATCH THE SHOW, BUT AT LEAST FINISH CROSSCHECKING THE NAMES OF THOSE WHO WERE REPORTED ON THE NEWS TODAY AND THOSE WHO HAVE BEEN KILLED.
I KNOW. I'LL GET ON TO THAT RIGHT AFTER OUR BELOVED MISA-MISA STARTS THE SHOW OFF WITH HER SONG.
MOST OF THE PEOPLE ARE TAKING A BREAK TODAY, SO IT WON'T HURT FOR US TO TAKE A LITTLE BREAK TOO.
I-I GUESS I'LL WATCH MISA-MISA THEN, IF YOU PUT IT THAT WAY.
NOW YOU'RE TALKING, IDE!
SO LIGHT, MISA-MISA'S REALLY GOING TO BE ANNOUNCING THE PERSON SHE'S ENGAGED TO AS MR A, AN OFFICE WORKER?
IT MUST BE TOUGH FOR YOU, LIGHT.
WELL... YES...I'VE DECIDED TO LET MISA DO AS SHE LIKES.

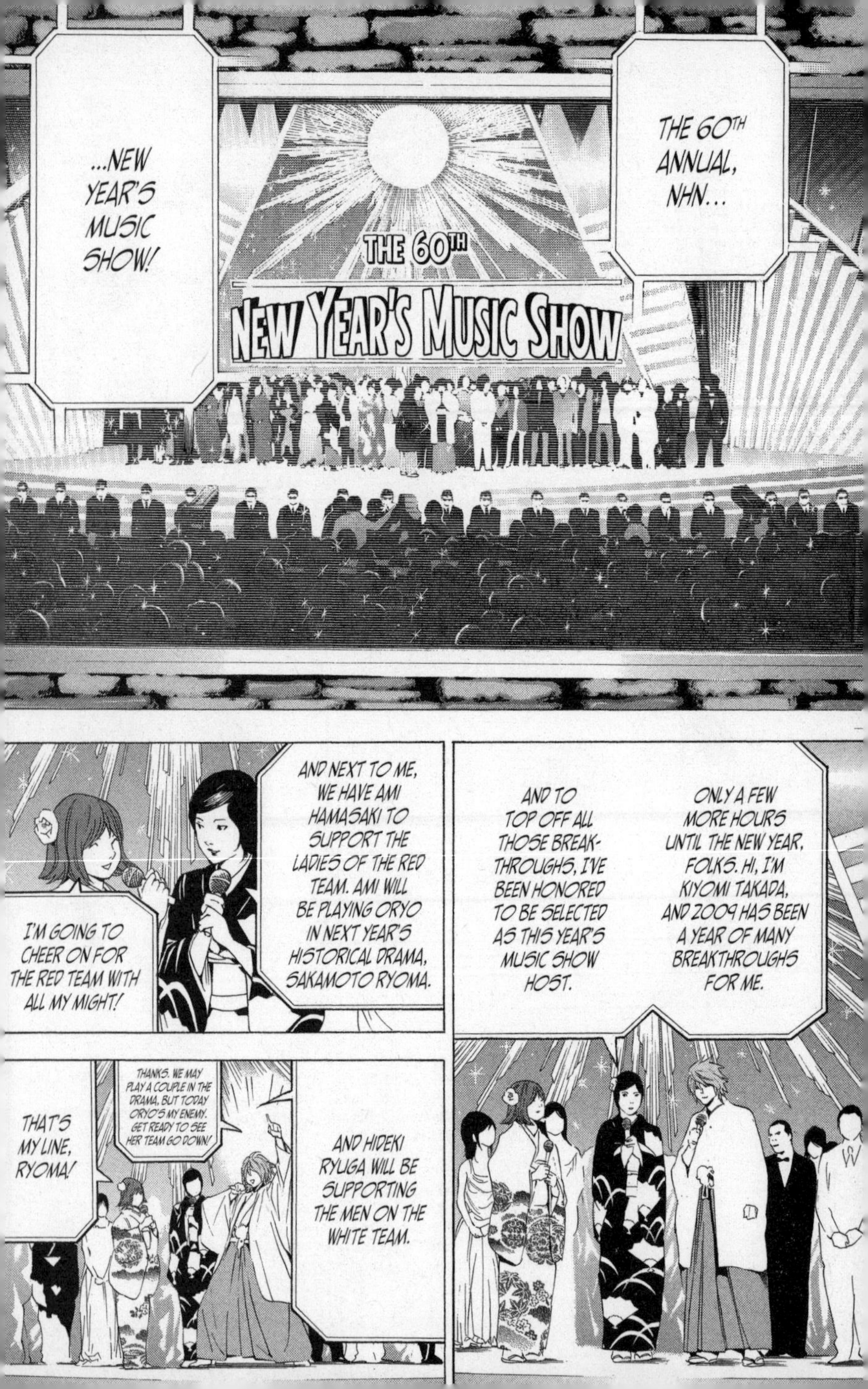
THE 60TH ANNUAL, NHN...
THE 60TH
NEW YEAR'S MUSIC SHOW
...NEW YEAR'S MUSIC SHOW!
ONLY A FEW MORE HOURS UNTIL THE NEW YEAR, FOLKS. HI, I'M KIYOMI TAKADA, AND 2009 HAS BEEN A YEAR OF MANY BREAKTHROUGHS FOR ME.
AND TO TOP OFF ALL THOSE BREAKTHROUGHS, I'VE BEEN HONORED TO BE SELECTED AS THIS YEAR'S MUSIC SHOW HOST.
AND NEXT TO ME, WE HAVE AMI HAMASAKI TO SUPPORT THE LADIES OF THE RED TEAM. AMI WILL BE PLAYING ORYO IN NEXT YEAR'S HISTORICAL DRAMA, SAKAMOTO RYOMA.
I'M GOING TO CHEER ON FOR THE RED TEAM WITH ALL MY MIGHT!
AND HIDEKI RYUGA WILL BE SUPPORTING THE MEN ON THE WHITE TEAM.
THANKS. WE MAY PLAY A COUPLE IN THE DRAMA, BUT TODAY ORYO'S MY ENEMY. GET READY TO SEE HER TEAM GO DOWN!
THAT'S MY LINE, RYOMA!

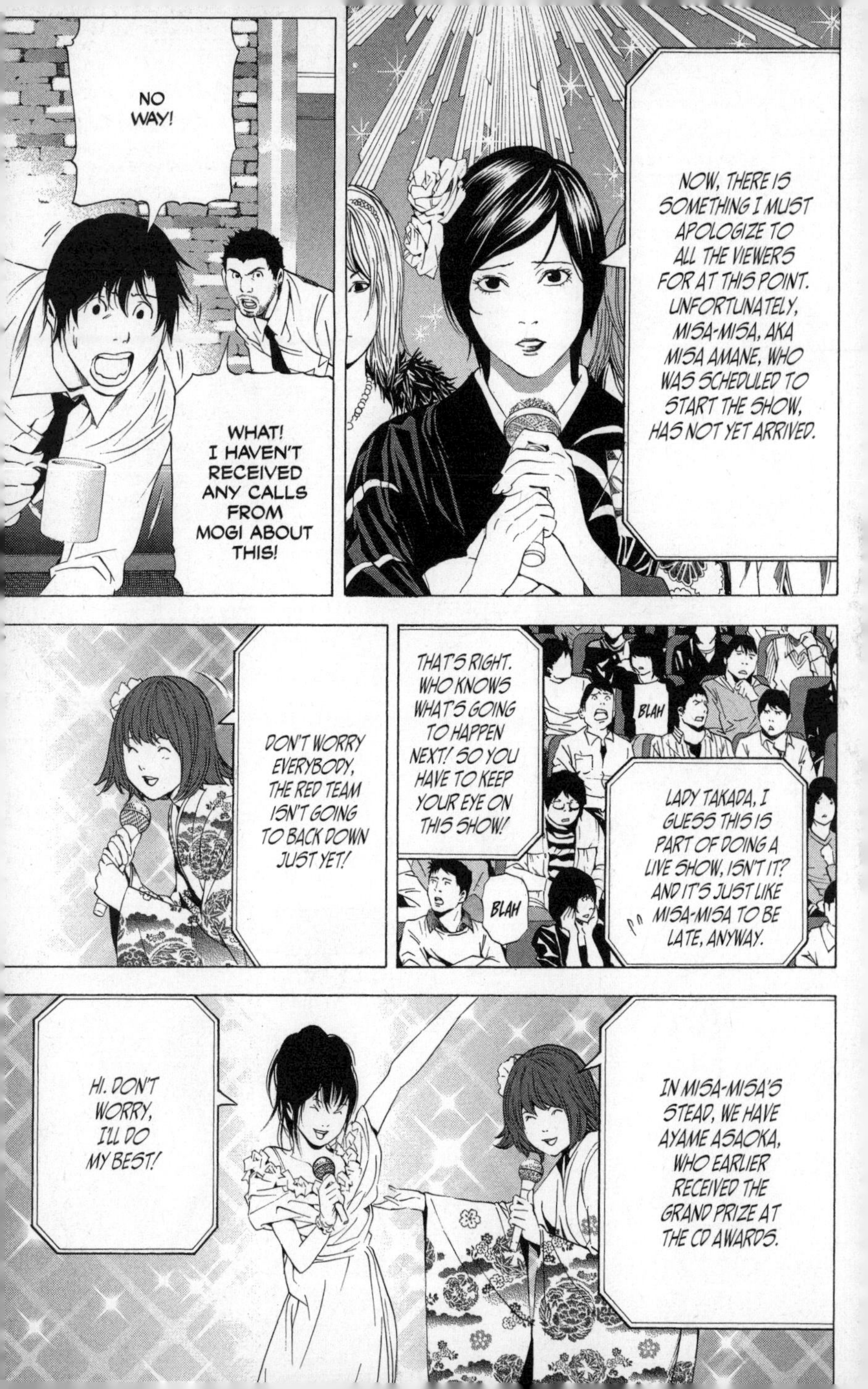
NOW, THERE IS SOMETHING I MUST APOLOGIZE TO ALL THE VIEWERS FOR AT THIS POINT. UNFORTUNATELY, MISA-MISA, AKA MISA AMANE, WHO WAS SCHEDULED TO START THE SHOW, HAS NOT YET ARRIVED.
NO WAY!
WHAT! I HAVEN'T RECEIVED ANY CALLS FROM MOGI ABOUT THIS!
THAT'S RIGHT. WHO KNOWS WHAT'S GOING TO HAPPEN NEXT! SO YOU HAVE TO KEEP YOUR EYE ON THIS SHOW!
BLAH
LADY TAKADA, I GUESS THIS IS PART OF DOING A LIVE SHOW, ISN'T IT? AND IT'S JUST LIKE MISA-MISA TO BE LATE, ANYWAY.
BLAH
DON'T WORRY EVERYBODY, THE RED TEAM ISN'T GOING TO BACK DOWN JUST YET!
IN MISA-MISA'S STEAD, WE HAVE AYAME ASAOKA, WHO EARLIER RECEIVED THE GRAND PRIZE AT THE CD AWARDS.
HI. DON'T WORRY, I'LL DO MY BEST!

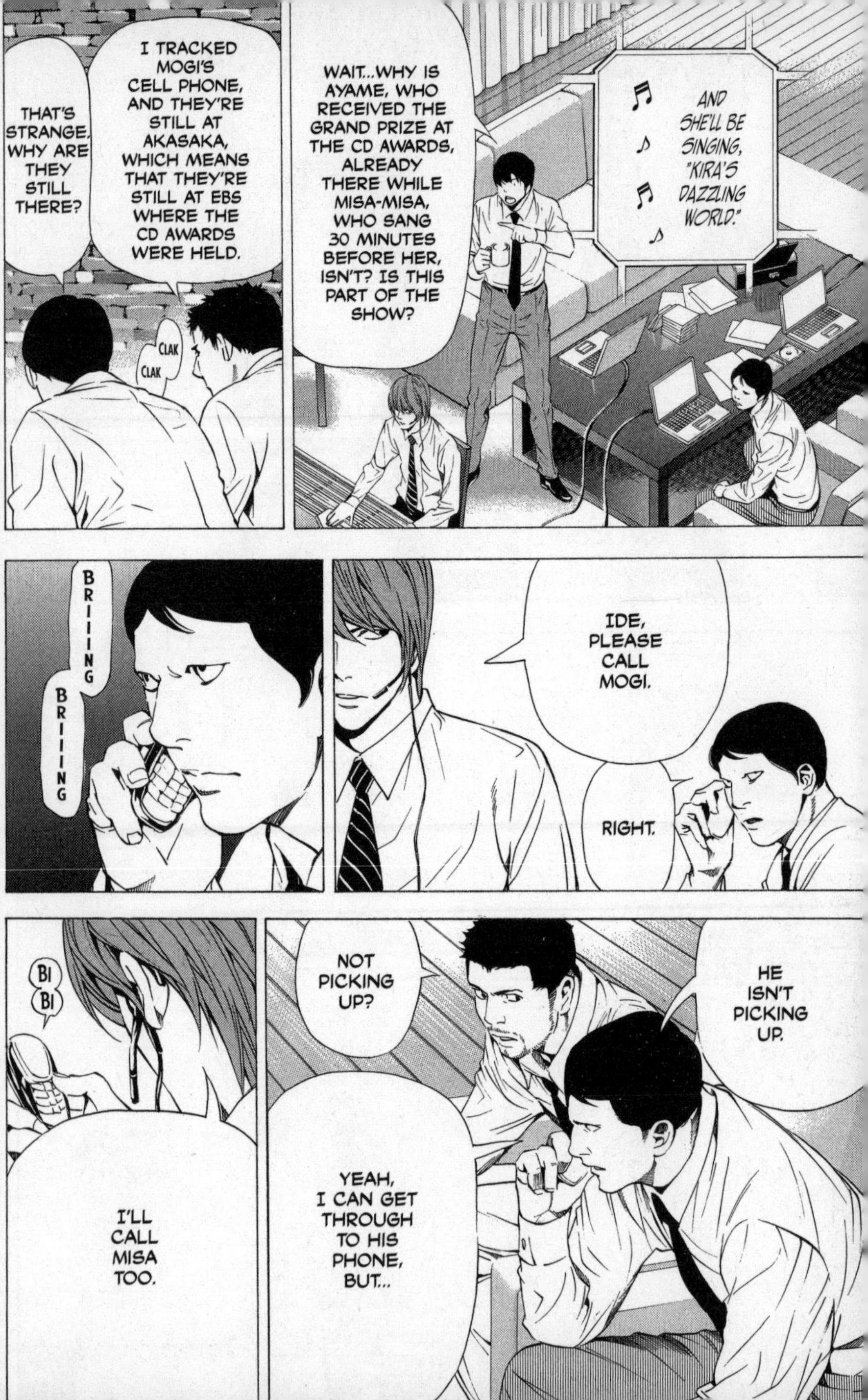
AND SHE'LL BE SINGING, "KIRA'S DAZZLING WORLD."
WAIT...WHY IS AYAME, WHO RECEIVED THE GRAND PRIZE AT THE CD AWARDS, ALREADY THERE WHILE MISA-MISA, WHO SANG 30 MINUTES BEFORE HER, ISN'T? IS THIS PART OF THE SHOW?
I TRACKED MOGI'S CELL PHONE, AND THEY'RE STILL AT AKASAKA, WHICH MEANS THAT THEY'RE STILL AT EBS WHERE THE CD AWARDS WERE HELD.
THAT'S STRANGE, WHY ARE THEY STILL THERE?
CLAK
CLAK
IDE, PLEASE CALL MOGI.
RIGHT.
BRIIING
BRIIING
HE ISN'T PICKING UP.
NOT PICKING UP?
YEAH, I CAN GET THROUGH TO HIS PHONE, BUT...
BI
BI
I'LL CALL MISA TOO.

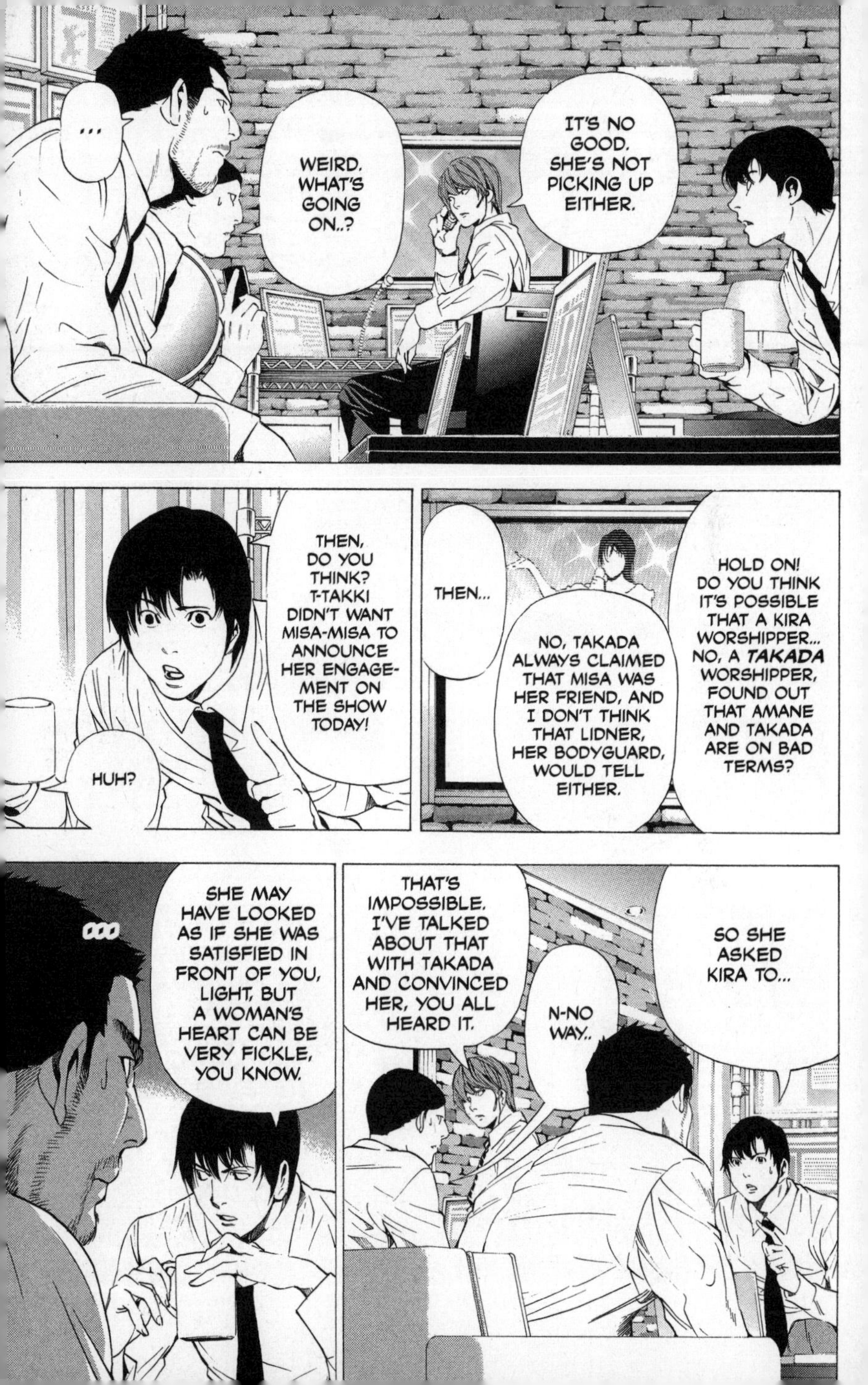
IT'S NO GOOD. SHE'S NOT PICKING UP EITHER.
WEIRD. WHAT'S GOING ON..?
...
HOLD ON! DO YOU THINK IT'S POSSIBLE THAT A KIRA WORSHIPPER... NO, A *TAKADA* WORSHIPPER, FOUND OUT THAT AMANE AND TAKADA ARE ON BAD TERMS?
NO, TAKADA ALWAYS CLAIMED THAT MISA WAS HER FRIEND, AND I DON'T THINK THAT LIDNER, HER BODYGUARD, WOULD TELL EITHER.
THEN...
THEN, DO YOU THINK? T-TAKKI DIDN'T WANT MISA-MISA TO ANNOUNCE HER ENGAGEMENT ON THE SHOW TODAY!
HUH?
SO SHE ASKED KIRA TO...
N-NO WAY..
THAT'S IMPOSSIBLE. I'VE TALKED ABOUT THAT WITH TAKADA AND CONVINCED HER, YOU ALL HEARD IT.
SHE MAY HAVE LOOKED AS IF SHE WAS SATISFIED IN FRONT OF YOU, LIGHT, BUT A WOMAN'S HEART CAN BE VERY FICKLE, YOU KNOW.

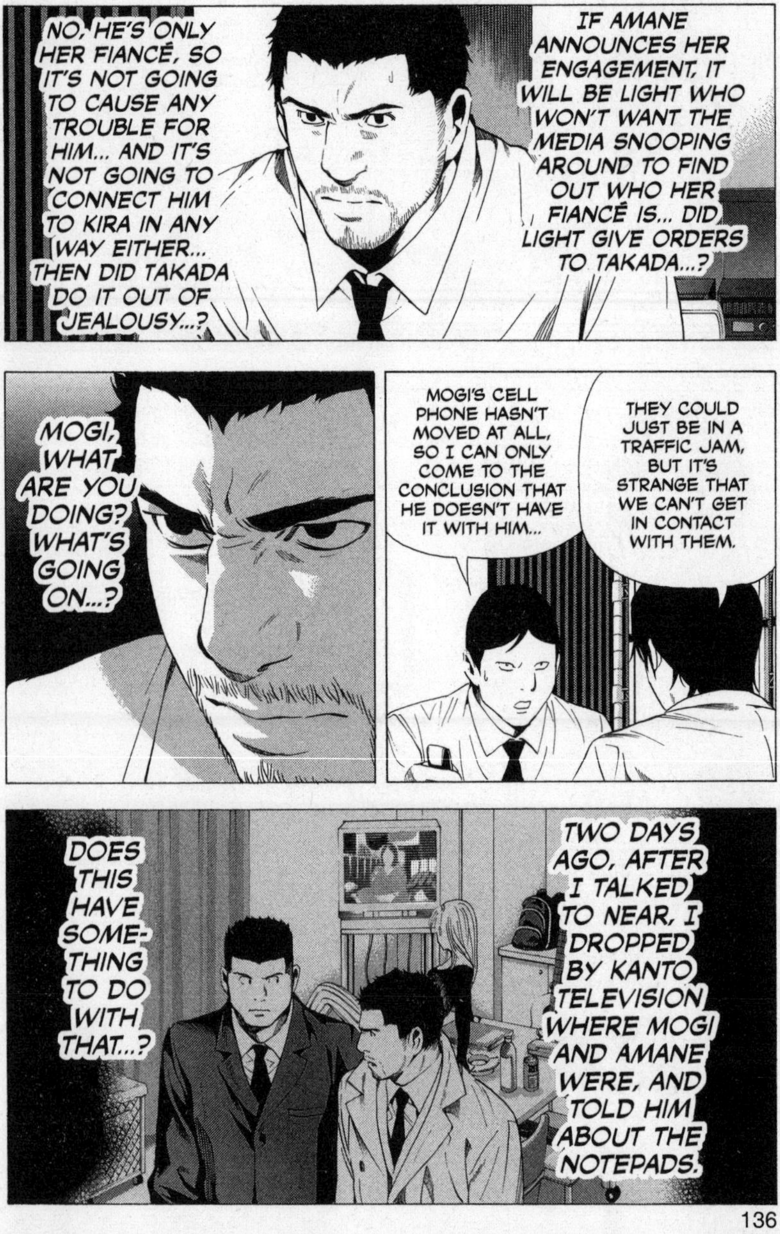
IF AMANE ANNOUNCES HER ENGAGEMENT, IT WILL BE LIGHT WHO WON'T WANT THE MEDIA SNOOPING AROUND TO FIND OUT WHO HER FIANCÉ IS... DID LIGHT GIVE ORDERS TO TAKADA...?
NO, HE'S ONLY HER FIANCÉ, SO IT'S NOT GOING TO CAUSE ANY TROUBLE FOR HIM... AND IT'S NOT GOING TO CONNECT HIM TO KIRA IN ANY WAY EITHER... THEN DID TAKADA DO IT OUT OF JEALOUSY...?
THEY COULD JUST BE IN A TRAFFIC JAM, BUT IT'S STRANGE THAT WE CAN'T GET IN CONTACT WITH THEM.
MOGI'S CELL PHONE HASN'T MOVED AT ALL, SO I CAN ONLY COME TO THE CONCLUSION THAT HE DOESN'T HAVE IT WITH HIM...
MOGI, WHAT ARE YOU DOING? WHAT'S GOING ON...?
TWO DAYS AGO, AFTER I TALKED TO NEAR, I DROPPED BY KANTO TELEVISION WHERE MOGI AND AMANE WERE, AND TOLD HIM ABOUT THE NOTEPADS.
DOES THIS HAVE SOME-THING TO DO WITH THAT...?

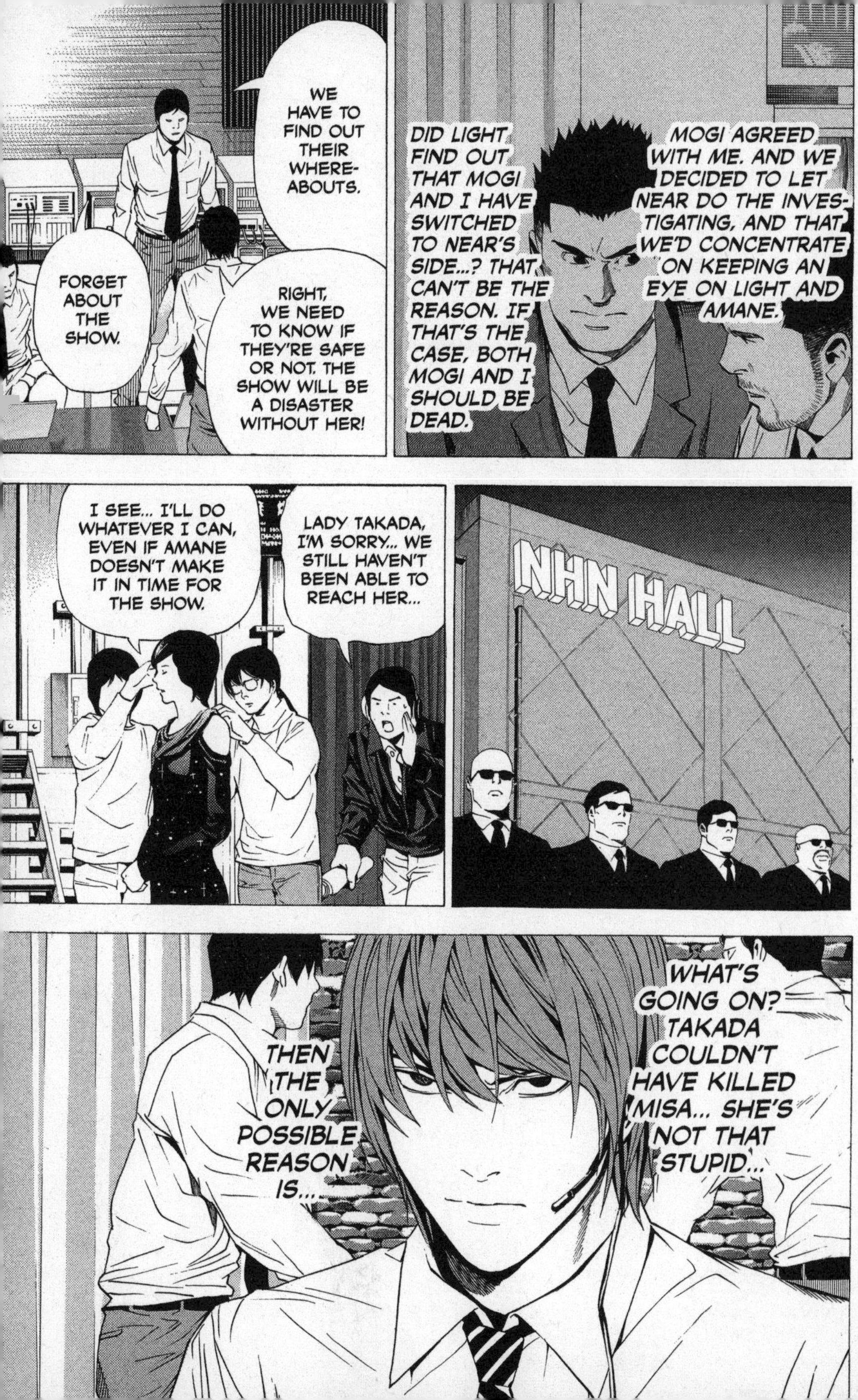
MOGI AGREED WITH ME. AND WE DECIDED TO LET NEAR DO THE INVESTIGATING, AND THAT WE'D CONCENTRATE ON KEEPING AN EYE ON LIGHT AND AMANE.
DID LIGHT FIND OUT THAT MOGI AND I HAVE SWITCHED TO NEAR'S SIDE...? THAT CAN'T BE THE REASON. IF THAT'S THE CASE, BOTH MOGI AND I SHOULD BE DEAD.
WE HAVE TO FIND OUT THEIR WHEREABOUTS.
FORGET ABOUT THE SHOW.
RIGHT, WE NEED TO KNOW IF THEY'RE SAFE OR NOT. THE SHOW WILL BE A DISASTER WITHOUT HER!
NHN HALL
LADY TAKADA, I'M SORRY... WE STILL HAVEN'T BEEN ABLE TO REACH HER...
I SEE... I'LL DO WHATEVER I CAN, EVEN IF AMANE DOESN'T MAKE IT IN TIME FOR THE SHOW.
WHAT'S GOING ON? TAKADA COULDN'T HAVE KILLED MISA... SHE'S NOT THAT STUPID...
THEN THE ONLY POSSIBLE REASON IS...

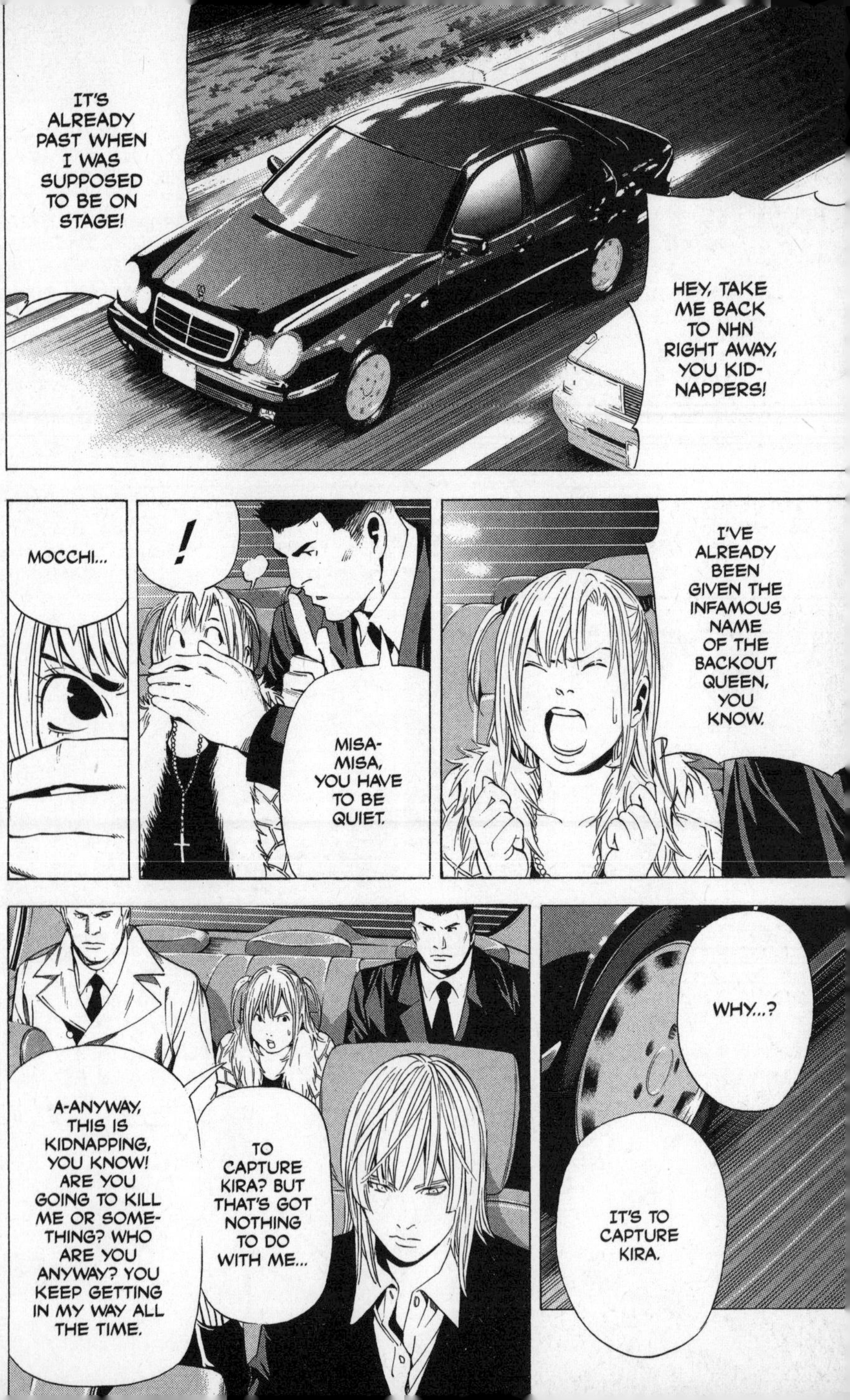
IT'S ALREADY PAST WHEN I WAS SUPPOSED TO BE ON STAGE!
HEY, TAKE ME BACK TO NHN RIGHT AWAY, YOU KID-NAPPERS!
I'VE ALREADY BEEN GIVEN THE INFAMOUS NAME OF THE BACKOUT QUEEN, YOU KNOW.
!
MISA-MISA, YOU HAVE TO BE QUIET.
MOCCHI...
WHY...?
IT'S TO CAPTURE KIRA.
TO CAPTURE KIRA? BUT THAT'S GOT NOTHING TO DO WITH ME...
A-ANYWAY, THIS IS KIDNAPPING, YOU KNOW! ARE YOU GOING TO KILL ME OR SOME-THING? WHO ARE YOU ANYWAY? YOU KEEP GETTING IN MY WAY ALL THE TIME.

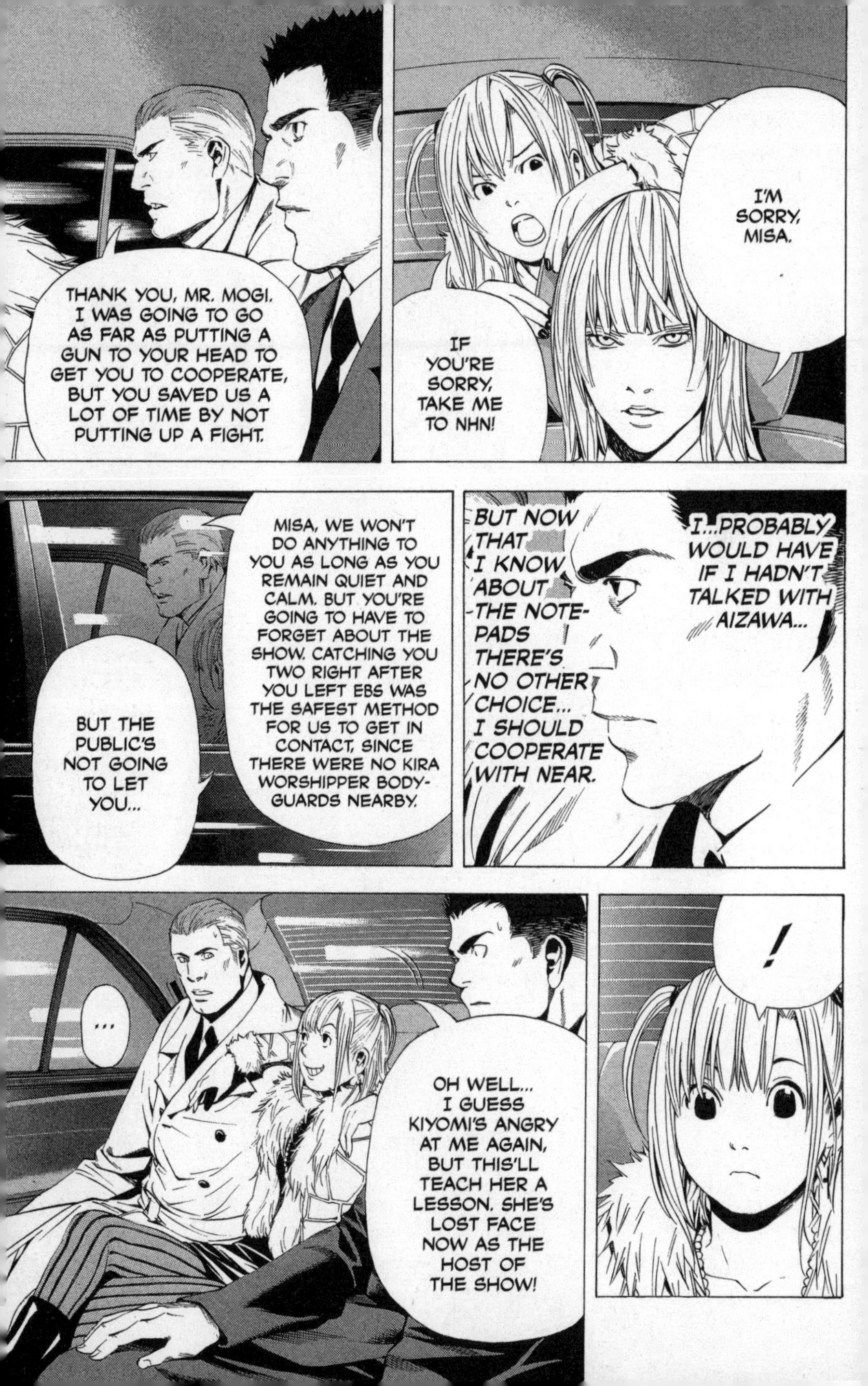
I'M SORRY, MISA.
IF YOU'RE SORRY, TAKE ME TO NHN!
THANK YOU, MR. MOGI. I WAS GOING TO GO AS FAR AS PUTTING A GUN TO YOUR HEAD TO GET YOU TO COOPERATE, BUT YOU SAVED US A LOT OF TIME BY NOT PUTTING UP A FIGHT.
I...PROBABLY WOULD HAVE IF I HADN'T TALKED WITH AIZAWA...
BUT NOW THAT I KNOW ABOUT THE NOTE-PADS THERE'S NO OTHER CHOICE... I SHOULD COOPERATE WITH NEAR.
MISA, WE WON'T DO ANYTHING TO YOU AS LONG AS YOU REMAIN QUIET AND CALM. BUT YOU'RE GOING TO HAVE TO FORGET ABOUT THE SHOW. CATCHING YOU TWO RIGHT AFTER YOU LEFT EBS WAS THE SAFEST METHOD FOR US TO GET IN CONTACT, SINCE THERE WERE NO KIRA WORSHIPPER BODY-GUARDS NEARBY.
BUT THE PUBLIC'S NOT GOING TO LET YOU...
!
OH WELL... I GUESS KIYOMI'S ANGRY AT ME AGAIN, BUT THIS'LL TEACH HER A LESSON. SHE'S LOST FACE NOW AS THE HOST OF THE SHOW!
...

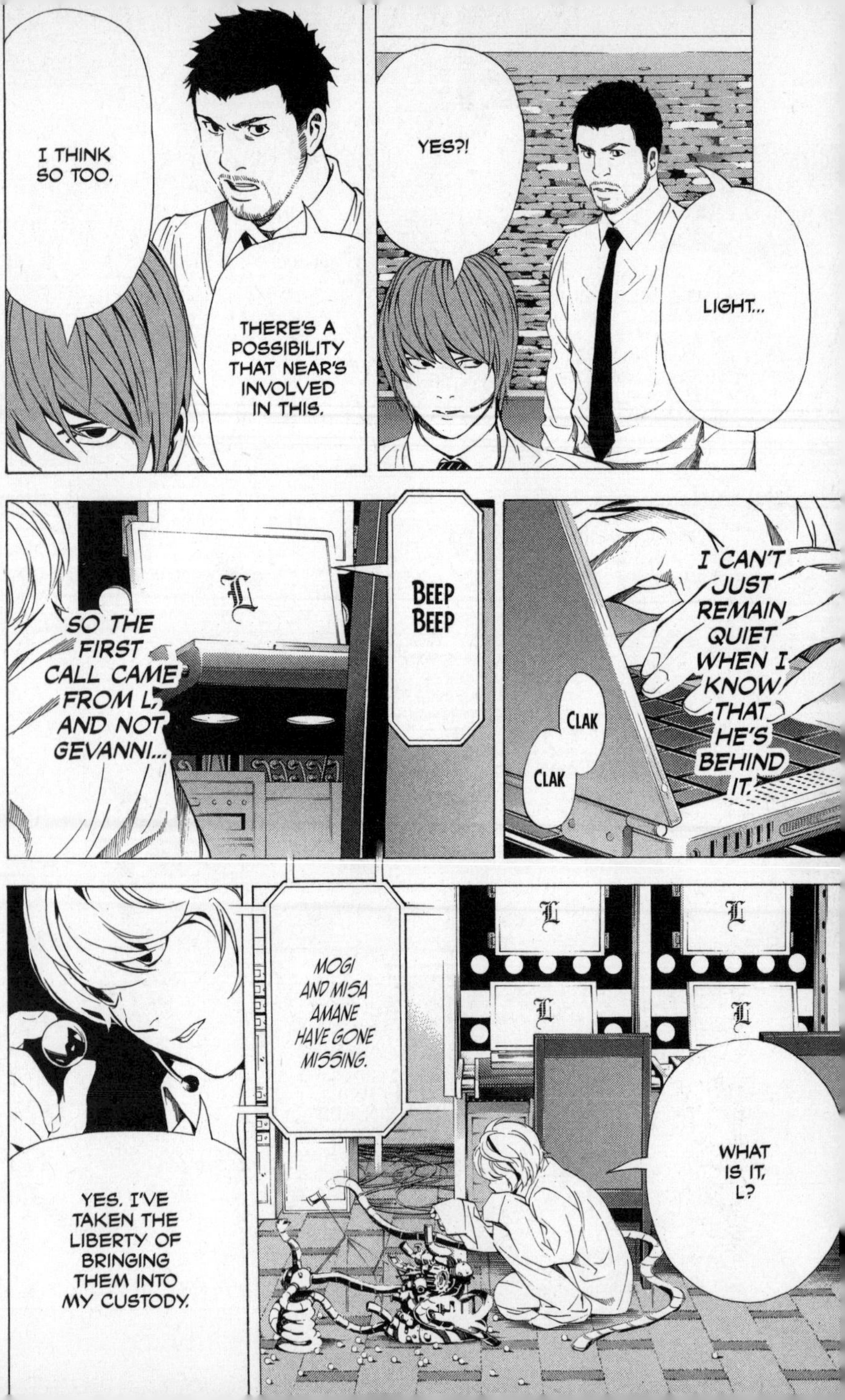
LIGHT...
YES?!
THERE'S A POSSIBILITY THAT NEAR'S INVOLVED IN THIS.
I THINK SO TOO.
I CAN'T JUST REMAIN QUIET WHEN I KNOW THAT HE'S BEHIND IT.
CLAK
CLAK
BEEP BEEP
SO THE FIRST CALL CAME FROM L, AND NOT GEVANNI...
WHAT IS IT, L?
MOGI AND MISA AMANE HAVE GONE MISSING.
YES. I'VE TAKEN THE LIBERTY OF BRINGING THEM INTO MY CUSTODY.

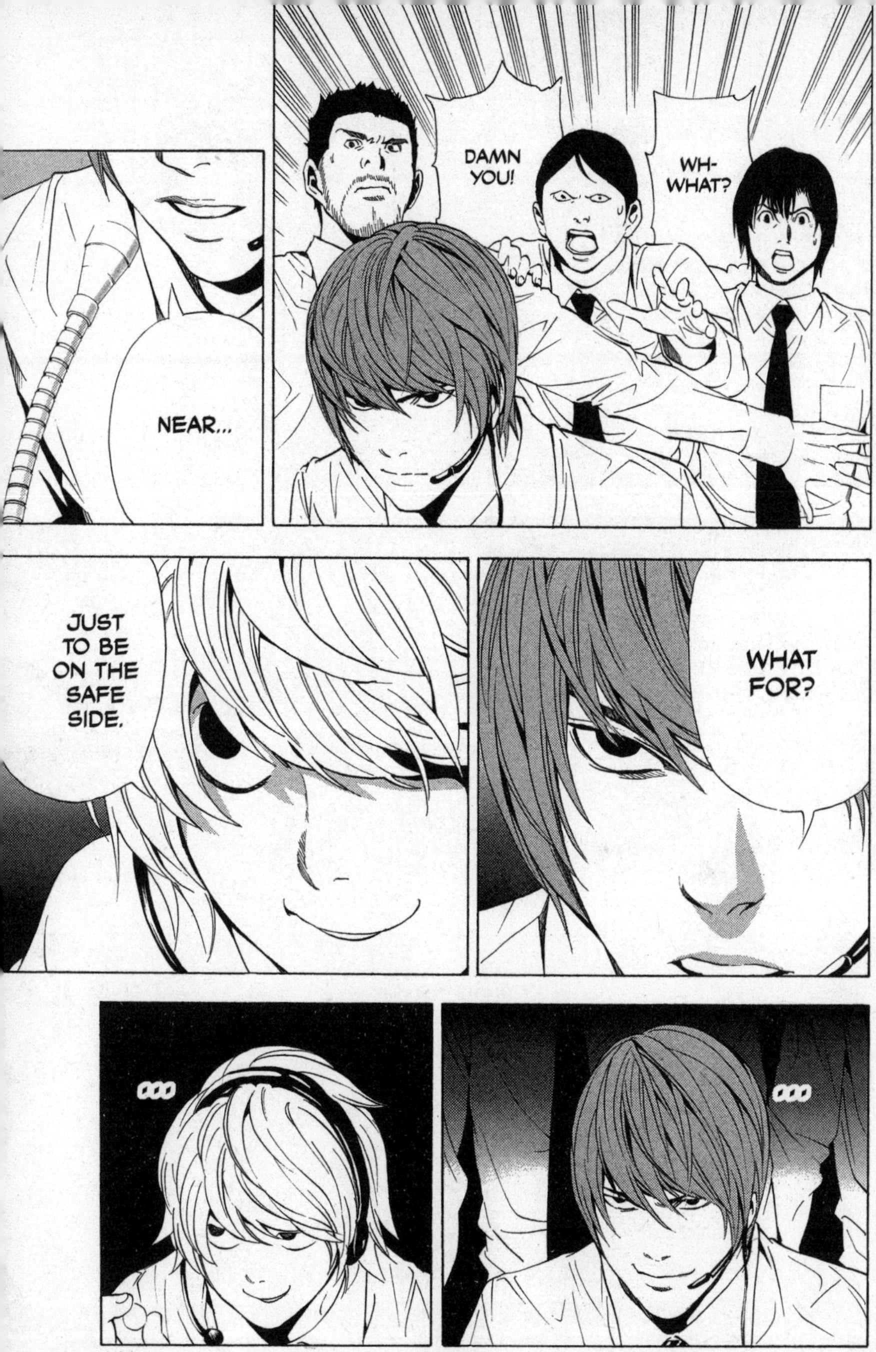
WH- WHAT?
DAMN YOU!
NEAR...
WHAT FOR?
JUST TO BE ON THE SAFE SIDE.
...
...

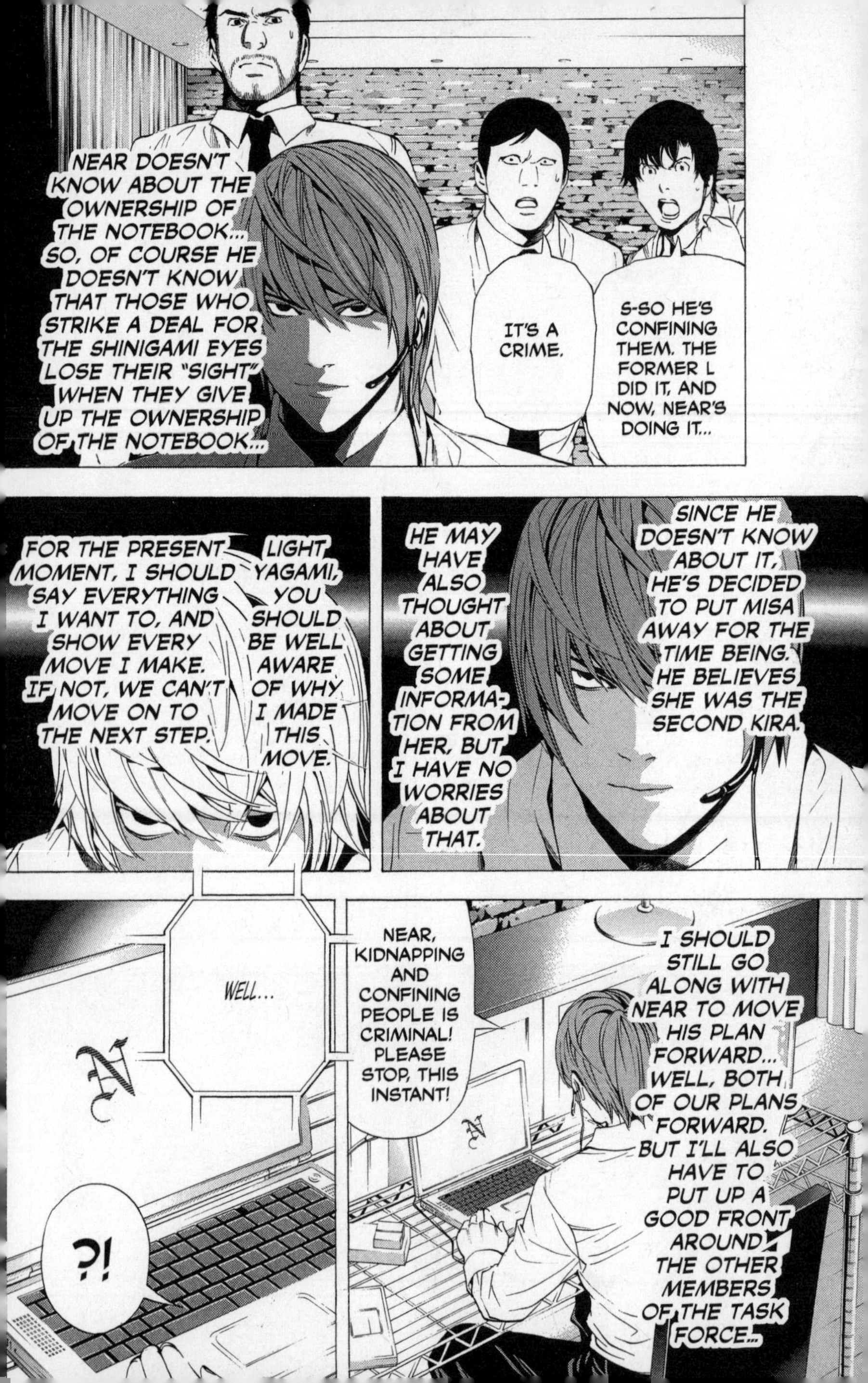
S-SO HE'S CONFINING THEM. THE FORMER L DID IT, AND NOW, NEAR'S DOING IT...
IT'S A CRIME.
NEAR DOESN'T KNOW ABOUT THE OWNERSHIP OF THE NOTEBOOK... SO, OF COURSE HE DOESN'T KNOW THAT THOSE WHO STRIKE A DEAL FOR THE SHINIGAMI EYES LOSE THEIR "SIGHT" WHEN THEY GIVE UP THE OWNERSHIP OF THE NOTEBOOK...
SINCE HE DOESN'T KNOW ABOUT IT, HE'S DECIDED TO PUT MISA AWAY FOR THE TIME BEING. HE BELIEVES SHE WAS THE SECOND KIRA.
HE MAY HAVE ALSO THOUGHT ABOUT GETTING SOME INFORMATION FROM HER, BUT I HAVE NO WORRIES ABOUT THAT.
LIGHT YAGAMI, YOU SHOULD BE WELL AWARE OF WHY I MADE THIS MOVE.
FOR THE PRESENT MOMENT, I SHOULD SAY EVERYTHING I WANT TO, AND SHOW EVERY MOVE I MAKE. IF NOT, WE CAN'T MOVE ON TO THE NEXT STEP.
I SHOULD STILL GO ALONG WITH NEAR TO MOVE HIS PLAN FORWARD... WELL, BOTH OF OUR PLANS FORWARD. BUT I'LL ALSO HAVE TO PUT UP A GOOD FRONT AROUND THE OTHER MEMBERS OF THE TASK FORCE...
NEAR, KIDNAPPING AND CONFINING PEOPLE IS CRIMINAL! PLEASE STOP, THIS INSTANT!
WELL...
?!

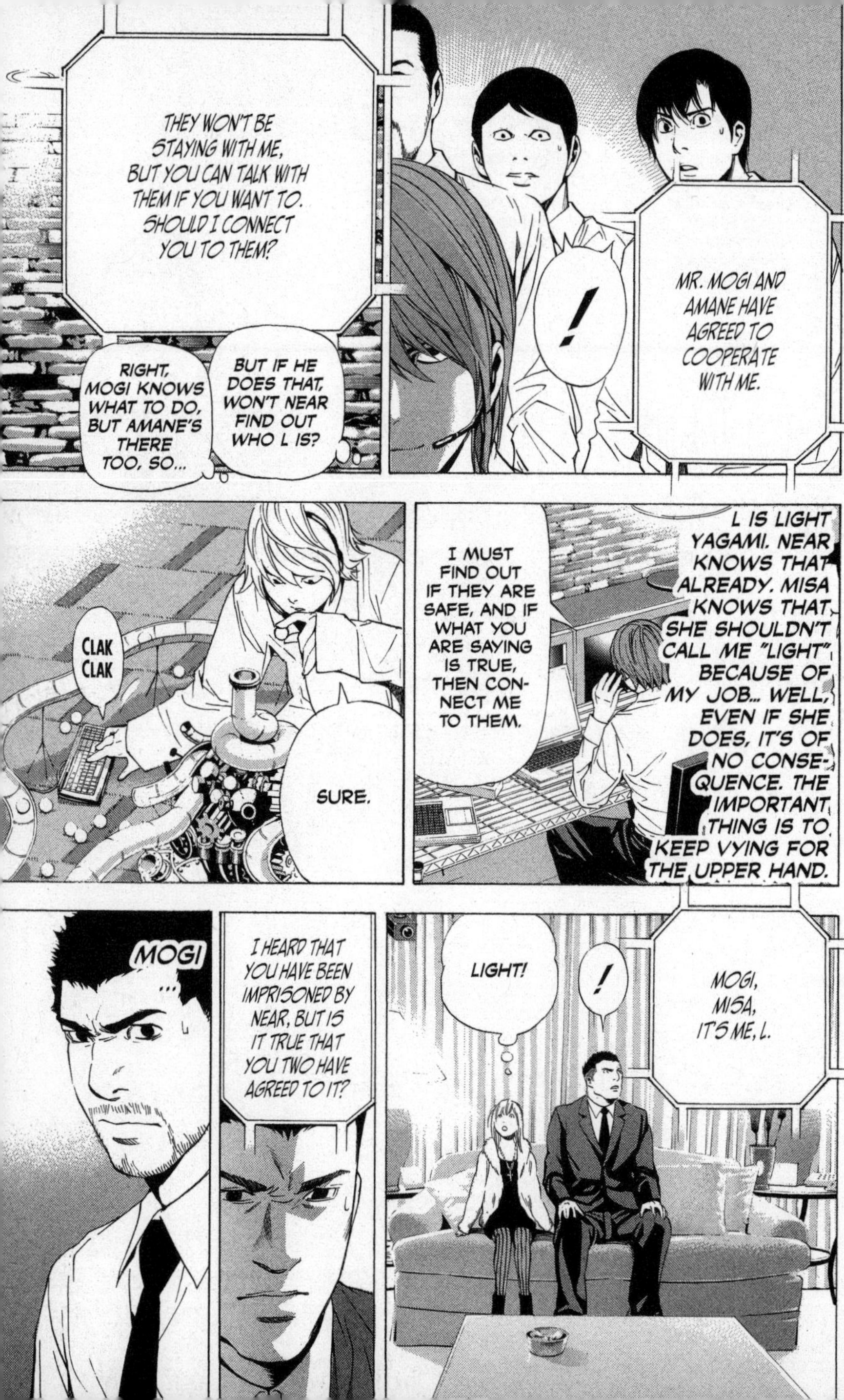
MR. MOGI AND AMANE HAVE AGREED TO COOPERATE WITH ME.
!
THEY WON'T BE STAYING WITH ME, BUT YOU CAN TALK WITH THEM IF YOU WANT TO. SHOULD I CONNECT YOU TO THEM?
BUT IF HE DOES THAT, WON'T NEAR FIND OUT WHO L IS?
RIGHT, MOGI KNOWS WHAT TO DO, BUT AMANE'S THERE TOO, SO...
L IS LIGHT YAGAMI. NEAR KNOWS THAT ALREADY. MISA KNOWS THAT SHE SHOULDN'T CALL ME "LIGHT" BECAUSE OF MY JOB... WELL, EVEN IF SHE DOES, IT'S OF NO CONSE-QUENCE. THE IMPORTANT THING IS TO KEEP VYING FOR THE UPPER HAND.
I MUST FIND OUT IF THEY ARE SAFE, AND IF WHAT YOU ARE SAYING IS TRUE, THEN CON-NECT ME TO THEM.
SURE.
CLAK CLAK
MOGI, MISA, IT'S ME, L.
!
LIGHT!
I HEARD THAT YOU HAVE BEEN IMPRISONED BY NEAR, BUT IS IT TRUE THAT YOU TWO HAVE AGREED TO IT?
MOGI
...

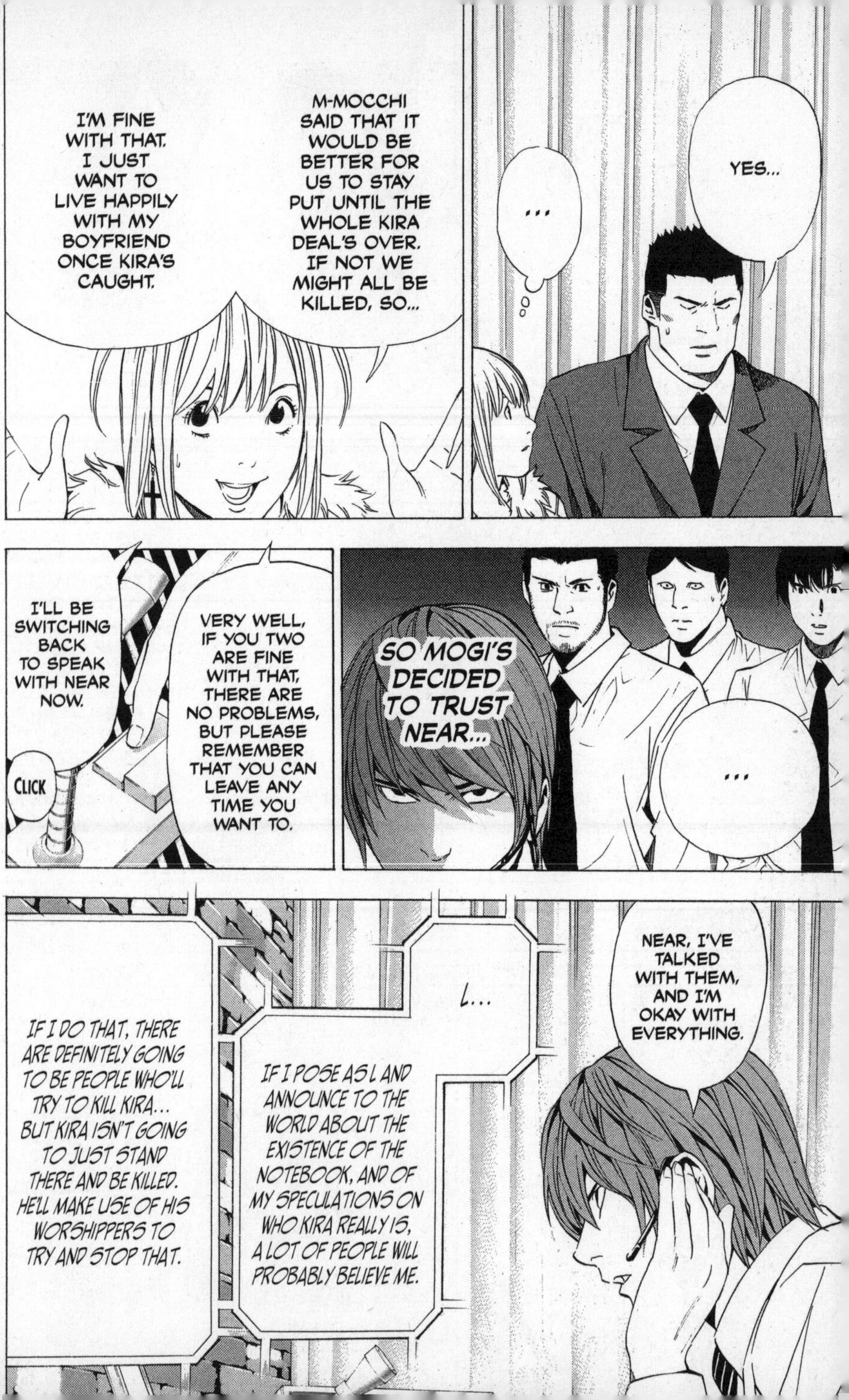
YES...
...
M-MOCCHI SAID THAT IT WOULD BE BETTER FOR US TO STAY PUT UNTIL THE WHOLE KIRA DEAL'S OVER. IF NOT WE MIGHT ALL BE KILLED, SO...
I'M FINE WITH THAT. I JUST WANT TO LIVE HAPPILY WITH MY BOYFRIEND ONCE KIRA'S CAUGHT.
SO MOGI'S DECIDED TO TRUST NEAR...
...
VERY WELL, IF YOU TWO ARE FINE WITH THAT, THERE ARE NO PROBLEMS, BUT PLEASE REMEMBER THAT YOU CAN LEAVE ANY TIME YOU WANT TO.
I'LL BE SWITCHING BACK TO SPEAK WITH NEAR NOW.
CLICK
NEAR, I'VE TALKED WITH THEM, AND I'M OKAY WITH EVERYTHING.
L...
IF I POSE AS L AND ANNOUNCE TO THE WORLD ABOUT THE EXISTENCE OF THE NOTEBOOK, AND OF MY SPECULATIONS ON WHO KIRA REALLY IS, A LOT OF PEOPLE WILL PROBABLY BELIEVE ME.
IF I DO THAT, THERE ARE DEFINITELY GOING TO BE PEOPLE WHO'LL TRY TO KILL KIRA... BUT KIRA ISN'T GOING TO JUST STAND THERE AND BE KILLED. HE'LL MAKE USE OF HIS WORSHIPPERS TO TRY AND STOP THAT.

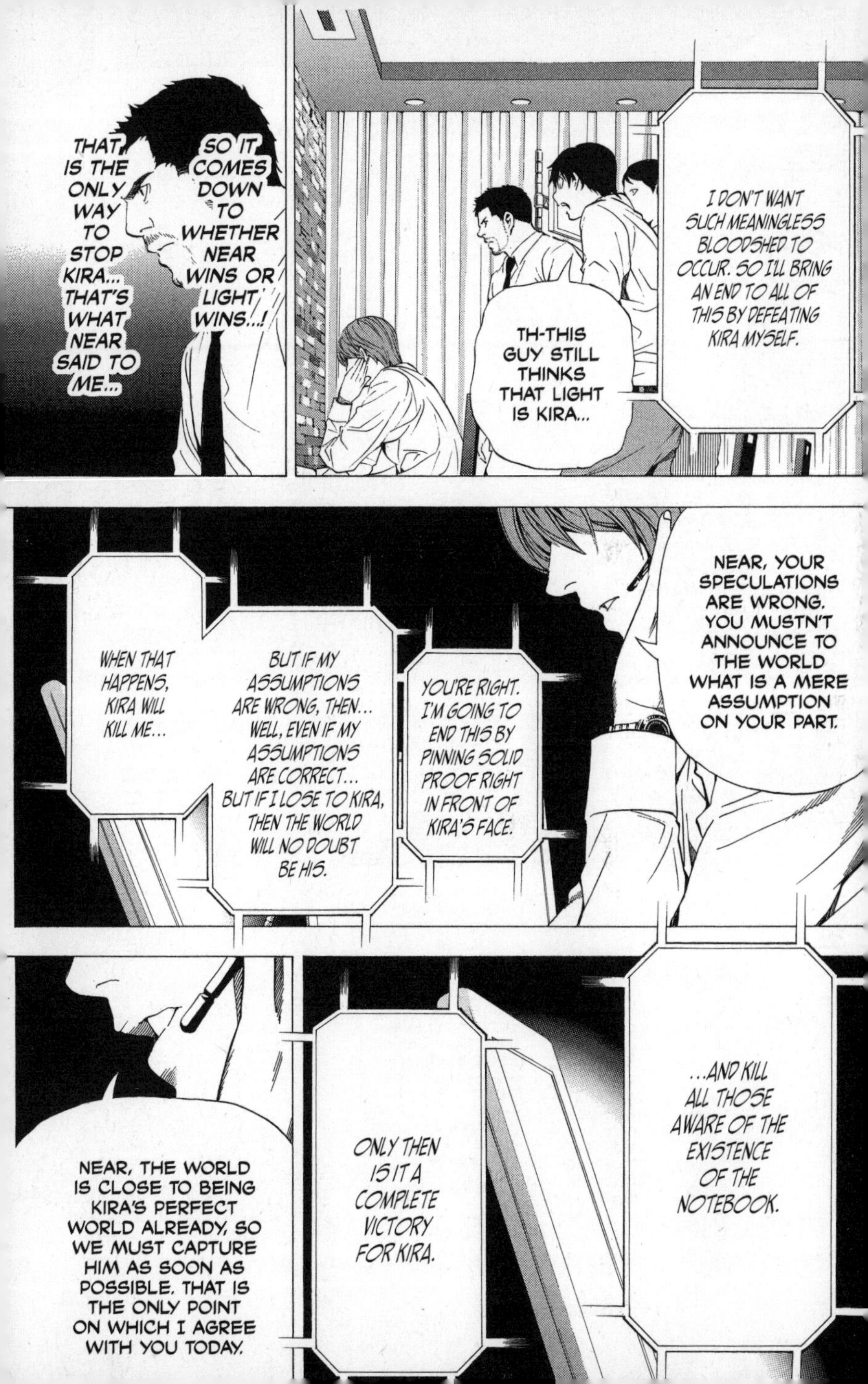
I DON'T WANT SUCH MEANINGLESS BLOODSHED TO OCCUR. SO I'LL BRING AN END TO ALL OF THIS BY DEFEATING KIRA MYSELF.
TH-THIS GUY STILL THINKS THAT LIGHT IS KIRA...
SO IT COMES DOWN TO WHETHER NEAR WINS OR LIGHT WINS...!
THAT IS THE ONLY WAY TO STOP KIRA... THAT'S WHAT NEAR SAID TO ME...
NEAR, YOUR SPECULATIONS ARE WRONG. YOU MUSTN'T ANNOUNCE TO THE WORLD WHAT IS A MERE ASSUMPTION ON YOUR PART.
YOU'RE RIGHT. I'M GOING TO END THIS BY PINNING SOLID PROOF RIGHT IN FRONT OF KIRA'S FACE.
BUT IF MY ASSUMPTIONS ARE WRONG, THEN... WELL, EVEN IF MY ASSUMPTIONS ARE CORRECT... BUT IF I LOSE TO KIRA, THEN THE WORLD WILL NO DOUBT BE HIS.
WHEN THAT HAPPENS, KIRA WILL KILL ME...
...AND KILL ALL THOSE AWARE OF THE EXISTENCE OF THE NOTEBOOK.
ONLY THEN IS IT A COMPLETE VICTORY FOR KIRA.
NEAR, THE WORLD IS CLOSE TO BEING KIRA'S PERFECT WORLD ALREADY, SO WE MUST CAPTURE HIM AS SOON AS POSSIBLE. THAT IS THE ONLY POINT ON WHICH I AGREE WITH YOU TODAY.

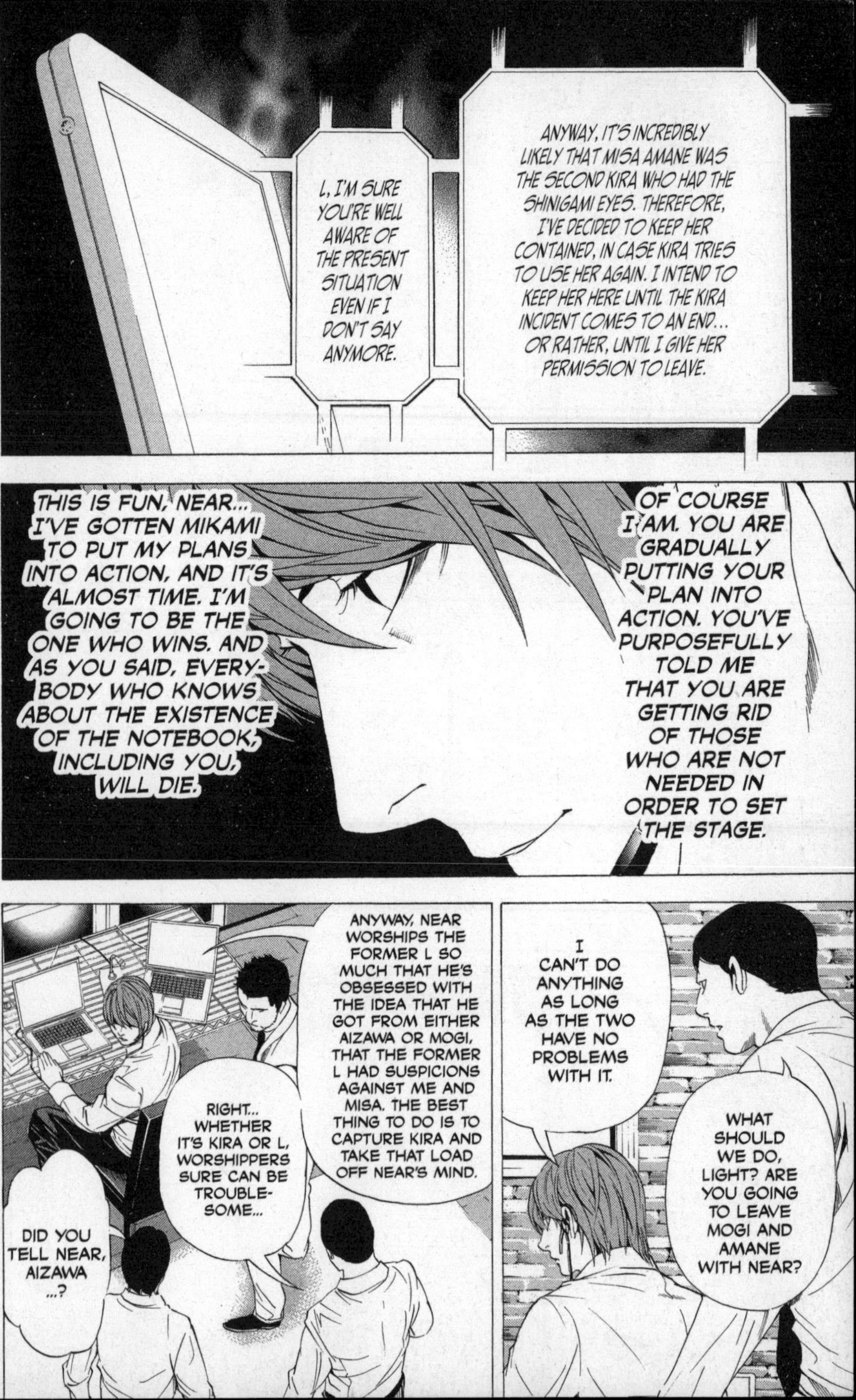
ANYWAY, IT'S INCREDIBLY LIKELY THAT MISA AMANE WAS THE SECOND KIRA WHO HAD THE SHINIGAMI EYES. THEREFORE, I'VE DECIDED TO KEEP HER CONTAINED, IN CASE KIRA TRIES TO USE HER AGAIN. I INTEND TO KEEP HER HERE UNTIL THE KIRA INCIDENT COMES TO AN END... OR RATHER, UNTIL I GIVE HER PERMISSION TO LEAVE.
L, I'M SURE YOU'RE WELL AWARE OF THE PRESENT SITUATION EVEN IF I DON'T SAY ANYMORE.
OF COURSE I AM. YOU ARE GRADUALLY PUTTING YOUR PLAN INTO ACTION. YOU'VE PURPOSEFULLY TOLD ME THAT YOU ARE GETTING RID OF THOSE WHO ARE NOT NEEDED IN ORDER TO SET THE STAGE.
THIS IS FUN, NEAR... I'VE GOTTEN MIKAMI TO PUT MY PLANS INTO ACTION, AND IT'S ALMOST TIME. I'M GOING TO BE THE ONE WHO WINS. AND AS YOU SAID, EVERYBODY WHO KNOWS ABOUT THE EXISTENCE OF THE NOTEBOOK, INCLUDING YOU, WILL DIE.
WHAT SHOULD WE DO, LIGHT? ARE YOU GOING TO LEAVE MOGI AND AMANE WITH NEAR?
I CAN'T DO ANYTHING AS LONG AS THE TWO HAVE NO PROBLEMS WITH IT.
ANYWAY, NEAR WORSHIPS THE FORMER L SO MUCH THAT HE'S OBSESSED WITH THE IDEA THAT HE GOT FROM EITHER AIZAWA OR MOGI, THAT THE FORMER L HAD SUSPICIONS AGAINST ME AND MISA. THE BEST THING TO DO IS TO CAPTURE KIRA AND TAKE THAT LOAD OFF NEAR'S MIND.
RIGHT... WHETHER IT'S KIRA OR L, WORSHIPPERS SURE CAN BE TROUBLESOME...
DID YOU TELL NEAR, AIZAWA ...?

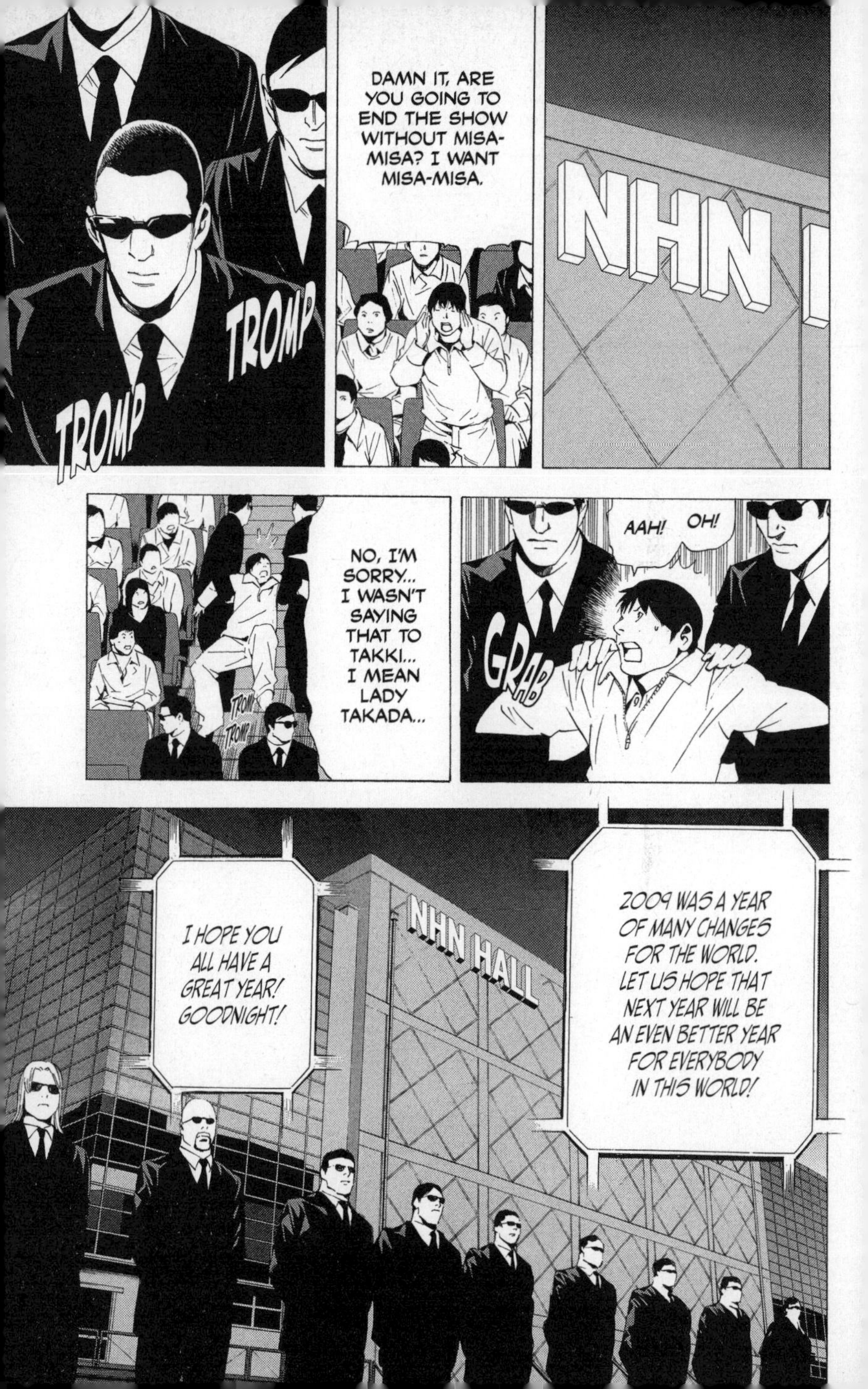
NHN
DAMN IT, ARE YOU GOING TO END THE SHOW WITHOUT MISA-MISA? I WANT MISA-MISA.
TROMP
TROMP
AAH! OH!
GRAB
NO, I'M SORRY... I WASN'T SAYING THAT TO TAKKI... I MEAN LADY TAKADA...
TROMP
TROMP
2009 WAS A YEAR OF MANY CHANGES FOR THE WORLD. LET US HOPE THAT NEXT YEAR WILL BE AN EVEN BETTER YEAR FOR EVERYBODY IN THIS WORLD!
NHN HALL
I HOPE YOU ALL HAVE A GREAT YEAR! GOODNIGHT!

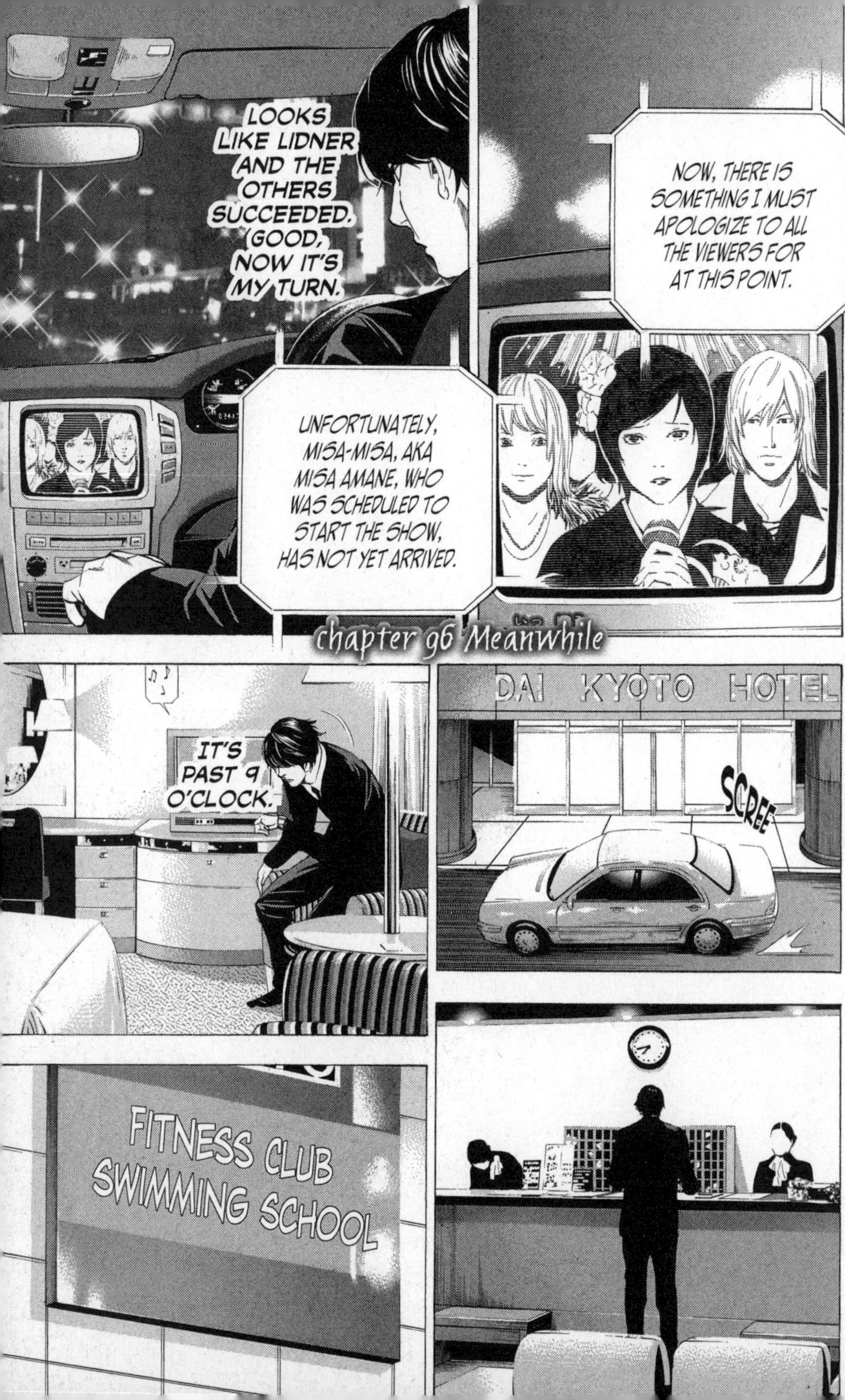
NOW, THERE IS SOMETHING I MUST APOLOGIZE TO ALL THE VIEWERS FOR AT THIS POINT.
LOOKS LIKE LIDNER AND THE OTHERS SUCCEEDED. GOOD, NOW IT'S MY TURN.
UNFORTUNATELY, MISA-MISA, AKA MISA AMANE, WHO WAS SCHEDULED TO START THE SHOW, HAS NOT YET ARRIVED.
chapter 96 Meanwhile
DAI KYOTO HOTEL
SCREE
IT'S PAST 9 O'CLOCK.
FITNESS CLUB
SWIMMING SCHOOL

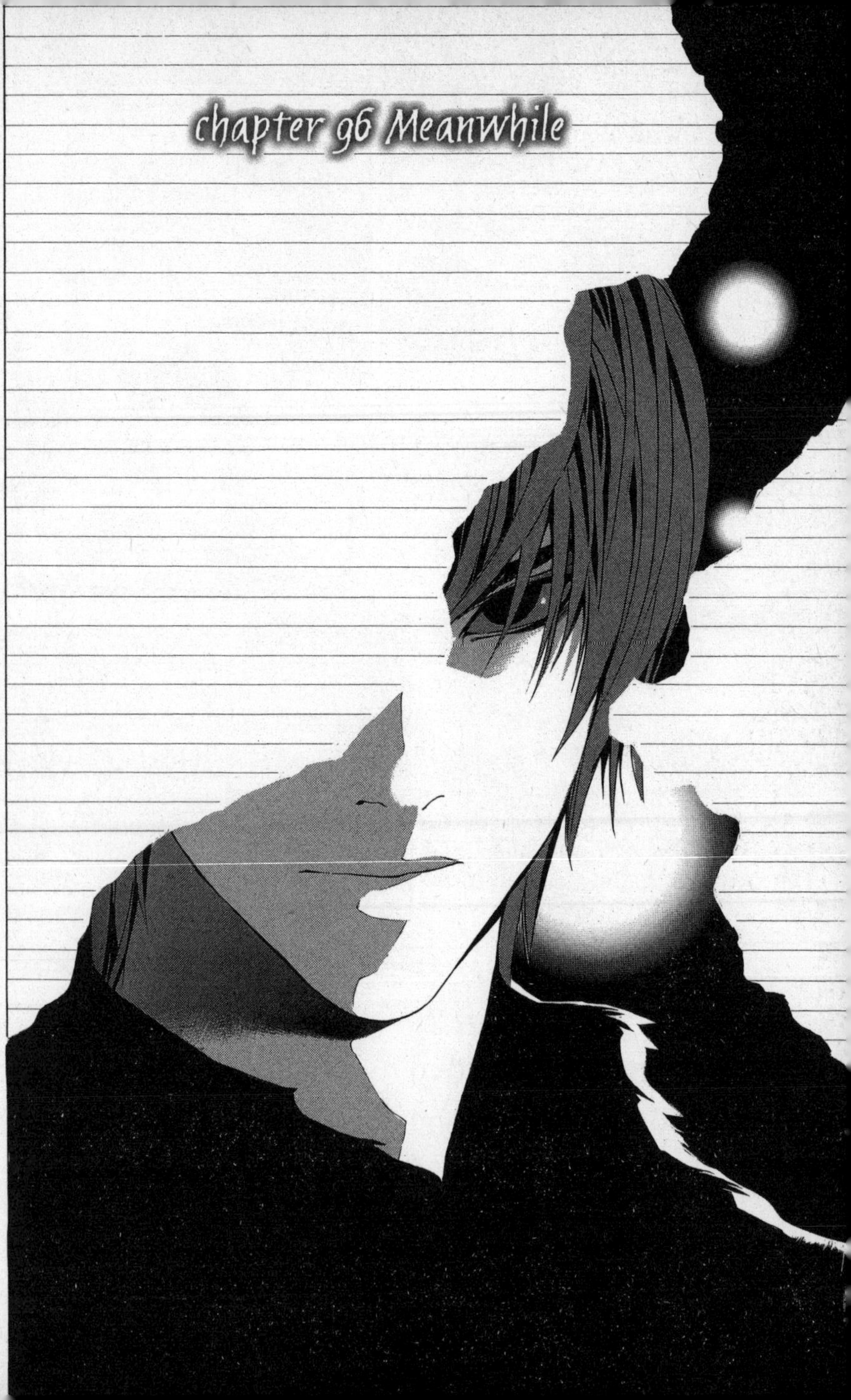
chapter 96 Meanwhile

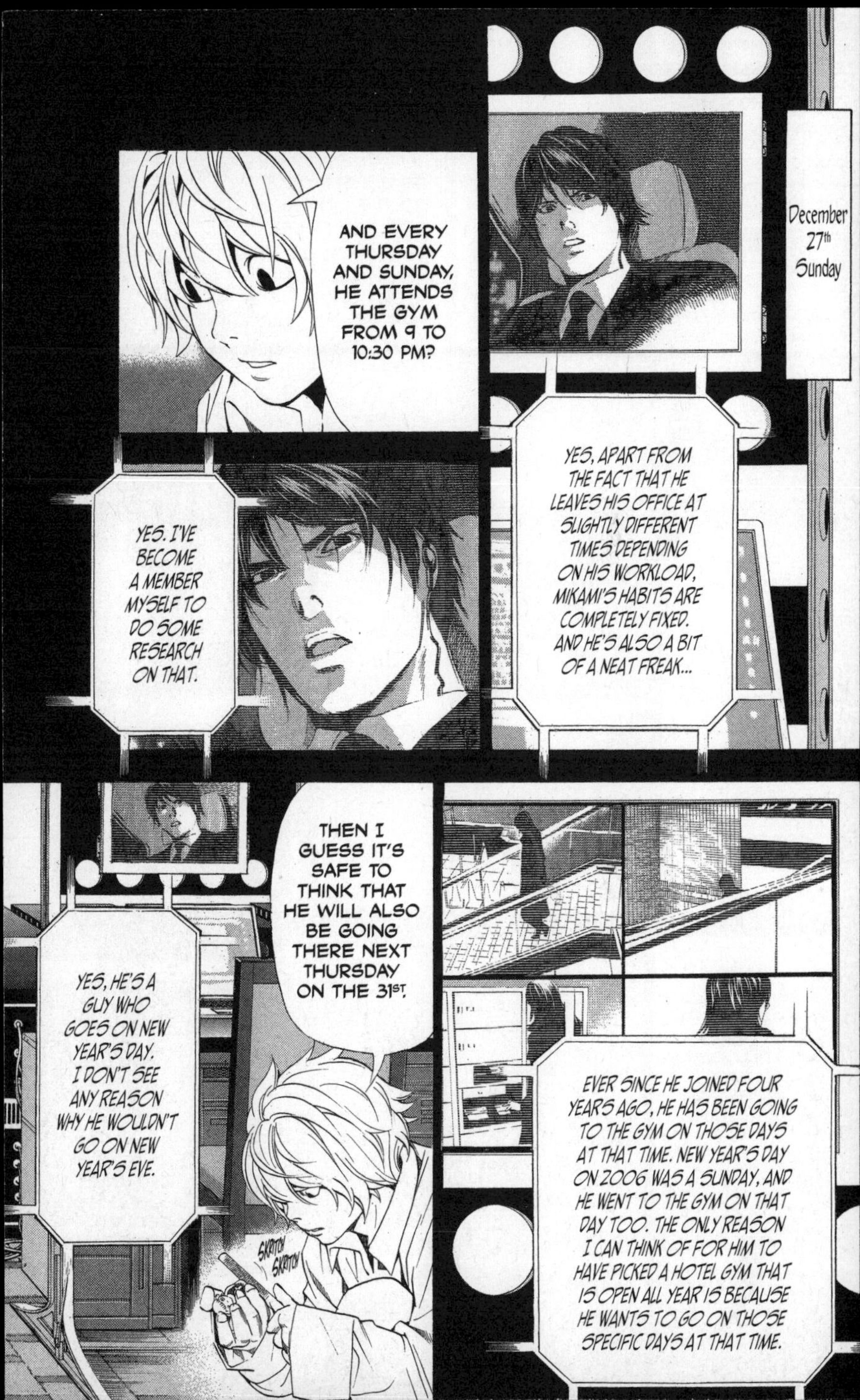
December 27th Sunday
YES, APART FROM THE FACT THAT HE LEAVES HIS OFFICE AT SLIGHTLY DIFFERENT TIMES DEPENDING ON HIS WORKLOAD, MIKAMI'S HABITS ARE COMPLETELY FIXED. AND HE'S ALSO A BIT OF A NEAT FREAK...
AND EVERY THURSDAY AND SUNDAY, HE ATTENDS THE GYM FROM 9 TO 10:30 PM?
YES. I'VE BECOME A MEMBER MYSELF TO DO SOME RESEARCH ON THAT.
EVER SINCE HE JOINED FOUR YEARS AGO, HE HAS BEEN GOING TO THE GYM ON THOSE DAYS AT THAT TIME. NEW YEAR'S DAY ON 2006 WAS A SUNDAY, AND HE WENT TO THE GYM ON THAT DAY TOO. THE ONLY REASON I CAN THINK OF FOR HIM TO HAVE PICKED A HOTEL GYM THAT IS OPEN ALL YEAR IS BECAUSE HE WANTS TO GO ON THOSE SPECIFIC DAYS AT THAT TIME.
THEN I GUESS IT'S SAFE TO THINK THAT HE WILL ALSO BE GOING THERE NEXT THURSDAY ON THE 31ST.
SKRITCH SKRITCH
YES, HE'S A GUY WHO GOES ON NEW YEAR'S DAY. I DON'T SEE ANY REASON WHY HE WOULDN'T GO ON NEW YEAR'S EVE.

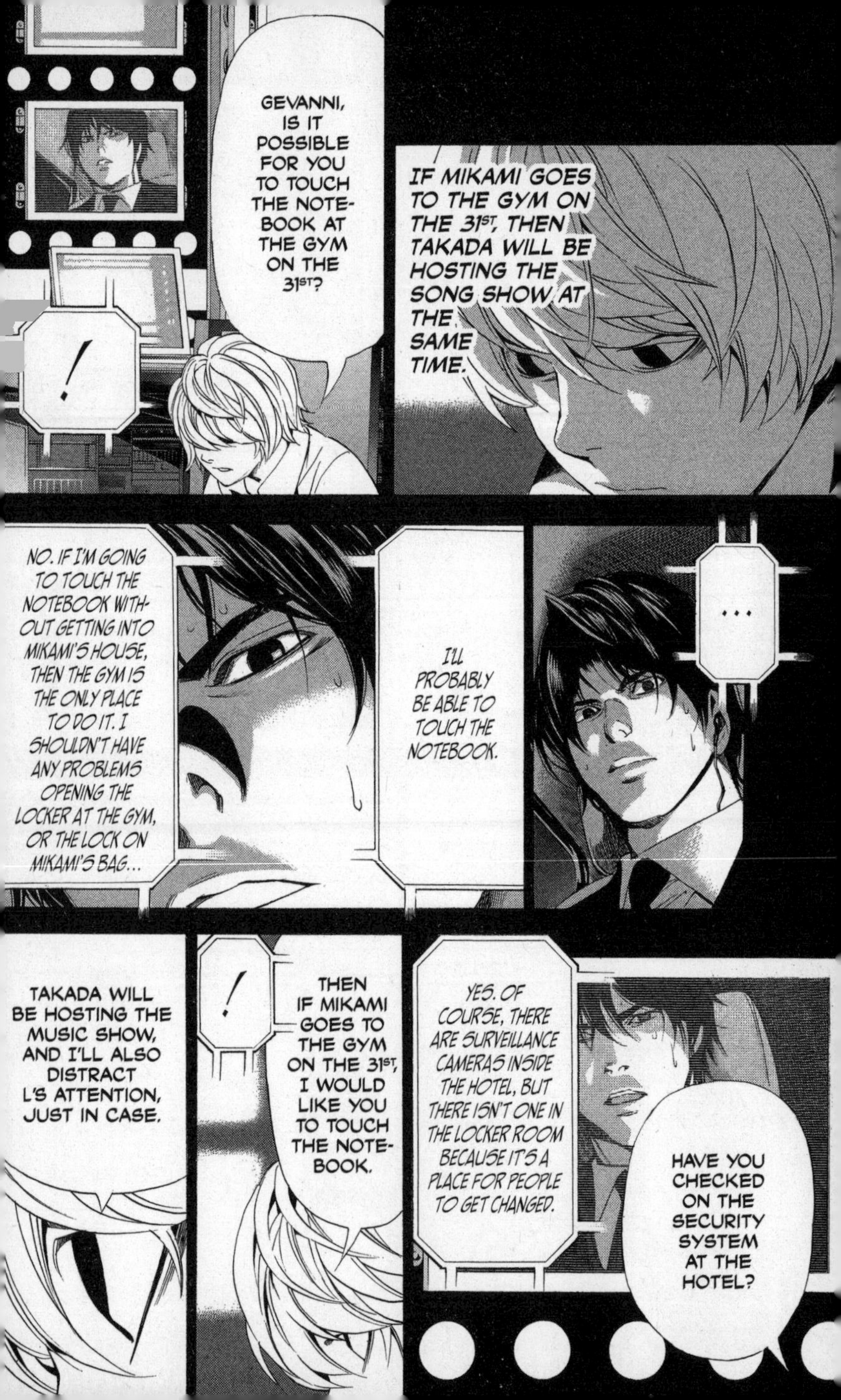
IF MIKAMI GOES TO THE GYM ON THE 31ST, THEN TAKADA WILL BE HOSTING THE SONG SHOW AT THE SAME TIME.
GEVANNI, IS IT POSSIBLE FOR YOU TO TOUCH THE NOTE-BOOK AT THE GYM ON THE 31ST?
!
...
I'LL PROBABLY BE ABLE TO TOUCH THE NOTEBOOK.
NO. IF I'M GOING TO TOUCH THE NOTEBOOK WITH-OUT GETTING INTO MIKAMI'S HOUSE, THEN THE GYM IS THE ONLY PLACE TO DO IT. I SHOULDN'T HAVE ANY PROBLEMS OPENING THE LOCKER AT THE GYM, OR THE LOCK ON MIKAMI'S BAG...
HAVE YOU CHECKED ON THE SECURITY SYSTEM AT THE HOTEL?
YES. OF COURSE, THERE ARE SURVEILLANCE CAMERAS INSIDE THE HOTEL, BUT THERE ISN'T ONE IN THE LOCKER ROOM BECAUSE IT'S A PLACE FOR PEOPLE TO GET CHANGED.
!
THEN IF MIKAMI GOES TO THE GYM ON THE 31ST, I WOULD LIKE YOU TO TOUCH THE NOTE-BOOK.
TAKADA WILL BE HOSTING THE MUSIC SHOW, AND I'LL ALSO DISTRACT L'S ATTENTION, JUST IN CASE.

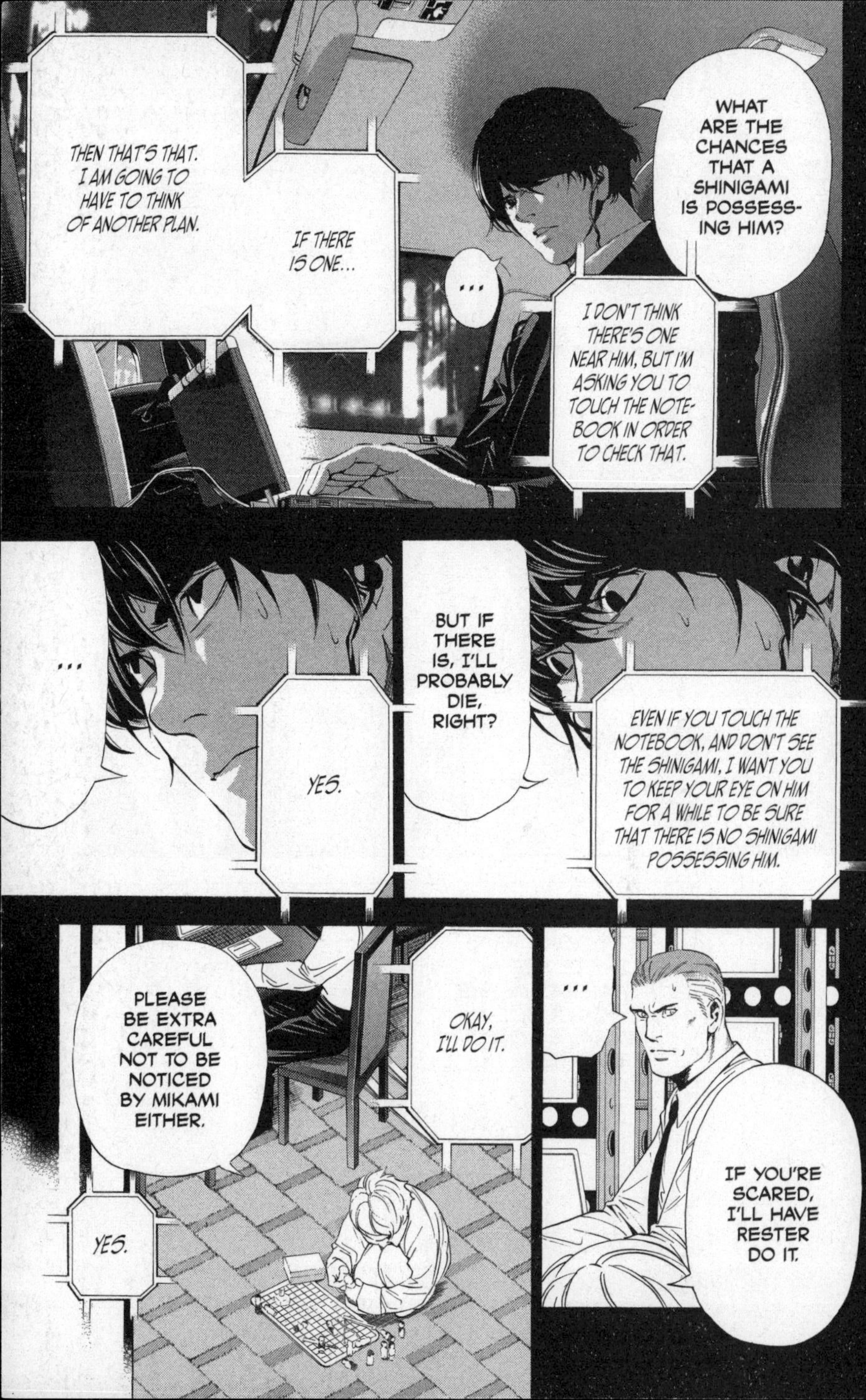
WHAT ARE THE CHANCES THAT A SHINIGAMI IS POSSESSING HIM?
I DON'T THINK THERE'S ONE NEAR HIM, BUT I'M ASKING YOU TO TOUCH THE NOTEBOOK IN ORDER TO CHECK THAT.
...
THEN THAT'S THAT. I AM GOING TO HAVE TO THINK OF ANOTHER PLAN.
IF THERE IS ONE...
EVEN IF YOU TOUCH THE NOTEBOOK, AND DON'T SEE THE SHINIGAMI, I WANT YOU TO KEEP YOUR EYE ON HIM FOR A WHILE TO BE SURE THAT THERE IS NO SHINIGAMI POSSESSING HIM.
BUT IF THERE IS, I'LL PROBABLY DIE, RIGHT?
YES.
...
...
IF YOU'RE SCARED, I'LL HAVE RESTER DO IT.
OKAY, I'LL DO IT.
PLEASE BE EXTRA CAREFUL NOT TO BE NOTICED BY MIKAMI EITHER.
YES.

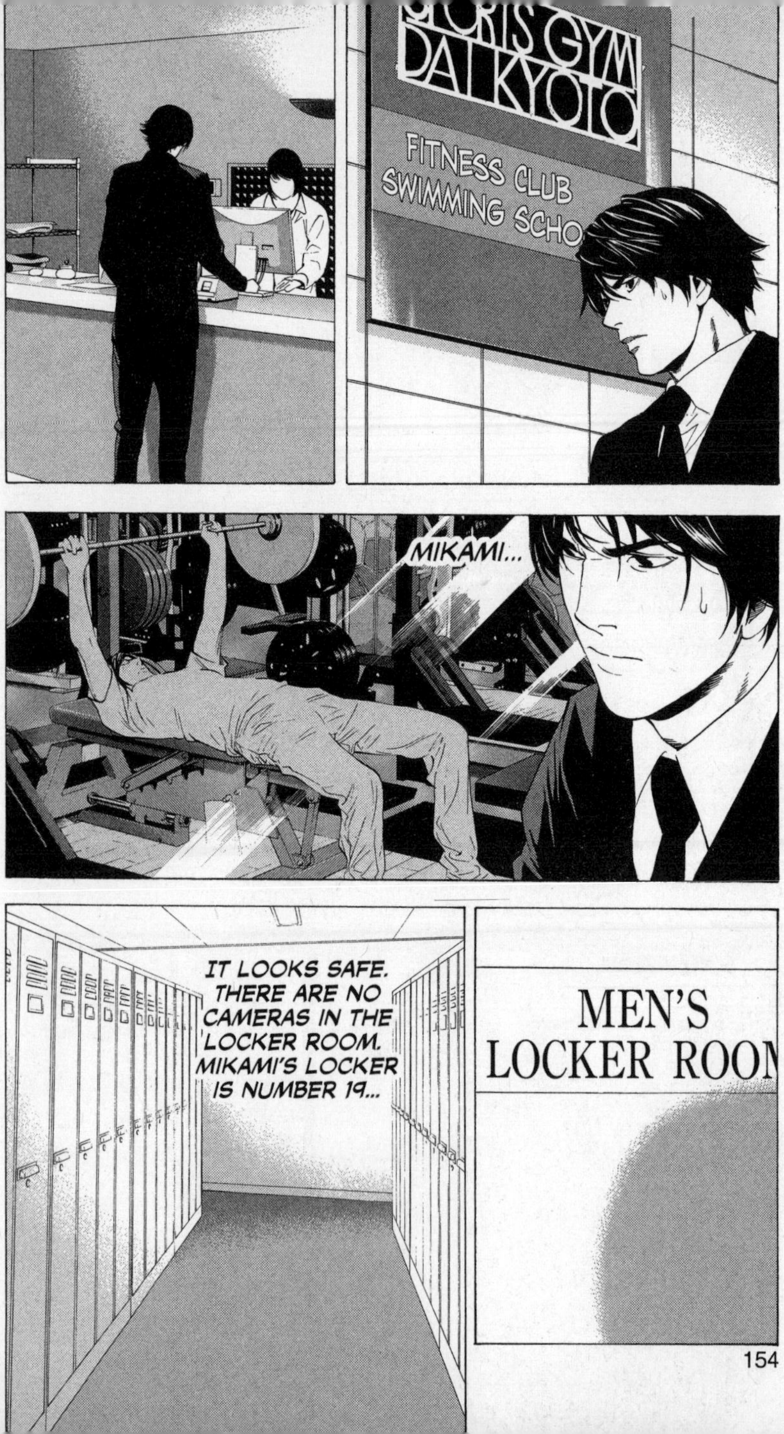
SPORTS GYM
DAI KYOTO
FITNESS CLUB
SWIMMING SCHO
MIKAMI...
MEN'S
LOCKER ROOM
IT LOOKS SAFE. THERE ARE NO CAMERAS IN THE LOCKER ROOM. MIKAMI'S LOCKER IS NUMBER 19...

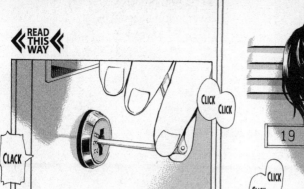

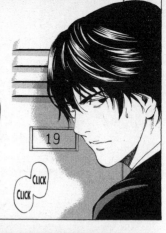

READ THIS WAY
19
CLICK
CLICK
CLICK
CLICK
CLACK
...
CLICK
CLICK
CLACK
IF A SHINIGAMI IS POSSESSING MIKAMI...
NO, IF THERE WAS ONE, I'M DEAD EITHER WAY BY NOW. I MAY AS WELL TOUCH IT.
SNAK

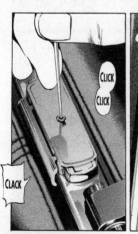

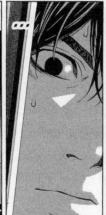

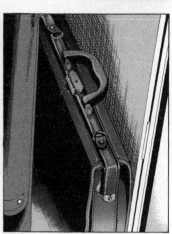

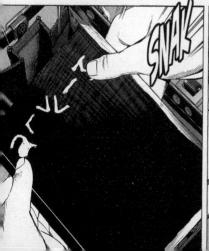

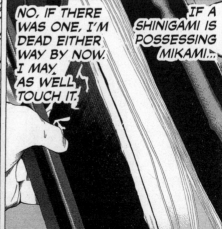

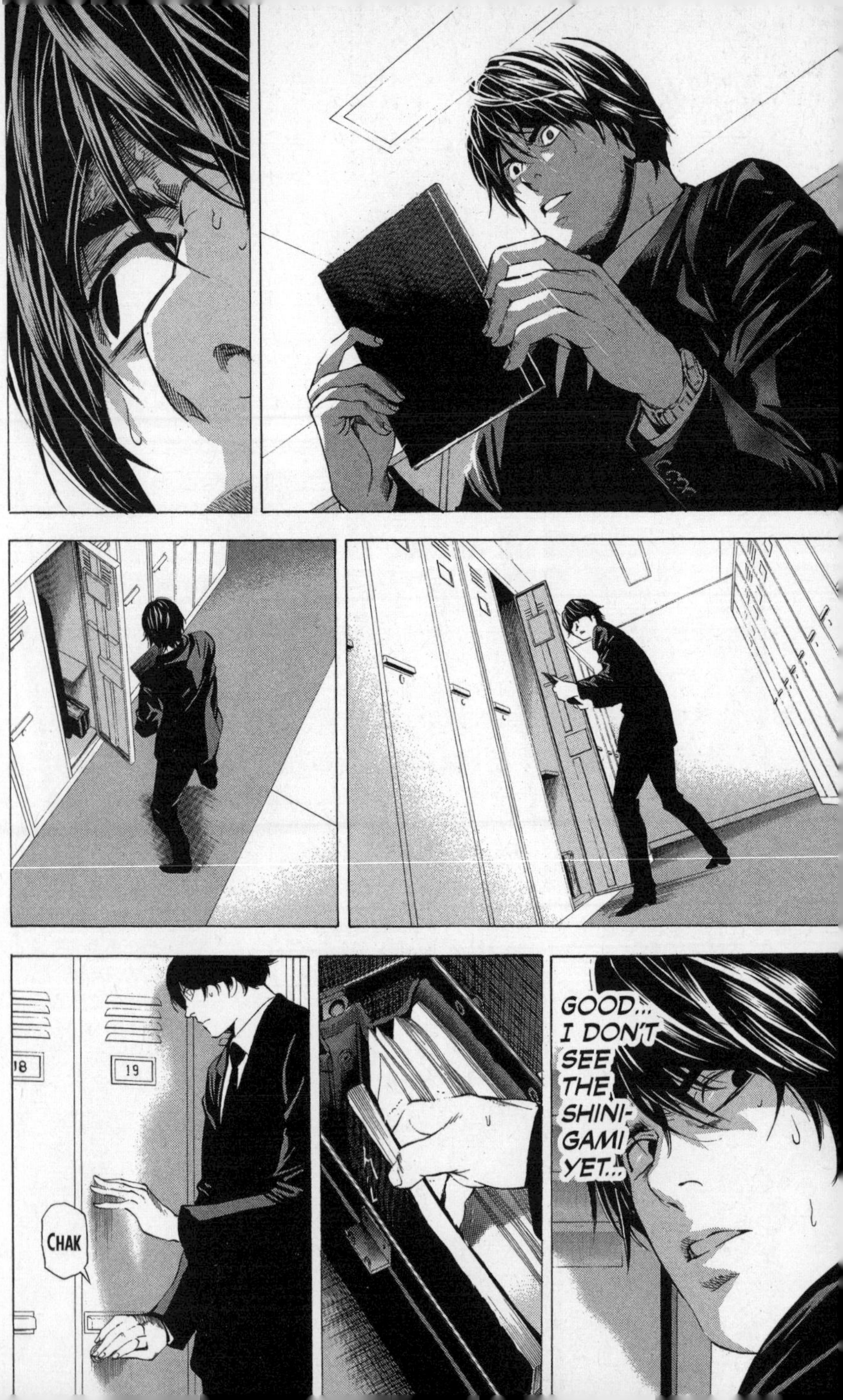
GOOD... I DON'T SEE THE SHINIGAMI YET...
CHAK
18
19

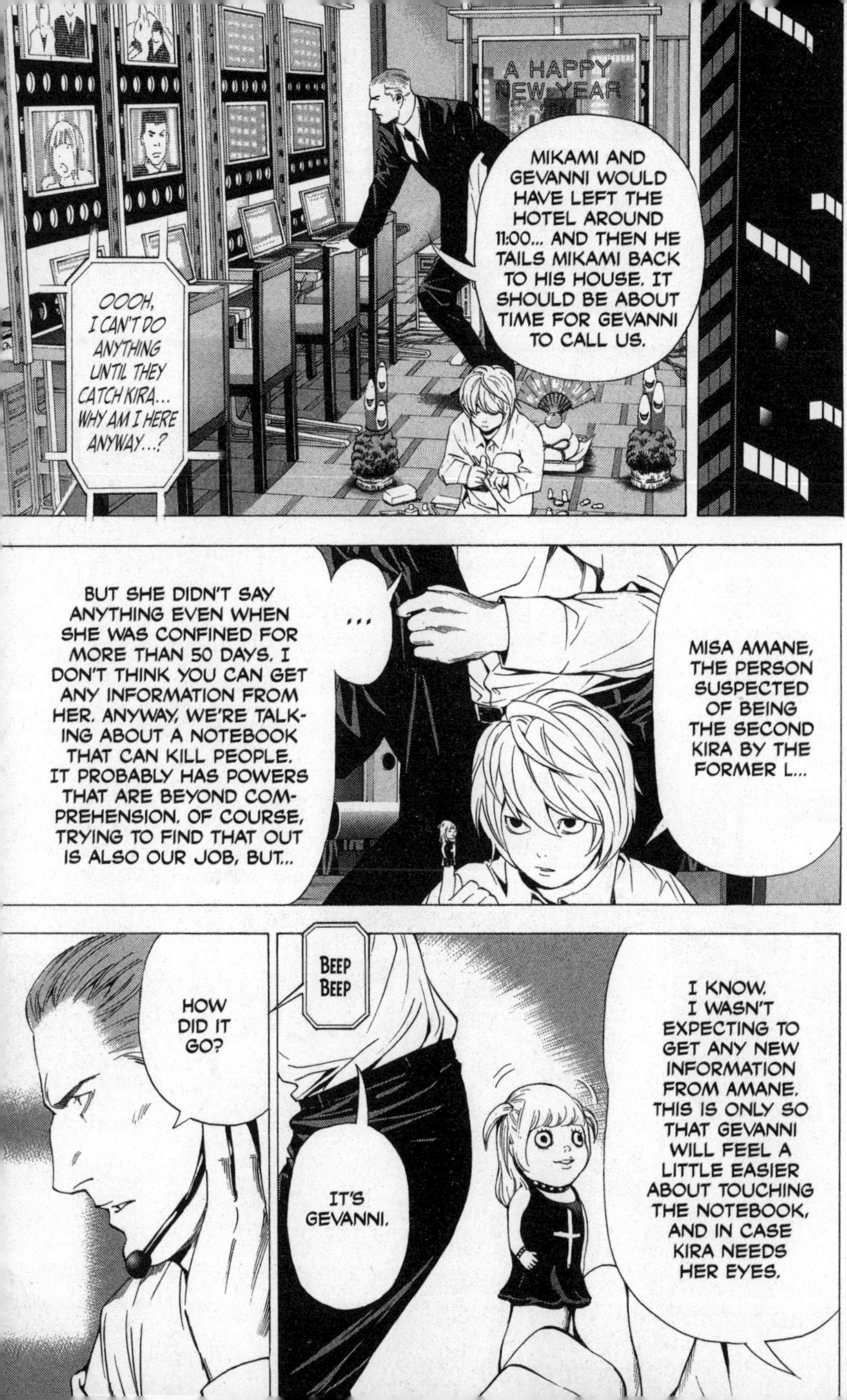
A HAPPY NEW YEAR
MIKAMI AND GEVANNI WOULD HAVE LEFT THE HOTEL AROUND 11:00... AND THEN HE TAILS MIKAMI BACK TO HIS HOUSE. IT SHOULD BE ABOUT TIME FOR GEVANNI TO CALL US.
OOOH, I CAN'T DO ANYTHING UNTIL THEY CATCH KIRA... WHY AM I HERE ANYWAY...?
MISA AMANE, THE PERSON SUSPECTED OF BEING THE SECOND KIRA BY THE FORMER L...
...
BUT SHE DIDN'T SAY ANYTHING EVEN WHEN SHE WAS CONFINED FOR MORE THAN 50 DAYS. I DON'T THINK YOU CAN GET ANY INFORMATION FROM HER. ANYWAY, WE'RE TALKING ABOUT A NOTEBOOK THAT CAN KILL PEOPLE. IT PROBABLY HAS POWERS THAT ARE BEYOND COMPREHENSION. OF COURSE, TRYING TO FIND THAT OUT IS ALSO OUR JOB, BUT...
I KNOW. I WASN'T EXPECTING TO GET ANY NEW INFORMATION FROM AMANE. THIS IS ONLY SO THAT GEVANNI WILL FEEL A LITTLE EASIER ABOUT TOUCHING THE NOTEBOOK, AND IN CASE KIRA NEEDS HER EYES.
BEEP BEEP
IT'S GEVANNI.
HOW DID IT GO?

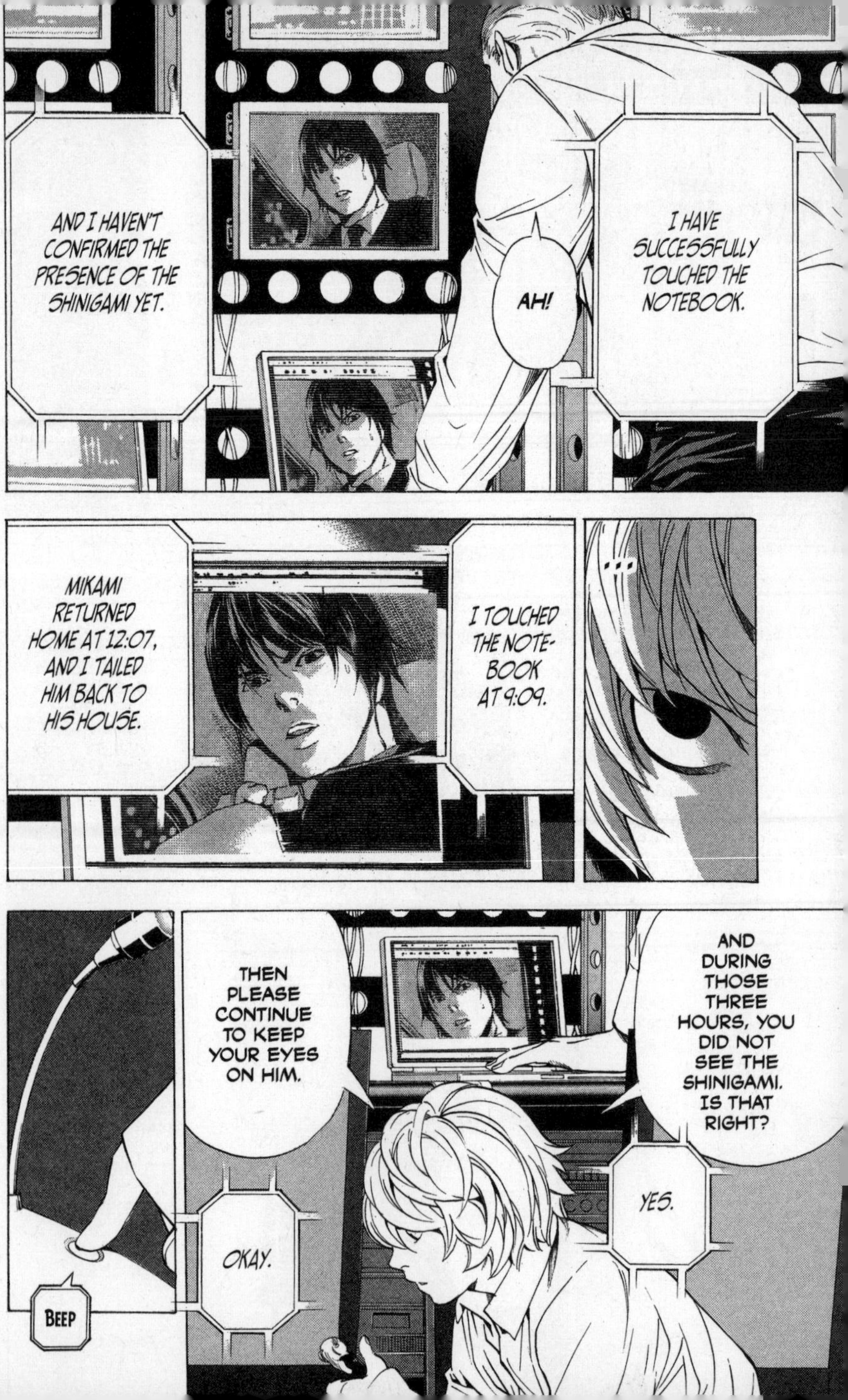
I HAVE SUCCESSFULLY TOUCHED THE NOTEBOOK.
AH!
AND I HAVEN'T CONFIRMED THE PRESENCE OF THE SHINIGAMI YET.
...
I TOUCHED THE NOTE-BOOK AT 9:09.
MIKAMI RETURNED HOME AT 12:07, AND I TAILED HIM BACK TO HIS HOUSE.
AND DURING THOSE THREE HOURS, YOU DID NOT SEE THE SHINIGAMI. IS THAT RIGHT?
YES.
THEN PLEASE CONTINUE TO KEEP YOUR EYES ON HIM.
OKAY.
BEEP

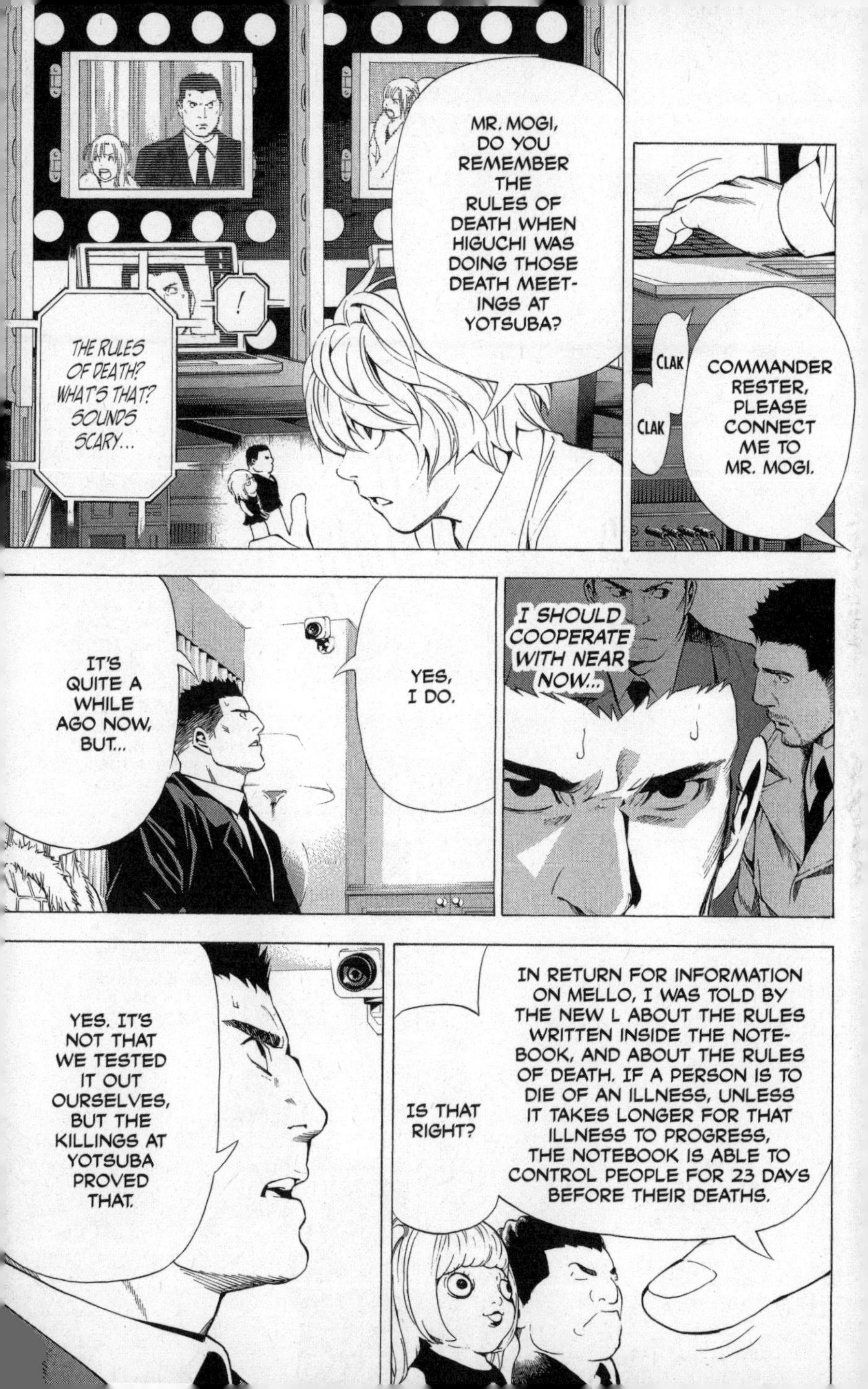
CLAK
CLAK
COMMANDER RESTER, PLEASE CONNECT ME TO MR. MOGI.
MR. MOGI, DO YOU REMEMBER THE RULES OF DEATH WHEN HIGUCHI WAS DOING THOSE DEATH MEET-INGS AT YOTSUBA?
!
THE RULES OF DEATH? WHAT'S THAT? SOUNDS SCARY...
I SHOULD COOPERATE WITH NEAR NOW...
YES, I DO.
IT'S QUITE A WHILE AGO NOW, BUT...
IN RETURN FOR INFORMATION ON MELLO, I WAS TOLD BY THE NEW L ABOUT THE RULES WRITTEN INSIDE THE NOTE-BOOK, AND ABOUT THE RULES OF DEATH. IF A PERSON IS TO DIE OF AN ILLNESS, UNLESS IT TAKES LONGER FOR THAT ILLNESS TO PROGRESS, THE NOTEBOOK IS ABLE TO CONTROL PEOPLE FOR 23 DAYS BEFORE THEIR DEATHS.
IS THAT RIGHT?
YES. IT'S NOT THAT WE TESTED IT OUT OURSELVES, BUT THE KILLINGS AT YOTSUBA PROVED THAT.

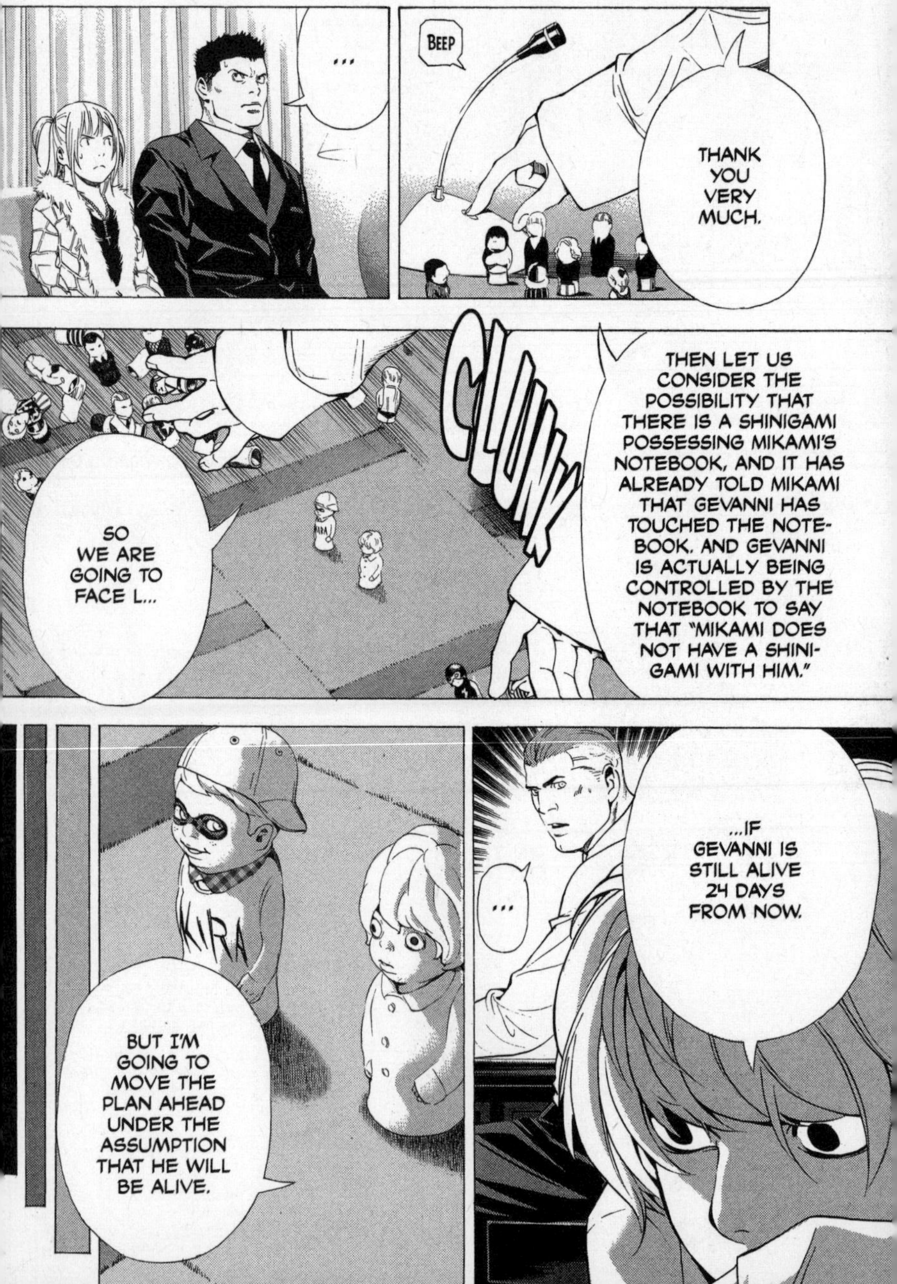
BEEP
THANK YOU VERY MUCH.
...
THEN LET US CONSIDER THE POSSIBILITY THAT THERE IS A SHINIGAMI POSSESSING MIKAMI'S NOTEBOOK, AND IT HAS ALREADY TOLD MIKAMI THAT GEVANNI HAS TOUCHED THE NOTEBOOK. AND GEVANNI IS ACTUALLY BEING CONTROLLED BY THE NOTEBOOK TO SAY THAT "MIKAMI DOES NOT HAVE A SHINIGAMI WITH HIM."
CLUNK
SO WE ARE GOING TO FACE L...
...IF GEVANNI IS STILL ALIVE 24 DAYS FROM NOW.
...
BUT I'M GOING TO MOVE THE PLAN AHEAD UNDER THE ASSUMPTION THAT HE WILL BE ALIVE.

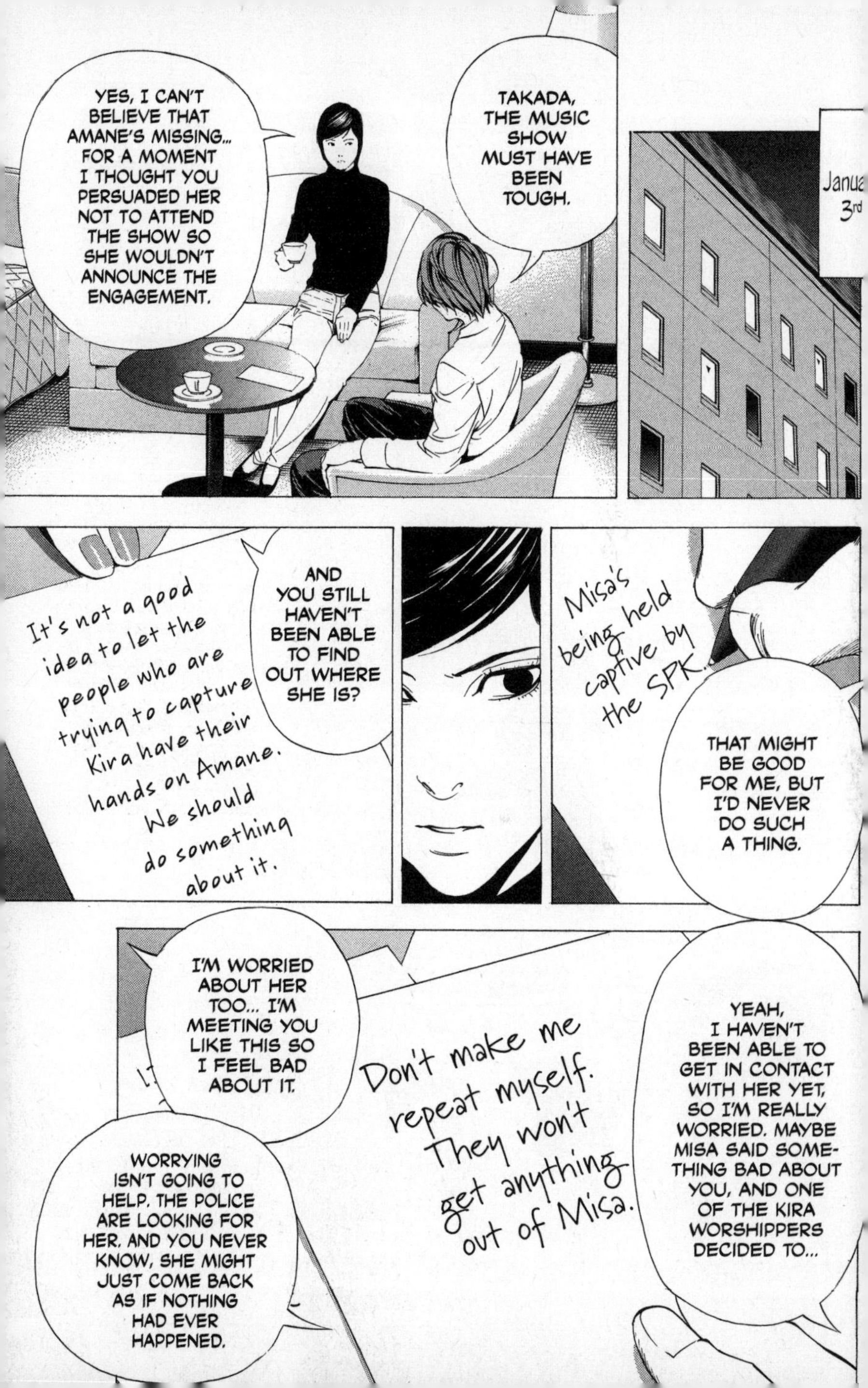
Janua
3rd
TAKADA, THE MUSIC SHOW MUST HAVE BEEN TOUGH.
YES, I CAN'T BELIEVE THAT AMANE'S MISSING... FOR A MOMENT I THOUGHT YOU PERSUADED HER NOT TO ATTEND THE SHOW SO SHE WOULDN'T ANNOUNCE THE ENGAGEMENT.
Misa's being held captive by the SPK...
THAT MIGHT BE GOOD FOR ME, BUT I'D NEVER DO SUCH A THING.
AND YOU STILL HAVEN'T BEEN ABLE TO FIND OUT WHERE SHE IS?
It's not a good idea to let the people who are trying to capture Kira have their hands on Amane. We should do something about it.
YEAH, I HAVEN'T BEEN ABLE TO GET IN CONTACT WITH HER YET, SO I'M REALLY WORRIED. MAYBE MISA SAID SOME-THING BAD ABOUT YOU, AND ONE OF THE KIRA WORSHIPPERS DECIDED TO...
Don't make me repeat myself. They won't get anything out of Misa.
I'M WORRIED ABOUT HER TOO... I'M MEETING YOU LIKE THIS SO I FEEL BAD ABOUT IT.
WORRYING ISN'T GOING TO HELP. THE POLICE ARE LOOKING FOR HER. AND YOU NEVER KNOW, SHE MIGHT JUST COME BACK AS IF NOTHING HAD EVER HAPPENED.

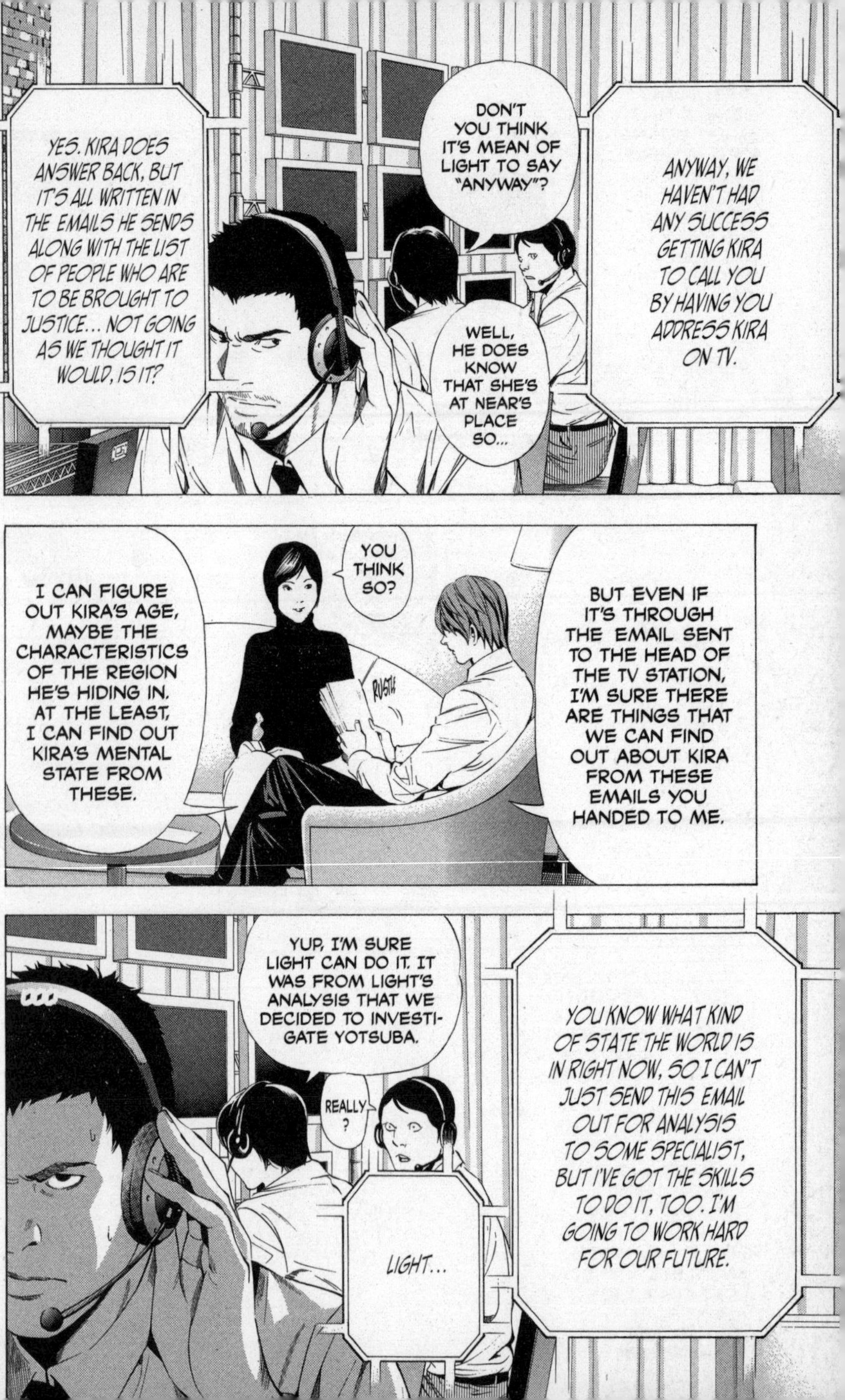

ANYWAY, WE HAVEN'T HAD ANY SUCCESS GETTING KIRA TO CALL YOU BY HAVING YOU ADDRESS KIRA ON TV.
DON'T YOU THINK IT'S MEAN OF LIGHT TO SAY "ANYWAY"?
YES. KIRA DOES ANSWER BACK, BUT IT'S ALL WRITTEN IN THE EMAILS HE SENDS ALONG WITH THE LIST OF PEOPLE WHO ARE TO BE BROUGHT TO JUSTICE... NOT GOING AS WE THOUGHT IT WOULD, IS IT?
WELL, HE DOES KNOW THAT SHE'S AT NEAR'S PLACE SO...
BUT EVEN IF IT'S THROUGH THE EMAIL SENT TO THE HEAD OF THE TV STATION, I'M SURE THERE ARE THINGS THAT WE CAN FIND OUT ABOUT KIRA FROM THESE EMAILS YOU HANDED TO ME.
RUSTLE
YOU THINK SO?
I CAN FIGURE OUT KIRA'S AGE, MAYBE THE CHARACTERISTICS OF THE REGION HE'S HIDING IN. AT THE LEAST, I CAN FIND OUT KIRA'S MENTAL STATE FROM THESE.
YOU KNOW WHAT KIND OF STATE THE WORLD IS IN RIGHT NOW, SO I CAN'T JUST SEND THIS EMAIL OUT FOR ANALYSIS TO SOME SPECIALIST, BUT I'VE GOT THE SKILLS TO DO IT, TOO. I'M GOING TO WORK HARD FOR OUR FUTURE.
YUP, I'M SURE LIGHT CAN DO IT. IT WAS FROM LIGHT'S ANALYSIS THAT WE DECIDED TO INVESTI-GATE YOTSUBA.
REALLY?
LIGHT...

READ THIS WAY

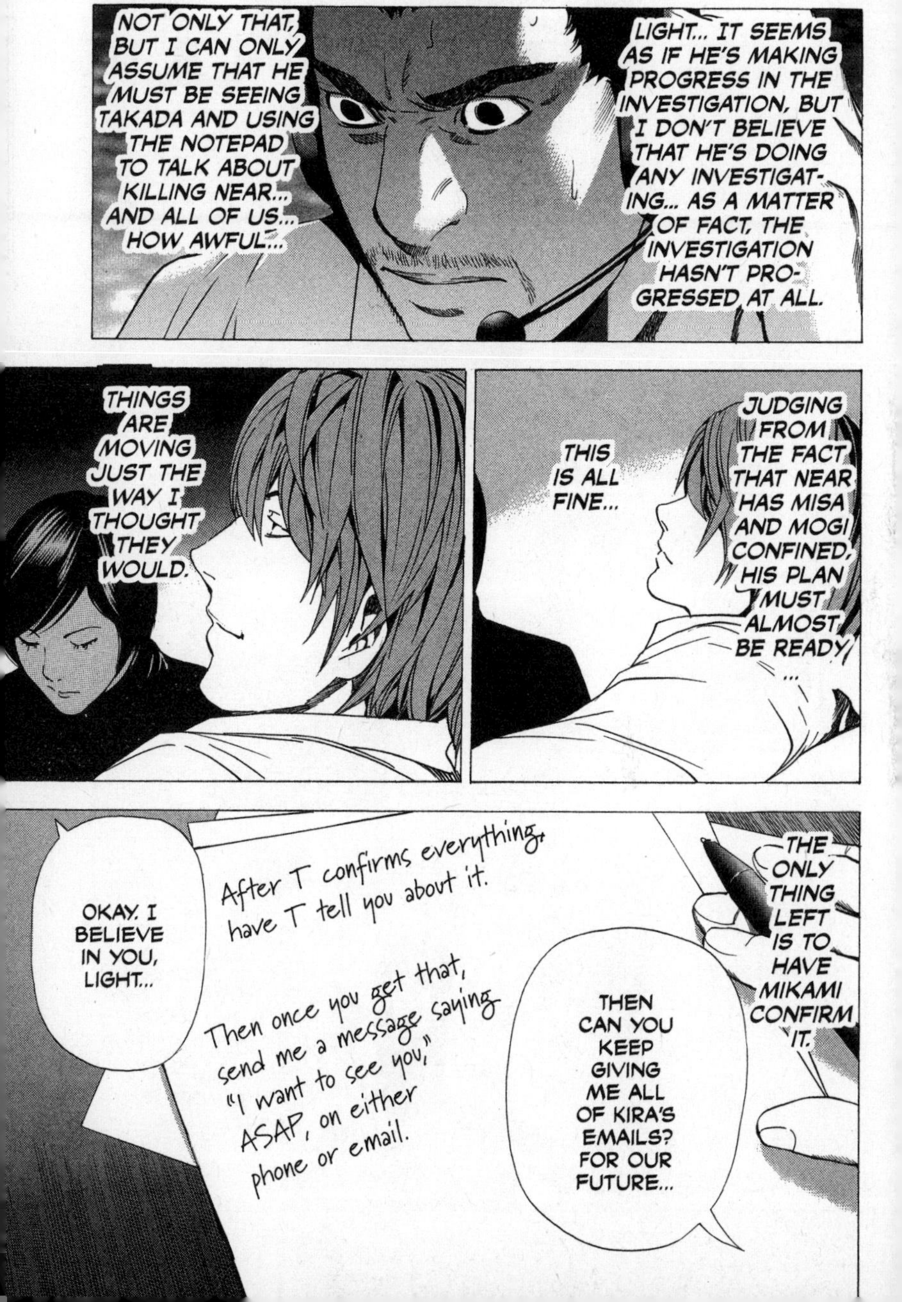

LIGHT... IT SEEMS AS IF HE'S MAKING PROGRESS IN THE INVESTIGATION, BUT I DON'T BELIEVE THAT HE'S DOING ANY INVESTIGATING... AS A MATTER OF FACT, THE INVESTIGATION HASN'T PROGRESSED AT ALL.
NOT ONLY THAT, BUT I CAN ONLY ASSUME THAT HE MUST BE SEEING TAKADA AND USING THE NOTEPAD TO TALK ABOUT KILLING NEAR... AND ALL OF US... HOW AWFUL...
JUDGING FROM THE FACT THAT NEAR HAS MISA AND MOGI CONFINED, HIS PLAN MUST ALMOST BE READY...
THIS IS ALL FINE...
THINGS ARE MOVING JUST THE WAY I THOUGHT THEY WOULD.
THE ONLY THING LEFT IS TO HAVE MIKAMI CONFIRM IT.
THEN CAN YOU KEEP GIVING ME ALL OF KIRA'S EMAILS? FOR OUR FUTURE...
After T confirms everything, have T tell you about it.
Then once you get that, send me a message saying "I want to see you," ASAP, on either phone or email.
OKAY. I BELIEVE IN YOU, LIGHT...

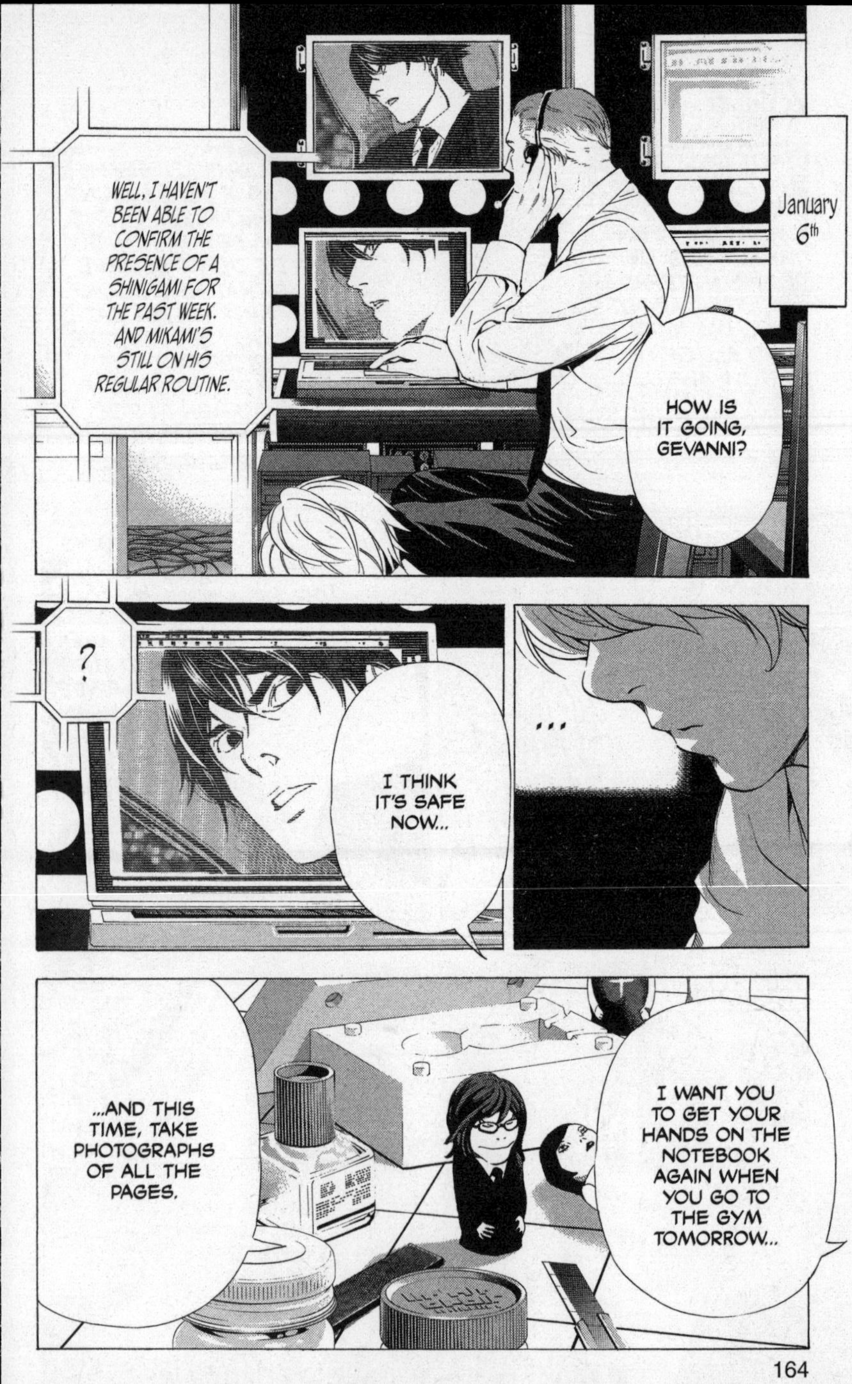
January 6th
HOW IS IT GOING, GEVANNI?
WELL, I HAVEN'T BEEN ABLE TO CONFIRM THE PRESENCE OF A SHINIGAMI FOR THE PAST WEEK. AND MIKAMI'S STILL ON HIS REGULAR ROUTINE.
...
?
I THINK IT'S SAFE NOW...
I WANT YOU TO GET YOUR HANDS ON THE NOTEBOOK AGAIN WHEN YOU GO TO THE GYM TOMORROW...
...AND THIS TIME, TAKE PHOTOGRAPHS OF ALL THE PAGES.

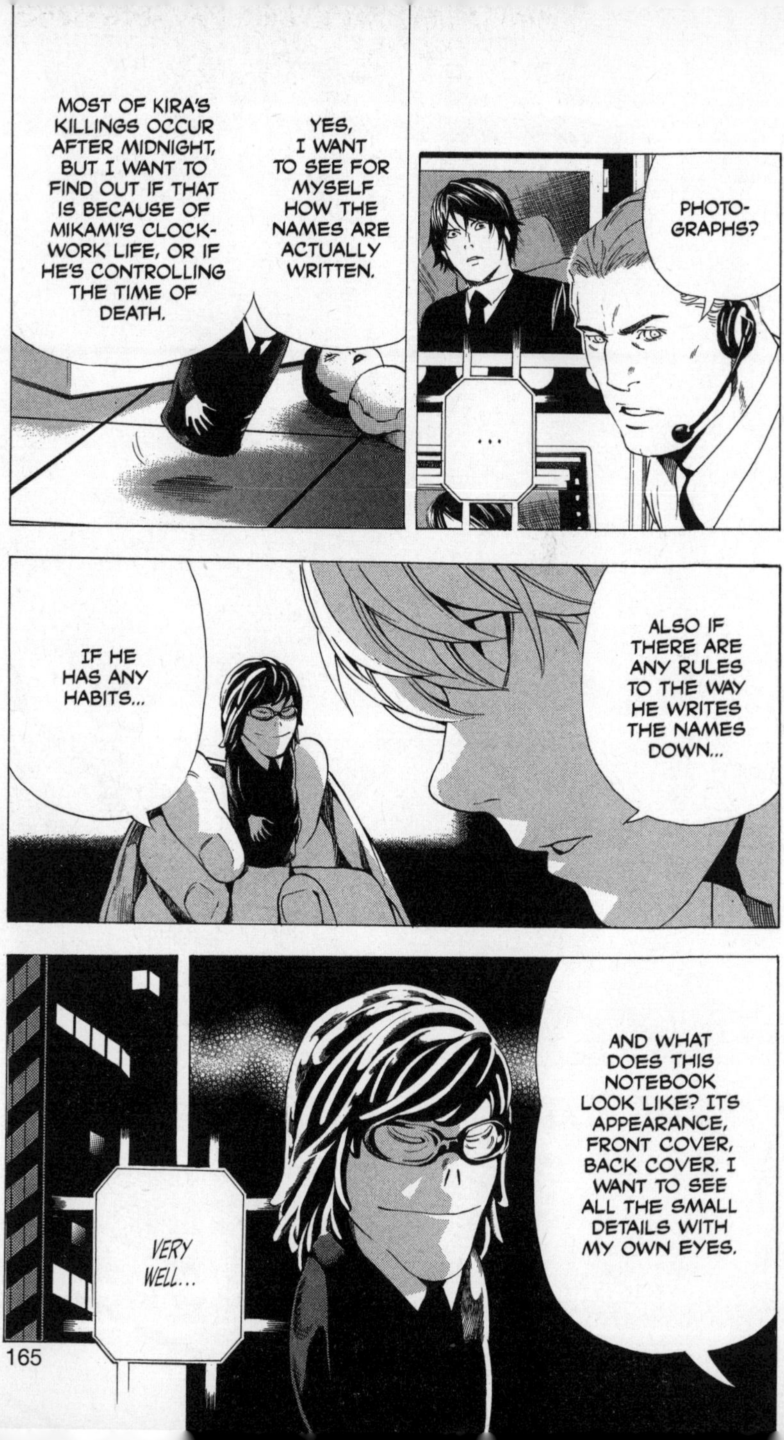

PHOTOGRAPHS?
...
YES, I WANT TO SEE FOR MYSELF HOW THE NAMES ARE ACTUALLY WRITTEN.
MOST OF KIRA'S KILLINGS OCCUR AFTER MIDNIGHT, BUT I WANT TO FIND OUT IF THAT IS BECAUSE OF MIKAMI'S CLOCKWORK LIFE, OR IF HE'S CONTROLLING THE TIME OF DEATH.
ALSO IF THERE ARE ANY RULES TO THE WAY HE WRITES THE NAMES DOWN...
IF HE HAS ANY HABITS...
AND WHAT DOES THIS NOTEBOOK LOOK LIKE? ITS APPEARANCE, FRONT COVER, BACK COVER. I WANT TO SEE ALL THE SMALL DETAILS WITH MY OWN EYES.
VERY WELL...

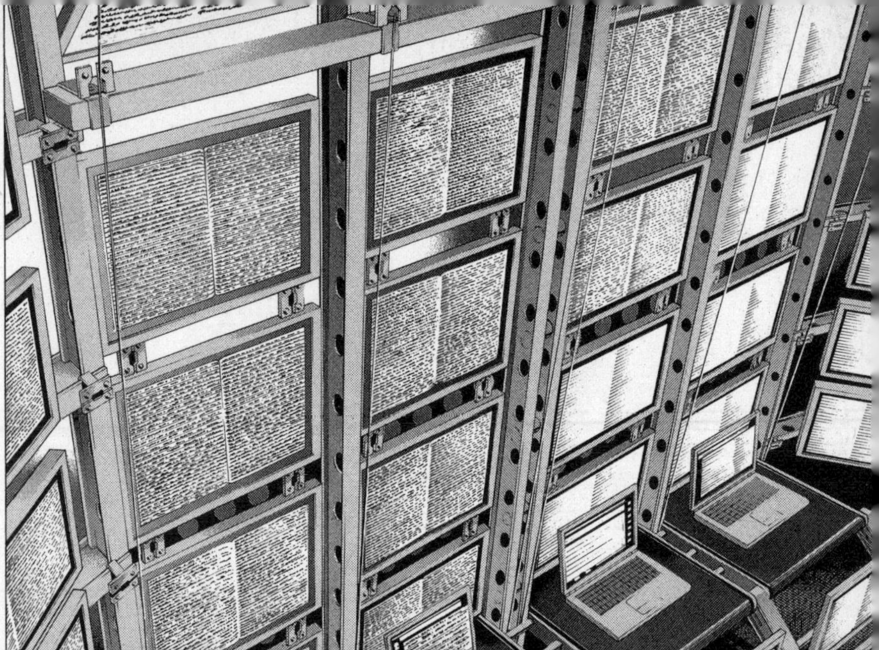

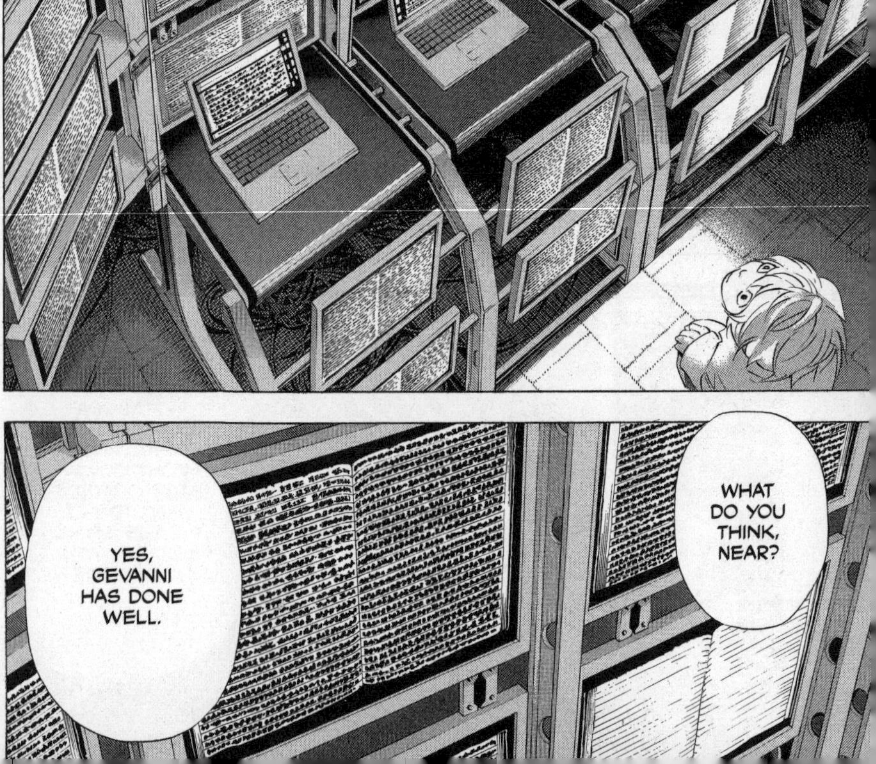
WHAT DO YOU THINK, NEAR?
YES, GEVANNI HAS DONE WELL.

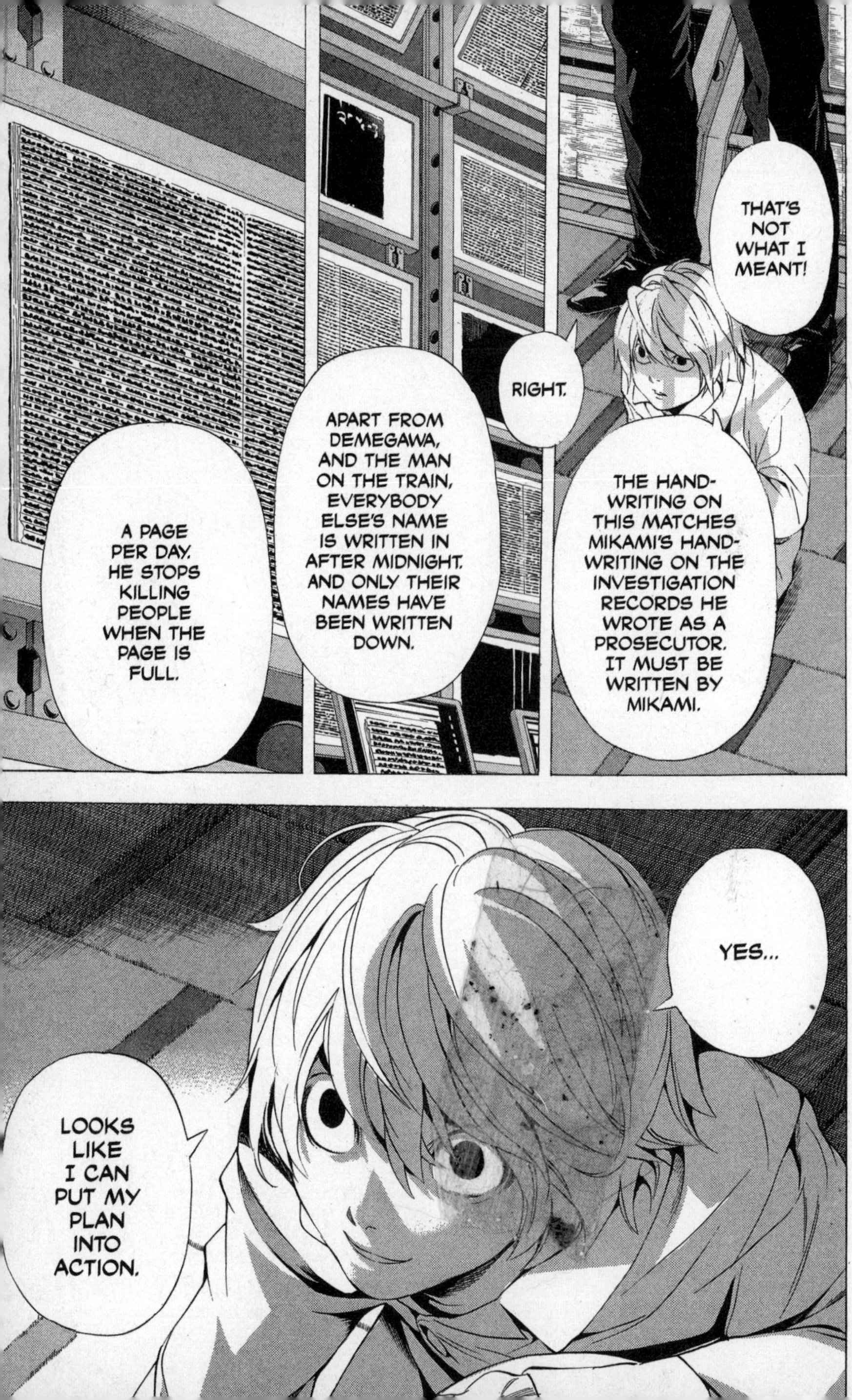

THAT'S NOT WHAT I MEANT!
RIGHT.
THE HAND-WRITING ON THIS MATCHES MIKAMI'S HAND-WRITING ON THE INVESTIGATION RECORDS HE WROTE AS A PROSECUTOR. IT MUST BE WRITTEN BY MIKAMI.
APART FROM DEMEGAWA, AND THE MAN ON THE TRAIN, EVERYBODY ELSE'S NAME IS WRITTEN IN AFTER MIDNIGHT. AND ONLY THEIR NAMES HAVE BEEN WRITTEN DOWN.
A PAGE PER DAY. HE STOPS KILLING PEOPLE WHEN THE PAGE IS FULL.
YES...
LOOKS LIKE I CAN PUT MY PLAN INTO ACTION.

DEATH NOTE
HOW to USE it
LXIV

o The following situations are the cases where a god of death that has brought the DEATH NOTE into the human world is allowed to return to the world of gods of death.

人間界にデスノートを持ち込んだ死神が死神界へ戻っていいのは

1. When the god of death has seen the end of the first owner of the DEATH NOTE brought into the human world, and has written that human's name on his/her own DEATH NOTE.

1．人間界に持ち込んだノートの最初の所有者となった人間の最期を見届け、
自分のノートにその人間の名前を書いた時。

2. When the DEATH NOTE which has been brought in is destroyed, like burned, and cannot be used by humans anymore.

2．持ち込んだノートが燃える等して人間が使えなくなった時。

3. If nobody claims the ownership of the DEATH NOTE and it is unnecessary to haunt anyone.

3．誰も所有権を持たず、憑く必要がなくなった時。

4. If, for any reason, the god of death possessing the DEATH NOTE has been replaced by another god of death.

4．何らかの理由で持ち込んだノートに憑く死神が交代した時。

5. When the god of death loses track of the DEATH NOTE which he/she possesses, cannot identify which human is owning the DEATH NOTE, or cannot locate where the owner is, and therefore needs to find such information through the hole in the world of gods of death.

5．自分が憑くそのノート自体への場所や、所有する人間が誰なのか、また所有者の居場所がわからなくなり、死神界の穴からそれを探す時。

Even in the situations 2, 3, and 4 above, gods of death are obliged to confirm the death of the first owner and write down that human's name in his/her DEATH NOTE even when he/she is in the world of gods of death.

2、3、4の場合でも、自分が最初に譲渡した人間の死は、
死神界からでも確認し自分のノートに書き込む義務がある。

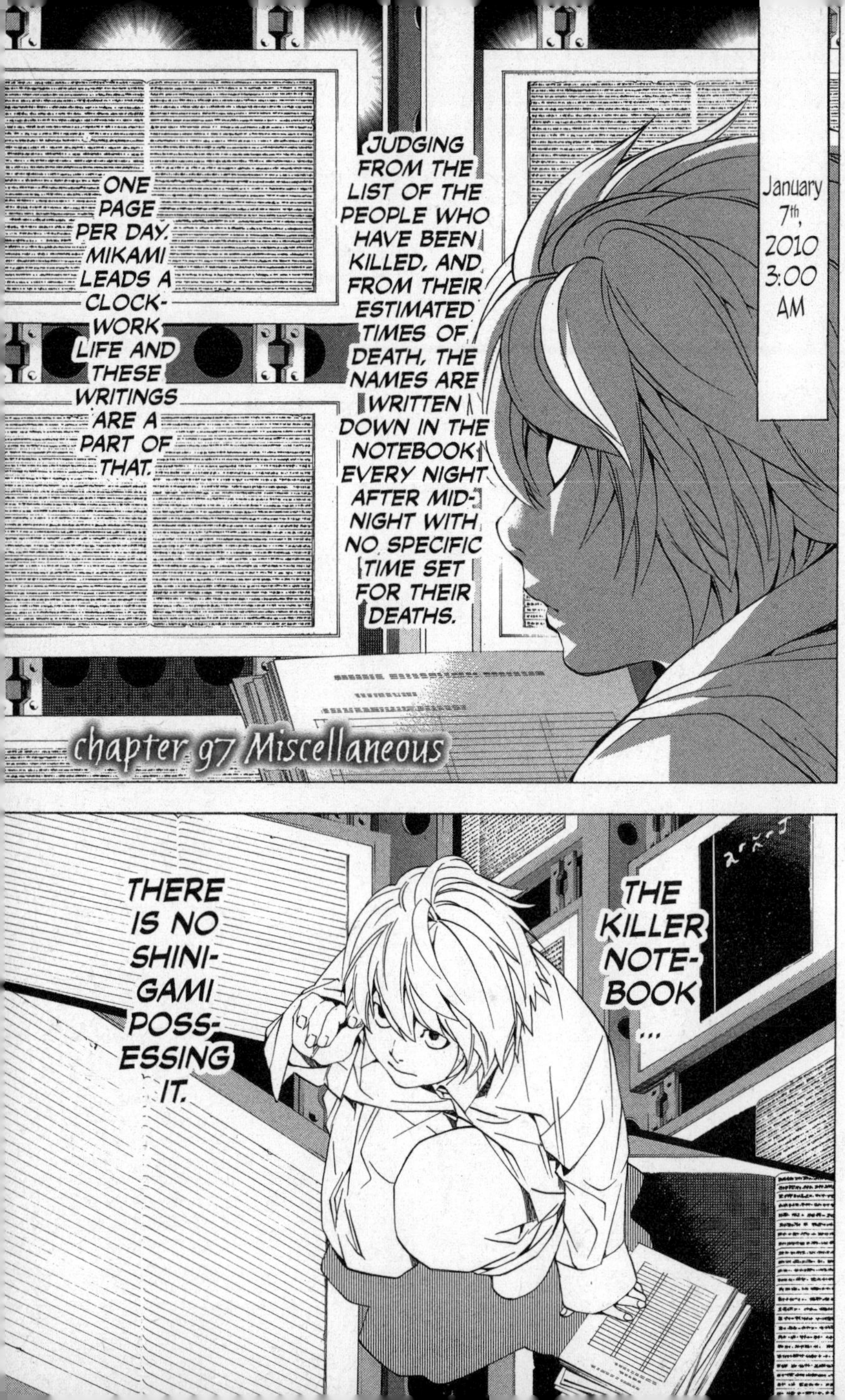
January 7th, 2010 3:00 AM
JUDGING FROM THE LIST OF THE PEOPLE WHO HAVE BEEN KILLED, AND FROM THEIR ESTIMATED TIMES OF DEATH, THE NAMES ARE WRITTEN DOWN IN THE NOTEBOOK EVERY NIGHT AFTER MIDNIGHT WITH NO SPECIFIC TIME SET FOR THEIR DEATHS.
ONE PAGE PER DAY. MIKAMI LEADS A CLOCKWORK LIFE AND THESE WRITINGS ARE A PART OF THAT.
chapter 97 Miscellaneous
THE KILLER NOTEBOOK...
THERE IS NO SHINIGAMI POSSESSING IT.

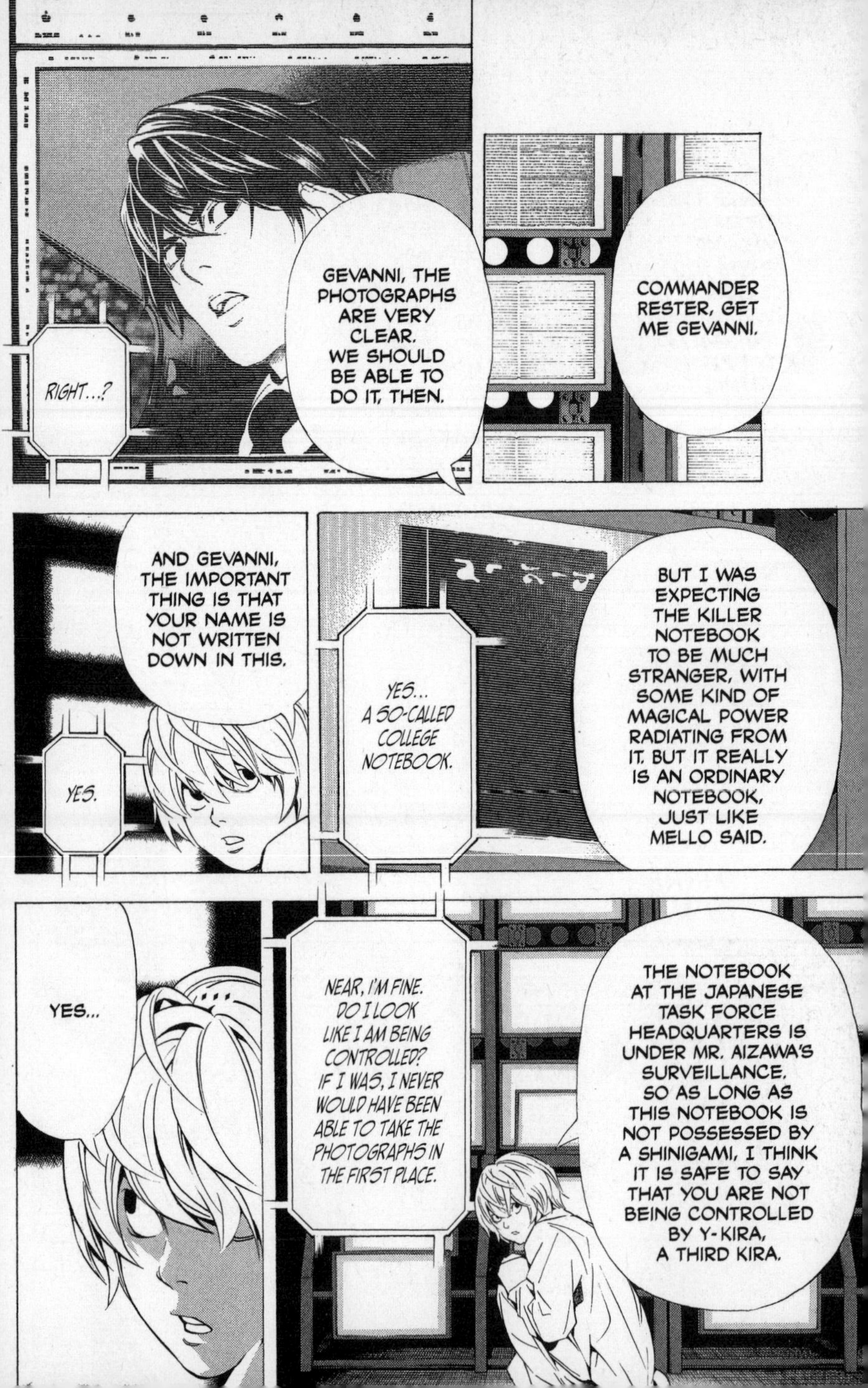
COMMANDER RESTER, GET ME GEVANNI.
GEVANNI, THE PHOTOGRAPHS ARE VERY CLEAR. WE SHOULD BE ABLE TO DO IT, THEN.
RIGHT...?
BUT I WAS EXPECTING THE KILLER NOTEBOOK TO BE MUCH STRANGER, WITH SOME KIND OF MAGICAL POWER RADIATING FROM IT. BUT IT REALLY IS AN ORDINARY NOTEBOOK, JUST LIKE MELLO SAID.
YES... A SO-CALLED COLLEGE NOTEBOOK.
AND GEVANNI, THE IMPORTANT THING IS THAT YOUR NAME IS NOT WRITTEN DOWN IN THIS.
YES.
THE NOTEBOOK AT THE JAPANESE TASK FORCE HEADQUARTERS IS UNDER MR. AIZAWA'S SURVEILLANCE. SO AS LONG AS THIS NOTEBOOK IS NOT POSSESSED BY A SHINIGAMI, I THINK IT IS SAFE TO SAY THAT YOU ARE NOT BEING CONTROLLED BY Y-KIRA, A THIRD KIRA.
NEAR, I'M FINE. DO I LOOK LIKE I AM BEING CONTROLLED? IF I WAS, I NEVER WOULD HAVE BEEN ABLE TO TAKE THE PHOTOGRAPHS IN THE FIRST PLACE.
...
YES...

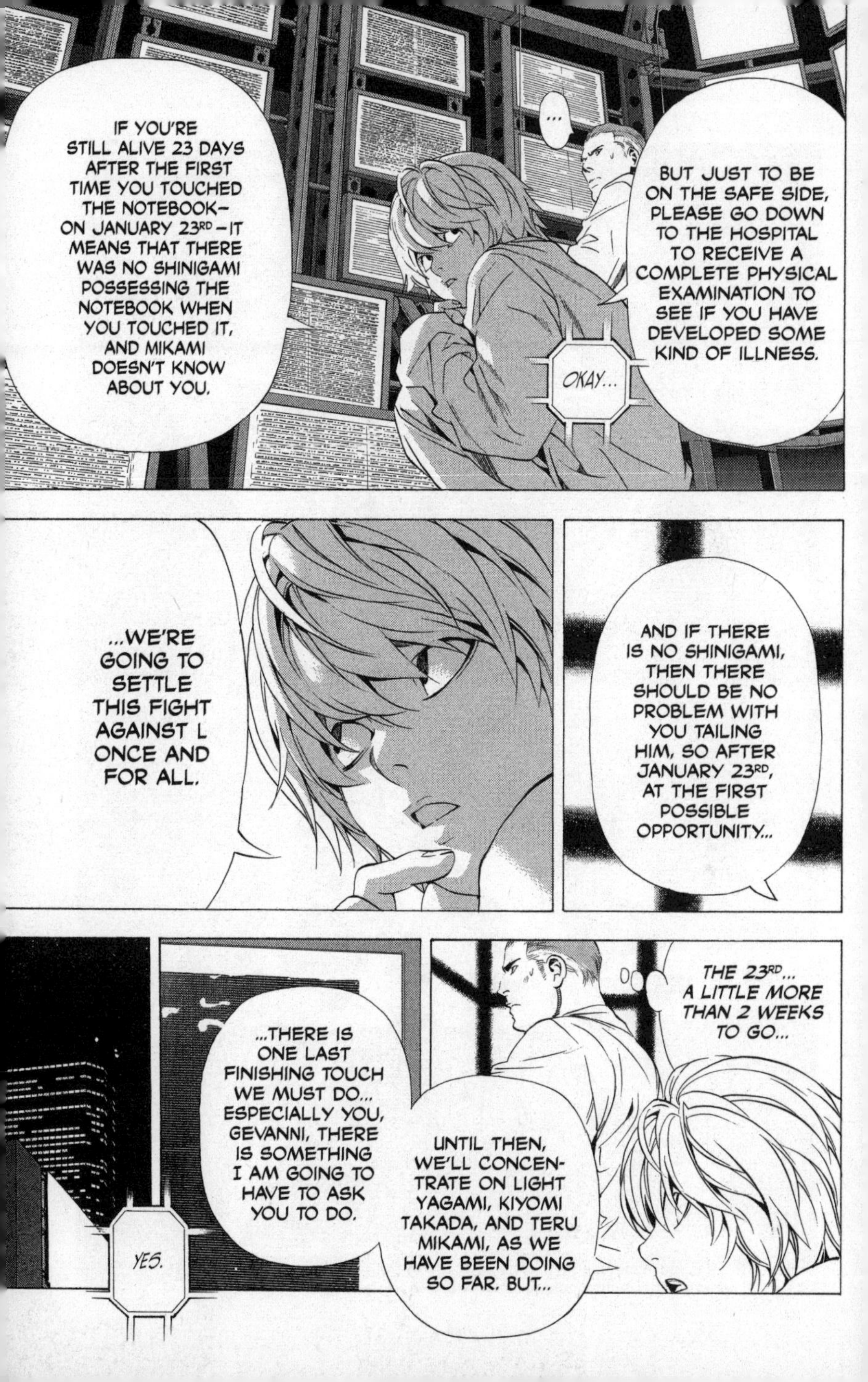
IF YOU'RE STILL ALIVE 23 DAYS AFTER THE FIRST TIME YOU TOUCHED THE NOTEBOOK— ON JANUARY 23RD —IT MEANS THAT THERE WAS NO SHINIGAMI POSSESSING THE NOTEBOOK WHEN YOU TOUCHED IT, AND MIKAMI DOESN'T KNOW ABOUT YOU.
...
BUT JUST TO BE ON THE SAFE SIDE, PLEASE GO DOWN TO THE HOSPITAL TO RECEIVE A COMPLETE PHYSICAL EXAMINATION TO SEE IF YOU HAVE DEVELOPED SOME KIND OF ILLNESS.
OKAY...
AND IF THERE IS NO SHINIGAMI, THEN THERE SHOULD BE NO PROBLEM WITH YOU TAILING HIM, SO AFTER JANUARY 23RD, AT THE FIRST POSSIBLE OPPORTUNITY...
...WE'RE GOING TO SETTLE THIS FIGHT AGAINST L ONCE AND FOR ALL.
THE 23RD... A LITTLE MORE THAN 2 WEEKS TO GO...
UNTIL THEN, WE'LL CONCENTRATE ON LIGHT YAGAMI, KIYOMI TAKADA, AND TERU MIKAMI, AS WE HAVE BEEN DOING SO FAR. BUT...
...THERE IS ONE LAST FINISHING TOUCH WE MUST DO... ESPECIALLY YOU, GEVANNI, THERE IS SOMETHING I AM GOING TO HAVE TO ASK YOU TO DO.
YES.

chapter 97 Miscellaneous

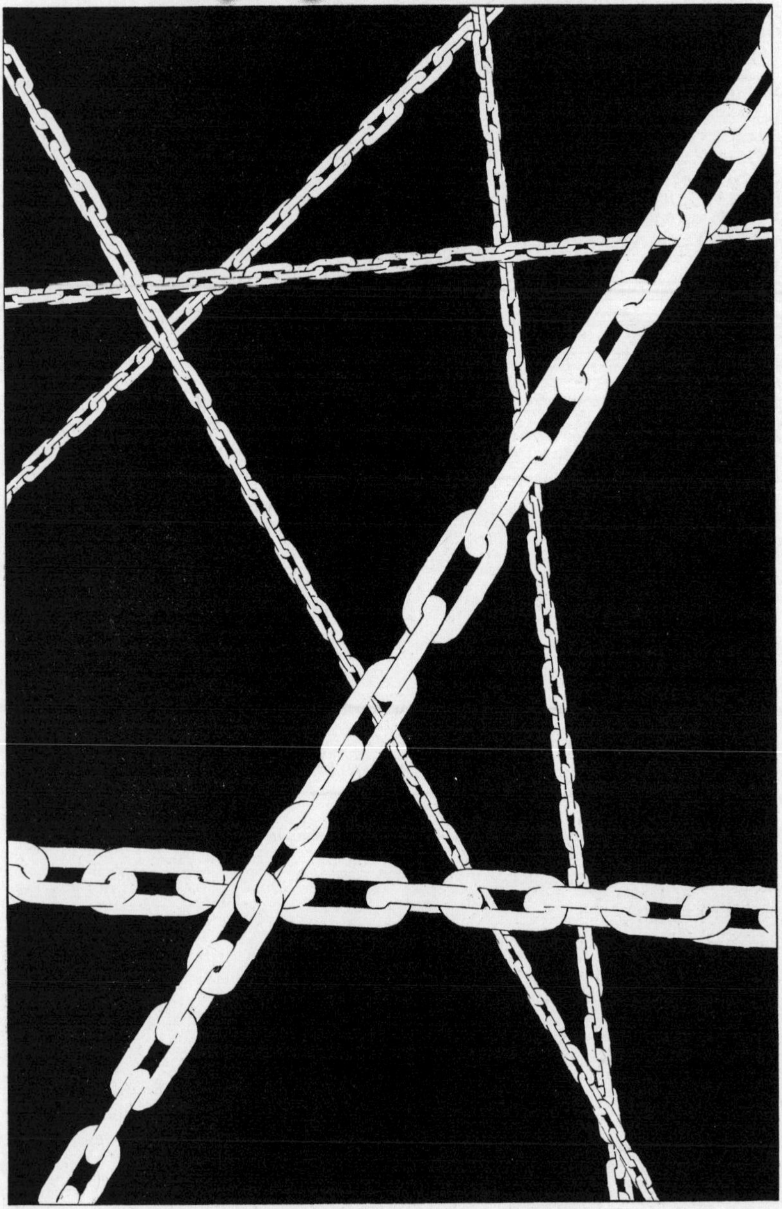

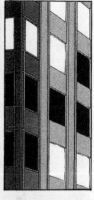

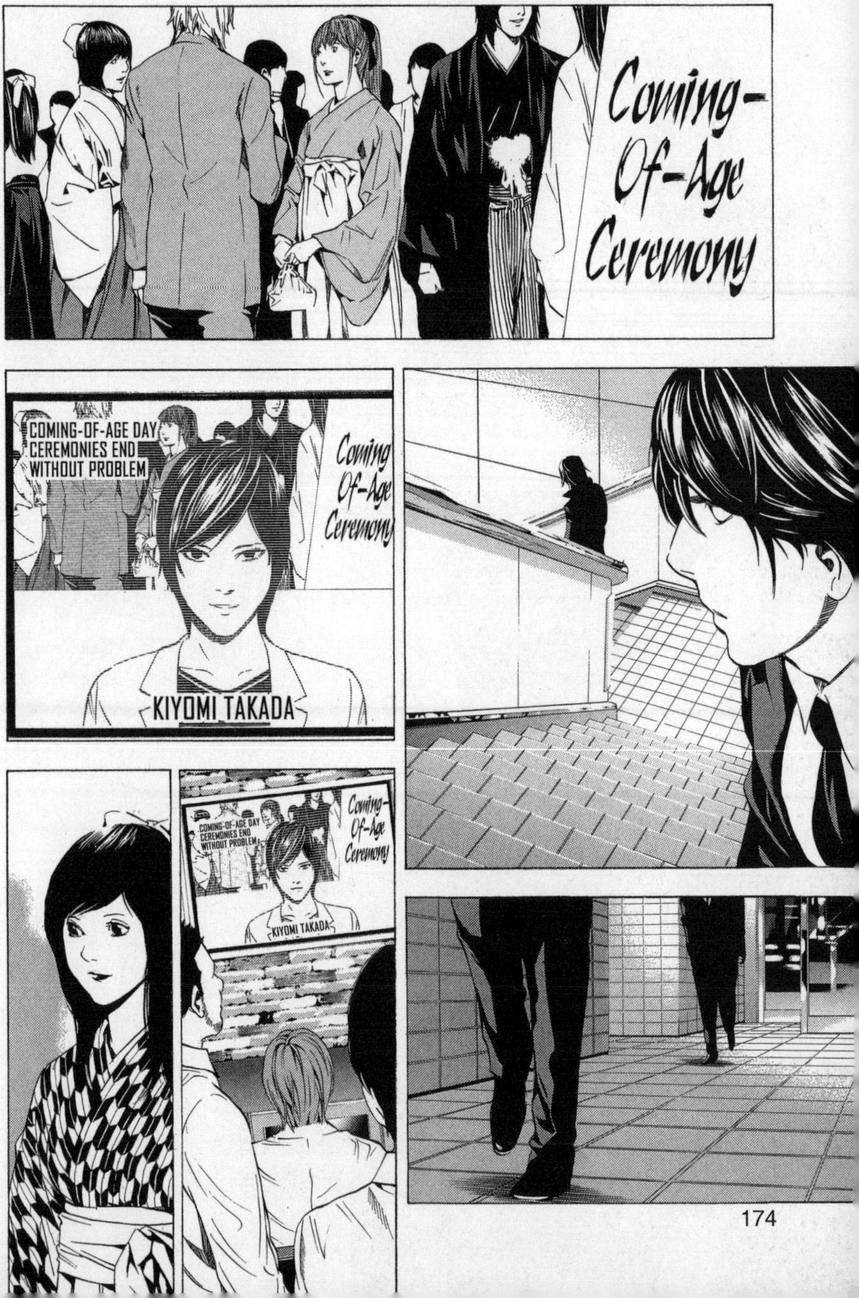
Coming-
Of-Age
Ceremony
COMING-OF-AGE DAY
CEREMONIES END
WITHOUT PROBLEM
Coming-
Of-Age
Ceremony
KIYOMI TAKADA
COMING-OF-AGE DAY
CEREMONIES END
WITHOUT PROBLEM
Coming-
Of-Age
Ceremony
KIYOMI TAKADA

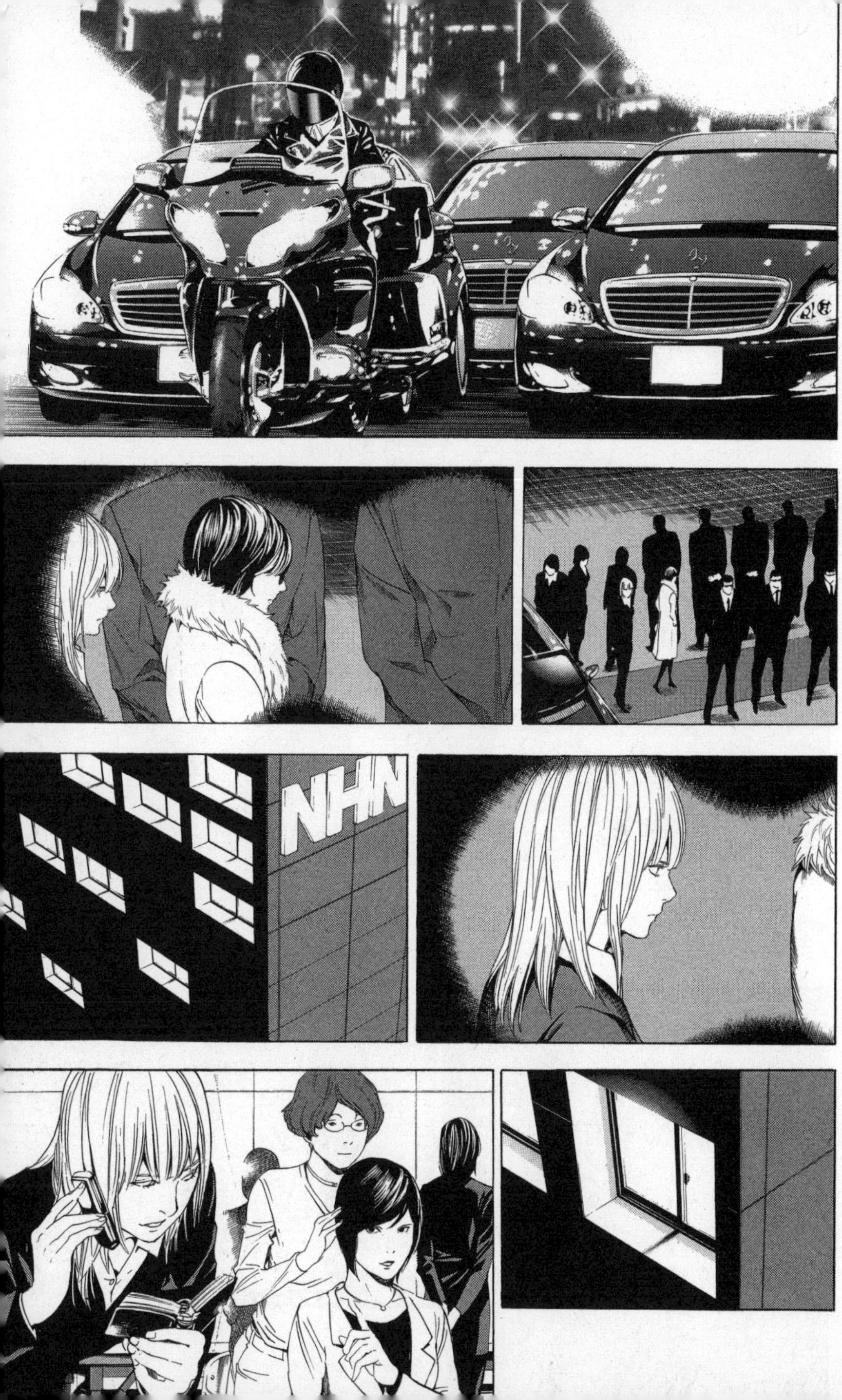
NHN

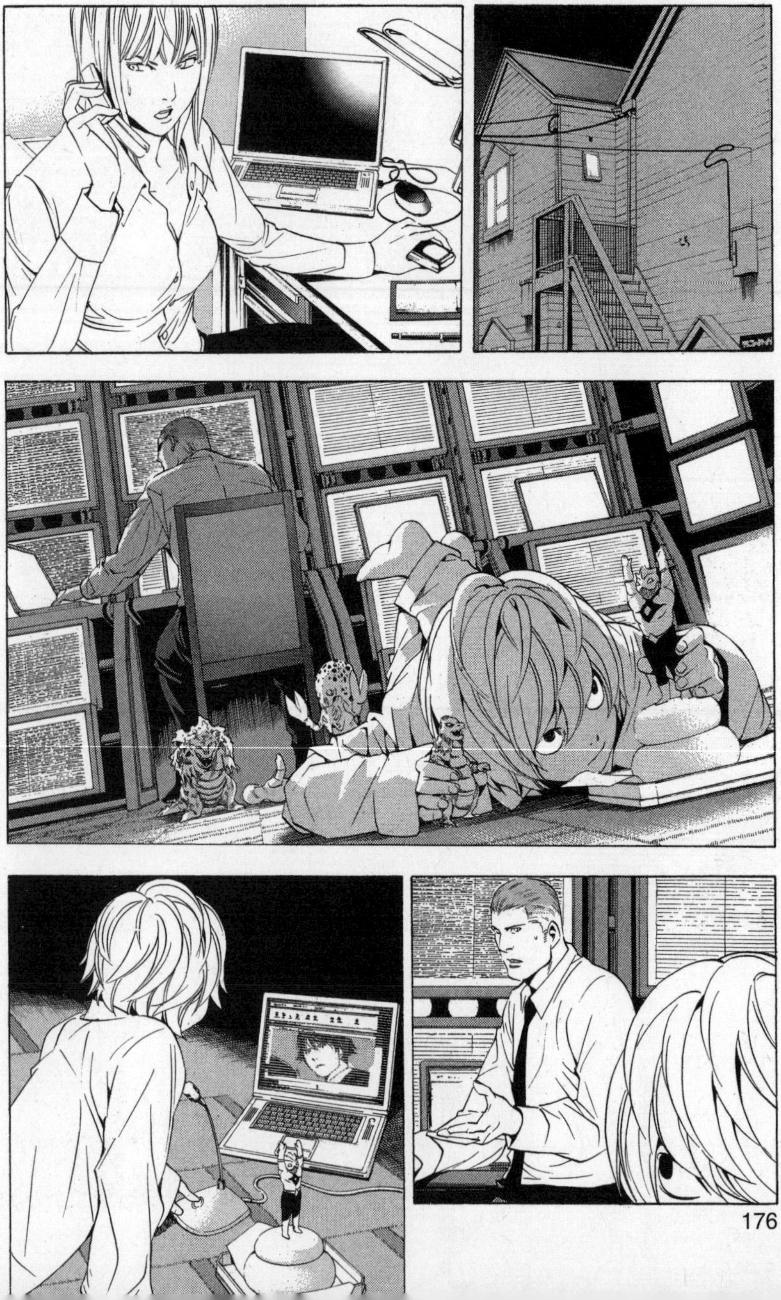

READ THIS WAY

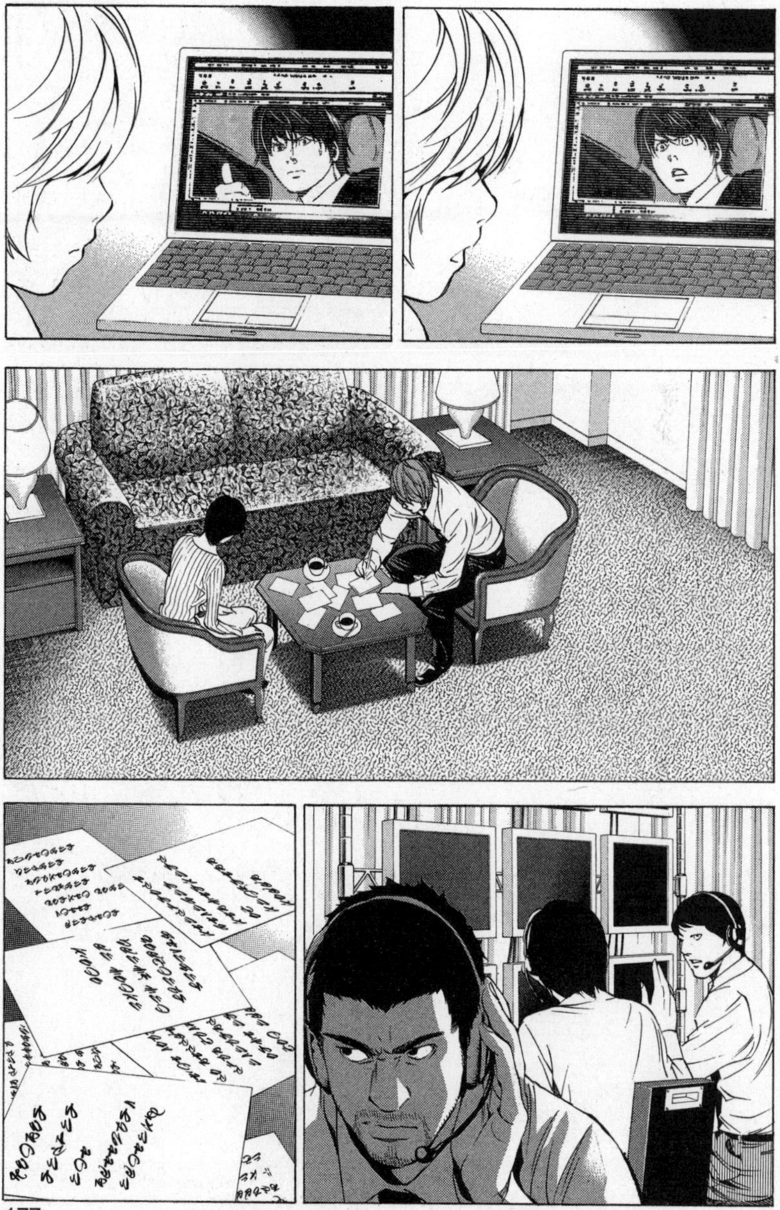

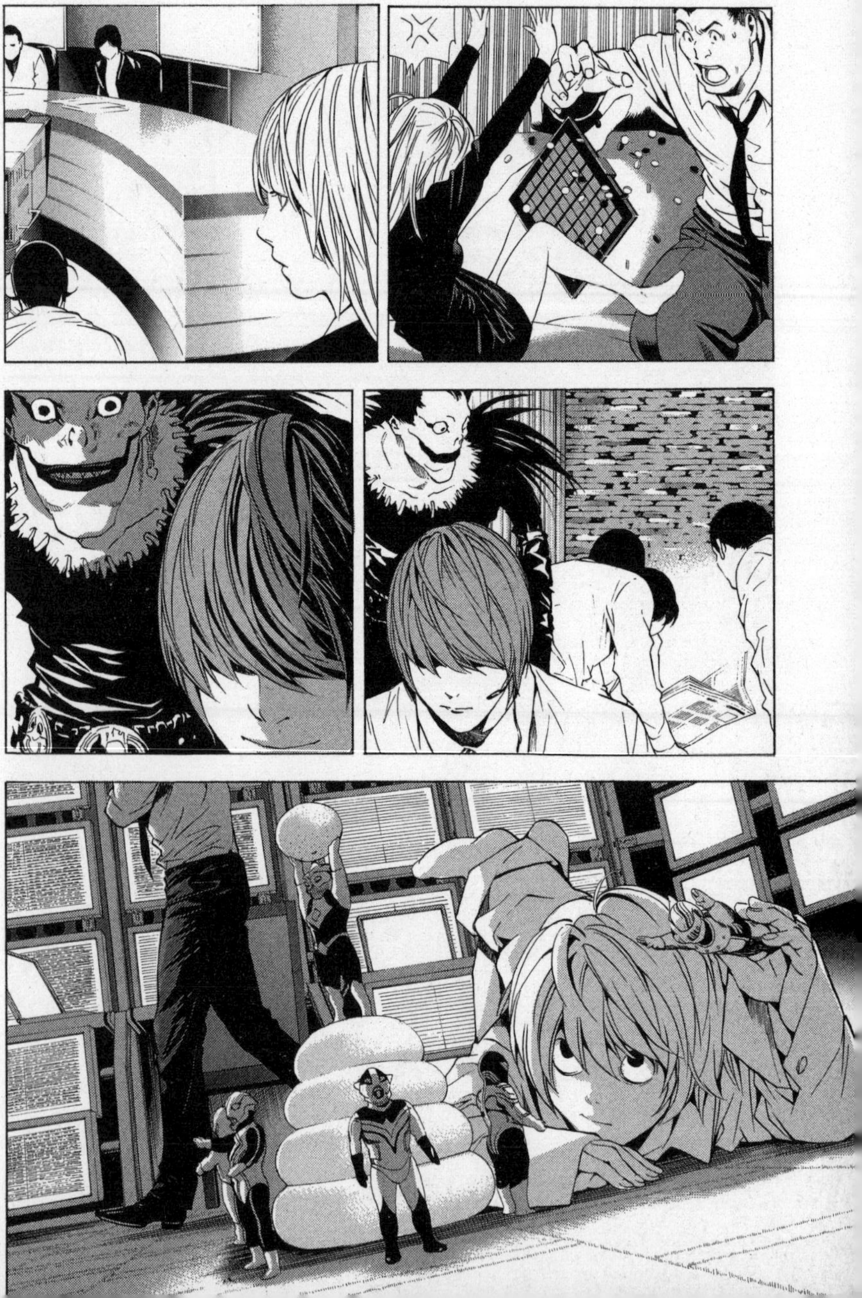

READ THIS WAY

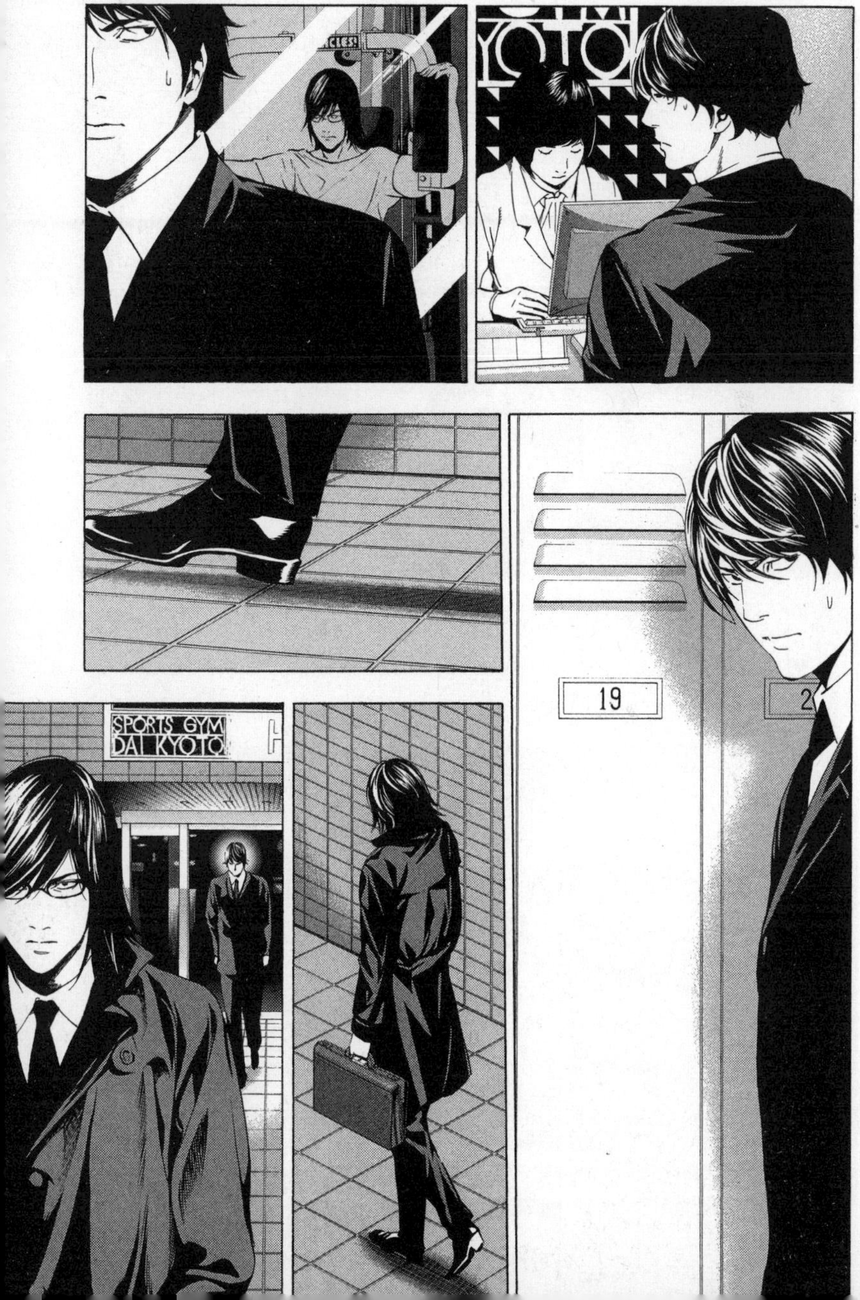
19
SPORTS GYM
DAI KYOTO

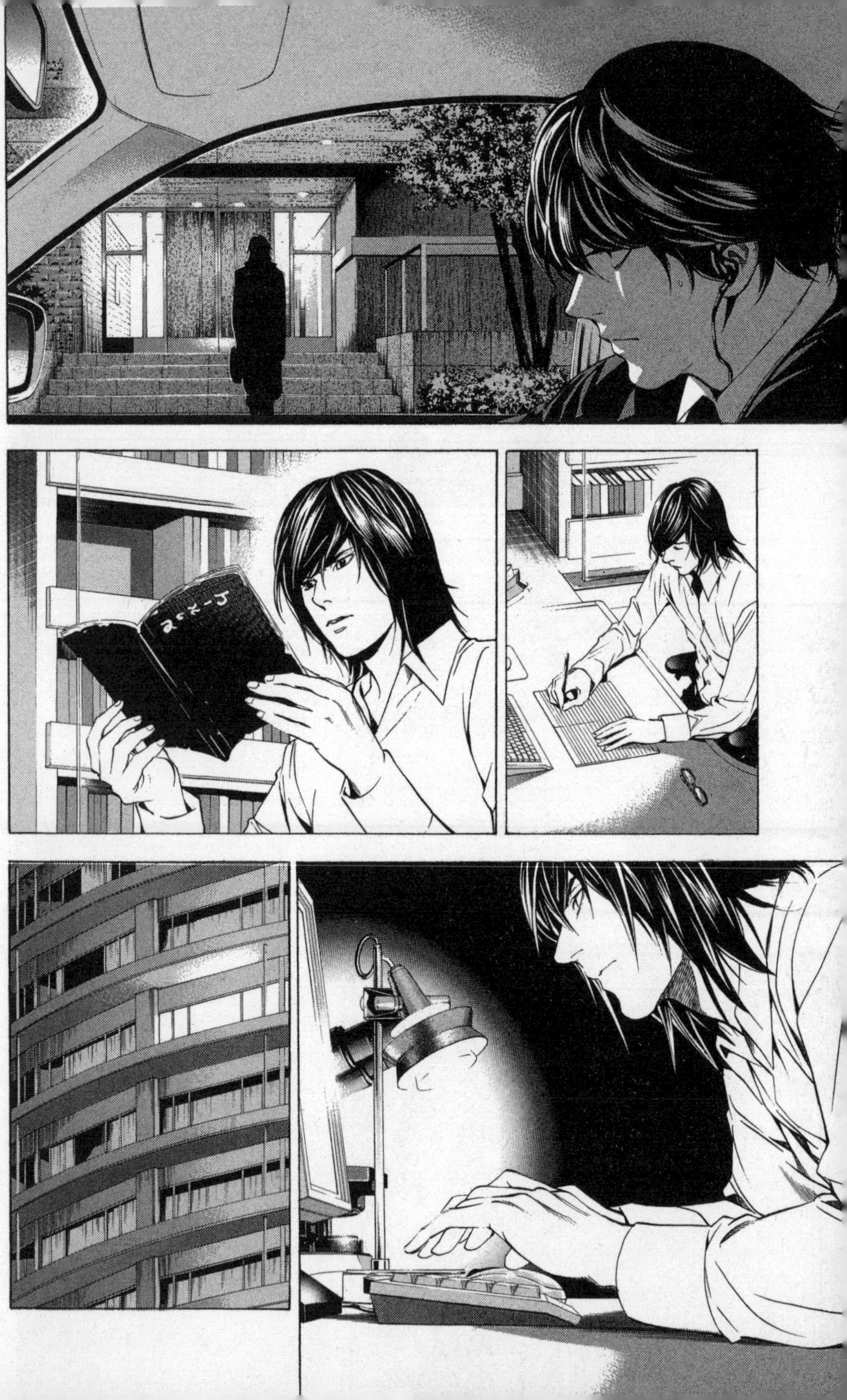

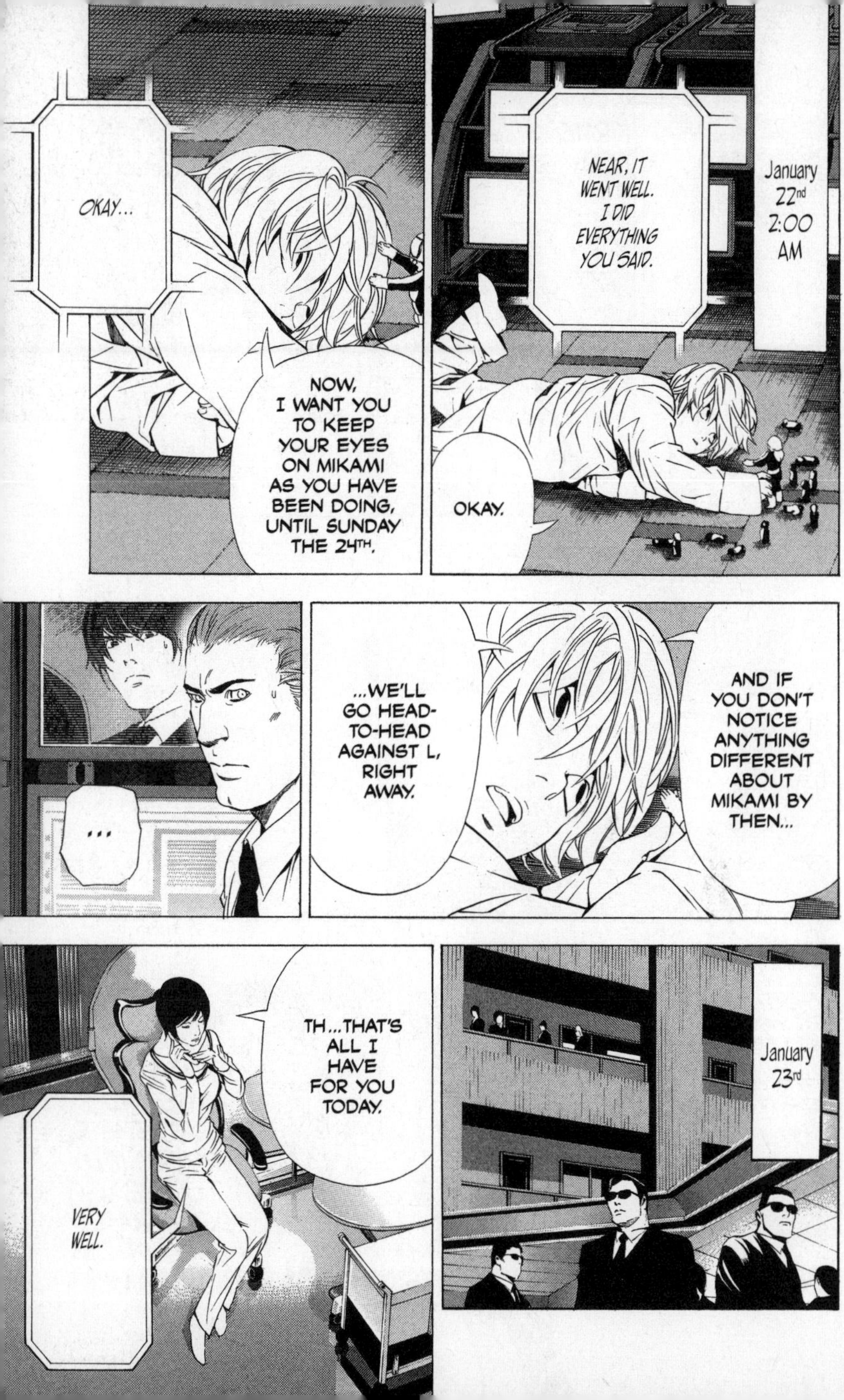
January 22nd 2:00 AM
NEAR, IT WENT WELL. I DID EVERYTHING YOU SAID.
OKAY.
NOW, I WANT YOU TO KEEP YOUR EYES ON MIKAMI AS YOU HAVE BEEN DOING, UNTIL SUNDAY THE 24TH.
OKAY...
AND IF YOU DON'T NOTICE ANYTHING DIFFERENT ABOUT MIKAMI BY THEN...
...WE'LL GO HEAD-TO-HEAD AGAINST L, RIGHT AWAY.
...
January 23rd
TH...THAT'S ALL I HAVE FOR YOU TODAY.
VERY WELL.

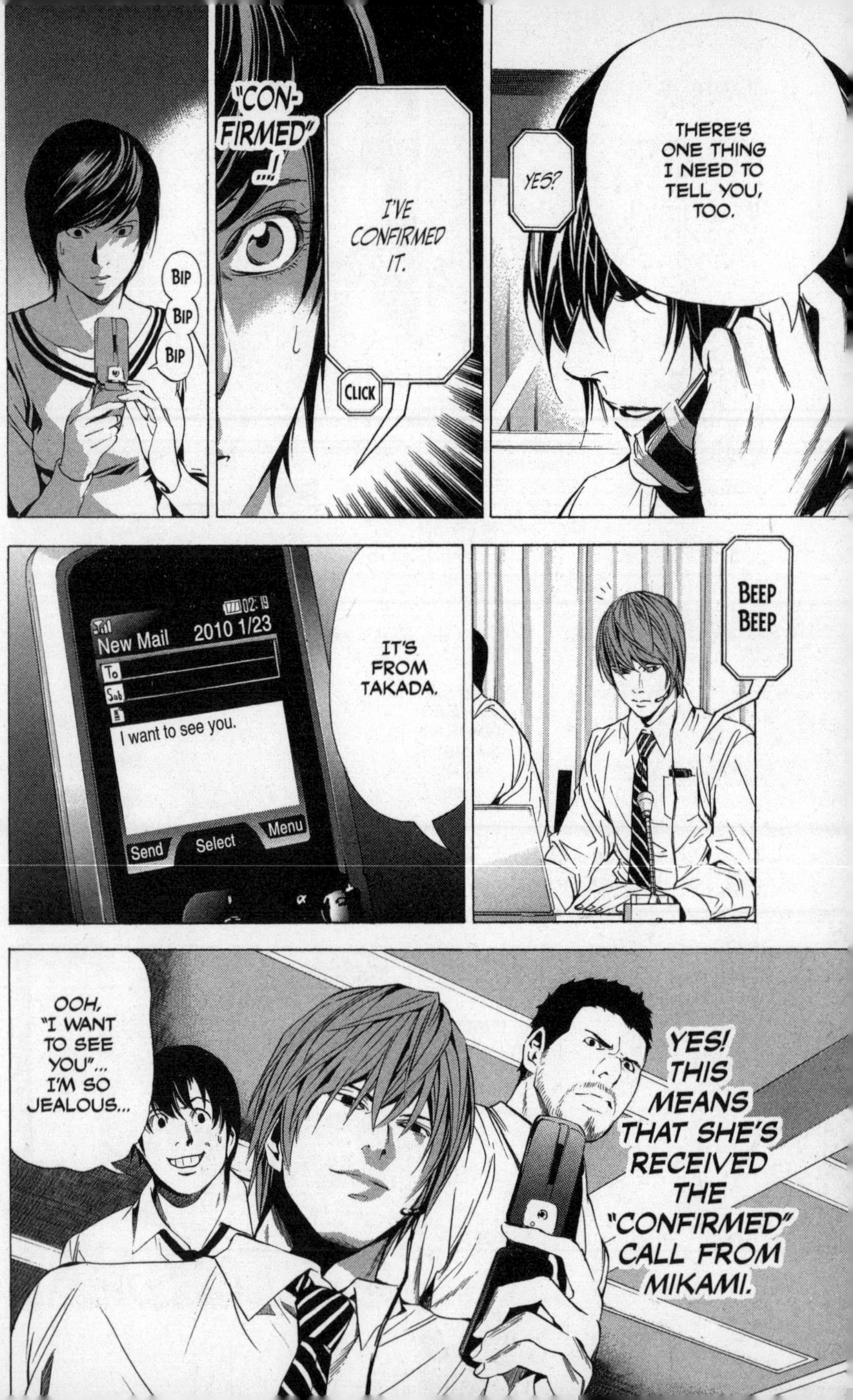

THERE'S ONE THING I NEED TO TELL YOU, TOO.
YES?
I'VE CONFIRMED IT.
"CON-FIRMED" ...!
CLICK
BIP
BIP
BIP
BEEP BEEP
IT'S FROM TAKADA.
02:19
New Mail 2010 1/23
To
Sub
I want to see you.
Send
Select
Menu
YES! THIS MEANS THAT SHE'S RECEIVED THE "CONFIRMED" CALL FROM MIKAMI.
OOH, "I WANT TO SEE YOU"... I'M SO JEALOUS...

READ THIS WAY

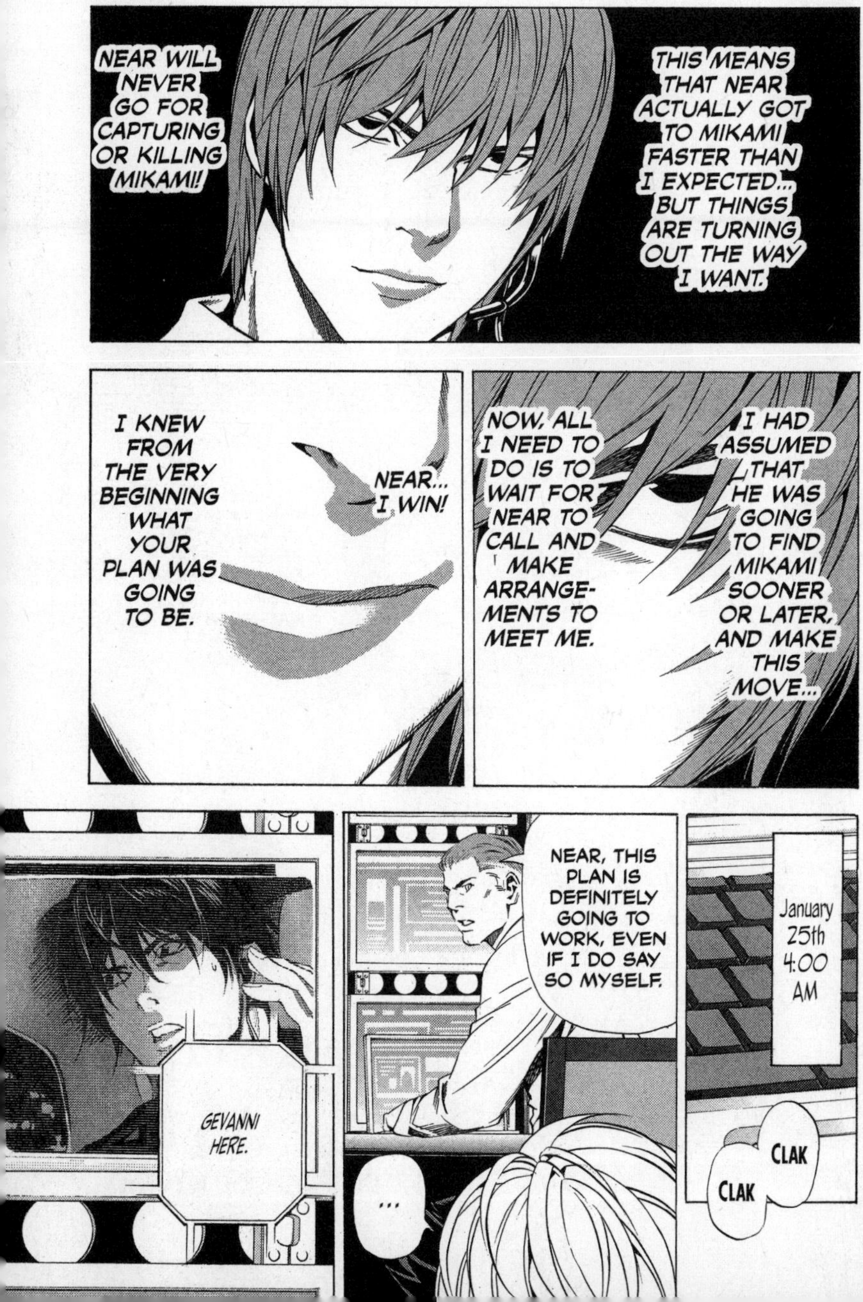
THIS MEANS THAT NEAR ACTUALLY GOT TO MIKAMI FASTER THAN I EXPECTED... BUT THINGS ARE TURNING OUT THE WAY I WANT.
NEAR WILL NEVER GO FOR CAPTURING OR KILLING MIKAMI!
I HAD ASSUMED THAT HE WAS GOING TO FIND MIKAMI SOONER OR LATER, AND MAKE THIS MOVE...
NOW, ALL I NEED TO DO IS TO WAIT FOR NEAR TO CALL AND MAKE ARRANGE-MENTS TO MEET ME.
NEAR... I WIN!
I KNEW FROM THE VERY BEGINNING WHAT YOUR PLAN WAS GOING TO BE.
January 25th 4:00 AM
CLAK
CLAK
NEAR, THIS PLAN IS DEFINITELY GOING TO WORK, EVEN IF I DO SAY SO MYSELF.
...
GEVANNI HERE.

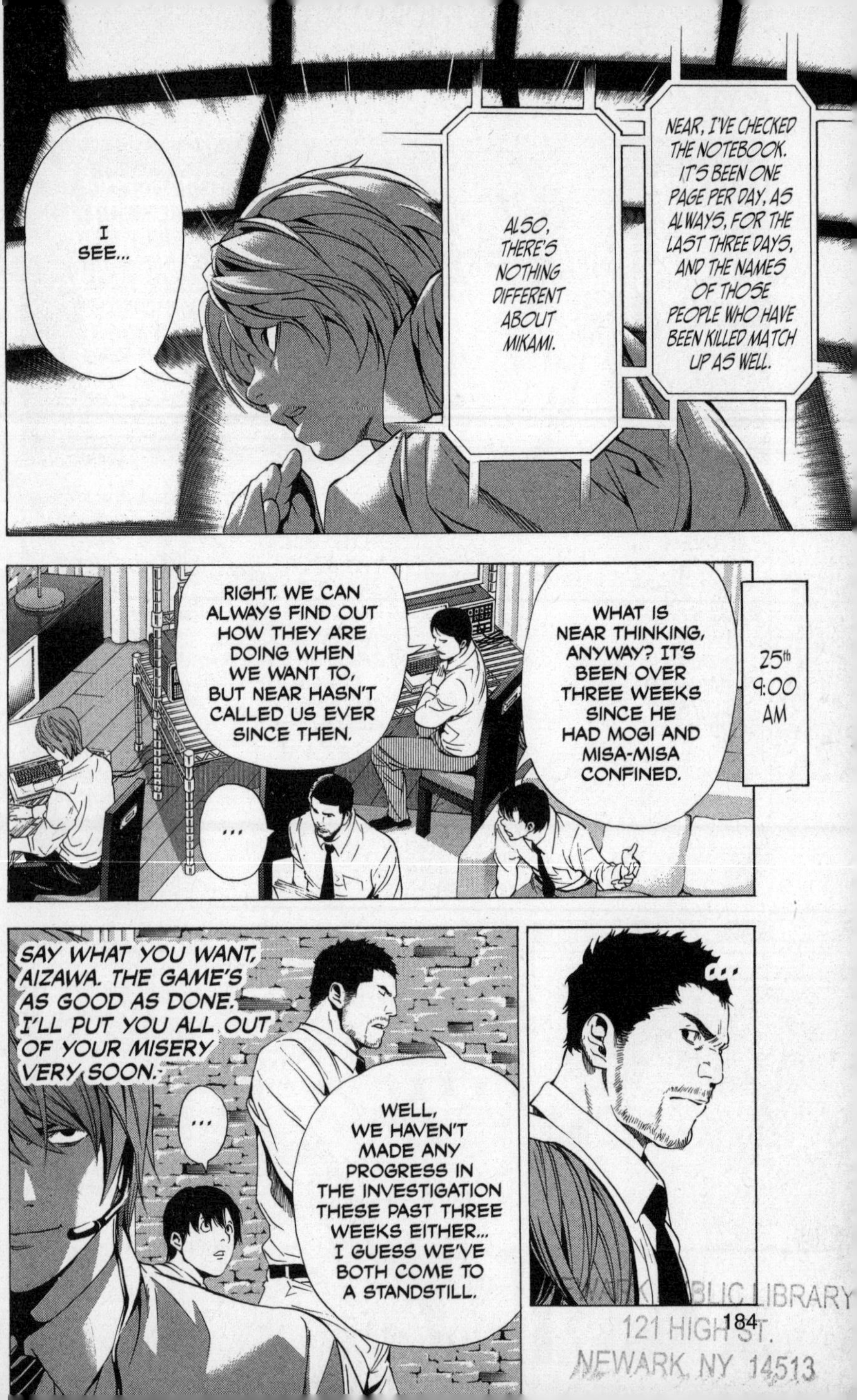
NEAR, I'VE CHECKED THE NOTEBOOK. IT'S BEEN ONE PAGE PER DAY, AS ALWAYS, FOR THE LAST THREE DAYS, AND THE NAMES OF THOSE PEOPLE WHO HAVE BEEN KILLED MATCH UP AS WELL.
ALSO, THERE'S NOTHING DIFFERENT ABOUT MIKAMI.
I SEE...
25th 9:00 AM
WHAT IS NEAR THINKING, ANYWAY? IT'S BEEN OVER THREE WEEKS SINCE HE HAD MOGI AND MISA-MISA CONFINED.
RIGHT. WE CAN ALWAYS FIND OUT HOW THEY ARE DOING WHEN WE WANT TO, BUT NEAR HASN'T CALLED US EVER SINCE THEN.
...
...
WELL, WE HAVEN'T MADE ANY PROGRESS IN THE INVESTIGATION THESE PAST THREE WEEKS EITHER... I GUESS WE'VE BOTH COME TO A STANDSTILL.
SAY WHAT YOU WANT, AIZAWA. THE GAME'S AS GOOD AS DONE. I'LL PUT YOU ALL OUT OF YOUR MISERY VERY SOON.
...

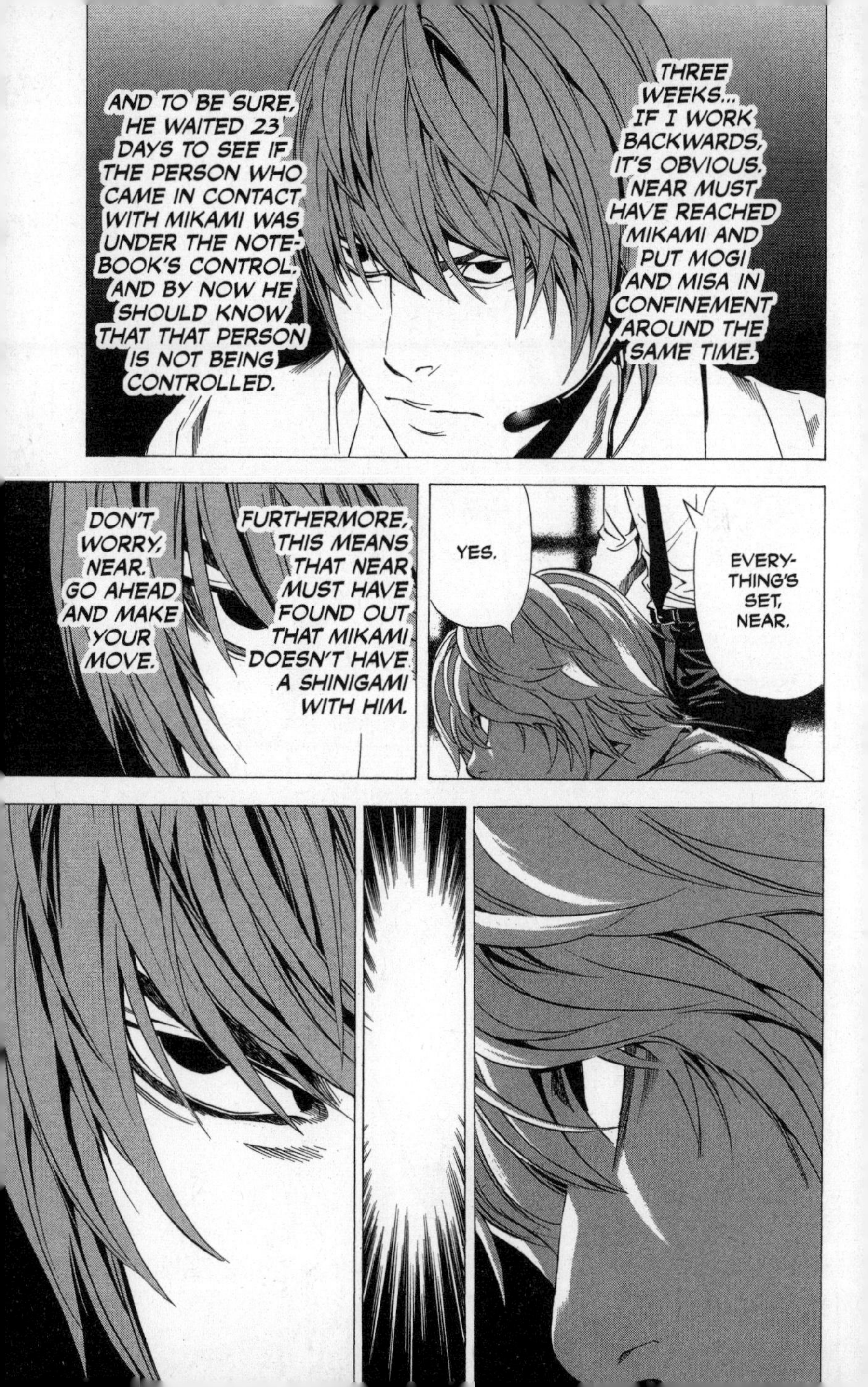
THREE WEEKS... IF I WORK BACKWARDS, IT'S OBVIOUS. NEAR MUST HAVE REACHED MIKAMI AND PUT MOGI AND MISA IN CONFINEMENT AROUND THE SAME TIME.
AND TO BE SURE, HE WAITED 23 DAYS TO SEE IF THE PERSON WHO CAME IN CONTACT WITH MIKAMI WAS UNDER THE NOTE-BOOK'S CONTROL. AND BY NOW HE SHOULD KNOW THAT THAT PERSON IS NOT BEING CONTROLLED.
EVERY-THING'S SET, NEAR.
YES.
FURTHERMORE, THIS MEANS THAT NEAR MUST HAVE FOUND OUT THAT MIKAMI DOESN'T HAVE A SHINIGAMI WITH HIM.
DON'T WORRY, NEAR. GO AHEAD AND MAKE YOUR MOVE.

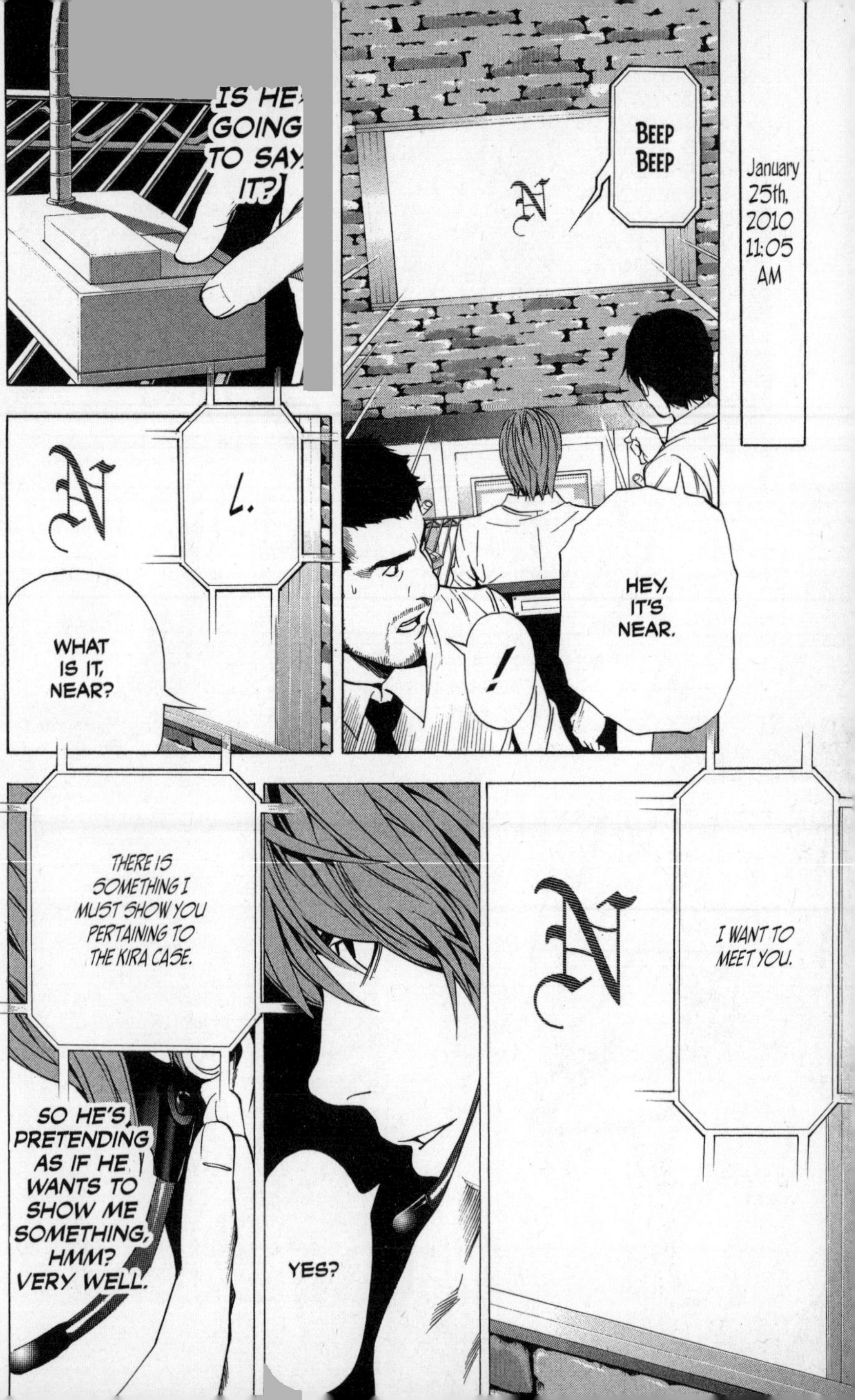

January 25th, 2010 11:05 AM
BEEP BEEP
HEY, IT'S NEAR.
!
IS HE GOING TO SAY IT?
L.
WHAT IS IT, NEAR?
I WANT TO MEET YOU.
YES?
THERE IS SOMETHING I MUST SHOW YOU PERTAINING TO THE KIRA CASE.
SO HE'S PRETENDING AS IF HE WANTS TO SHOW ME SOMETHING, HMM? VERY WELL.

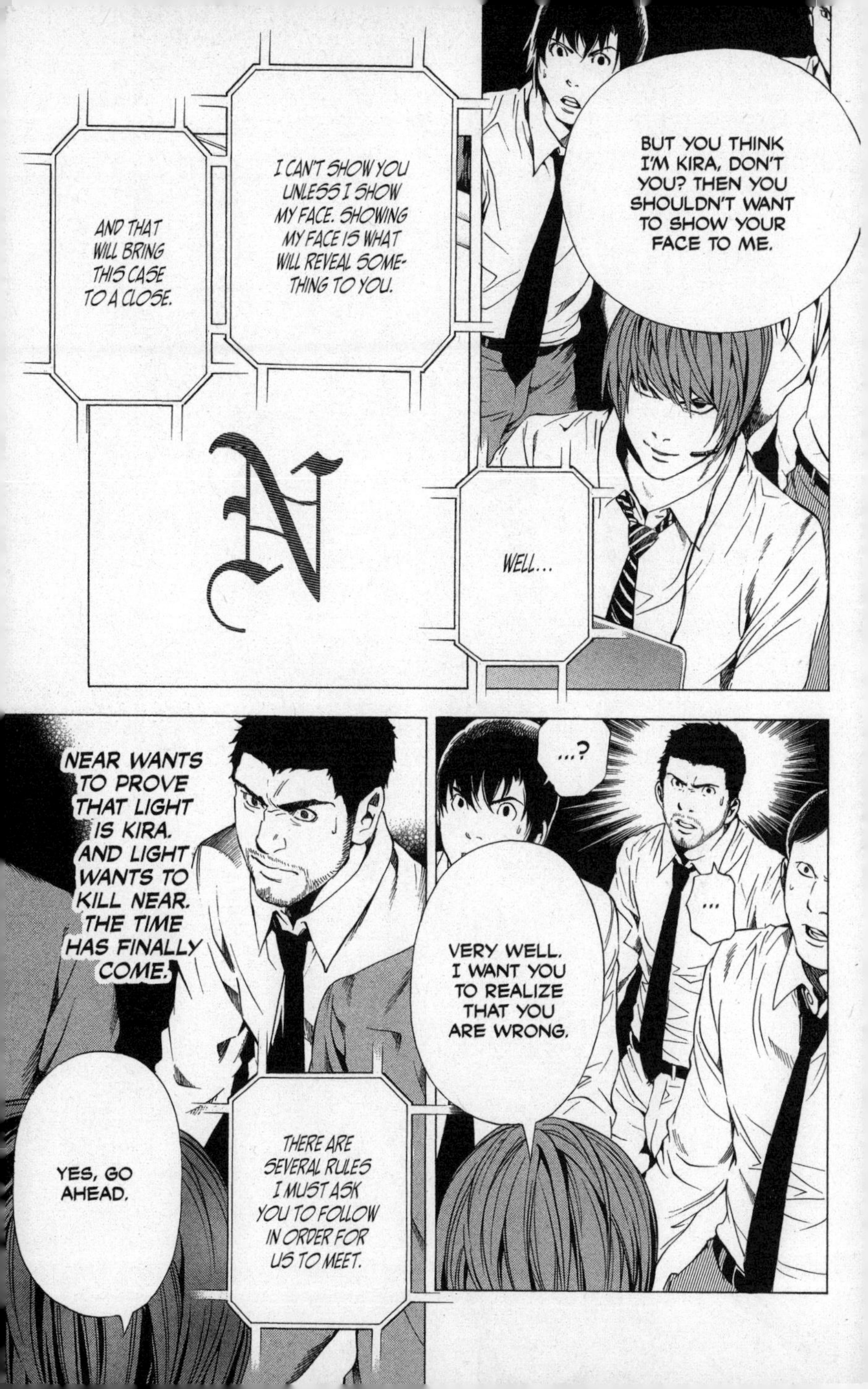
BUT YOU THINK I'M KIRA, DON'T YOU? THEN YOU SHOULDN'T WANT TO SHOW YOUR FACE TO ME.
WELL...
I CAN'T SHOW YOU UNLESS I SHOW MY FACE. SHOWING MY FACE IS WHAT WILL REVEAL SOME-THING TO YOU.
AND THAT WILL BRING THIS CASE TO A CLOSE.
N
...?
VERY WELL. I WANT YOU TO REALIZE THAT YOU ARE WRONG.
...
NEAR WANTS TO PROVE THAT LIGHT IS KIRA. AND LIGHT WANTS TO KILL NEAR. THE TIME HAS FINALLY COME.
THERE ARE SEVERAL RULES I MUST ASK YOU TO FOLLOW IN ORDER FOR US TO MEET.
YES, GO AHEAD.

DEATH NOTE
How to use it
LXV

- In the world of gods of death there are a few copies of what humans may call user guidebook for using the DEATH NOTE in the human world. However, the guidebook is not allowed to be delivered to humans.

デスノートの人間界でいう取扱説明書的な物は死神界に数冊存在するが、それを人間に渡す事は許されない。

- It is perfectly okay for gods of death to read the guidebook for him/herself and teach humans about its contents, no matter what the content may be.

それを自分が読み人間に教える事は、その内容がいかなるものでも全く問題ない。

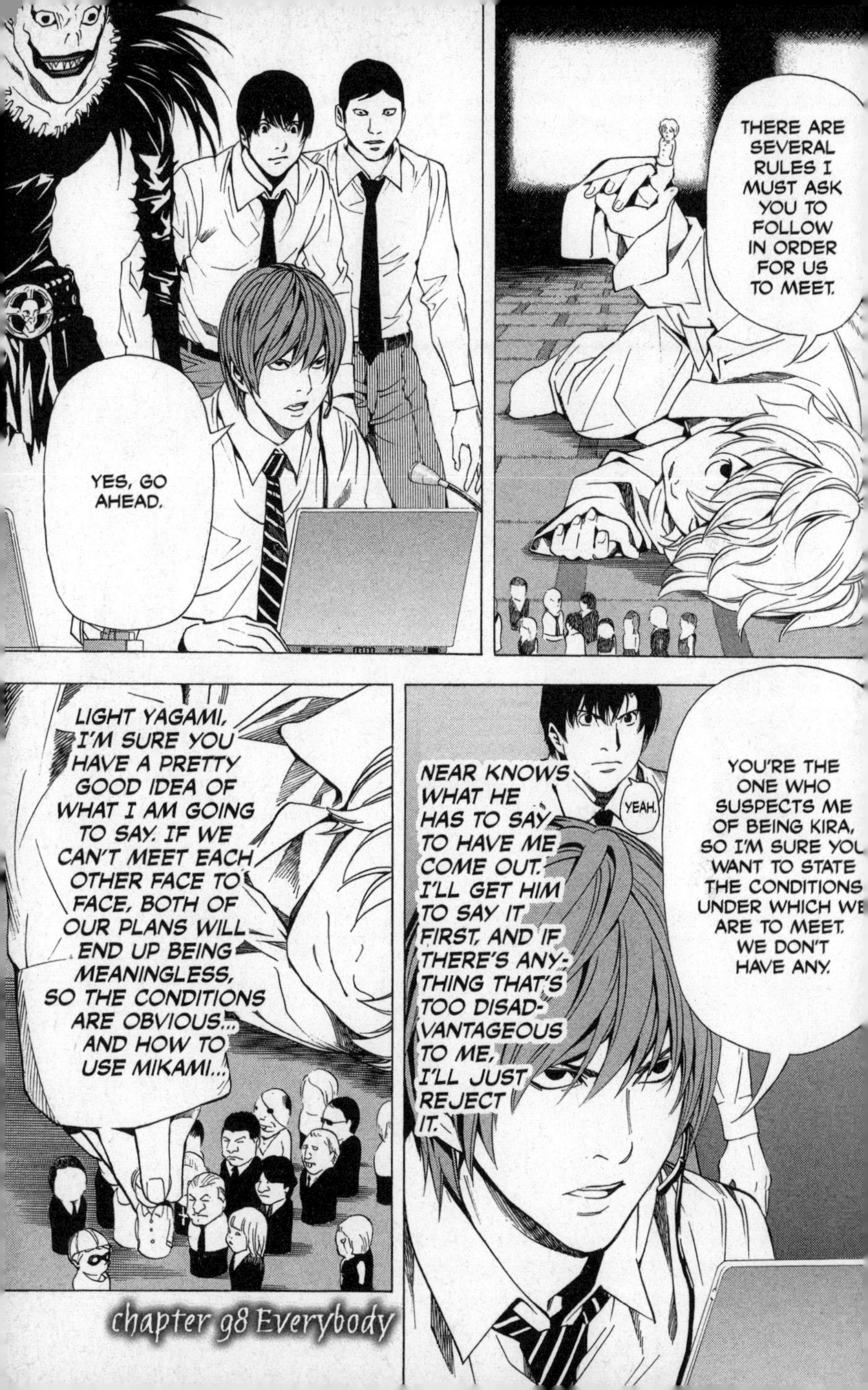

THERE ARE SEVERAL RULES I MUST ASK YOU TO FOLLOW IN ORDER FOR US TO MEET.
YES, GO AHEAD.
YOU'RE THE ONE WHO SUSPECTS ME OF BEING KIRA, SO I'M SURE YOU WANT TO STATE THE CONDITIONS UNDER WHICH WE ARE TO MEET. WE DON'T HAVE ANY.
YEAH.
NEAR KNOWS WHAT HE HAS TO SAY TO HAVE ME COME OUT. I'LL GET HIM TO SAY IT FIRST, AND IF THERE'S ANY-THING THAT'S TOO DISAD-VANTAGEOUS TO ME, I'LL JUST REJECT IT.
LIGHT YAGAMI, I'M SURE YOU HAVE A PRETTY GOOD IDEA OF WHAT I AM GOING TO SAY. IF WE CAN'T MEET EACH OTHER FACE TO FACE, BOTH OF OUR PLANS WILL END UP BEING MEANINGLESS, SO THE CONDITIONS ARE OBVIOUS... ...AND HOW TO USE MIKAMI...
chapter 98 Everybody

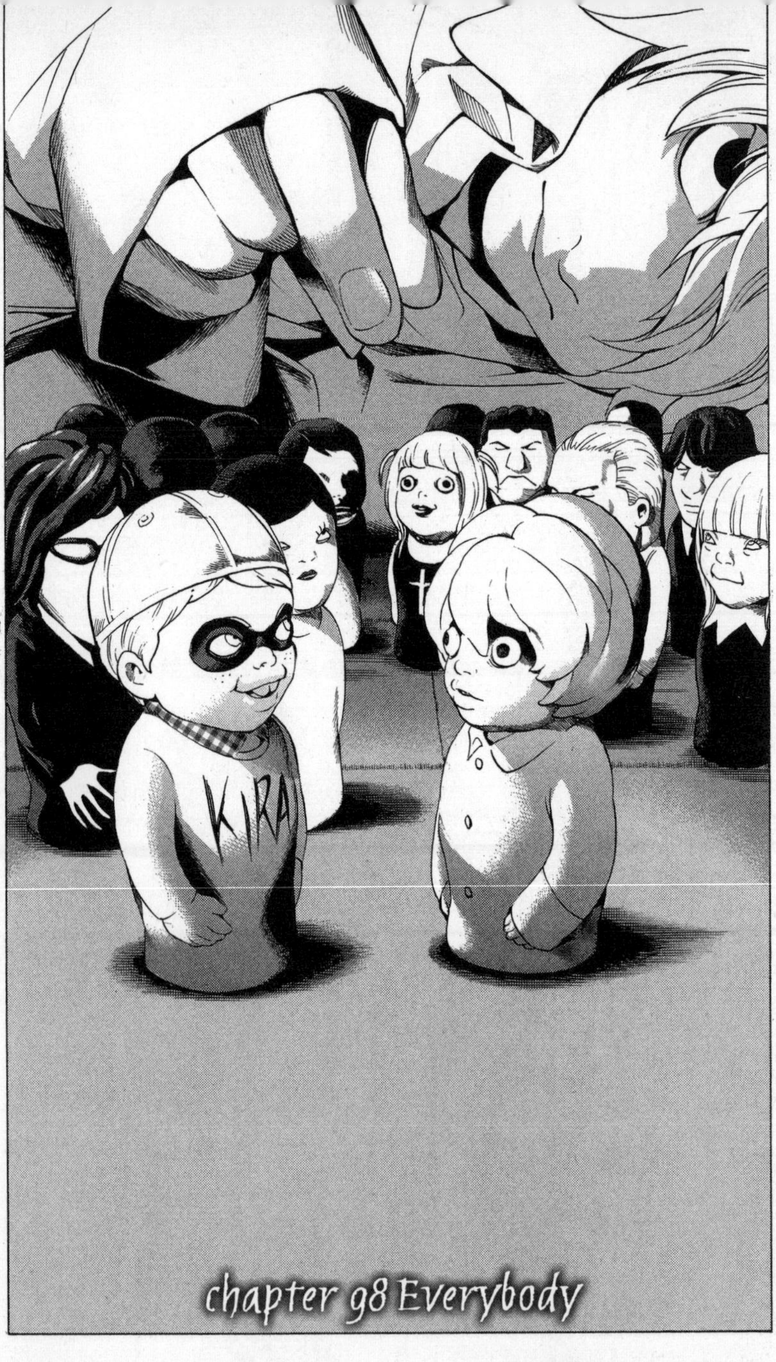
KIRA

chapter 98 Everybody

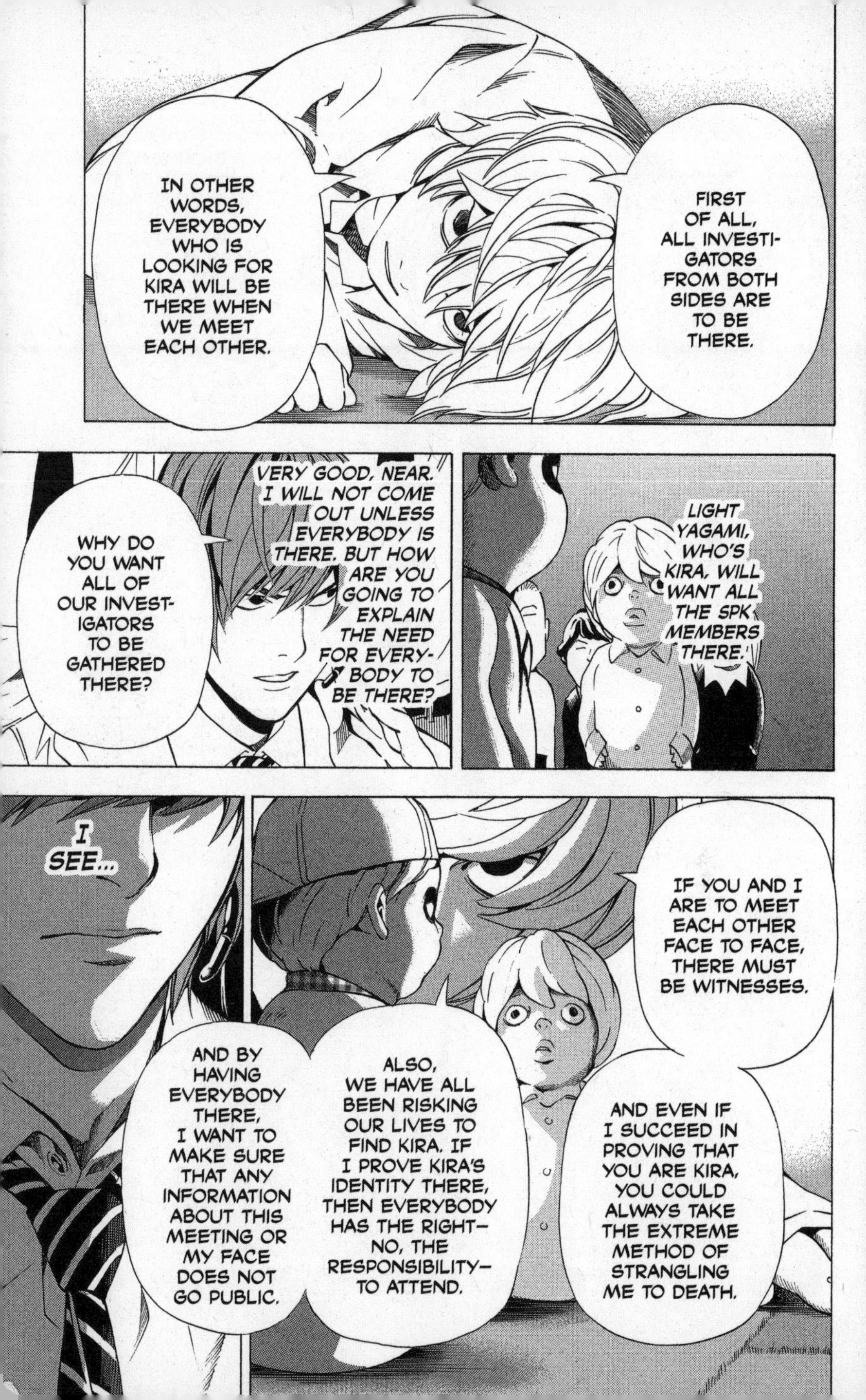
FIRST OF ALL, ALL INVESTI-GATORS FROM BOTH SIDES ARE TO BE THERE.
IN OTHER WORDS, EVERYBODY WHO IS LOOKING FOR KIRA WILL BE THERE WHEN WE MEET EACH OTHER.
LIGHT YAGAMI, WHO'S KIRA, WILL WANT ALL THE SPK MEMBERS THERE.
VERY GOOD, NEAR. I WILL NOT COME OUT UNLESS EVERYBODY IS THERE. BUT HOW ARE YOU GOING TO EXPLAIN THE NEED FOR EVERY-BODY TO BE THERE?
WHY DO YOU WANT ALL OF OUR INVEST-IGATORS TO BE GATHERED THERE?
IF YOU AND I ARE TO MEET EACH OTHER FACE TO FACE, THERE MUST BE WITNESSES.
AND EVEN IF I SUCCEED IN PROVING THAT YOU ARE KIRA, YOU COULD ALWAYS TAKE THE EXTREME METHOD OF STRANGLING ME TO DEATH.
ALSO, WE HAVE ALL BEEN RISKING OUR LIVES TO FIND KIRA. IF I PROVE KIRA'S IDENTITY THERE, THEN EVERYBODY HAS THE RIGHT— NO, THE RESPONSIBILITY— TO ATTEND.
AND BY HAVING EVERYBODY THERE, I WANT TO MAKE SURE THAT ANY INFORMATION ABOUT THIS MEETING OR MY FACE DOES NOT GO PUBLIC.
I SEE...

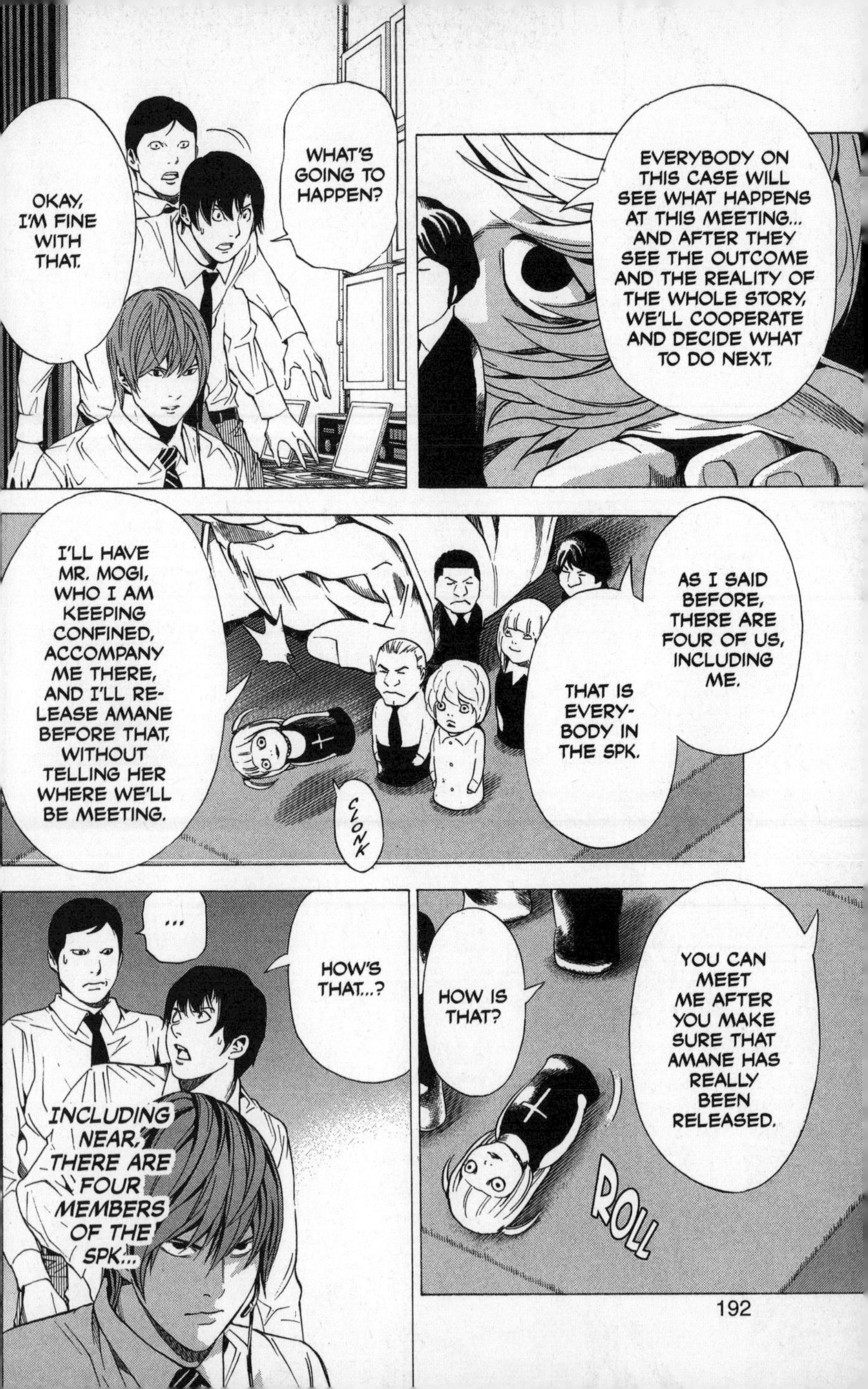
EVERYBODY ON THIS CASE WILL SEE WHAT HAPPENS AT THIS MEETING... AND AFTER THEY SEE THE OUTCOME AND THE REALITY OF THE WHOLE STORY, WE'LL COOPERATE AND DECIDE WHAT TO DO NEXT.
WHAT'S GOING TO HAPPEN?
OKAY, I'M FINE WITH THAT.
AS I SAID BEFORE, THERE ARE FOUR OF US, INCLUDING ME.
THAT IS EVERY-BODY IN THE SPK.
CLONK
I'LL HAVE MR. MOGI, WHO I AM KEEPING CONFINED, ACCOMPANY ME THERE, AND I'LL RE-LEASE AMANE BEFORE THAT, WITHOUT TELLING HER WHERE WE'LL BE MEETING.
YOU CAN MEET ME AFTER YOU MAKE SURE THAT AMANE HAS REALLY BEEN RELEASED.
HOW IS THAT?
ROLL
HOW'S THAT...?
...
INCLUDING NEAR, THERE ARE FOUR MEMBERS OF THE SPK...

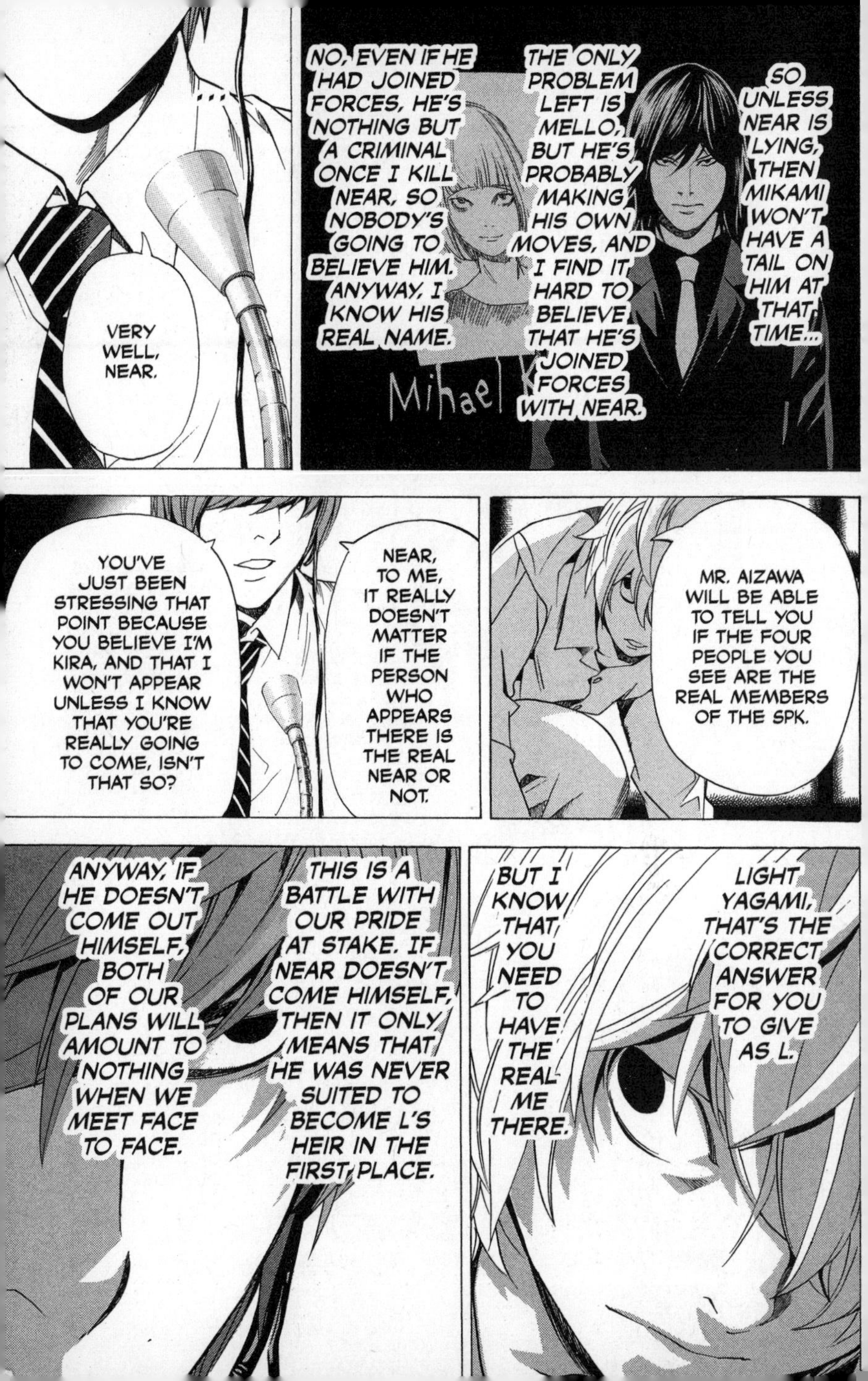
SO UNLESS NEAR IS LYING, THEN MIKAMI WON'T HAVE A TAIL ON HIM AT THAT TIME...
THE ONLY PROBLEM LEFT IS MELLO, BUT HE'S PROBABLY MAKING HIS OWN MOVES, AND I FIND IT HARD TO BELIEVE THAT HE'S JOINED FORCES WITH NEAR.
NO, EVEN IF HE HAD JOINED FORCES, HE'S NOTHING BUT A CRIMINAL ONCE I KILL NEAR, SO NOBODY'S GOING TO BELIEVE HIM. ANYWAY, I KNOW HIS REAL NAME.
Mihael K
...
VERY WELL, NEAR.
MR. AIZAWA WILL BE ABLE TO TELL YOU IF THE FOUR PEOPLE YOU SEE ARE THE REAL MEMBERS OF THE SPK.
NEAR, TO ME, IT REALLY DOESN'T MATTER IF THE PERSON WHO APPEARS THERE IS THE REAL NEAR OR NOT.
YOU'VE JUST BEEN STRESSING THAT POINT BECAUSE YOU BELIEVE I'M KIRA, AND THAT I WON'T APPEAR UNLESS I KNOW THAT YOU'RE REALLY GOING TO COME, ISN'T THAT SO?
LIGHT YAGAMI, THAT'S THE CORRECT ANSWER FOR YOU TO GIVE AS L.
BUT I KNOW THAT YOU NEED TO HAVE THE REAL ME THERE.
THIS IS A BATTLE WITH OUR PRIDE AT STAKE. IF NEAR DOESN'T COME HIMSELF, THEN IT ONLY MEANS THAT HE WAS NEVER SUITED TO BECOME L'S HEIR IN THE FIRST PLACE.
ANYWAY, IF HE DOESN'T COME OUT HIMSELF, BOTH OF OUR PLANS WILL AMOUNT TO NOTHING WHEN WE MEET FACE TO FACE.

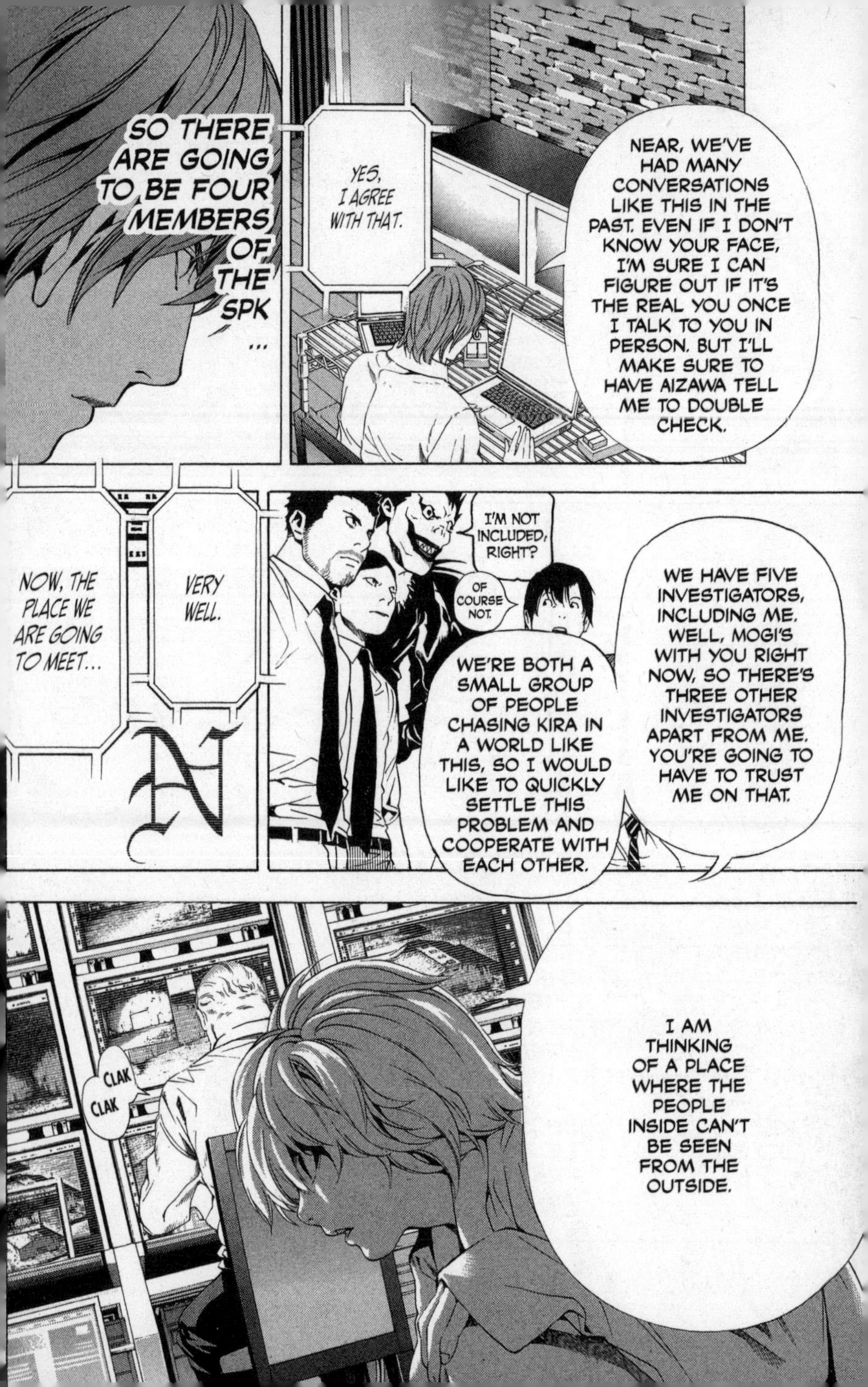
NEAR, WE'VE HAD MANY CONVERSATIONS LIKE THIS IN THE PAST. EVEN IF I DON'T KNOW YOUR FACE, I'M SURE I CAN FIGURE OUT IF IT'S THE REAL YOU ONCE I TALK TO YOU IN PERSON. BUT I'LL MAKE SURE TO HAVE AIZAWA TELL ME TO DOUBLE CHECK.
YES, I AGREE WITH THAT.
SO THERE ARE GOING TO BE FOUR MEMBERS OF THE SPK ...
WE HAVE FIVE INVESTIGATORS, INCLUDING ME. WELL, MOGI'S WITH YOU RIGHT NOW, SO THERE'S THREE OTHER INVESTIGATORS APART FROM ME. YOU'RE GOING TO HAVE TO TRUST ME ON THAT.
I'M NOT INCLUDED, RIGHT?
OF COURSE NOT.
WE'RE BOTH A SMALL GROUP OF PEOPLE CHASING KIRA IN A WORLD LIKE THIS, SO I WOULD LIKE TO QUICKLY SETTLE THIS PROBLEM AND COOPERATE WITH EACH OTHER.
VERY WELL.
NOW, THE PLACE WE ARE GOING TO MEET...
I AM THINKING OF A PLACE WHERE THE PEOPLE INSIDE CAN'T BE SEEN FROM THE OUTSIDE.
CLAK
CLAK

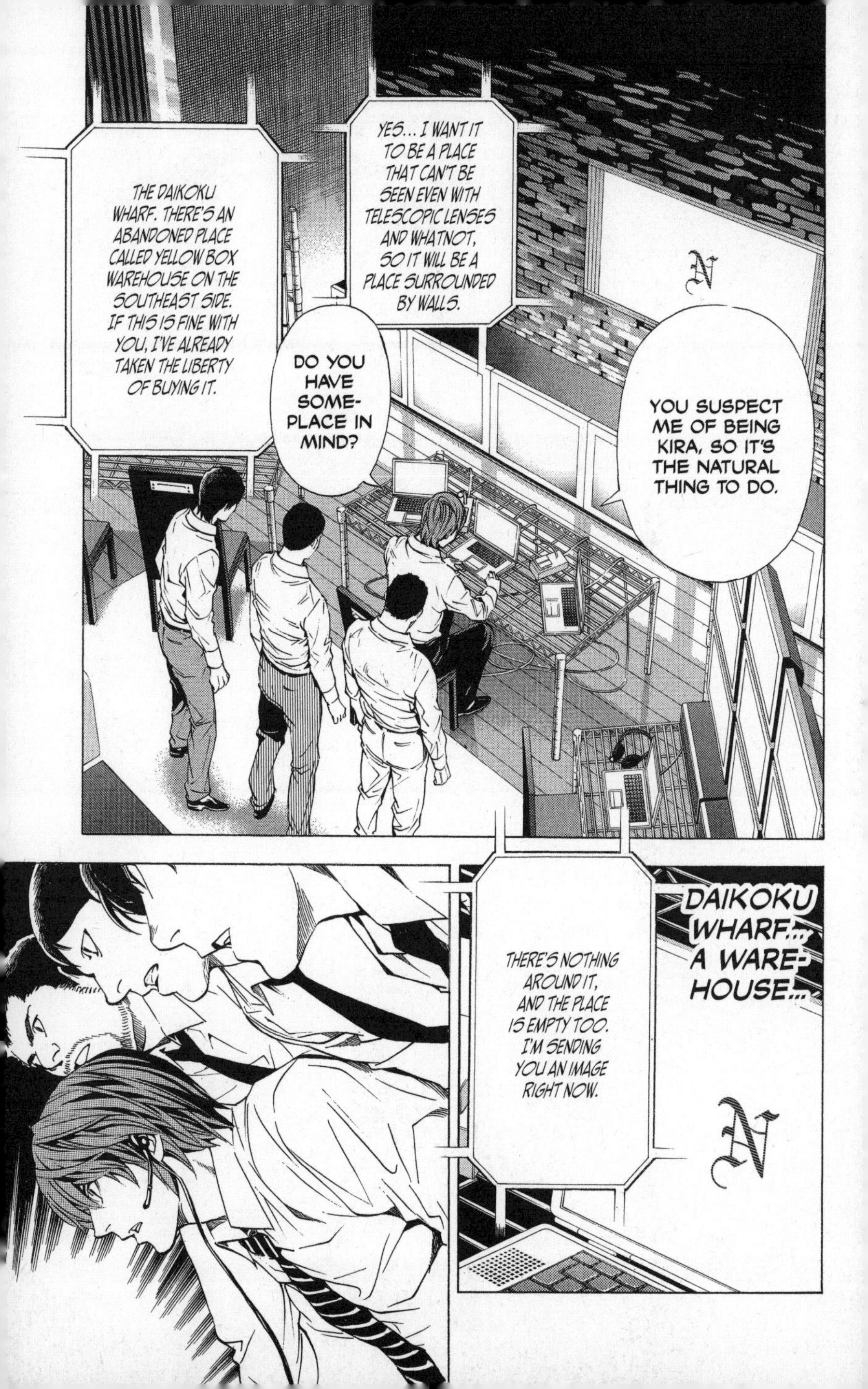
YOU SUSPECT ME OF BEING KIRA, SO IT'S THE NATURAL THING TO DO.
N
YES... I WANT IT TO BE A PLACE THAT CAN'T BE SEEN EVEN WITH TELESCOPIC LENSES AND WHATNOT, SO IT WILL BE A PLACE SURROUNDED BY WALLS.
DO YOU HAVE SOME-PLACE IN MIND?
THE DAIKOKU WHARF. THERE'S AN ABANDONED PLACE CALLED YELLOW BOX WAREHOUSE ON THE SOUTHEAST SIDE. IF THIS IS FINE WITH YOU, I'VE ALREADY TAKEN THE LIBERTY OF BUYING IT.
DAIKOKU WHARF... A WARE-HOUSE...
N
THERE'S NOTHING AROUND IT, AND THE PLACE IS EMPTY TOO. I'M SENDING YOU AN IMAGE RIGHT NOW.

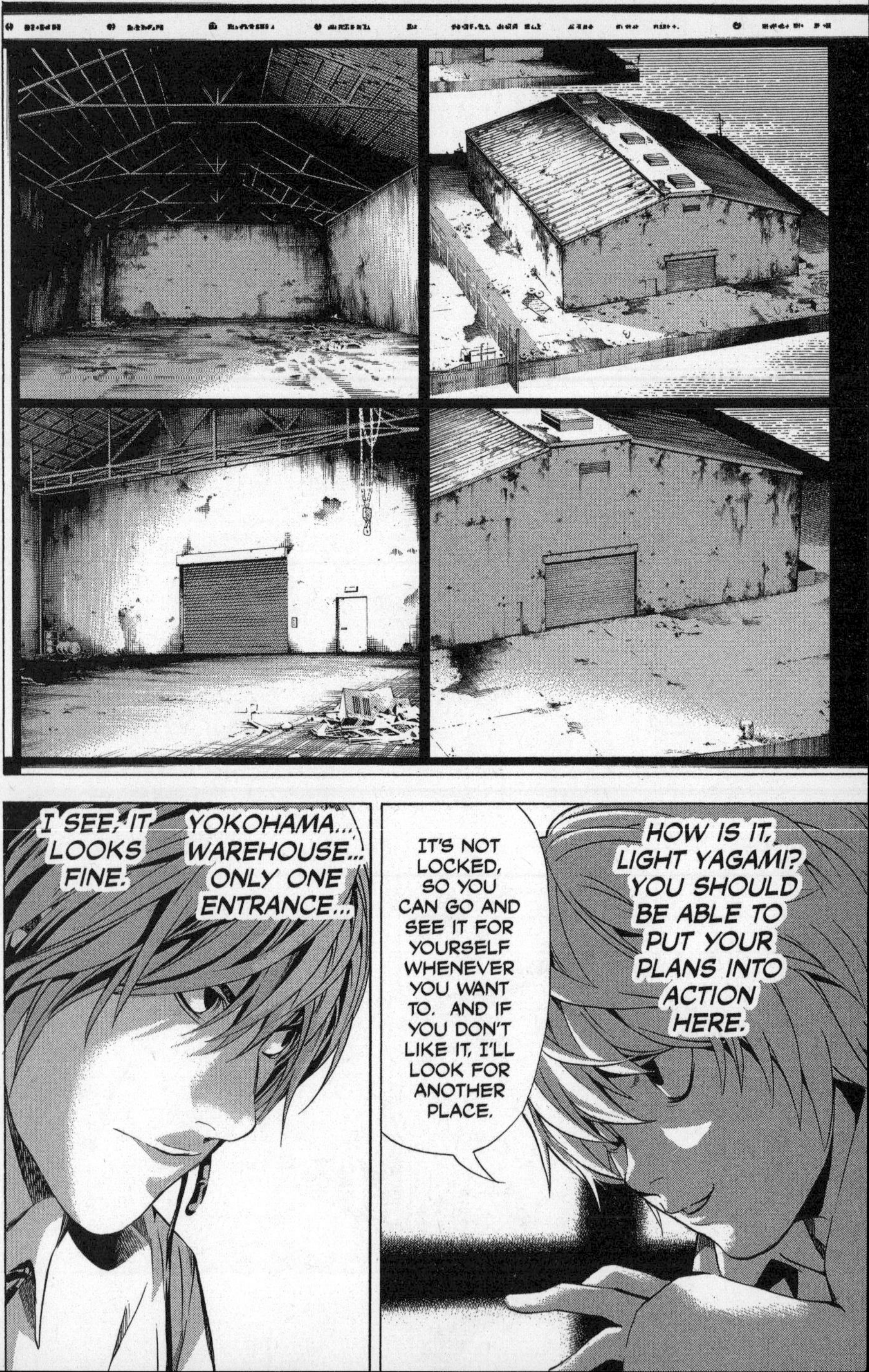
HOW IS IT, LIGHT YAGAMI? YOU SHOULD BE ABLE TO PUT YOUR PLANS INTO ACTION HERE.
IT'S NOT LOCKED, SO YOU CAN GO AND SEE IT FOR YOURSELF WHENEVER YOU WANT TO. AND IF YOU DON'T LIKE IT, I'LL LOOK FOR ANOTHER PLACE.
YOKOHAMA... WAREHOUSE... ONLY ONE ENTRANCE...
I SEE, IT LOOKS FINE.

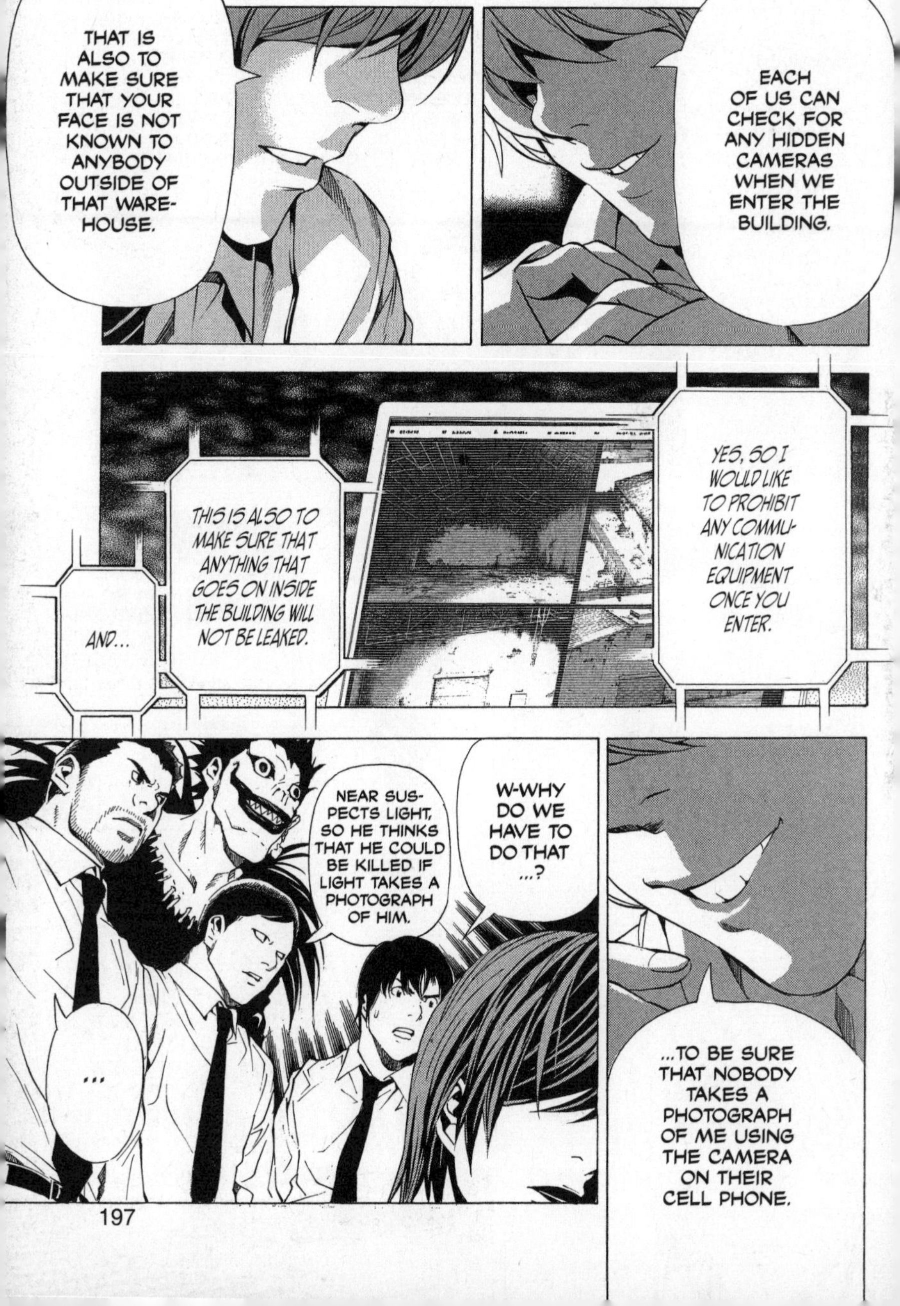
EACH OF US CAN CHECK FOR ANY HIDDEN CAMERAS WHEN WE ENTER THE BUILDING.
THAT IS ALSO TO MAKE SURE THAT YOUR FACE IS NOT KNOWN TO ANYBODY OUTSIDE OF THAT WARE-HOUSE.
YES, SO I WOULD LIKE TO PROHIBIT ANY COMMU-NICATION EQUIPMENT ONCE YOU ENTER.
THIS IS ALSO TO MAKE SURE THAT ANYTHING THAT GOES ON INSIDE THE BUILDING WILL NOT BE LEAKED.
AND...
...TO BE SURE THAT NOBODY TAKES A PHOTOGRAPH OF ME USING THE CAMERA ON THEIR CELL PHONE.
W-WHY DO WE HAVE TO DO THAT ...?
NEAR SUS-PECTS LIGHT, SO HE THINKS THAT HE COULD BE KILLED IF LIGHT TAKES A PHOTOGRAPH OF HIM.
...

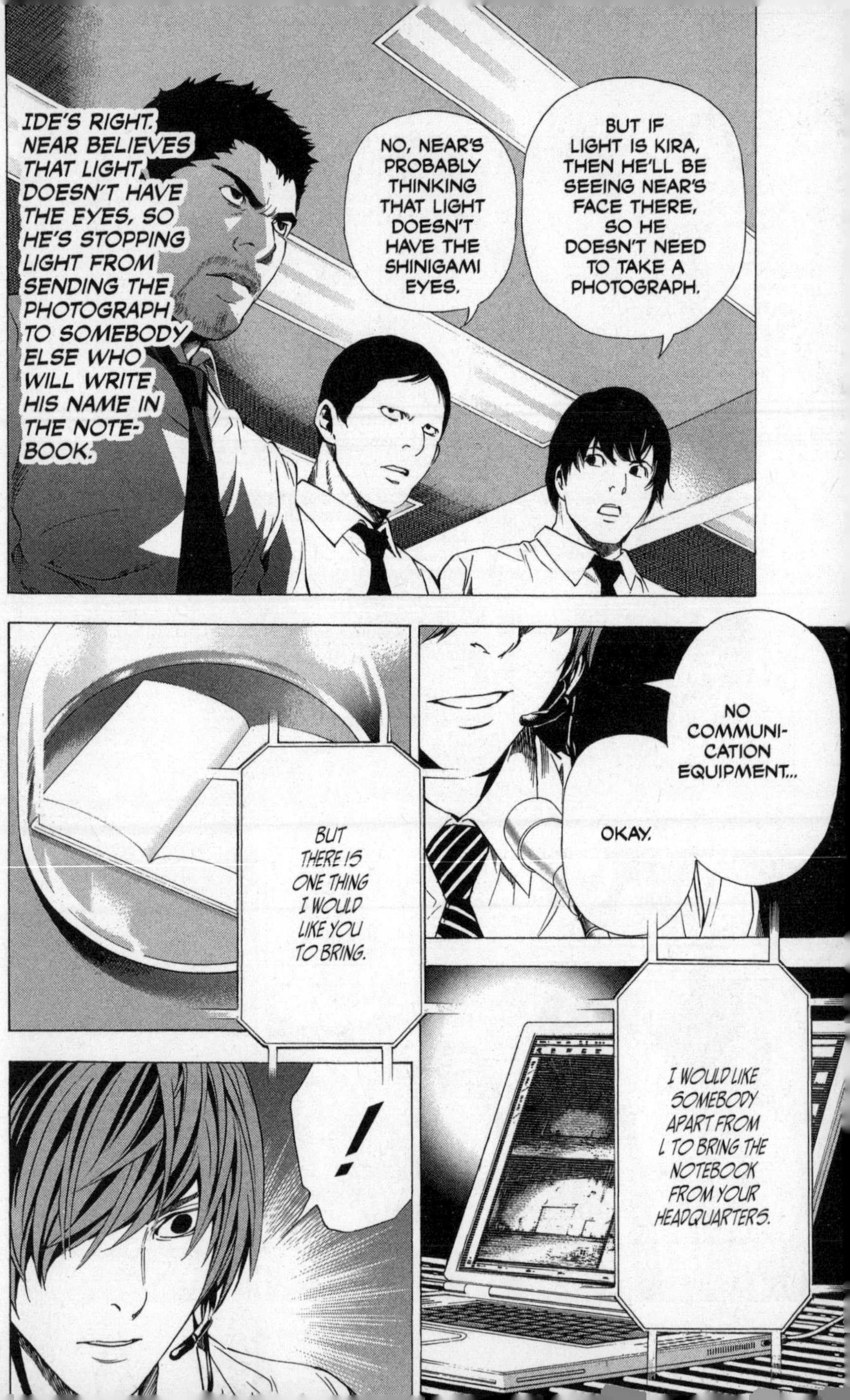
BUT IF LIGHT IS KIRA, THEN HE'LL BE SEEING NEAR'S FACE THERE, SO HE DOESN'T NEED TO TAKE A PHOTOGRAPH.
NO, NEAR'S PROBABLY THINKING THAT LIGHT DOESN'T HAVE THE SHINIGAMI EYES.
IDE'S RIGHT. NEAR BELIEVES THAT LIGHT DOESN'T HAVE THE EYES, SO HE'S STOPPING LIGHT FROM SENDING THE PHOTOGRAPH TO SOMEBODY ELSE WHO WILL WRITE HIS NAME IN THE NOTE-BOOK.
NO COMMUNI-CATION EQUIPMENT...
OKAY.
BUT THERE IS ONE THING I WOULD LIKE YOU TO BRING.
I WOULD LIKE SOMEBODY APART FROM L TO BRING THE NOTEBOOK FROM YOUR HEADQUARTERS.
!

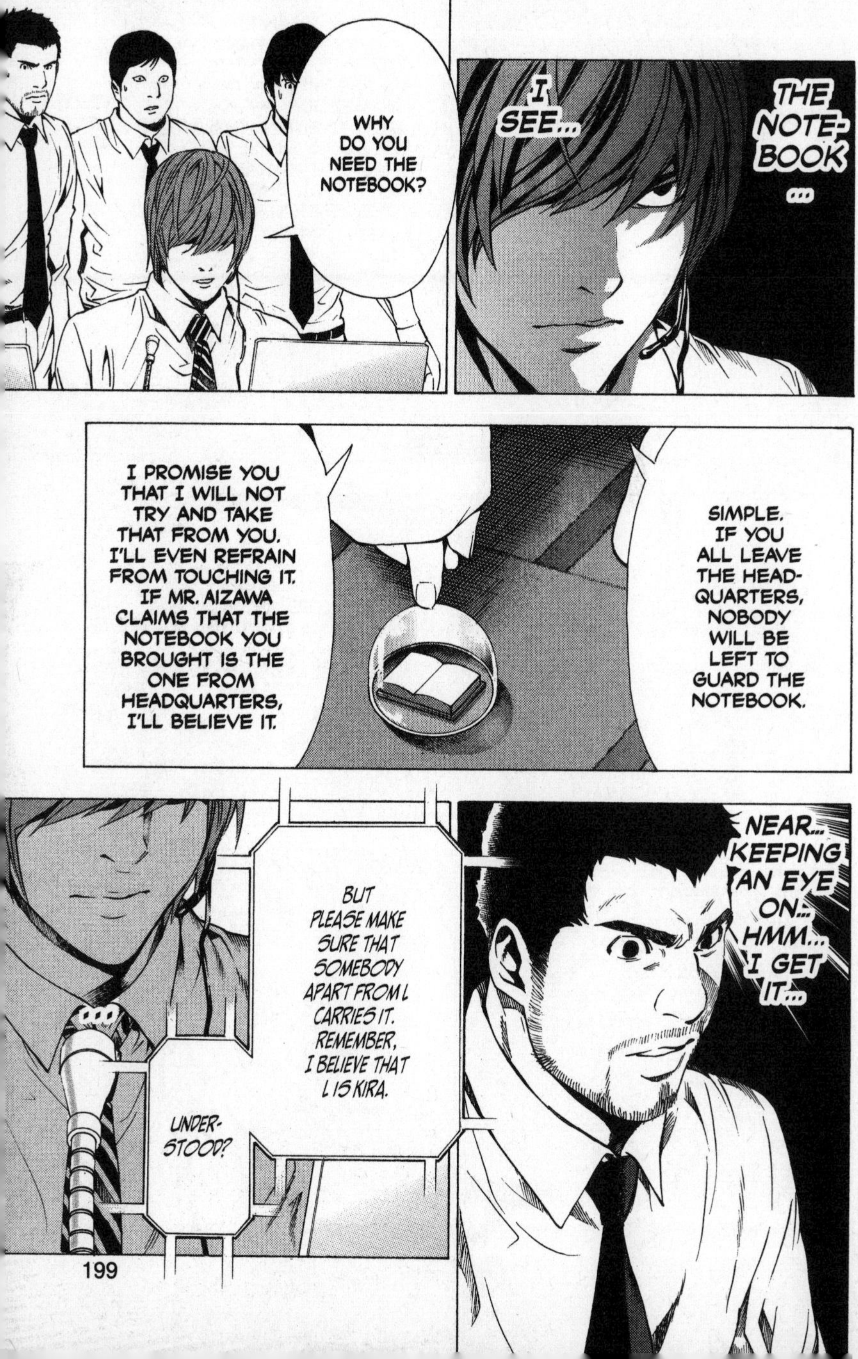
THE NOTE-BOOK...
I SEE...
WHY DO YOU NEED THE NOTEBOOK?
SIMPLE. IF YOU ALL LEAVE THE HEAD-QUARTERS, NOBODY WILL BE LEFT TO GUARD THE NOTEBOOK.
I PROMISE YOU THAT I WILL NOT TRY AND TAKE THAT FROM YOU. I'LL EVEN REFRAIN FROM TOUCHING IT. IF MR. AIZAWA CLAIMS THAT THE NOTEBOOK YOU BROUGHT IS THE ONE FROM HEADQUARTERS, I'LL BELIEVE IT.
NEAR... KEEPING AN EYE ON... HMM... I GET IT...
BUT PLEASE MAKE SURE THAT SOMEBODY APART FROM L CARRIES IT. REMEMBER, I BELIEVE THAT L IS KIRA.
UNDER-STOOD?
...

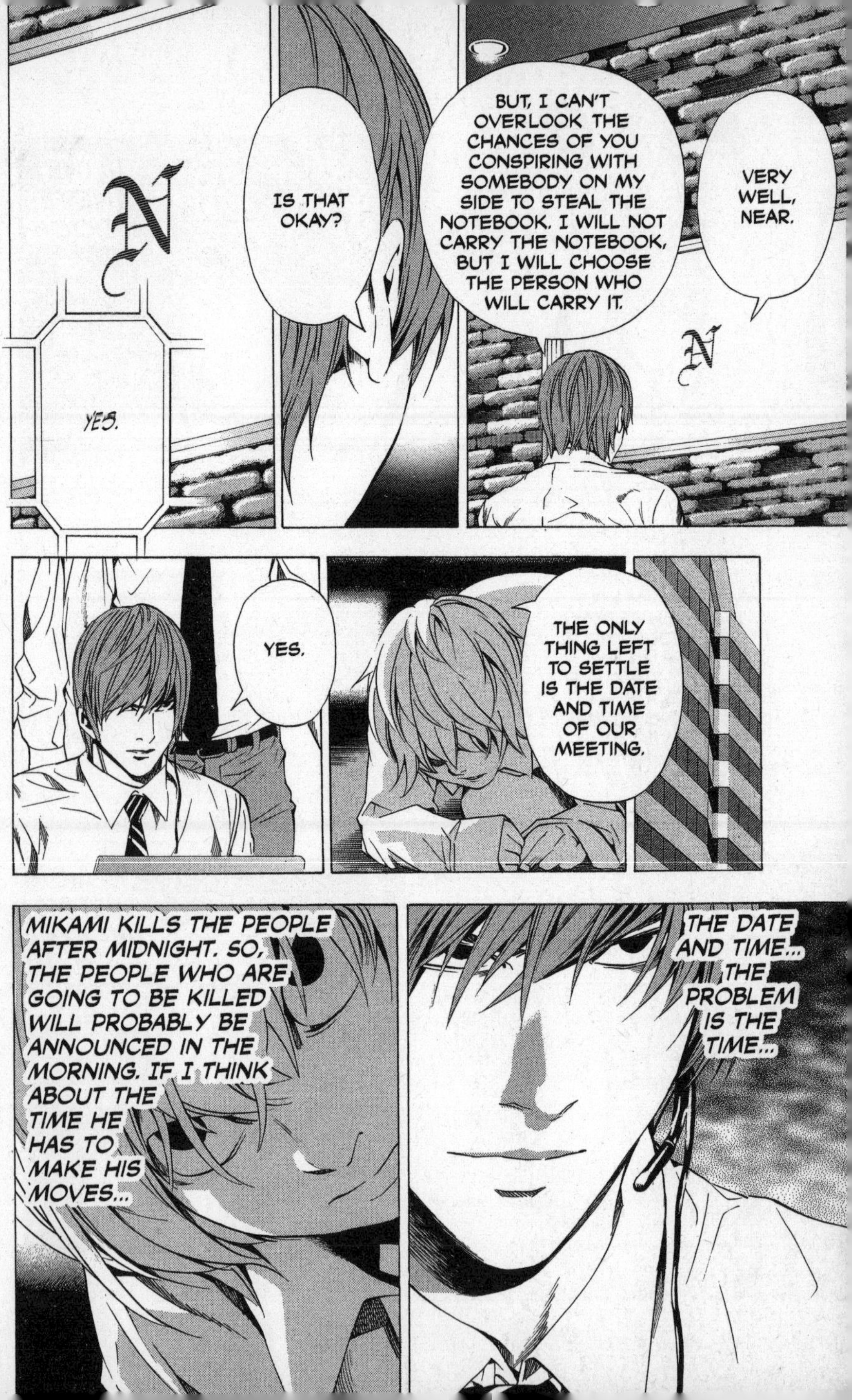
VERY WELL, NEAR.
BUT, I CAN'T OVERLOOK THE CHANCES OF YOU CONSPIRING WITH SOMEBODY ON MY SIDE TO STEAL THE NOTEBOOK. I WILL NOT CARRY THE NOTEBOOK, BUT I WILL CHOOSE THE PERSON WHO WILL CARRY IT.
IS THAT OKAY?
YES.
THE ONLY THING LEFT TO SETTLE IS THE DATE AND TIME OF OUR MEETING.
YES.
THE DATE AND TIME... THE PROBLEM IS THE TIME...
MIKAMI KILLS THE PEOPLE AFTER MIDNIGHT. SO, THE PEOPLE WHO ARE GOING TO BE KILLED WILL PROBABLY BE ANNOUNCED IN THE MORNING. IF I THINK ABOUT THE TIME HE HAS TO MAKE HIS MOVES...

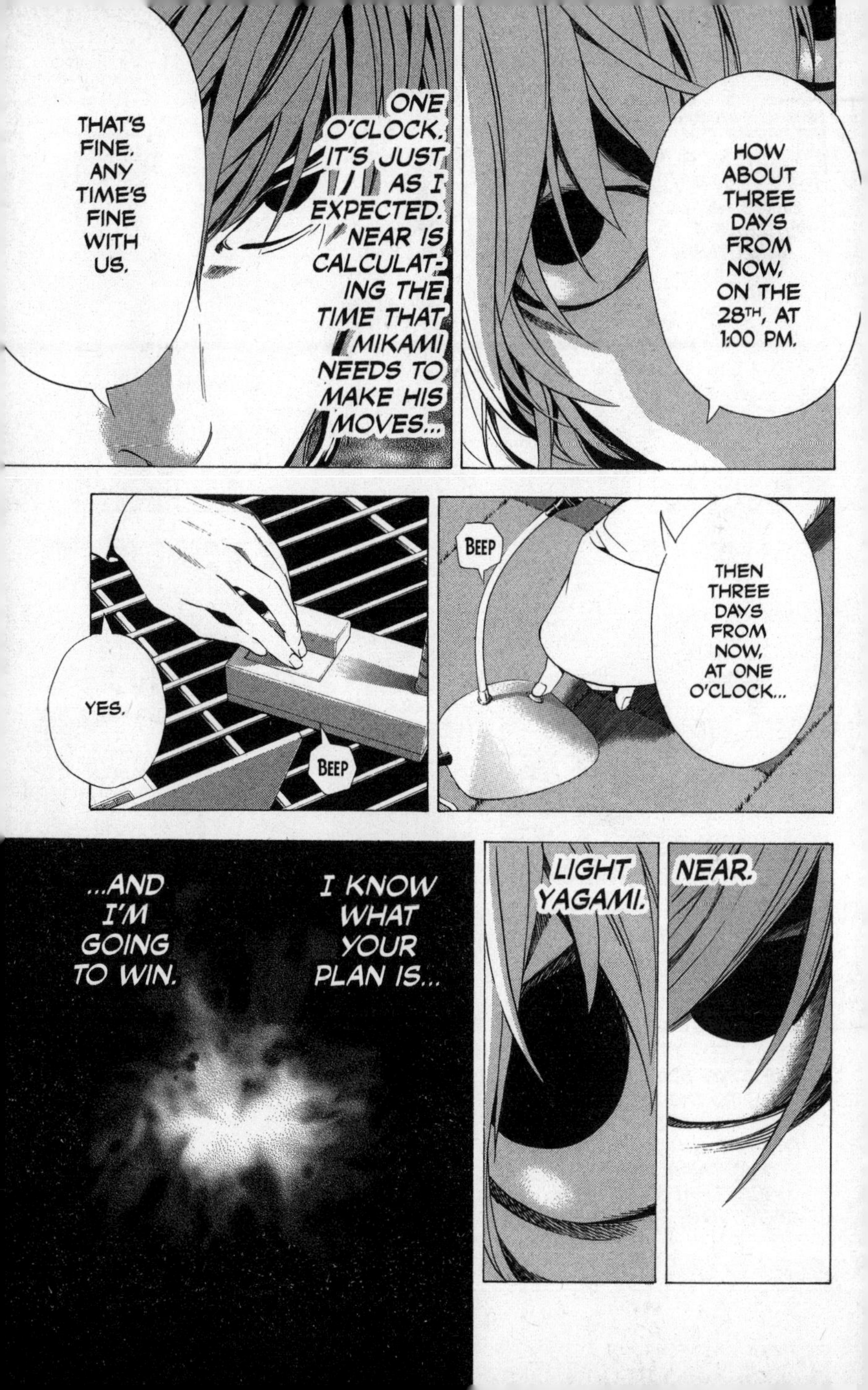
HOW ABOUT THREE DAYS FROM NOW, ON THE 28TH, AT 1:00 PM.
ONE O'CLOCK. IT'S JUST AS I EXPECTED. NEAR IS CALCULATING THE TIME THAT MIKAMI NEEDS TO MAKE HIS MOVES...
THAT'S FINE. ANY TIME'S FINE WITH US.
BEEP
THEN THREE DAYS FROM NOW, AT ONE O'CLOCK...
YES.
BEEP
NEAR.
LIGHT YAGAMI.
I KNOW WHAT YOUR PLAN IS...
...AND I'M GOING TO WIN.

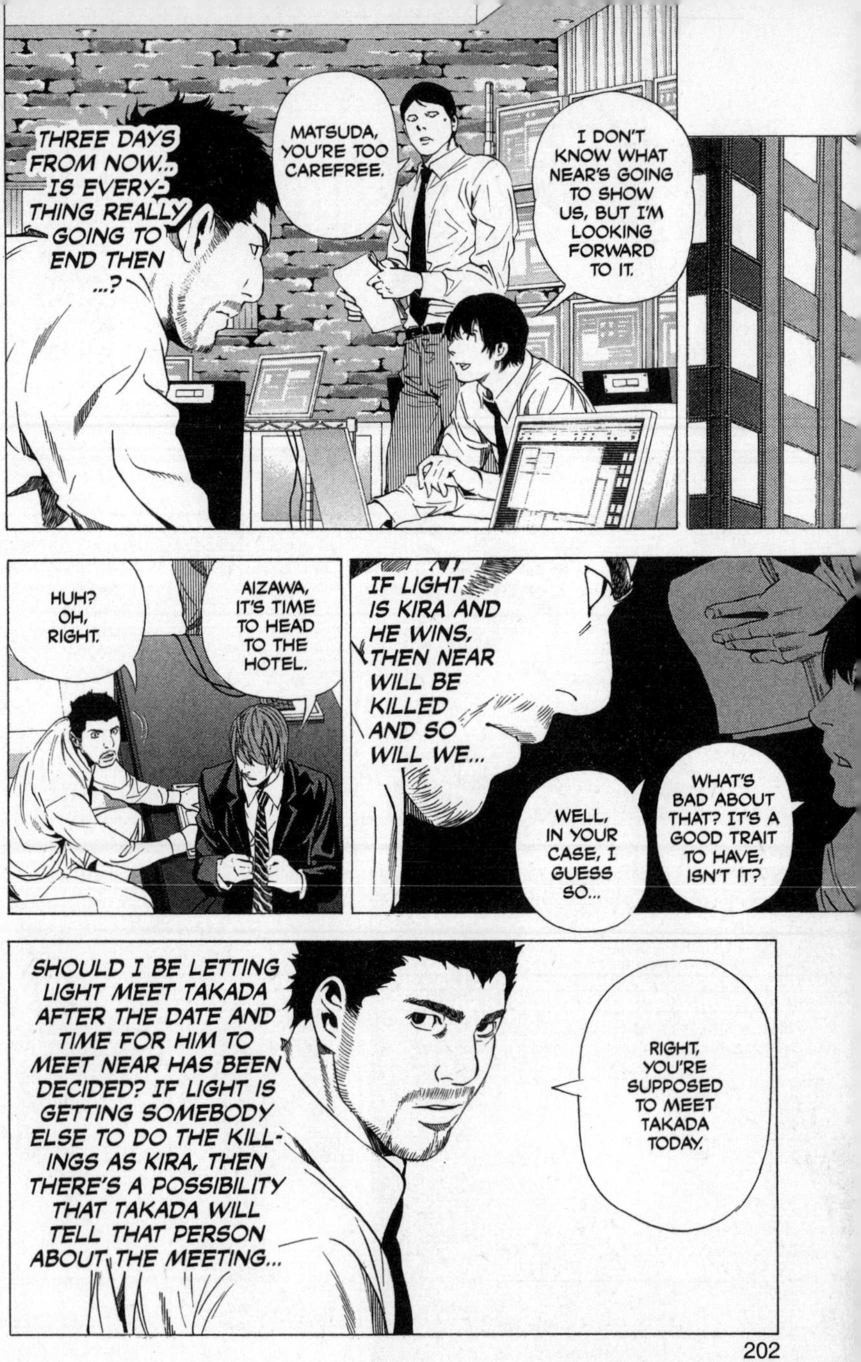
I DON'T KNOW WHAT NEAR'S GOING TO SHOW US, BUT I'M LOOKING FORWARD TO IT.
MATSUDA, YOU'RE TOO CAREFREE.
THREE DAYS FROM NOW... IS EVERYTHING REALLY GOING TO END THEN ...?
WHAT'S BAD ABOUT THAT? IT'S A GOOD TRAIT TO HAVE, ISN'T IT?
WELL, IN YOUR CASE, I GUESS SO...
IF LIGHT IS KIRA AND HE WINS, THEN NEAR WILL BE KILLED AND SO WILL WE...
AIZAWA, IT'S TIME TO HEAD TO THE HOTEL.
HUH? OH, RIGHT.
RIGHT, YOU'RE SUPPOSED TO MEET TAKADA TODAY.
SHOULD I BE LETTING LIGHT MEET TAKADA AFTER THE DATE AND TIME FOR HIM TO MEET NEAR HAS BEEN DECIDED? IF LIGHT IS GETTING SOMEBODY ELSE TO DO THE KILLINGS AS KIRA, THEN THERE'S A POSSIBILITY THAT TAKADA WILL TELL THAT PERSON ABOUT THE MEETING...

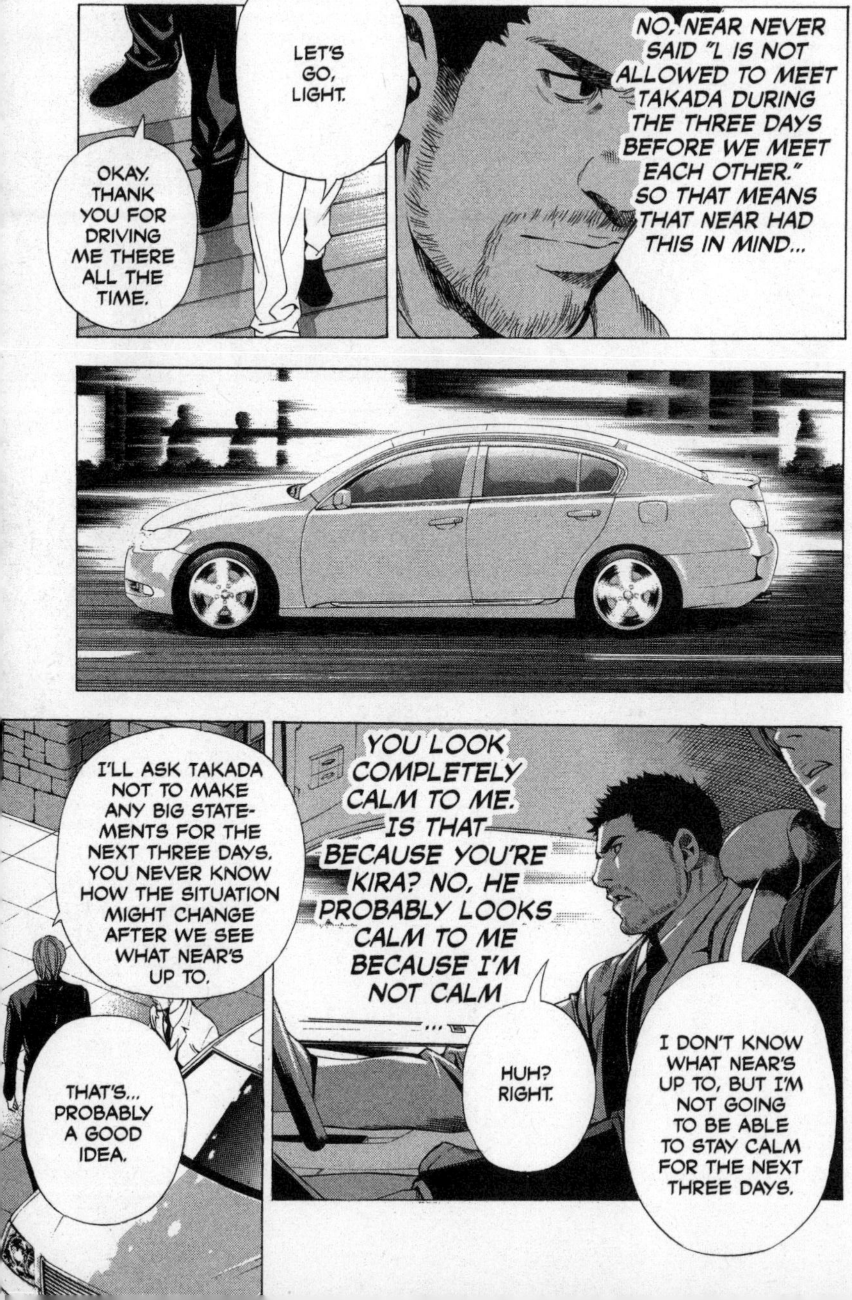

NO, NEAR NEVER SAID "L IS NOT ALLOWED TO MEET TAKADA DURING THE THREE DAYS BEFORE WE MEET EACH OTHER." SO THAT MEANS THAT NEAR HAD THIS IN MIND...
LET'S GO, LIGHT.
OKAY. THANK YOU FOR DRIVING ME THERE ALL THE TIME.
YOU LOOK COMPLETELY CALM TO ME. IS THAT BECAUSE YOU'RE KIRA? NO, HE PROBABLY LOOKS CALM TO ME BECAUSE I'M NOT CALM
I DON'T KNOW WHAT NEAR'S UP TO, BUT I'M NOT GOING TO BE ABLE TO STAY CALM FOR THE NEXT THREE DAYS.
HUH? RIGHT.
I'LL ASK TAKADA NOT TO MAKE ANY BIG STATEMENTS FOR THE NEXT THREE DAYS. YOU NEVER KNOW HOW THE SITUATION MIGHT CHANGE AFTER WE SEE WHAT NEAR'S UP TO.
THAT'S... PROBABLY A GOOD IDEA.

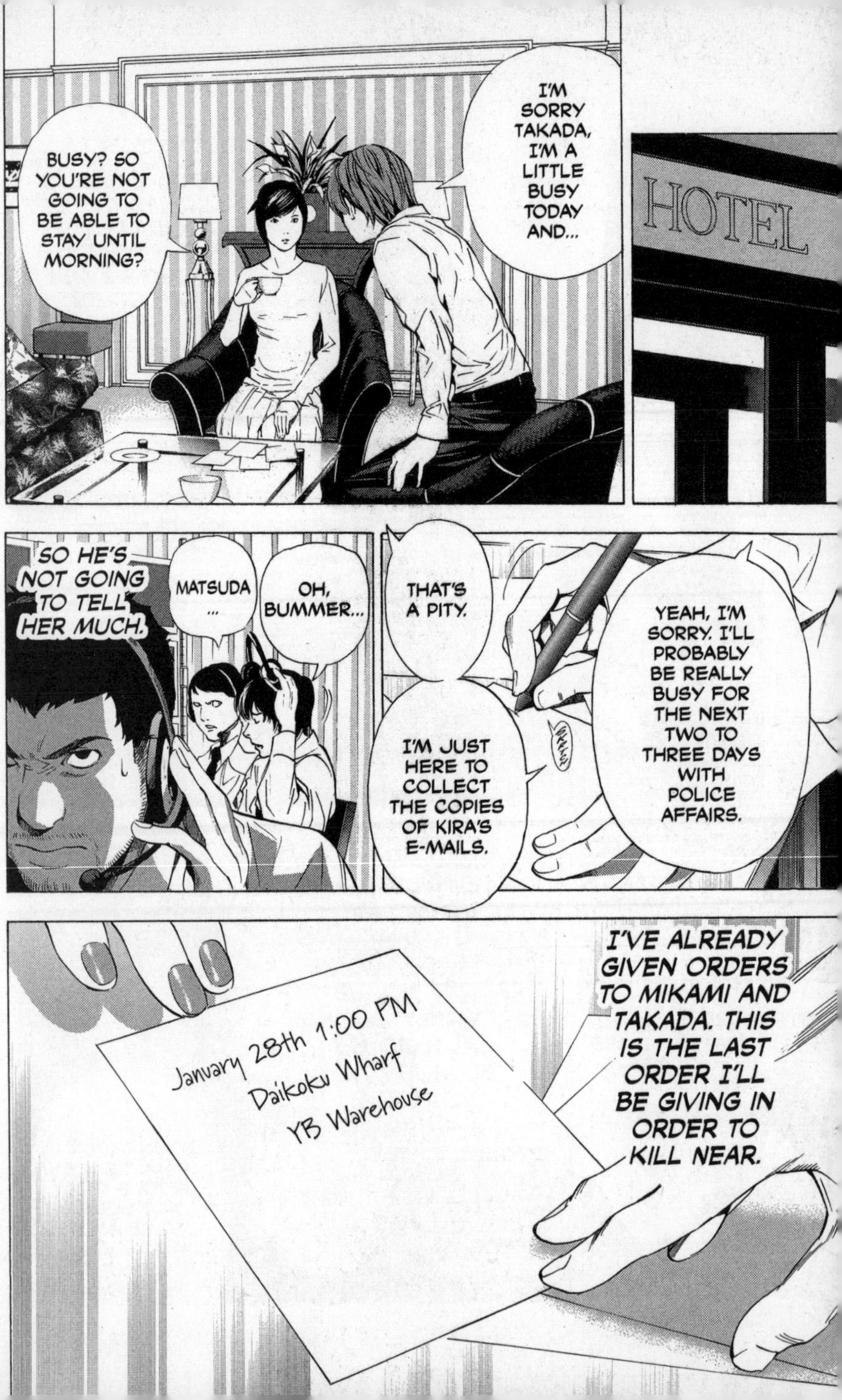
HOTEL
I'M SORRY TAKADA, I'M A LITTLE BUSY TODAY AND...
BUSY? SO YOU'RE NOT GOING TO BE ABLE TO STAY UNTIL MORNING?
YEAH, I'M SORRY. I'LL PROBABLY BE REALLY BUSY FOR THE NEXT TWO TO THREE DAYS WITH POLICE AFFAIRS.
THAT'S A PITY.
I'M JUST HERE TO COLLECT THE COPIES OF KIRA'S E-MAILS.
OH, BUMMER...
MATSUDA ...
SO HE'S NOT GOING TO TELL HER MUCH.
I'VE ALREADY GIVEN ORDERS TO MIKAMI AND TAKADA. THIS IS THE LAST ORDER I'LL BE GIVING IN ORDER TO KILL NEAR.
January 28th 1:00 PM
Daikoku Wharf
YB Warehouse

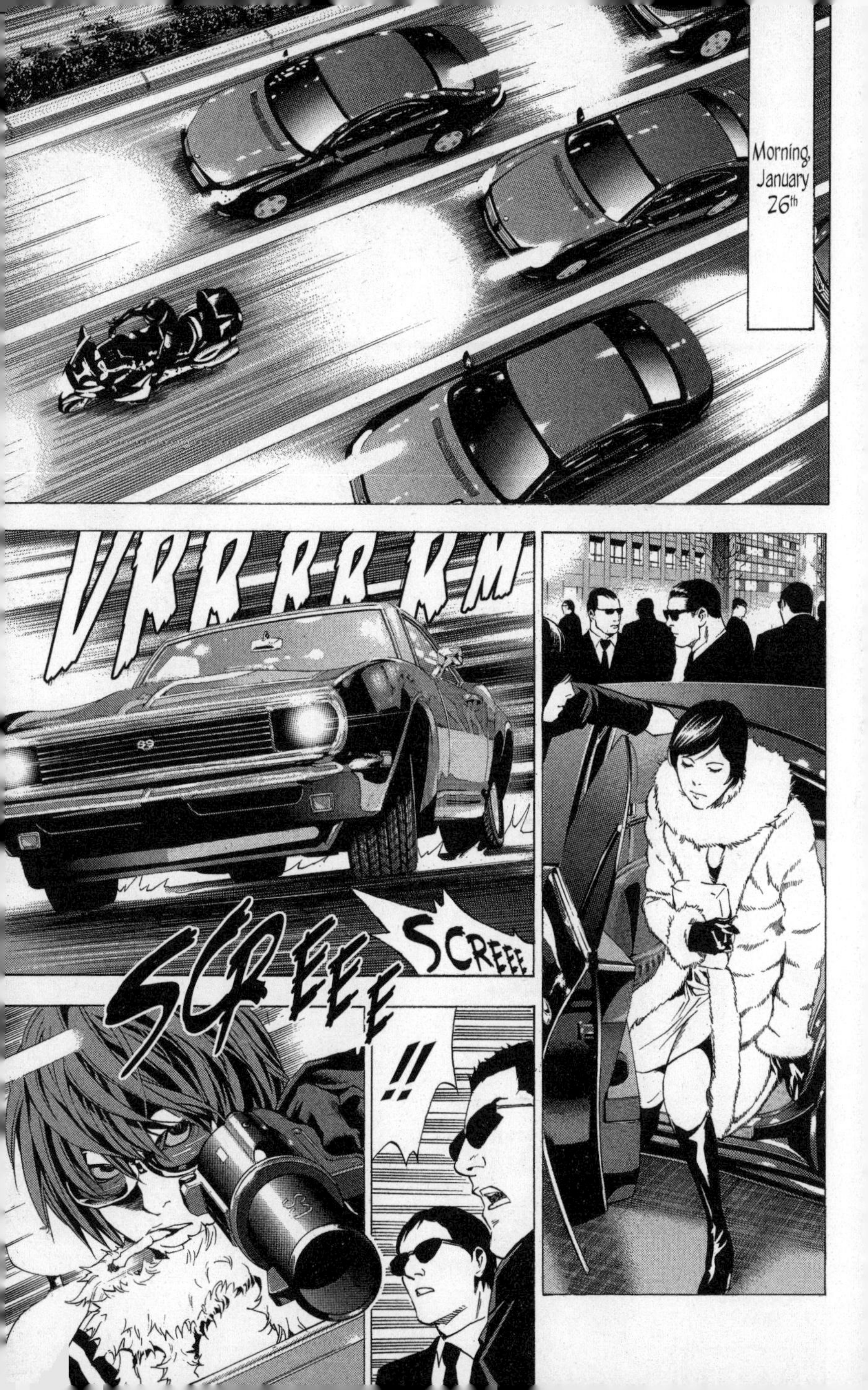

Morning, January 26th
VRRRRRM
SCREEE
SCREEE
!!

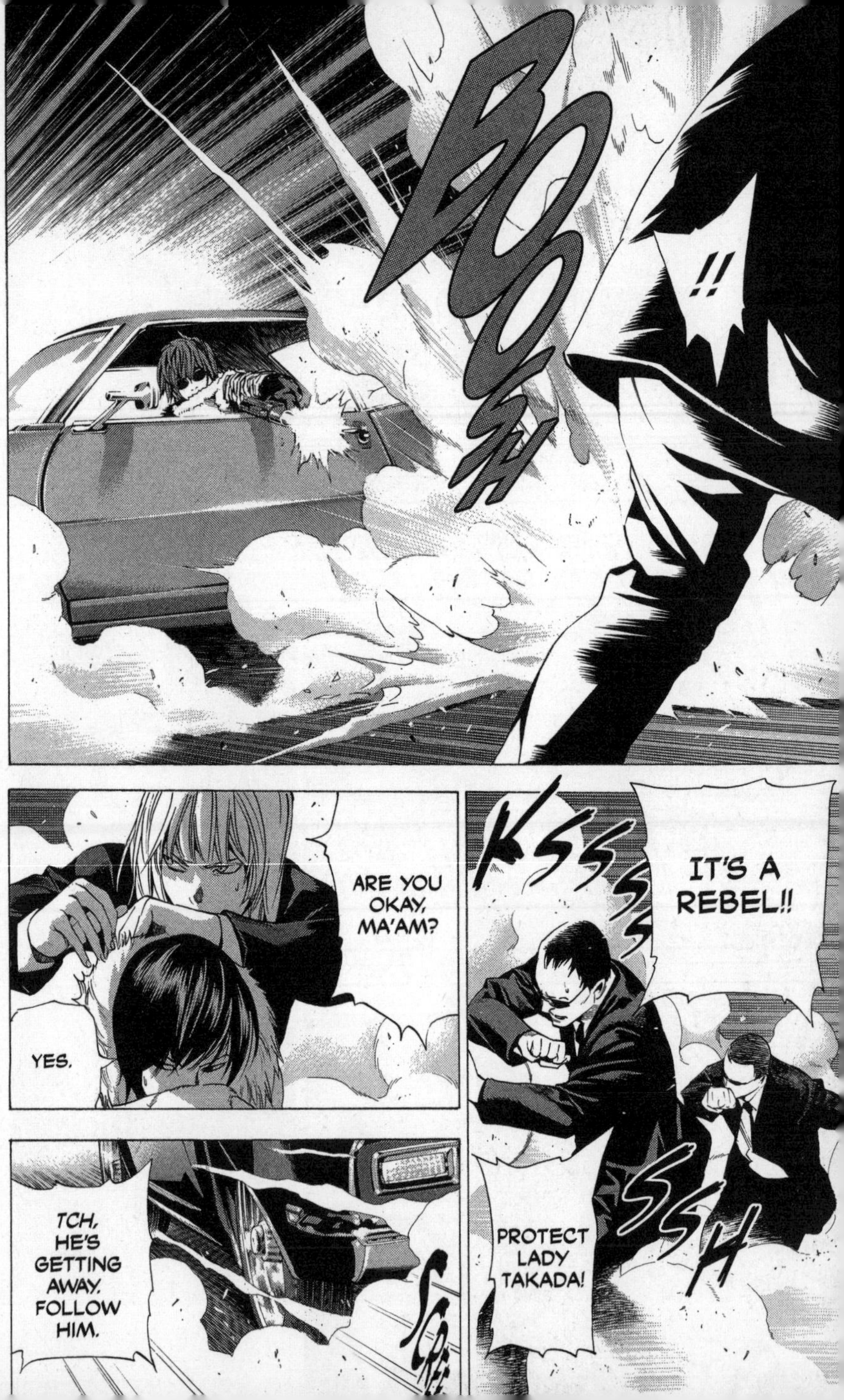
BOOSH
!!
KSSSSS
SSH
IT'S A REBEL!!
PROTECT LADY TAKADA!
ARE YOU OKAY, MA'AM?
YES.
TCH, HE'S GETTING AWAY. FOLLOW HIM.

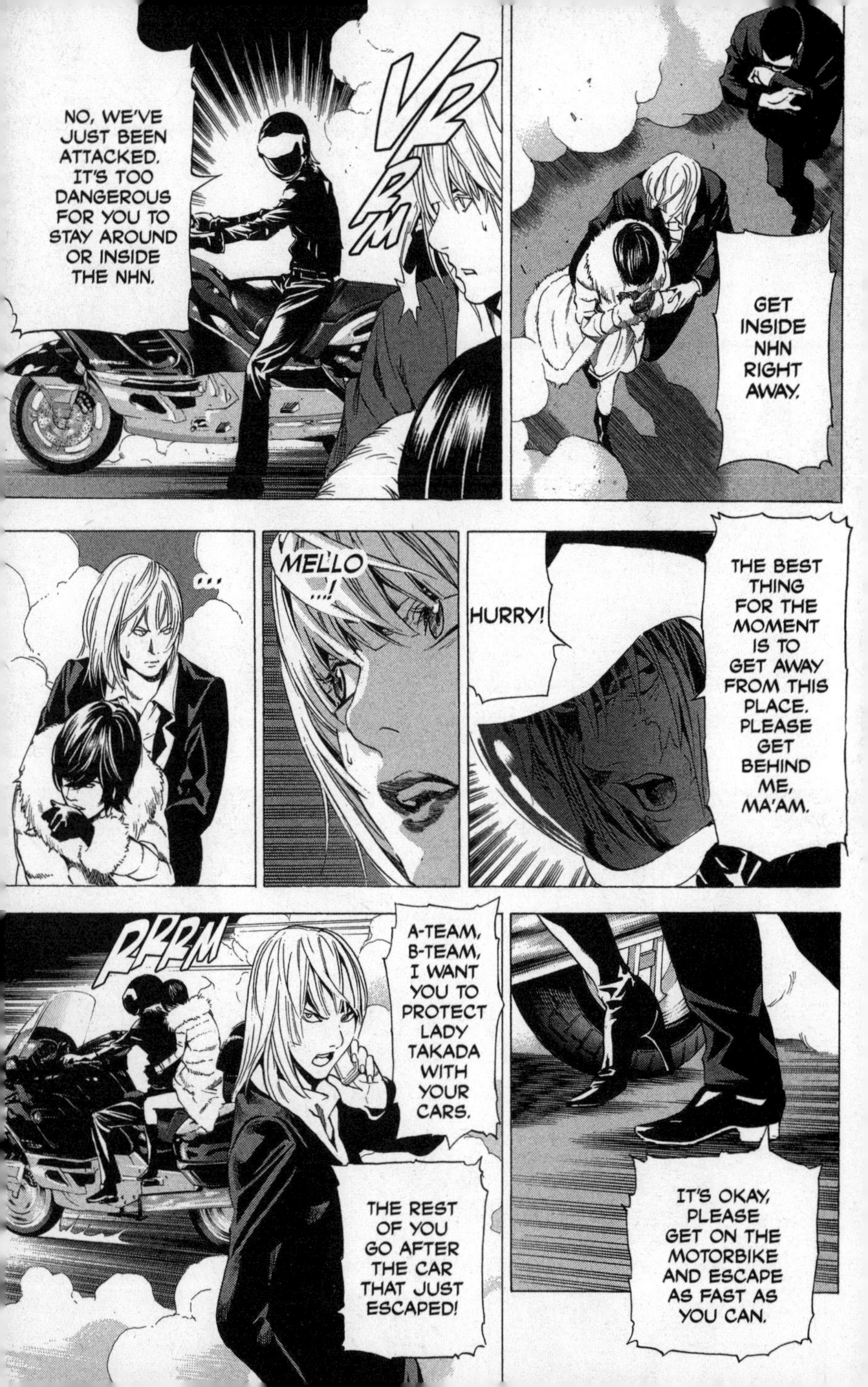
GET INSIDE NHN RIGHT AWAY.
VRRM
NO, WE'VE JUST BEEN ATTACKED. IT'S TOO DANGEROUS FOR YOU TO STAY AROUND OR INSIDE THE NHN.
THE BEST THING FOR THE MOMENT IS TO GET AWAY FROM THIS PLACE. PLEASE GET BEHIND ME, MA'AM.
HURRY!
MELLO ...!
...
IT'S OKAY, PLEASE GET ON THE MOTORBIKE AND ESCAPE AS FAST AS YOU CAN.
A-TEAM, B-TEAM, I WANT YOU TO PROTECT LADY TAKADA WITH YOUR CARS.
RRRM
THE REST OF YOU GO AFTER THE CAR THAT JUST ESCAPED!

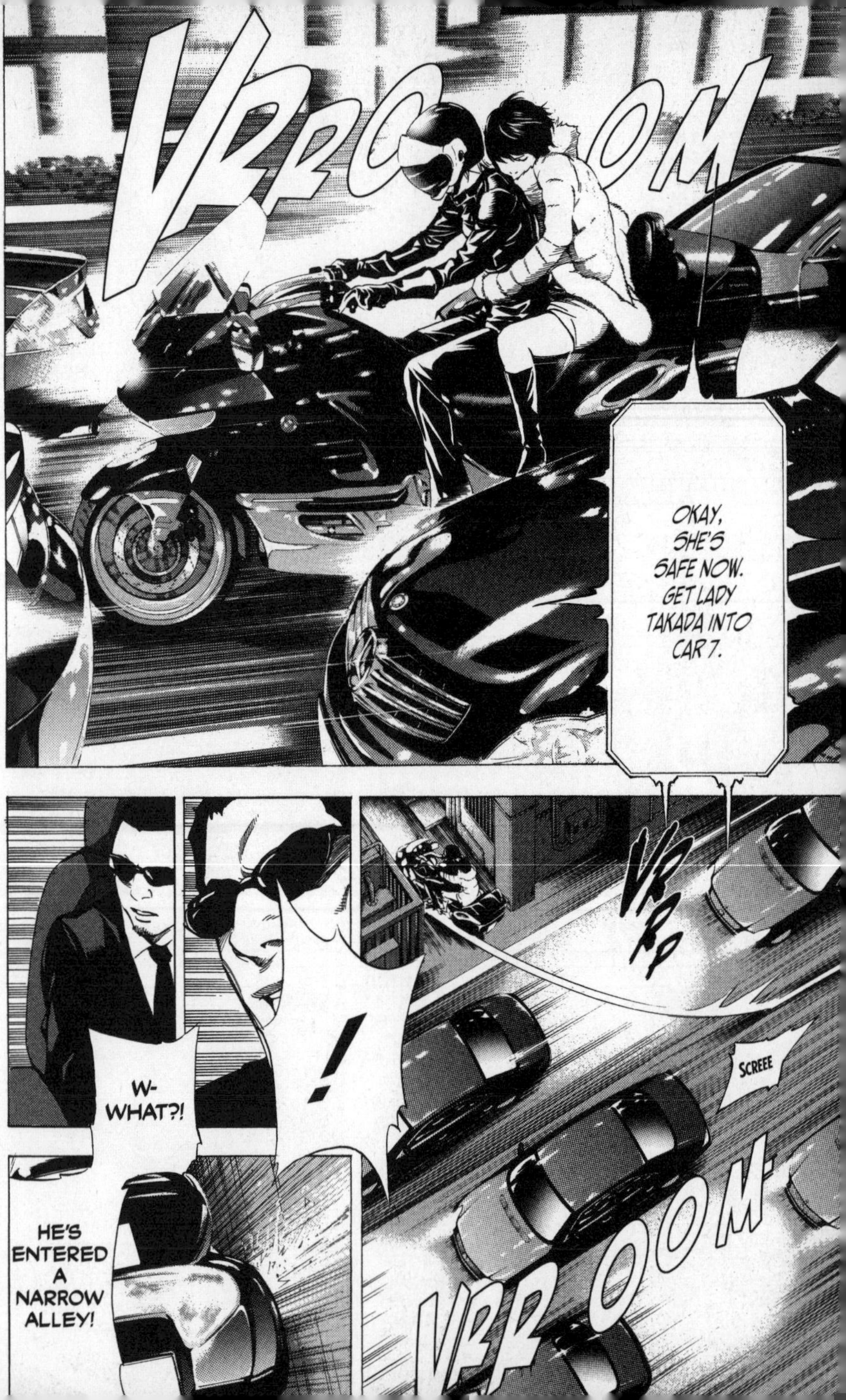
VRROOOM
OKAY, SHE'S SAFE NOW. GET LADY TAKADA INTO CAR 7.
VRRR
SCREEE
VRROOOM
!
W-WHAT?!
HE'S ENTERED A NARROW ALLEY!

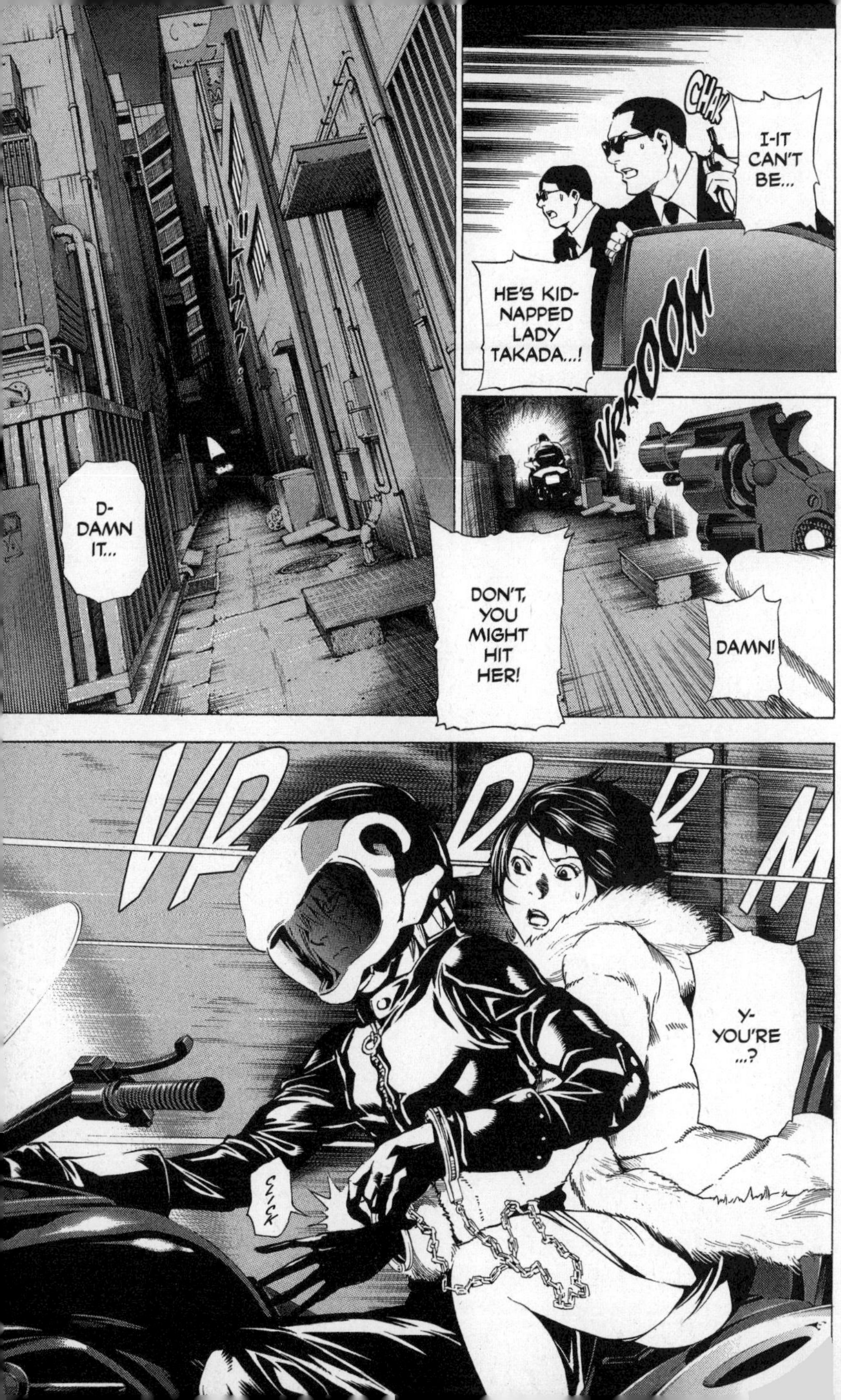
CHAK
I-IT CAN'T BE...
HE'S KID-NAPPED LADY TAKADA...!
VRROOM
DAMN!
DON'T, YOU MIGHT HIT HER!
D-DAMN IT...
VROOM
Y-YOU'RE ...?
CLICK

DEATH NOTE
How to use it
LXVI

- Some limited number of DEATH NOTES have white or red front covers, but they would make no difference in their effects, as compared with the black cover DEATH NOTES.

デスノートには白や赤の表紙の物も稀にあるが、
使い方や効力は黒表紙の物と一切変わらない。

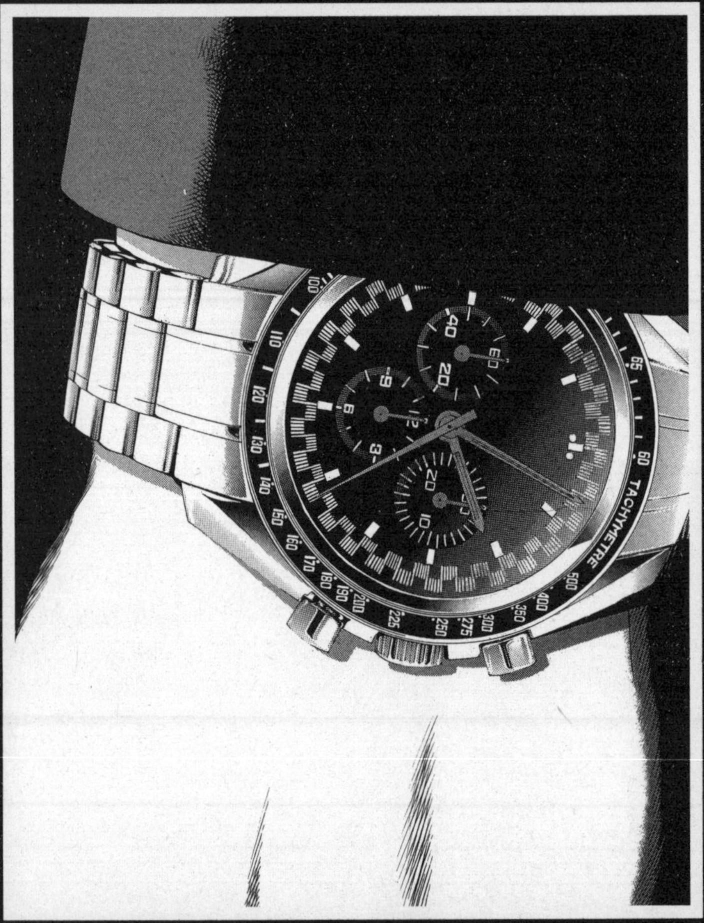
TACHYMETRE

In the Next Volume

The End Is Nigh

Available Now

You're Reading in the Wrong Direction!!

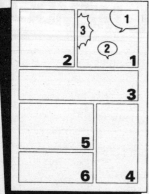

Whoops! Guess what? You're starting at the wrong end of the comic!

...It's true! In keeping with the original Japanese format, **Death Note** is meant to be read from right to left, starting in the upper-right corner.

Unlike English, which is read from left to right, Japanese is read from right to left, meaning that action, sound effects and word-balloon order are completely reversed... something which can make readers unfamiliar with Japanese feel pretty backwards themselves. For this reason, manga or Japanese comics published in the U.S. in English have sometimes been published "flopped"–that is, printed in exact reverse order, as though seen from the other side of a mirror.

By flopping pages, U.S. publishers can avoid confusing readers, but the compromise is not without its downside. For one thing, a character in a flopped manga series who once wore in the original Japanese version a T-shirt emblazoned with "M A Y" (as in "the merry month of") now wears one which reads "Y A M"! Additionally, many manga creators in Japan are themselves unhappy with the process, as some feel the mirror-imaging of their art alters their original intentions.

We are proud to bring you Tsugumi Ohba & Takeshi Obata's **Death Note** in the original unflopped format. For now, though, turn to the other side of the book and let the quest begin...!

–Editor